Piety and Power in Ireland
1760–1960
Essays in Honour of Emmet Larkin

Piety and Power in Ireland

1760–1960

Essays in honour of
Emmet Larkin

Edited by
Stewart J. Brown
and David W. Miller

THE INSTITUTE OF IRISH STUDIES
THE QUEEN'S UNIVERSITY OF BELFAST

UNIVERSITY OF NOTRE DAME PRESS
NOTRE DAME, INDIANA

The Institute of Irish Studies
The Queen's University of Belfast

University of Notre Dame Press
Notre Dame, Indiana

© Stewart J. Brown and David W. Miller 2000

All rights reserved. No parts of this publication may be reproduced,
stored in a retrieval system, or transmitted, in any form or by any means,
electronic, mechanical, photocopying, recording or otherwise,
without prior permission of the publisher.

British Library Cataloguing-In-Publication Data.
A catalogue record for this book
is available from the British Library.

ISBN 0 85389 743 3

Published in the United States in 2000 by
University of Notre Dame Press
Notre Dame, Indiana 46556

All rights reserved.

A record of the Library of Congress Cataloging-in-Publication Data
is available upon request from the Library of Congress.

ISBN 0-268-03863-5

Printed by ColourBooks Ltd, Dublin
Typeset by Carole Lynch
Design by Dunbar Design

Contents

Contributors	VI
Acknowledgements	VII
Abbreviations	VIII
Introduction Stewart J. Brown and David W. Miller	1

POWER

1. Priests, Pikes and Patriots: The Irish Catholic Church and Political Violence from the Whiteboys to the Fenians — 16
   Donal A. Kerr
2. British Liberal Politics and Irish Liberalism after O'Connell — 43
   George L. Bernstein
3. 1875: Faith or Fatherland? The Contested Symbolism of Irish Nationalism — 65
   Hugh F. Kearney
4. Imagining the Nation in Irish Historical Fiction, c.1870–c.1925 — 81
   Lawrence W. McBride
5. The *Irish Peasant* and the Conflict Between Irish-Ireland and the Catholic Bishops, 1903–10 — 108
   Frank A. Biletz
6. On the Birth of the Modern Irish State: The Larkin Thesis — 130
   J.J. Lee

PIETY

7. Mass Attendance in Ireland in 1834 — 158
   David W. Miller
8. The New Reformation Movement in the Church of Ireland, 1801–29 — 180
   Stewart J. Brown
9. Social Catholicism in England in the Age of the Devotional Revolution — 209
   Josef L. Altholz
10. The Genealogy of Irish Modernism: The Case of W.B. Yeats — 220
    Thomas William Heyck
11. The Peak of Marianism in Ireland, 1930–60 — 252
    James S. Donnelly, Jr

Emmet Larkin: A Memoir — 284
    Lawrence J. McCaffrey

Principal Works of Emmet Larkin (to 1998) — 295
    Helen Mulvey

Index — 297

Contributors

Josef L. Altholz is professor of history at the University of Minnesota.
George L. Bernstein is associate professor of history at Tulane University.
Frank A. Biletz is a lecturer in history at Loyola University, Chicago.
Stewart J. Brown is professor of ecclesiastical history at the University of Edinburgh.
James S. Donnelly, Jr is professor of history at the University of Wisconsin–Madison.
Thomas William Heyck is professor of history at Northwestern University.
Hugh F. Kearney is the Carroll Amundson professor emeritus of British history at the University of Pittsburgh.
Donal A. Kerr is professor of ecclesiastical history at the National University of Ireland, Maynooth.
J.J. Lee is professor of history at University College, Cork.
Lawrence W. McBride is professor of history at Illinois State University.
Lawrence J. McCaffrey is professor emeritus of history at Loyola University, Chicago.
David W. Miller is professor of history at Carnegie Mellon University.
Helen Mulvey is professor emerita of history at Connecticut College.

Acknowledgments

The editors wish to acknowledge with gratitude a generous subvention from the Georges Lurcy Charitable and Educational Trust toward the publication of this work. Acknowledgements by individual authors will be found in footnotes at the beginning of the respective contributions.

Abbreviations

A.H.R.	*American Historical Review*
B.L.,…Add. MSS	British Library,…Additional Manuscripts
I.E.R.	*Irish Ecclesiastical Record*
I.H.S.	*Irish Historical Studies*
Keogh, *French disease*	Dáire Keogh, *The French disease: The Catholic Church and Irish radicalism, 1790–1800* (Dublin, 1993).
Keogh, *Vatican, bishops, Irish politics*	Dermot Keogh, *The Vatican, the bishops and Irish politics 1919–1939* (Cambridge, 1986).
Keogh, *Ireland & Vatican*	Dermot Keogh, *Ireland and the Vatican: the politics and diplomacy of church-state relations, 1922–1960* (Cork, 1995)
Kerr, *Peel, priests, & politics*	D.A. Kerr, *Peel, priests, and politics: Sir Robert Peel's administration and the Roman Catholic Church in Ireland, 1841–1846* (Oxford, 1982)
Kerr, *'Nation of beggars'?*	D.A. Kerr, *'A Nation of beggars'?: priests, people and politics in famine Ireland, 1846–1852* (Oxford, 1994)
Larkin, *R. C. Ch. 1850–60*	Emmet Larkin, *The making of the Roman Catholic Church in Ireland, 1850–1860* (Chapel Hill, North Carolina, 1980)
Larkin, *R. C. Ch. 1860–70*	Emmet Larkin, *The consolidation of the Roman Catholic Church in Ireland, 1860–1870* (Chapel Hill and London, 1987)
Larkin, *R. C. Ch. 1870–74*	Emmet Larkin, *The Roman Catholic Church and the home rule movement in Ireland, 1870–1874* (Chapel Hill and London, 1990)
Larkin, *R. C. Ch. 1874–78*	Emmet Larkin, *The Roman Catholic Church and the emergence of the modern Irish political system, 1874–1878* (Washington, DC, and Dublin, 1996)
Larkin, *R. C. Ch. 1878–86*	Emmet Larkin, *The Roman Catholic Church and the creation of the modern Irish state, 1878–1886* (Philadelphia and Dublin, 1975)
Larkin, *R. C. Ch. 1886–88*	Emmet Larkin, *The Roman Catholic Church and the plan of campaign in Ireland, 1886–1888* (Cork, 1978)

Abbreviations

Larkin, *R. C. Ch. 1888–91*	Emmet Larkin, *The Roman Catholic Church in Ireland and the fall of Parnell, 1888–1891* (Chapel Hill and Liverpool, 1979)
Miller, *Church, state & nation*	D.W. Miller, *Church, state and nation in Ireland, 1898–1921* (Dublin, 1973).
N.L.I.	National Library of Ireland
P.R.O.	Public Record Office of England
Whyte, *Church & state*	J.H. Whyte, *Church and state in Ireland, 1923–1970* (Dublin, 1971)

EMMET LARKIN

Introduction

STEWART J. BROWN AND DAVID W. MILLER

THE NAME EMMET LARKIN seldom evokes an indifferent response; throughout his career both the man and his work have often prompted diametrically opposed reactions – both deep affection and open antagonism toward the man, both unqualified admiration and sharp criticism for his work. The editors of this volume – as well as the other contributors no doubt – are among those who hold Emmet in affectionate regard. While neither of us can claim total objectivity toward his work, however, in assembling this collection and in writing this introduction to it we have sought to place his main professional achievement in a perspective which is critical as well as empathetic. That achievement is, of course, his pioneering study of the Roman Catholic church in modern Ireland.

While Larkin was turning his 1957 doctoral dissertation into a book,[1] he faced the issue of choosing a topic for a second project. Unlike most young historians, he very consciously chose a topic not for a book but for a career. Early in his research he envisaged the product as a five-volume work on the Irish Catholic church from 1780 to 1918, and by the early 1970s he had drafted one of the five projected volumes. This volume, covering 1878–91, was so massive that he eventually divided it into three volumes and decided

---

1. Emmet Larkin, *James Larkin: Irish labour leader, 1876–1947* (London, 1965).

that to carry out his project at the level of detail which the subject deserved would require much more than five volumes. So far seven volumes, covering the period 1850–91, have appeared.

What is most likely to strike the reader who dips into this corpus for the first time is its style, which Larkin characterises as a 'mosaic': he makes heavy use of quotations, especially from the very rich archives of episcopal correspondence, and invites the reader to contemplate the picture which he constructs from these colourful fragments of raw evidence. Some readers find this technique richly rewarding; others are annoyed by it. It certainly makes heavy demands on the reader. The persistent reader who stays the course for a volume or more will discover that Larkin has built an overarching structure from which to discern patterns in the mosaic.

Larkin projected that structure in a 1962 article[2] which at the time drew attention perhaps more for the author's audacity in publishing correspondence from the Propaganda Archives containing allegations of sexual and other misconduct by priests, than for the bold conceptualisation which he offered under the conventional-sounding title 'Church and state in Ireland in the nineteenth century'. The title might have led an unwary reader to expect a piece of constitutional history recounting the process which, over several decades, led to the state going out of the religion business in 1869 by simultaneously disendowing the Church of Ireland and converting certain financial commitments which it had made to the two principal non-established churches – Roman Catholic and Presbyterian – into one-time, lump-sum severance payments: end of story. Instead, the reader confronted a mind-bending analysis in which there were two churches – neither of which was Protestant – and two states – one of which, according to more conventional accounts, wouldn't exist at all until 1922.

Implicit in Larkin's distinction between a 'Roman church' and an 'Irish church' was the national Catholic hierarchy's struggle to determine their own political destiny without interference from their ecclesiastical superiors in Rome. That struggle rises to the status of a 'church-state' issue because of the repeated efforts of the 'British State' throughout the century to exploit Rome's desire for diplomatic relations to influence the Holy See's dealings with its Irish hierarchy. Of course the main reason for these efforts was the British state's desire to bolster its own authority in Ireland – ultimately to avert being replaced by an 'Irish State'. What was to make Larkin's use of the

---

2. 'Church and state in Ireland in the nineteenth century' in *Church History*, xxxi, no. 3 (Sept. 1962), 294–306.

latter term provocative was the claim which he would develop in his *magnum opus* that by 1886 an Irish state was not merely virtual – as a generation of Fenians had sworn – but 'real'.³

To understand why that claim was important for Larkin we should attend to the terms 'party of the Constitution' and 'party of the Revolution'⁴ which he coined to refer to what contemporaries called 'constitutional' and 'physical force' nationalism. It could certainly be argued that for many constitutional nationalists, including bishops, 'constitutional' was essentially a synonym for 'non-violent', not an expression of special regard for or interest in that curious amalgam of law, convention and reverence for tradition known in British political discourse as 'the constitution'. For Larkin, however, that very constitution was a sort of metaphor for the object of his quest: the rules of the game, i.e. those understandings and practices by which the principal players in nationalist politics came to conduct themselves by the end of the nineteenth century. He thus cast his projected study of the Irish Catholic church in the mould of constitutional history.

This choice was a felicitous solution to the serious problem of how to hold a career-long project together and give it intelligible form. In a 1975 article⁵ in which he laid out his views on the social foundations of modern Irish nationalism, Larkin also elaborated his 1962 analysis by delineating the 'constitutional' arrangements of the Irish state in which the king, lords and commons of British constitutional discourse were replaced by the leader, the bishops and the party. The three volumes which he published during 1975–79 were structured around the emergence of the new tripartite system of checks and balances in the period 1878–91. The central event of this period was a 'concordat'⁶ in which the bishops agreed to support the party and its leader in return for assurances that in matters relevant to the church's interests – specifically education – the party would take its lead from the bishops.

The powerfully-stated argument of the 1878–91 volumes, then, set Larkin's agenda for the next phase of his project to which he turned his attention in the mid 1970s: the church during the Irish career of Paul Cardinal Cullen, 1850–78. How did the three components of the 'Irish political system' evolve to the point where they were capable of the constitution-forming transactions described in the 1878–91 volumes? For the ebbtide of nationalist politics in the 1850s and 1860s, Larkin's central task was to

---

3. See, e.g., *R. C. Ch. 1886–88*, p. xiii.
4. 'Church and state', p. 305.
5. 'Church, state and nation in modern Ireland' in *A.H.R.*, lxxx, no. 5 (Dec. 1975), pp 1244–95.
6. *R. C. Ch. 1876–86*, p. 396.

explain how the 'Irish church' established its autonomy *vis-à-vis* the 'Roman church'. Paradoxically Cullen, the arch-romaniser, is cast in the role of principal agent of this process by virtue of his successful efforts to isolate John MacHale, archbishop of Tuam, whose embarrassingly public conflict with Daniel Murray, archbishop of Dublin, during the 1830s and 1840s, had split the hierarchy and rendered the Irish church especially vulnerable to Roman interference.[7]

Despite Cullen's masterful efforts to gather all the reins of power in the Irish church into his own hands, 'the bishops as a body'[8] emerge as a power in their own right, especially after their experience of living and acting together for several months at the first Vatican Council in 1870. Meanwhile, Larkin recounts the hierarchy's policy of opposition – under Cullen's leadership and against MacHale's recurrent subversion – to the physical force nationalism represented by the Fenians. The appearance in the 1870s under the rubric of 'home rule' of a party capable of mobilising for constitutional nationalism many of those sympathetic to fenianism enables the bishops as a body to take the first tentative steps toward playing their part in the Irish political system. In the 1874–78 volume Larkin provides the keystone which holds together the two separately-composed components of the seven-volume corpus. As a means for giving form and structure to a massive lifework, the constitutional paradigm must be deemed a resounding success.

The key to the success of the conceptualisation is its suitability to the empirical task which the author had set for himself. Larkin was committed to reconstructing from raw correspondence the interactions of a political elite on an almost daily basis over several decades. That exercise was bound to turn up a welter of contingent, individual human agency. The great merit of constitutional history – especially as practised on a British-style unwritten constitution – is the fact that such historiography makes no claim to predict particular outcomes in political history. Rather it seeks to inform the writer or reader of political history of the evolving system of conventions and understandings which in any particular period constrain the conduct of individual political actors. It enabled Larkin to make intelligible a very complex series of individual decisions without creating a false sense of determinacy.

---

7. For Larkin's treatment of one phase of the conflict, see 'The quarrel among the Roman Catholic hierarchy over the national system of education in Ireland, 1838–41' in R.B. Browne, W.J. Roscelli and Richard Loftus (ed.), *The Celtic cross: studies in Irish culture and literature* (West Lafayette, IN, 1964), pp 121–46. The conflict has since been treated much more fully by one of our contributors, D.A. Kerr, in his two volumes, *Peel, priests, & politics* and *'Nation of beggars'?*
8. Larkin's first use of this term seems to occur in 'Church, state and nation', p. 1269

The same factor which so commends Larkin's choice of a conceptual framework – his commitment to an empirical undertaking which was bound to absorb his entire career – perhaps also provides a clue to its shortcomings. A young historian setting out today on an effort to discern the rules by which a group of actors in a political system regulated their conduct might well – in keeping with current fashions in the profession – consciously borrow the intellectual tools of social anthropology. Setting out in the 1950s, Larkin conceptualised his task in terms of the subdiscipline of constitutional history which was once highly respected but is today distinctly unfashionable within the historical profession. This fact, not to mention the forbidding magnitude of the product, has no doubt limited his readership. Perhaps a decision to devote a career to a single project necessarily entails defiance of fashion and a commitment to write as much for posterity as for one's own contemporaries. In any event, his choice of the constitutional paradigm probably served him better in explicating the continuities of evolutionary change than it would when applied to revolutionary change.[9]

Paradoxically, Larkin's other major contribution was a bold assertion of historical *dis*continuity. Perhaps the one major theme in his work which was unanticipated in the 1962 article was his concept of a 'devotional revolution'. In the third quarter of the nineteenth century, he argued in a 1972 article, Paul Cullen presided over the making of 'practicing Catholics of the Irish people in a generation'.[10] This provocative claim has attracted a good deal more attention than his equally bold construction of a political system for the de facto Irish state. The term 'devotional revolution' has become a commonplace in Irish historiography and the 1972 article has often been cited by scholars in other fields.[11] Nevertheless, there has been extensive debate about aspects of Larkin's argument, about the quantitative evidence for his thesis, and about the meaning of his findings. Desmond Keenan has questioned Larkin's chronology, pointing out devotional innovations which were introduced earlier than the mid nineteenth century.[12] Patrick Corish has called into question some of the ways in which Miller handled mass-attendance data on which Larkin's assertions of lax canonical practice before the Famine

---

9. See J.J. Lee's contribution to this volume.
10. Emmet Larkin, 'The devotional revolution in Ireland, 1850–75' in *A.H.R.*, lxxvii, no. 3 (June 1972), p. 650.
11. A search of the *Arts and Humanities Citation Index* database turns up citations of the devotional revolution article by students not only of Irish society, but of Britain, Germany, the United States, Canada, Australia and New Zealand.
12. *The Catholic church in nineteenth-century Ireland: a sociological study* (Dublin, 1983), pp 148–52, 243.

are founded.[13] Eugene Hynes has offered a sociological interpretation which downplays the agency of Cullen and attributes post-Famine piety to the values of the strong farmer class which came to dominate Irish society as the (presumably less observant) underclass of cottiers and labourers was eliminated by the Famine and by post-Famine emigration.[14]

By far the most searching criticism of the thesis, however, is Thomas McGrath's 1990 argument that the entire notion of a 'devotional revolution' ought to be replaced by a concept of 'tridentine evolution'.[15] In other words, the changes which occurred in Catholic religious practice in the nineteenth century ought to be seen as the working out of the decrees of the Council of Trent between the adjournment of that body in 1563 and the convening of the second Vatican Council in 1962. McGrath conceptualises this process as a top-down effort whose effects were obstructed by political circumstances until c. 1775. From that period until c. 1875 there was a strong tridentine renewal which was accelerated by the Famine. The result was 'the triumphant expression of the tridentine ideal' between 1875 and 1962 in Ireland. Larkin's mistake was to think he had discovered a 'devotional revolution' when he had only stumbled on 'the tail end of the tridentine renewal'.[16]

Why did Catholics throughout Ireland between 1875 and 1962 attend mass each week at rates which seem to have approached 100 per cent of those canonically obligated to do so? According to McGrath, the answer to this question is that in 1563 the Council of Trent decreed that it should be so. While McGrath's observation that 'historians such as Larkin' have focused on 'very narrow time-spans' is a fair criticism, many historians will probably be sceptical of an explanation which places the cause three centuries earlier than the effect. The mechanism by which he connects the effect with the cause is 'ecclesiastical administration and pastoral achievement' which were held in abeyance by exogenous factors for two centuries but then sprang into action when the penal laws were relaxed. Whether one finds this a convincing causal mechanism will depend on how one is disposed to conceive the causation of religious change.

In the wider arena of religious history, scholars have tended during the past three decades or so to attach relatively more significance to the behaviour of

---

13. *The Catholic community in the seventeenth and eighteenth centuries* (Dublin, 1981), p. 107; *The Irish Catholic experience: a historical survey* (Dublin, 1985), pp 166–9.
14. Eugene Hynes, 'The great hunger and Irish catholicism' in *Societas*, viii, no. 2 (Spring 1978), pp 137–56.
15. T.G. McGrath, 'The tridentine evolution of modern Irish catholicism, 1563–1962; A re-examination of the "devotional revolution" thesis' in Réamonn Ó Muirí (ed), *Irish church history today: Cumann Seanchais Ard Mhacha Seminar 10 March 1990* (Armagh, n.d.), pp 84–99
16. Ibid., pp 94–97.

the laity and less to the prescriptions of the clergy in conceptualising and explaining 'religion'. In Irish historiography this 'popular religion' approach is most clearly reflected in the recent work of Raymond Gillespie on the seventeenth century.[17] Gillespie argues that religious outcomes result from dialogue between the needs of the laity and what the competing formal religious systems had to offer in the religious marketplace.

Thus, for example, we would badly misunderstand what was happening in Irish anglicanism in the late eighteenth century if we paid attention to the prayer-book service read every Sunday in the parish church and ignored the parishioners down the road listening to the Methodist preacher denounce the rector as unconverted. Similarly, Ulster presbyterianism in the late eighteenth century should be seen as a religious system embracing not only the enlightened ministrations of the General Synod, but the 'holy fairs' in which Seceding ministers preached what they conceived to be true Presbyterian doctrine in the fields and served communion to country folk who understood themselves thereby to be renewing the Solemn League and Covenant. Moreover, as Schmidt has persuasively argued in the Scottish and American cases, the presence of the less godly at these events in a penumbra of drink, conviviality and courtship is far from irrelevant to their overall meaning.[18] The same approach would lead us to understand the religious system of Catholic Ireland that emerged from the penal laws in the late eighteenth century as including not only those beliefs and practices which the clergy had been trained to promote, but also the whole range of other activities – patterns, wakes, pilgrimages, etc. – which the faithful conceived as relevant to their relationship to the supernatural.

Interestingly, Larkin's 1972 formulation of the devotional revolution as the making of 'practicing Catholics of the Irish people', resembles McGrath's thinking in its tacit assumption that religion is whatever the religious professionals say it is. In recent years, however, as Larkin has turned his attention to writing a volume on the devotional revolution, he has clearly attended to the insights to be gained from the popular religion approach. For example, in a recent paper on the practice of stations – the priest's scheduled visits to well-to-do households to hear confessions, to say mass and to serve communion to parishioners of the neighbourhood – Larkin places the formal

---

17. *Devoted people: belief and religion in early modern Ireland* (Manchester, 1997). See also 'Popular and unpopular religion: a view from early modern Ireland' in J.S. Donnelly, Jr., and K.A. Miller (ed.), *Irish popular culture, 1650–1850* (Dublin, 1998), pp 30–49.
18. L.E. Schmidt, *Holy fairs: Scottish communions and American revivals in the early modern period* (Princeton, 1989).

sacramental occasion in an interpretative context which includes the feasting, drink and story-telling.[19] McGrath, by contrast, treats stations more as an interim adaptation pending conditions in which the tridentine ideal for the administration of confession, mass and communion might be implemented.[20]

Why does it matter whether the devotional changes which occurred in nineteenth century Ireland were a revolutionary discontinuity rather than the culmination of an evolutionary process which had been going on for 300 years? The claim is important because of possible conjunctures with other major discontinuities in modern Irish history. If it is true, then the devotional changes *might* have been causally related to the massive demographic discontinuity of the 1840s or perhaps even to the socio-economic discontinuity of 1878–1903. It would be hard to argue, however, for a causal relationship between the devotional changes and the major political discontinuities of either 1778–1800 or 1912–23.

The striking changes in recent years which have led many commentators to speak of contemporary Ireland as a post-Catholic society mark another discontinuity in compliance with devotional requirements (as well as other religious norms). When Larkin first advanced the devotional revolution hypothesis many readers were startled to learn that a disposition to extremely regular canonical practice was not an Irish personality trait which extended into the very remote past. The developments of the past decade suggest that what we might call hyper-Catholic Ireland may have an end as well as a beginning. It is fair to add that when he was developing the devotional revolution hypothesis around 1970 Larkin could hardly have foreseen how soon thereafter the devotional regime whose beginning he described would come to an end.

So we can now see that a period from the third quarter of the nineteenth century to the last quarter of the twentieth in Ireland constituted a single devotional regime. That regime spanned the last six decades or so of one constitutional regime and the first six of another. Although any link between his two great hypotheses – constitutional and devotional – is more implicit than explicit in Larkin's work, both he and his readers would have made a connection: surely a society whose members so faithfully followed their clergy's directives in the devotional sphere would have heeded those same clergy's admonitions to eschew violence and support democratic institutions

---

19. Emmet Larkin, 'The rise and fall of stations in Ireland, 1750–1850,' a paper delivered at a conference at the University of Rennes, 1996, and forthcoming in the proceedings of that conference.
20. 'Tridentine evolution', pp 95–6.

in the 1920s and 1930s. Perhaps so, but it does not follow that the society's political elite was acting upon conventions established among bishops, leader and party in the 1880s. But we can see more clearly the temporal limits of the constitutional regime which Larkin so brilliantly conceived and so eloquently explicated because we can now see so clearly the temporal limits of the devotional regime which neither he nor anyone else could have known when he drew our attention to it.

This volume in honour of Emmet Larkin is organised, then, around the two seminal theses that have shaped his mature work on the Catholic church in modern Irish politics – that of the role of the church in the creation of the modern Irish state, and that of the role of the church in defining a distinctive Irish national identity through the 'devotional revolution'. The various chapters explore different themes and adopt diverse historical approaches – political, social, ecclesiastical and literary. At the same time, they are united by their common engagement with aspects of Larkin's work on Irish culture and consciousness between the late eighteenth century and the present.

The first section includes six chapters dealing broadly with Larkin's 'church, state and nation' thesis. The section opens with a chapter by Donal Kerr on 'Priests, pikes and patriots: The Irish Catholic church and political violence from the Whiteboys to the Fenians'. He explores the Catholic hierarchy's responses to revolutionary politics from the late eighteenth to the late nineteenth century, with emphasis on the risings of 1798, 1848 and 1867. He rebuts allegations that the Catholic bishops were indifferent to the oppression suffered by the Irish Catholic community, or to legitimate nationalist aspirations. Rather, he maintains, Irish Catholic bishops opposed revolutionary violence as a threat to all lawfully constituted authority, as often ill-judged and irresponsible action that brought only more suffering upon the Catholic population, and as an impediment to more promising constitutional reform movements. The bishops' sphere of action in Ireland, moreover, was constrained by the influence and authority of the papacy, which, haunted by the anti-Christian violence of the French Revolution, opposed movements of revolutionary nationalism across Europe. The Irish hierarchy's opposition to political violence formed a major factor in development of the politics of consensus that Larkin has described in later nineteenth-century Ireland. In the second chapter, 'British Liberal politics and Irish liberalism after O'Connell', George Bernstein considers the period 1847 to 1865, when Irish politics remained very much under 'the shadow of Daniel O'Connell'. The chapter explores the question of why, despite O'Connell's commitment to the ideals of civil and religious liberty, the movement he initiated did not evolve into a strong Irish Liberal party in close alliance with the British Liberal party. Why, in short, did Irish liberalism not become part of a larger late-Victorian British liberal consensus, as happened with Scottish and Welsh liberalism? For Bernstein, while the liberal movements in Ireland and Britain shared many ideals, there were also crucial points of divergence – in attitudes regarding the role of the state in famine relief, in views on the place of the Catholic church within the United Kingdom, and in responses to the movement for Italian unification. These divergences were aggravated by the British Liberals' frequent expressions of contempt for what they viewed as the 'beggary' and 'opportunism' of the Irish. This was not helped by the lack of a mid Victorian Irish liberal leader of the stature of O'Connell, who could command the respect, if not the love, of British Liberal politicians. The weakness of Irish liberalism meant that it was O'Connell's catholicism and nationalism, more than his liberalism, that defined his enduring political legacy in Ireland after 1865.

The theme of O'Connell's political legacy is taken up by Hugh Kearney in his chapter, entitled '1875: faith or fatherland? The contested symbolism of Irish nationalism'. Here Kearney discusses the use of symbolism, ritual and rhetoric in the Dublin commemoration of the centenary of O'Connell's birth. As he demonstrates, the meaning of the event was disputed between the proponents of two differing perceptions of O'Connell's legacy. One group venerated the memory of O'Connell as champion of Catholic emancipation and advocate of a Catholic Irish nationalism. Their position was personified in the ultramontane archbishop of Dublin, Cardinal Paul Cullen. The other group celebrated O'Connell as the champion of the repeal of the union between Ireland and Britain and the proponent of a liberal and secular nationalism. The Protestant home ruler, Isaac Butt, became the representative figure for this position. The struggle between the advocates of a religious and a secular nationalism for the 'powerful political symbol' of O'Connell embittered the celebrations in 1875 and revealed the deep divisions in the nineteenth-century Irish national consciousness.

In the fourth chapter, 'Imagining the nation in Irish historical fiction, c.1870–1925', Lawrence McBride continues the exploration of the symbolism and rhetoric of cultural identity. For McBride, the large body of Irish popular fiction provides important evidence of Irish self-perceptions during the period which witnessed, according to Larkin, the emergence of the de facto Irish state and its transformation into the de jure state. By analysing the way in which popular novelists imagined Irish space and time, McBride delineates an 'imagined Irish community' that was communal rather than individualistic (or class-based), rural rather than urban, agrarian rather than industrial, traditionalist rather than progressive, Catholic rather than secular. The community was defined by unwritten social sanctions rather than statute law, and decision-making was based on consensus rather than majority rule. It was, in short, an 'imagined community' that fit in well with a Catholic constitutional nationalism, and with the political consensus of the de facto Irish state shaped by Charles Stewart Parnell between 1878 and 1891 through balancing the respective claims of leader, party and bishops.

In chapter five, 'The *Irish Peasant* and the conflict between Irish-Ireland and the Catholic bishops, 1903–10', Frank Biletz considers the cultural conflicts surrounding the de facto Irish state in the early twentieth century. As Biletz demonstrates, not everyone was pleased with the nature of that de facto state, and especially with the central role of the Catholic clergy in the new political consensus. The cultural nationalists of the Irish-Ireland movement challenged what they viewed as the tightening of an oppressive social control by the bishops – and they called for the revival of traditional popular culture, a greater role for lay intellectuals, more teaching of Irish language and culture in the schools, and commitment to the struggle for full Irish independence. The conflict between the more radical Irish-Ireland intelligentsia and the conservative Catholic hierarchy found expression in the controversies surrounding the *Irish Peasant*, one of the most influential of the Irish-Ireland newspapers. Under the forceful editorship of Patrick D. Kenny from 1903 to 1905, and W.P. Ryan from 1905 to 1910, the *Irish Peasant* championed cultural nationalism and confronted the Catholic hierarchy. It refused to accept Roman catholicism as fundamental to Irish identity and it demanded a more secular national education system. In the event, the bishops weathered the challenge from the *Irish Peasant*. But in responding to such challenges, the bishops embraced significant elements of cultural nationalism, and thus ensured that the Catholic church not only retained its place in the political consensus but also exercised a dominant role in Irish culture.

Finally, in chapter six, 'On the birth of the modern Irish state: the Larkin thesis', Joe Lee offers both an appreciation and a critical assessment of Larkin's seminal work on the consolidation of the de facto Irish state between 1878 and 1891. Larkin's thesis, Lee maintains, is both audacious and challenging, and, since its appearance in the 1970s, has had a profound impact on Irish historiography. Larkin's argument that Parnell created the modern Irish state by balancing and uniting the claims of leader, party and bishops is one that has commanded attention, not least as a conceptual tool for understanding Irish politics in the twentieth century. However, Lee also recommends caution. There can be a danger, he suggests, of developing a reductionist view of modern Irish history from Larkin's thesis. If, he asks, Parnell created the modern Irish state between 1878 and 1891, if these years did indeed witness the seminal event in modern Irish political history, are not subsequent events in Irish political history – the First World War, the Easter Rising, the war of independence, the Treaty and the civil war – reduced in importance? Do they not become minor events in the path toward actualising a political system already in place by 1891? Lee feels Irish political developments remained much more open to change after 1891. He also questions the extent to which the modern Irish state can be identified with the Parnellite political system. Analysis of the Parnellite system, he observes, does not reveal much about the territorial extent of the modern Irish state, the patterns of political leadership that developed after 1918, the limitations of the bishops' political influence outside the areas of sexual behaviour and education, the growing importance of public opinion, or the development of a competitive party system. In short, Lee concludes, the Parnellite political system did not define a single line of future political development for Ireland; rather, after 1891 there remained a wide range of possible paths of political change.

In the second section, the five chapters engage in various ways with Larkin's 'devotional revolution' thesis. In his chapter, 'Mass attendance in Ireland in 1834', David W. Miller revisits with more modern technology some data from the Report of the Commissioners of Public Instruction, Ireland, which he earlier utilised in a 1975 article. He offers a resolution of some of the problems which have plagued those who seek to interpret these data, and he produces a spatial visualisation of mass-attendance patterns before the Famine. This effort is a step toward the author's goal of testing a variety of hypotheses about religious practice which have been generated by the devotional revolution debate. Though such an analysis as he projects will necessarily be rooted in that single moment in time for which we have comprehensive mass-attendance data for the whole of Ireland, Miller suggests a way of conceptualising the problem in the *longue durée*. He thus proposes for a problem in historical causation a framework in time and space analogous to the one which McBride uses in his analysis of popular historical imagination.

In chapter eight, 'The new reformation movement in the Church of Ireland, 1801–29', Stewart Brown considers the early nineteenth-century movement to secure the conformity of the Irish population to the established church. During the first three decades of the nineteenth century, the state invested unprecedented amounts of public money in endeavouring to strengthen the established Church of Ireland – building and repairing churches and manses, creating parish schools, supporting educational and home mission societies, reducing pluralism and non-residence among the parish clergy. The aims were religious and political – to achieve at last the victory of the sixteenth-century Protestant Reformation in Ireland and to consolidate the United Kingdom around shared religious and moral values disseminated by the established Protestant church. Behind the new reformation movement was the assumption that the Irish majority was only nominally Catholic. Their condition had resulted from the failure of the established Church of Ireland to provide adequate pastoral care and a Bible-based popular education. With the Union of 1801 and the creation of a united church of England and Ireland, the established church in Ireland at last commanded the resources and parliamentary support to make its parish system work. The new reformation campaign reached its height in the early and mid 1820s, as both high church and evangelical supporters of the established church co-operated in the effort to achieve mass conversions and to halt the momentum for Catholic emancipation. The much-publicised wave of conversions in late 1826 and early 1827, however, soon receded. The new reformation campaigners, Brown argues, had been misled about the nature of popular Irish catholicism. As they discovered, the devotional revolution was already well established by the 1820s, and the Irish majority were not merely nominal Catholics awaiting pastoral attention from the established church.

In chapter nine, Josef Altholz considers 'Social catholicism in England in the age of the devotional revolution'. What, he asks, were the defining social ideals and the social outreach of the English Catholic church, as it experienced waves of migration from Ireland, especially during the Famine years? Altholz perceives three main strands of Catholic social concern in England between the 1840s and the 1860s. The first was characterised by romanticism, and especially the romantic medievalism of the Catholic earl of Shrewsbury and the Catholic convert, Phillips de Lisle. The romantic medievalists proclaimed the Christian duty of giving to the poor because they were poor, but showed little awareness of the actual social conditions of industrialising Britain. They were more concerned with working for church reunion or reviving gothic architecture, than with identifying and alleviating the causes of poverty. The second strand of Catholic social concern was associated with two Catholic periodicals, the *Tablet* and the *Rambler*, and involved a more realistic approach to poverty, based upon practical social work at the parish level. It was, Altholz maintains, this parish-based education and social work that marked the beginning of effective engagement with the problems confronted by the Irish in England. The third strand was connected with the new ultramontanism that arrived with Nicholas Wiseman in the late 1840s, and which emphasised local missions, including emotional, open-air street preaching, followed up by the work of confraternities and devotional societies, as a means of reaching the Irish Catholic poor. For all this, Altholz concludes that Catholic social activities during this period remained inadequate and unsystematic. The concern was more with building the institutional church and encouraging devotion than with alleviating poverty. In this, English catholicism reflected the conservative ecclesiastical priorities of the devotional revolution in Ireland rather than the emerging social catholicism of the European continent.

The following two chapters consider the confrontation of the devotional revolution and the modern world, with its secular, cosmopolitan priorities. T.W. Heyck's chapter, 'The genealogy of Irish modernism: the case of W.B. Yeats', explores the question of Yeats's poetic identity and its Irish context. Was Yeats essentially a modernist poet – cosmopolitan, anti-historical, apolitical – or was he an Irish nationalist poet, a poet of cultural anti-colonialism? For Heyck, Yeats was a modernist, but his was a distinctive form of Irish modernism. Heyck demonstrates that while Yeats was drawn to Irish nationalism, his personal genealogy – his roots in a former coloniser group, his freethinking father's rejection of Christianity, his immersion in English literary culture – meant that he could not be part of the Catholic nationalism that we have seen developing out of the devotional revolution. Yet, alienated from English literary culture, he could also not be part of the modernism of the Bloomsbury literati. He thus developed his own version of Irish nationalism, based on a non-Christian religious expression and an idealised vision of a Celtic Irish culture unspoiled by the commercial society of England. It was, Heyck argues, largely his disillusionment with the conservative Catholic nationalism emerging from the devotional revolution that drove Yeats along his unique path to a distinctive Irish modernism. The interactions of the Ireland of the devotional revolution and the modern world are considered further by James Donnelly in 'The peak of Marianism in Ireland, 1930–60'. Donnelly maintains that the conservative Catholic nationalism of the devotional revolution, which Larkin maintained was consolidated between 1850 and 1870, reached its fullest flowering in the period 1930 to 1960, with Marian devotion now forming its central symbols, values and practices. This Marian devotion, he demonstrates, was fostered by the new media of film and radio, by the formation of rosary groups at workplaces and rosary crusades, and by the work of the Legion of Mary. Donnelly identifies three main influences behind this upsurge of Marian passion in Ireland – first, the Spanish civil war and the perceived anti-clericalism of the republican forces; second, the Cold War and the anti-Christian policies of communism, and third, the spread of dance halls, jazz music and other perceived threats to the moral purity of the Irish nation. Thus the defensive priorities of the devotional revolution, which Larkin observed in the reaction to the Famine and the waning of traditional Gaelic culture in the mid nineteenth century, were continued in Catholic Ireland's reaction to communism and secular, cosmopolitan culture in the mid twentieth century.

In chapter twelve, we move from the making of the modern Irish state and the devotional revolution – and consider Emmet Larkin, the man and the historian. Lawrence McCaffrey's 'Emmet Larkin: a memoir' provides a personal memoir and appreciation, based on their friendship of over forty years. McCaffrey gives particular attention to Larkin's leading role in the formation and development of the American Committee for Irish Studies, now the American Conference for Irish Studies, which has provided vital institutional support to the upsurge in Irish studies in recent decades. He also briefly discusses the historian's background – his family's roots in Ireland, his years in New York and Boston, his complex relations with the Catholic church, and his long association with the University of Chicago – and he offers a glimpse into Larkin's personal life. From McCaffrey's account, two themes emerge. The first is Larkin's essentially liberal (dare we say Gladstonian?) belief that great institutions – churches, universities, civil governments, parliaments – represent the collective struggles of generations and serve to elevate individuals with a vision of what humans can achieve. At their best, institutions are more than the sum of the individual humans who form them, and they inspire individuals to be more than what they are. The second is Larkin's deep respect for the vocation of the scholar-teacher and historian. One of the most abiding images of the man, for friends, colleagues and students, is his thorough-going professionalism. The volume concludes with Helen Mulvey's compilation of the 'Principal works of Emmet Larkin', which illustrates the magnitude and versatility of his writings, and the importance of his contributions to our understanding of the themes of 'piety and power' in the making of modern Ireland.

1

Priests, Pikes and Patriots:
The Irish Catholic Church and Political Violence from the Whiteboys to the Fenians

DONAL A. KERR*

In 'Ninety-Eight weren't the rebels excommunicated and wasn't Father John Murphy, that was burned alive by the yeomen, excommunicated? Didn't Archbishop Troy issue pastorals condemning the 'Ninety-eight men, and didn't he have prayers offered up in thanksgiving when poor Robert Emmet was captured? . . . Didn't they condemn the men of 'Forty-eight and tell the people to give up their crops and die of hunger in the ditches? . . . Weren't the Fenians excommunicated, and didn't the Catholic chaplains in Portland and Chatham join with the rest of the warders in driving Dr. Gallagher mad with torture? Brendan Behan to the prison chaplain, *The Borstal Boy.*

WHILE THE OUTBURST OF BRENDAN BEHAN finds an echo in the hearts of many latter-day nationalists to this day, the claim of Patrick Duigenan, that the great rebellion of 1798 was 'a popish plot', would also find many adherents.

---

*I am indebted to Monsignor James O'Brien of the Sacred Congregation for Bishops, Vatican City, for allowing me to consult his unpublished thesis 'The Irish hierarchy and the Fenian movement, 1858–1870: a study in the right to rebel.' I also wish to thank Dr Cadoc Leighton, Professor Stewart J. Brown and Dr Gerard Moran for help with this article.

Both interpretations can find substance in the tragic course of Irish history. On 23 May 1798, the ballad tells us, Fr John Murphy, of Kilcormack parish in Wexford, spurred up the rocks from his burnt-out chapel, gathered together a group of peasants armed with pikes, scythes and a few guns and routed two small detachments of His Majesty's forces, thus beginning the Wexford rebellion. Fifty years later, in July 1848, two priests outfaced Smith O'Brien, MP for Limerick, who was attempting to persuade Tipperary farmers and peasants at Mullinahone to take up arms; the clerics persuaded most of them to return home and so help destroy the Young Irelanders' forlorn hopes. At the time of the third revolutionary movement in this hundred-year span, the church appeared unambiguously hostile when, in the 1860s, the Irish bishops, led by Archbishop Paul Cullen, took a firm line against the Fenians. Yet, even then, ambivalence persisted, for some clerics remained sympathetic to the 'advanced' nationalists.[1]

Emmet Larkin, in his monumental studies on the church, has provided an excellent examination of the bishops' reaction to the Fenians. Several important recent studies have thrown new light on clerical involvement in 1798.[2]

---

1. P. Ua Laoghaire, *Mo sgéal féin* (Dublin, 1915), pp 112–21; P.A. Sheehan, *The graves at Kilmorna*. See too the fierce dispute between the parish priest and the curate in Séamas Ó Grianna, *Caisleáin óir*, (Cork, reprint 1976), p. 141. 'Sin', ar seisean [an sagart óg], 'an áit a dearn an chléir cearr riamh sa tír seo é. Bhí siad mar shílfeadh siad nach dtiocfadh an creideamh a choinneáil beo gan cuidiú na Sasana'; Sean O'Faolain, *The Irish* (London, 1947), pp 106–28.

2. Larkin, *R. C. Ch. 1860–1870*, pp 394–438, 641–85. Among works on the Irish church during the 1790s the following deserve special attention: R.F. Hayes, 'Priests in the independence movement of '98' in *I.E.R*, ser 5, lxvi, (1945) 258–70; Nicholas Furlong, *Fr. John Murphy of Boolavogue, 1753–1798* (Dublin, 1991); L.M. Cullen, 'The 1798 rebellion in Wexford: United Irishman organisation, membership, leadership' in Kevin Whelan and William Nolan, *Wexford: history and society: interdisciplinary essays on the history of an Irish county* (Dublin, 1987), pp 248–95; Kevin Whelan, 'The role of the Catholic priest in the 1798 rebellion in County Wexford', ibid. 296–315; Kevin Whelan, 'Catholics, Politicisation and the 1798 Rebellion' in Ó Muirí, *Irish church history today*; Keogh, *French disease*; Eamon O'Flaherty, 'Irish Catholics and the French Revolution' in Hugh Gough and David Dickson (ed.), *Ireland and the French Revolution* (Dublin, 1990), pp 52–67; V. J. McNally, *Reform, Revolution and Reaction: Archbishop Thomas Troy and the Catholic Church in Ireland, 1787–1817* (Lanham, MD, 1995); P. O'Donoghue, 'The Catholic Church and Ireland in an age of imperialism and rebellion, 1782–1803' (National University of Ireland, Ph.D. thesis, 1973).

On the church and the 1848 rebellion: Kerr, *'Nation of beggars?*, pp 122–65.

On the church and the Fenians: Donal McCartney, 'The church and Fenianism' in *University Review*, iv, (1967), 102–12; Tomás Ó Fiaich, 'The clergy and fenianism, 1860–70' in *I.E.R*, ser 5, cix (1968), 81–103; E.R. Norman, *The Catholic Church and Ireland in the age of rebellion: 1859–1873* (London, 1965); James O'Shea, *Priest, politics and society in post-Famine Ireland: a study of county Tipperary 1850–1891* (Dublin, 1983); R.V. Comerford, *The Fenians in context: Irish politics and society, 1848–82* (Dublin, 1985); G.P. Moran, *A radical priest in Mayo, Father Patrick Lavelle, 1825–86* (Dublin, 1994); O.P. Rafferty, 'The church, the state and the Fenian threat, 1861–75', (Oxford University D. Phil. thesis, 1996).

On the general problem: Oliver MacDonagh, *States of mind: a study of Anglo-Irish conflict, 1780–1980* (London, 1983) pp 90–103; Sheridan Gilley, 'The Catholic Church and revolution' in D.G. Boyce (ed.), *The revolution in Ireland, 1879–1923* (London, 1988), pp 157–72.

This chapter is an attempt to link, and extend, those two major episodes to see if, from the church's attitude over that century from the 1760s to the 1860s, any pattern emerges. In a sense, it will attempt to ascertain which of the admittedly extreme interpretations of Behan or Duigenan accords best with the facts. Did the Irish Catholic church deny all right to rebel or did its clergy espouse revolt, openly when they could, secretly when they could not? Particular attention will be paid to the attitude of those who bore most public responsibility for the church – the twenty-seven bishops – though most of them have left little record of their position. This Irish experience fits into the context of events on the continent and in the international Catholic church.

By the second half of the eighteenth century, the Irish church, having painfully re-established its position after the penal era, was again a vibrant community and a full hierarchy had been reconstituted. The political situation of the church was still unusual, for while some bishops were still Jacobite, others, in 1756, had prayers offered for the success of George III's armies. In the 1760s came the Whiteboy outbreak – a peasant protest whose targets included the excessive tithes of the parson and the dues of the priest. Whiteboyism, the first serious agrarian disturbances since the beginning of the century, was the first occasion for the clergy to react to violence that threatened the established order. Although a few priests were accused of being involved and Fr Nicholas Sheehy of Clogheen was executed, the evidence of their involvement was quite doubtful and the clergy in general opposed the movement strongly. Their condemnation of Whiteboyism was not on purely political grounds, but because it was a sinful revolt against the structure of society. A major motive, too, behind their condemnation was their concern to dispel charges of disloyalty – the constant theme of Protestant speeches and sermons.

As the disturbances continued, a leading bishop of the day, John Thomas Troy of Ossory, brought a new dimension to the problem. Troy, a Dominican, had begun his studies at the Dominican house of San Clemente in Rome in 1755. Some years before, in 1738, Pope Clement XII, had become alarmed at the spread of freemasonry in Jacobite circles in Rome and had officially condemned it in the Pontifical Constitution, *Providas*. In 1751, Pope Benedict XIV, in another Pontifical Constitution, *In Eminenti*, extended the condemnation to all similar secret societies. Three reasons were given for the condemnation of the freemasons. They constituted an oath-bound secret society, posed a threat to both state and church and fostered religious indifference. Troy, who would have been familiar with the papal decrees, now invoked them as the basis for his own condemnation of the secret society of the Whiteboys. He was comprehensive, however, in his approach to the problem for while he excommunicated the Whiteboys, he also threatened with immediate suspension from exercising the priesthood any priest who asked too much from his people. Troy appreciated and played a part in the steady advance Catholics had made towards civil liberties. On 6 May 1789, he had brought the cream of society, Protestant and Catholic, to Francis Street Chapel, his episcopal church, for a solemn *Te Deum* on George III's recovery of his health. The unique gathering included the duke of Leinster, the earl of Tyrone, Lords Belvedere, Portarlington, Bective, Tyrone, Carhampton, Headford, Clifden, Dysert, Arran, Dudley, Enniskillen, Thomas Connolly, speaker of the house of commons, La Touche, Gardiner, Lowther, Bushe, Grattan, the attorney general, the lord mayor and sheriffs of Dublin and others. Never before and perhaps never again would so many of the Protestant ascendancy come to a Catholic service.[3] All augured well for further progress towards Catholic emancipation and Catholic integration into the political and social community. The cautious Troy, 'the wily Trojan', as O'Connell called him later, wanted at all costs to avert any action by Catholics which would place at risk the recent concessions they had achieved or jeopardise their hopes for the future.

At the very time of Troy's extraordinary ecumenical triumph, events of great significance were taking place abroad that would pose a challenge to the Catholic church on the Continent and impinge also on the Irish church. On 5 May, the Estates General met in Versailles marking the beginning of the most momentous event of the century – the French Revolution. The oath to the Civil Constitution followed in the early spring of 1792 and split the nation and the church in France. Then the September massacres in 1792, the reign of terror in 1793–94, and the dechristianisation campaign antagonised the Catholic church world-wide.

As the revolution became more extreme the Irish bishops grew increasingly concerned. When Troy was criticised for presiding at the Catholic 'Convention', a title with revolutionary overtones for many, in February 1793, he attempted to rebut renewed charges of Catholic disloyalty, by issuing a pastoral letter entitled 'Duties of Christian citizens'. This important document was the first

---

3. *Faulkner's Dublin Journal*, 7 May 1789, cited in John Brady, *Catholics and catholicism in the eighteenth-century press* (Maynooth, 1965), pp 266–7; H. Peel, 'John Thomas Troy, Archbishop of Dublin, 1786–1823: a man of his times.' Unpublished lecture at Saint Patrick's College, Carlow, (1986), p. 11.

full statement of the relationship which a leading Catholic bishop believed should exist between Irish Catholics and their English Protestant king. Its opening tones recall Rousseau's trumpet call to freedom in the Social Contract. 'Liberty is good ... liberty is fruitful', wrote Troy, 'servitude' produces only 'degradation and turpitude'. The gospel of Christ is a law of liberty. True liberty, however, is the golden mean between unrestrained independence, on the one hand, and base slavery on the other. Reflecting both his own Thomism and the prevailing ethos, Troy understood society as necessary, its subversion as evil. Yet he sternly warned kings and ministers that they have their duties to their subjects and must render a strict account to the supreme Ruler. His emphasis, however, was on the respect Catholics should pay to their sovereign and to the laws – both instruments of God's providence. He took his proofs from scripture and the church fathers. Jesus had declared that we should render unto Caesar the things that are Caesar's; Saint Peter had warned the Christian to 'submit yourself for the sake of the Lord to the sovereign as supreme or to the governor as his deputy'; Saint Paul, and after him, the fathers of the church, Justin, Irenaeus, Tatian, Athenagoras, Gregory of Nazianzus had proclaimed the same doctrine. Obedience to legitimate authority, then, was a religious duty and for Troy the king, lord and commons of Ireland constituted the legitimate authority. The principles which Troy invoked were similar to those held by most bishops of the established church. Although dissenting voices existed, the Unitarian attorney, Samuel Heywood, observed in 1792 that 'passive obedience and non-resistance are still the avowed principles of the Church'.[4]

What weighed very much with Troy was the rebuttal of the charge of Catholic disloyalty and to it he devoted much of his pastoral. Catholics had recently received important benefits culminating in the relief act of 1793, which the British government was forcing, at that very moment, on a reluctant Irish Protestant parliament. At this same time, the bishops were also considering applying to the government for a further great concession – the establishment of a training college for their priests, now an urgent need after the closing of the Irish colleges in France. Troy and the bishops saw a link between Catholic loyalty and British liberality. No wonder he showered praise on George III, 'this most best of kings'. To bolster Catholic claims of loyalty Troy argued that Catholic religious principles were above all others the best calculated to inspire a reverence for constituted authority. To some of the bishops the memory of the penal laws was still fresh and, as Castlereagh had warned, what government had given, government could take back.

---

4. J.C.D. Clark, *English society 1688–1832* (London, 1985), p. 259.

Alarmed when the United Irishmen sought to swear the Defenders, who were Catholics, into their now revolutionary society, Troy and his fellow-bishops denounced the Defenders as a secret oath-bound society. The threat of revolution became real when at Christmas 1796 a French invading army entered Bantry Bay. The bishops were quick to warn against any co-operation with the French and in February 1797, Troy offered a solemn *Te Deum* for the country's deliverance. The sermon he preached was circulated as a pastoral letter to his diocese. To his former arguments of the religious duty of obedience to the state, he added a new theme: the excesses of the French Revolution.

> Do not approach the rotten tree of French liberty, if you desire to live. It bears forbidden fruit, fair to the eye but deadly to those who taste it. Rooted in corruption, it vegetates only to destroy. Evils innumerable lie concealed under its branches and shining foliage, bending under an exuberant weight of crimes. Such is the boasted tree of liberty, and such is its baleful fruit, presented to us covered over with the fairest flowers of … oratory, and under the imposing names of liberty, equality, amity and protection.

In opposing Jacobin revolution in Ireland, Troy was not 'unpatriotic'. Seen in the context of what the revolutionaries were inflicting on the Catholic church in that large section of Europe controlled by France, Troy could scarcely take any other stand. With the victories of their armies, the revolutionaries brought their anti-church legislation and spoliation into the Netherlands, Germany, Spain and Italy. When they defeated and occupied the Papal States of Pius VI, the Irish revolutionary leader, Wolfe Tone wrote: 'I am heartily rejoiced that that old priest is at last laid under contribution in his turn. Many a long century he and his predecessors have been fleecing all Europe, but the day of retribution is come at last; and besides, I am strongly tempted to hope that this is but the beginning of his sorrows'.[5]

His hopes came true for this incident proved indeed only the beginning of sorrows for the pope. In 1797 the revolutionaries arrested Pius VI, 'Citizen Pope', as they called him, transported the eighty-two year old pope over the Alps to Valence in an agonising journey that lasted five months. There, on 29 August 1799, Pius VI died. The officials who reported to the government the death of 'Giovanni Angelo Braschi, exercising the profession of pontiff', maintained that they were, no doubt, burying the last pope! To many it appeared to be the end of the papacy and the Roman church.

---

5. Wolfe Tone, diary entry 4 July 1796, cited in R. Barry O'Brien (ed.), *The autobiography of Theobald Wolfe Tone, 1763–1798* (London, 1893), ii, 65. Tone wanted General Clarke to put pressure on the pope to write to Troy to secure the support of the Irish clergy for the United Irishmen or their neutrality.

Troy's warnings may have convinced most clergy but he proved unable to steer all of them away from revolutionary ideas. Young clerics were the most vulnerable to the new intoxicating doctrines of the rights of man and a number of student-priests at Maynooth became involved with the United Irishmen. Ten of the sixty-nine students at the recently founded Royal College of Saint Patrick at Maynooth had taken the United Irishmen's oath, some when it was not a secret society. Eight of them pleaded their innocence but, after a meeting of the board of trustees, at which the archbishops of Dublin and Armagh, and the bishop of Cork, were present, all ten of them were expelled. A former student named Francis Hearn was sentenced to death for membership of the United Irishmen almost a year and a half after the rebellion in which he had taken no active part. The priest attending him at the scaffold, William Power, conducted a macabre interrogation. Where did he receive his revolutionary ideas? By reading French pamphlets on liberty while he was in Louvain was his reply. Did Maynooth College give him any of those ideas, the priest then asked him? No, he replied, it gave only 'wholesome advices and sound Christian doctrines'. Power then told 'the multitude present of every rank, that my motive for putting these ... questions to him was precisely to vindicate religion from the many uncharitable aspersions cast upon it by narrow evil minded individuals, who are well known to pronounce the whole body of Catholics to be from principle ... disposed to promote disorder'. Again concern to rebut the charge of disloyalty is uppermost in the Catholic clergy's mind. During the 1798 period, then, the stance taken by the church was to condemn violence and revolution. The reasons for condemning revolt were threefold: the sinfulness of a revolt against legitimate authority and the established order; the fear that the atrocities of the French Jacobins and their campaign of dechristianisation might spill over to Ireland; and the fear that a rebellion would endanger the hard-won concessions of recent decades.

The motives of Troy (and the bishops in general) in denouncing violence and rebellion are relatively easy to establish. Some Irish clergy, most of whom had trained in France, had, like the French clergy, initially welcomed the revolution, but then the Terror and the attempts at dechristianisation had turned them against it. Many of them, now prompted or constrained by landlords and bishops, preached sermons enjoining loyalty and often suffered intimidation from United Irishmen as a result. Their exhortations had, apparently, some effect, for Dublin, a hot-bed of United Irishmen's activity, saw no serious outbreak and most of the country remained quiet. Many Irish clergy simply went quietly about their pastoral work during the period. Yet when the 1798 Rebellion erupted some 70 priests were accused of being involved. All were not equally guilty, some probably not guilty at all and the total constituted a small proportion of the 1800 priests in the country. The bishops generally were highly critical of the rebel priests, Troy calling them the scum of the church and complaining that they had greatly damaged it.

The most interesting account of priests involved in the rebellion is contained in the report James Caulfield, bishop of Ferns, sent to Troy concerning the Wexford priests. Some twenty priests in the Wexford area were accused of taking part in the rebellion but, according to Caulfield, nine were innocent although one or two of them might have spoken unwisely to prevent greater evil. Another was mentally disturbed. Caulfield told Troy that most of the others, even before the rebellion, were no longer on the active ministry, some had been in trouble with their superiors, generally over disobedience, drunkenness, and in two cases at least because they were 'giddy', that is, possessed of revolutionary ideas. Caulfield, who was conservative, had just come through a frightening experience in Wexford town and was intent to defend the reputation of the church. Although it is likely that many of the ten rebel priests fell into the category he assigned to them, it is also possible that some of them were convinced of the justice of their actions. Since what records exist come from hostile sources, however, the motivation of the clergy who participated in the 1798 Rebellion is difficult to establish with accuracy. Friendship or kinship with the United Irishmen existed in more than one instance, sympathy with the aspirations and fears of their parishioners, genuine republicanism of the French style, all may have been present. The local situation varied from diocese to diocese and parish to parish. In the west of Ireland, among the fifteen or so priests accused of involvement, *many* appear to have been genuine supporters of Humbert's invasion but whether as committed United Irishmen or as leaders of the Catholic population who looked to the French for the deliverance from Protestant domination is not clear.[6]

In contrast to later-day 'patriot priests', only one of them – James O'Coigley, an Armagh priest – left any account of his actions. Even he is not explicit on his motives apart from saying that on his escape from the revolution in France, he deplored the persecution of Catholics that he had witnessed in Ulster. He believed a civil war was in progress and that religion was made the pretext, to the great profit of the government. O'Coigley was motivated by the ideal of the United Irishmen whose aim Tone had defined as the destruction of English interference in Ireland to be achieved by uniting

---

6. Keogh, *French disease*, pp 182–6.

Protestant, Catholic and Dissenter. The Augustinian friar, John Martin, in a confession made after his arrest, said he had 'entered into engagement with the United Irishmen to obtain their rights, thinking themselves an injured people' and because he believed that they intended to 'put all units on a level' and 'to dissolve all establishments'.[7] Those priests who espoused rebellion, however, constituted a tiny minority. Unrelenting opposition to rebellion was certainly the stand of the Irish church leaders during those tumultuous years. The appalling slaughter during the rebellion and terrible loyalist reprisals deepened the horror most clerics felt for revolution.

In the early decades of the nineteenth century, the Catholic church in Europe, while it continued in strong reaction against the excesses of the revolution, experienced a remarkable revival. Ireland shared in this new confidence of the European church and a new generation of Catholic leaders emerged. One of the most remarkable of them and one of the ablest bishops of his age was James Warren Doyle, bishop of Kildare and Leighlin, or 'JKL'. From 1822 on, Doyle had begun a remarkable series of lengthy 'Letters' vindicating the 'religious and civil principles' of Catholics.[8] Through his letters and his forceful evidence before a number of parliamentary committees and royal commissions, Doyle played a significant part in persuading educated British opinion of the justice of Irish Catholic claims. In 1824, anxious to promote Christian unity in Ireland but also to force the government to investigate and remedy the unhappy state of Ireland, Doyle appeared to challenge the line taken by Troy on civil obedience:

> The minister of England cannot look to the exertions of the Catholic priesthood ... they may yield for a moment to the influence of nature, though it be opposed to grace. The clergy, with few exceptions, are from the ranks of the people, they inherit their feelings, they are not, as formerly, brought up under despotic governments, and they have imbibed the doctrines of Locke and Paley more deeply than those of Bellarmin, or even Bossuet, on the divine right of kings; they know much more of the principles of the Constitution than they do of passive obedience. If a rebellion were raging from Carrickfergus to Cape Clear, no sentence of excommunication would ever be fulminated by a Catholic prelate.[9]

---

7. Ibid., pp 187–96.
8. *A vindication of the religious and civil principles of the Irish Catholics* ... (Dublin, 1823) was one of the earliest and most significant of these letters.
9. J.W. Doyle, *Letter to Robertson* [sic] *esq. M.P. on a union of the Catholics and Protestant churches* (Dublin, 1824). Thomas McGrath, 'Politics, interdenominational relations and education in the public ministry of James Doyle, OSA, 1819–1834', (Hull Univ., Ph.D. thesis, 1992), pp 31–41 gives a full analysis of this important letter.

There was a shocked reaction among conservatives. In Maynooth College, the senior professor of theology, Louis Delahogue, exclaimed in disbelief, 'Mon Dieu, il prêche la révolution' to the chorus of the equally astounded colleague, François Anglade, 'La révolution, la révolution!'. To clear the church of any such suspicion the four professors of theology at Maynooth issued a statement demonstrating how they fulfilled their duty of training priests as loyal citizens:

> In discharging this solemn duty we have been guided by the unchangeable principles of the Catholic religion, plainly and forcibly contained in the precepts of St Peter and St Paul. Our commentaries on these texts cannot be better conveyed than in the language of Tertullian. 'Christians are aware who has conferred their power on the Emperors: they know it is God, after whom they are first in rank. We Christians invoke on all the Emperors, the blessings of long life, a prosperous reign, domestic security, a brave army, a devoted senate, and a moral people.'

The eighteenth-century bishops and priests, and indeed many of Doyle's contemporaries like Delahogue, belonged to the *ancien régime* and accepted the hierarchical order of society and the divine right of kings. Delahogue and Anglade, who had taught in Gallican seminaries in France, set the theological tone for the first two generations of Maynooth priests. Contemporary France was witnessing, in the writings of De Maistre, a powerful restatement of those ideas. Doyle, however, marks a change, for although his aim in the letter was to paint in dramatic terms the danger of allowing misrule to continue, yet he was also changing the terms of reference as regards rebellion. He told a parliamentary commission in 1832 that 'if we are prevented from pursuing a right because in pursuing that right evils may arise, we must abandon ourselves to utter despotism'. If Doyle was correct in claiming that the clergy had now imbibed the doctrines of Locke, this swing was of great significance. Doyle himself had read Locke during his training in Portugal and later insisted on placing some of Locke's works on the programme for the students for the priesthood at Saint Patrick's College, Carlow. His concept of allegiance rested on the notion of a contract between ruler and ruled, a view which through Hobbes, became one dear to Locke and Rousseau and other leading writers of the Enlightenment. Doyle was not far removed from Whig views.

A private letter which Doyle wrote shortly after O'Connell had won his famous victory at the Clare election, reveals that he had not excluded rebellion from his thoughts.

> We are a divided people.... We are unlike ... to any people who ever obtained independence in despite of a powerful state. And the advantages we possess cannot be made available to that great purpose. I have made the calculation a thousand times and I always came to the conclusion 'tis impossible and ought not to be attempted. We must proceed on another course, there is less risk in it. Change not less important than revolutions may be effected without the sword ... the power of knowledge is able to effect in a peaceable manner what heretofore could only be produced by war.... I would prefer a lesser degree of happiness than is possible than to see her [Ireland?] thrown into a furnace having no assurance of her escape from it.[10]

Perhaps too much should not be read into a private letter and, in any case, Doyle made it clear that he was firmly committed to peaceful pressure. To what extent other bishops shared his views is not clear.

By the 1840s Catholics were more self-confident thanks, in part, to Catholic emancipation and the leadership of Doyle, MacHale and O'Connell. O'Connell had won over the clergy to his campaign for repeal of the Union, largely because he channelled the discontent of their people away from violence into constitutional agitation. 'The [national] spirit', a priest wrote, 'weaned by O'Connell from the midnight folly of rebellion – taught by him the secret of moral power'. An old friend of O'Connell and his key political helper in Waterford for over a quarter of a century, Fr John Sheehan, wrote to him in 1845 'There is no part of your doctrine as an agitator which I admire more than you saying that you would not bring about the greatest possible good at the expense of one drop of human blood'. In 1846, when the dispute broke out between the Young Irelanders and O'Connell on the abstract question of the legitimacy of force to achieve political ends, the clergy rallied to O'Connell.[11] Bishop Cantwell of Meath warned that '[T]he Catholic members, be they Young or Old Ireland, who could advocate the resort to physical force in the debates of an association that has enrolled the great majority of the Bishops and Clergy of Ireland, must be regardless of their duties as Christians'. 'To pursue a course of physical force', he concluded, 'would prove fatal to the temporal and eternal welfare of the flocks committed to our pastoral care'.[12] O'Higgins' comment was more dismissive: 'we have no physical force men in this diocese. Neither have we, thank God,

---

10. Doyle to [?Robert Cassidy], 13 Apr. 1829, (Kildare and Leighlin Diocesan Archives, File 1829/25), cited in McGrath, 'Doyle', pp 114–15.
11. For the Young Ireland period, Dennis Gwynn, *Young Ireland and 1848* (Cork, 1949); R.P. Davis, *The Young Ireland movement* (Dublin, 1987); Kerr, *'Nation of beggars?*, pp 126–30.
12. *Tablet*, 31 July 1846.

any schoolboy philosophers, false and sanguinary Repealers or Voltairian newspapers'.[13] Other O'Connellite bishops followed suit. The fiery MacHale distanced himself from any suspicion of physical force: 'with the advocates of physical force and sanguinary revolution we disown all sympathy'.[14]

It is all the more surprising that the run-up to the rebellion of 1848 is, arguably, the only period in Irish history since the seventeenth century, in which one finds a substantial number of clerics, including one bishop, apparently defending the right to rebel. The 1848 rebellion has understandably been written off as 'a cabbage-patch rebellion', but its place in the context of the 'Springtime of the Nations' and the debate on the issues raised make it deserving of more interest. From early in 1848, many priests spoke publicly in ominously revolutionary tones. At a meeting in Limerick on 3 April Rev. Dr O'Brien promised that the priest would 'brave any danger to wrest their [his countrymen's] souls and bodies from the debasement, destitution, and destruction of foreign rule'. A Limerick priest declared that it was 'far better to die as men died in Berlin, Vienna, and Paris than that another million should die the death of Skibbereen'. On 9 April, at a meeting at Causeway, Kerry, Rev. Mathias McMahon spoke of Ireland 'at last preparing in earnest to get rid of the robber rule of England'. Fr O'Sullivan, the parish priest of Killorglin, went further. At a Repeal meeting in Killarney attended by seven priests, he declared:

> Louis Philippe was a bad man and therefore a determined people armed and hurled him from the pinnacle of greatness. But, bad though he was, no man in France died of famine. Was that the case under the 'base, bloody, and brutal Whigs'? Seek the answer from the millions of our poor countrymen who are rotting in their graves because of the misrule of England.... if their constitutional appeal [were] treated with ridicule, he for one ... was prepared to take his stand with the people.

One bishop took an equally strong line. Edward Maginn, coadjutor and acting bishop of Derry, told George Poulet Scrope, MP for Stroud, who had exposed the horrors of evictions in parliament, that 'sooner than allow their [the people's] present misery to continue, like the archbishop of Milan, I would rather grasp the cross and the green flag of Ireland and rescue my country, or perish with its people'. Fr James Birmingham of Borrisokane gave this dramatic advice to the people: 'First make your peace with God....

---

13. Ibid., 8 Aug. 1846.
14. Ibid.

Secondly – arm quietly.... When ... your liberties as well as your lives shall be invaded ... let every man ... make a vow ... to lessen ... by one man at least, the enemies of my native land and to die'.[15] Fr John Kenyon harangued a mass meeting in Templederry, in support of Mitchel, Meagher and Smith O'Brien, the imprisoned Young Irelanders, and elicited a promise from the aroused crowd to die for the arrested men. '[E]very man', he proclaimed, 'ought to conquer this government that is lying like a load of lead on the heart of his country ... or die'.[16] Kenyon, too, took up the theory of a social contract. Others, like Fr Coughlan of Waterford, spelt out this line of thought: 'in allegiance there is a contract, and should either party fail to supply the due conditions, then it falls to the ground.... it is pretty clear that *one* of the contracting parties was found wanting. The unworthy death of some 800,000 honest men attest it'.

Fr Hughes, in Mayo, cited Paley to the effect that 'the duty of allegiance is neither unlimited or unconditional'. The views expressed by Coughlan and Hughes, as well as the more influential Kenyon, give substance to Doyle's comment on the influence of Locke and Paley. Even allowing for the rhetoric, the language used in 1848 was startlingly strong. The score or more who expressed such views represent a small percentage of the 3000 priests but there is evidence that many more shared those views.[17] How can we explain this change from the universal support for O'Connell's policy of non-violence?

The events that sharpened clerical language were partly domestic, partly European. A million or so had died in the previous year and a half. After the Gregory quarter-acre clause came into operation matters worsened and evictions soared from between 3500 and 3600 in 1846 to 6026 in 1847 and 9657 in 1848. Violence increased and landlords and agents were assassinated. When Major Mahon was murdered in County Roscommon the parish priest, Michael MacDermott, was accused of being responsible because, it was alleged, he had declared from the altar that 'Major Mahon was worst than Cromwell, and yet he lives'. Press and parliament denounced the priests as instigators of assassination. It was publicly suggested that in every parish where a landlord was shot, the parish priest should be hanged, and the foreign secretary, Lord Palmerston, made the same suggestion privately. In Rome, Lord Minto presented the accusation against McDermott and the priests as facts and secured a reproof to the clergy from a startled Pius IX. No

---

15. *Nation*, 15 Apr. 1848.
16. Ibid., 22 Apr. 1848.
17. Kerr, *'Nation of beggars'?*, pp 135–6.

proof could be found for the accusation against McDermott which was almost certainly unfounded. The accusations against the priests proved counter-productive. The clergy who, obedient to O'Connell, had supported the Whig government and endeavoured to persuade the starving peasants not to break the law, were outraged. A letter from a timid non-political bishop, Edmund French of Kilmacduagh to Paul Cullen, rector of the Irish College in Rome, merits citing at length:

> ... the yellings of the poor, on the Roads, in the streets of our Towns, at all our Houses ... the heart-rending scenes in the Houses of the poor, lying sick of fever, starvation, of inanition and want, are the daily prospects of our Clergy.... In one parish alone there were twenty-one deaths of heads of Families in four days ... they all died with the utmost resignation to the Will of God blessing the Priest for a very small temporary help. These are the scenes constantly witnessed by our Clergy in the South and West of Ireland!!! and alas if we dare describe these afflictions of our people and our own Agonies at their heartrending sufferings, we are stamped by our Enemies of this English Press and the leading Members of Parliament as 'Surplissed [sic] Ruffians and Instigators of the Murder of the Landed Gentry and the Exterminators of the People'!!![18]

Frustration at famine deaths, anger at ruthless evictions and fury at being accused of instigating assassination, might not have triggered off clerical revolutionary language were it not for an outside factor – the 1848 revolutions in Europe and the church's attitude to them. In France, after Louis Philippe had been toppled in February, the clergy blessed trees of liberty; in Milan the archbishop appeared on the barricades; in the papal states clerics sported the Italian tricolour cockade, an action which only two years earlier would have brought a charge of sedition. Most important was the attitude of the pope. In 1846, a Liberal pope, the only eventuality Metternich had not provided for, had ascended the papal throne – Pius IX. He immediately granted an amnesty, established a *consulta* (parliament) and courageously challenged Austria when Radetzky's army paraded truculently through Ferrara in July 1847. When Pius concluded a speech with the stirrings words 'God bless Italy', his words were hailed as blessing Italian national aspirations. 'The ferment [of patriotism] penetrated the seminaries ... and drove many priests and religious brothers to take a rifle in their hand as if in that way they could reconcile the love of their country and the priestly mission.'[19] The first months of 1848 – the Springtime of the Nations – was

---

18. French to Cullen, 16 Feb. 1848 (Archives of the Pontifical Irish College, Rome, Cullen Papers).
19. Giacomo Martina, *Pio IX 1846–50* (Rome, 1974), pp 197–8.

quite extraordinary in Europe as revolution spread from country to country. Lacordaire could well speak of 'Dieu et Liberté'. What would happen in Ireland? Cornewall Lewis exclaimed in some dread that 'The sparks blown over Europe by the French Revolution find a train of disaffection towards the English connexion ready laid in Ireland'. Would the Irish clergy set the match? Smith O'Brien returned from France, enthused by the co-operation of the priests in the new regime and devoutly hoping that the Irish priests would imitate them. Certainly, during the months from March to June, despite the efforts of bishops and government, many spoke out publicly as if they would. As late as July 1848, the able Fr Thaddeus O'Malley made a powerful effort to win over the bishops:

> The great and striking moral phenomena of our day is the almost simultaneous resurrection throughout all Europe of oppressed Nationalities.... The Catholic church in other lands has given to the holy cause of National freedom its heroes or its martyrs, each confronting danger differently in different circumstances – the Lombard bishop braving death as a soldier because the battle was to be won – the Frank braving death as a pacificator because the battle was won. With such examples, with the still higher example of our noble Chief Pontiff, who has preserved the Catholic religion in Italy, by making himself the head apostle of Italian freedom, is it for you, my Lords, to shrink from a struggle the most righteous of all?'[20]

O'Malley was a cleric of great ability whom the government had appointed rector of the University of Malta despite Rome's disapproval. His independent line had brought him into collision with church authorities before but Archbishop Murray, who recognised his ability, was well-disposed to him. This time, however, Murray was not impressed by his arguments. Murray had long opposed rebellion and was suspicious of the Repeal agitation, fearing it would lead in that direction. In March 1848, he had complained to Cullen, whom he knew to be an ardent supporter of Repeal, of the applause given to Alexandre Ledru Rollin, now one of the leaders of the revolution in France, who was again promising support for Ireland: 'The Man who in 1843 offered armed assistance from a foreign Country to our Irish Repealers, and who was therefore rejected by O'Connell, was publicly cheered at a meeting in Dublin last night. I always feared that our movement would lead to such fatal result, which may God avert'. [21]

The clergy were not confining themselves, he feared, to 'the sphere of their clerical duty' and were joining the confederate clubs. Murray, appalled at

---

20. *Nation*, 15 July 1848.
21. Murray to Cullen, 8 April 1848, copy, (Dublin Diocesan Archives, Murray Papers).

their behaviour, insisted that as servants of the prince of peace, they should abhor violence. As a last resort, Murray finally went public in the newspapers, warning the people of the horrific sufferings during the rebellion of 1798 which he had observed at first hand: 'Fifty years ago I witnessed the miseries which a convulsion ... inflicted on the political, social and moral condition of this unhappy country. Can anyone be surprised that a thrill of horror should rush through my soul at the thought of the recurrence of such a calamity? May God in his mercy avert it!'[22]

Bishop Kennedy of Killaloe also acted decisively against the two most prominent priest-supporters of Young Ireland in his diocese, John Kenyon and James Birmingham. Kennedy now entered into a discussion on the legitimacy of rebellion, with Laurence Renehan, president of Maynooth.[23] Both accepted that in certain circumstances rebellion could be justifiable but agreed that encouragement to rebel at that moment was criminal. Renehan based his reply on the question of the legality or illegality of the Act of Union. In accepting the legitimacy of the government, he used an argument not mentioned earlier: that of 'prescription', or right obtained by long-continued usage. '[T]hough I believe the Act of Union to have been most corruptly, unjustly, iniquitously procured', he wrote, 'yet after so long an acquiescence I would be *conscientiously* afraid to ... treat it ... as a nullity'. On more practical grounds, he denounced the 'unpriestly and scandalous incentives' of those priests whose rhetoric could seduce the people to 'the gallows or a bloody grave'.[24] Kennedy's opposition was based on similar pragmatic grounds. If the clergy preached rebellion, the result, he feared, would be civil war 'which few would be willing to face except that unhappy class who are so steeped in misery as to be ... persuaded that no change could be worse for them'. Neither of them took up the question of the government's alleged breach of contract in permitting so many to die of famine nor did they refer to the events abroad. In contrast to bishops in the 1790s they were not concerned about the revival of the penal laws or about proving their loyalty. They now drew a distinction between crown and government which the bishops in the 1790s had not dared to draw. The question of secret oath-bound societies did not surface for the Young Irelanders were not secret.

If the revolutions in Europe encouraged some priests to threaten rebellion in Ireland, when those revolutions became more extreme, the Irish priests

---

22. *Tablet*, 12 Apr. 1848.
23. Kennedy to Renehan, 2, 8 June 1848; Renehan to Kennedy, 4 June 1848 (Maynooth College Archives, Renehan Papers, 7/18/13).
24. Renehan to Kennedy, 4 June 1848, (Maynooth College Archives, Renehan Papers).

began to pull back. The shooting of Archbishop Affre of Paris at the barricades on 25 June 1848 marked the turning point and provided the 'media-conscious' lord lieutenant, Clarendon, with an admirable opportunity to exploit it in the press. He was successful and exultantly told Russell, the prime minister, that 'the priests have taken alarm at the death of the Archbishop of Paris, who, poor man, never did a better thing in his life than getting himself murdered'. '[Cooke Taylor and] I have kept up such an uninterrupted fire of anti-infidel articles founded upon the experience of all French revolutions that their Reverences have struck their flags and are coming over in flocks'. When the Young Irelanders did rebel in July not merely did the priests stand aloof but several were instrumental in persuading the people to steer clear of what they saw as insane folly. Fr Philip Fitzgerald, who rode up to the Widow McCormack's house in Ballingarry and persuaded the irresolute Smith O'Brien to abandon the siege and effectively abort the rebellion, explained his position later:

> On the one hand, a numerous army, well-appointed and disciplined and supplied with all the munitions of war, on the other an undisciplined and unarmed peasantry, without leaders of any knowledge or experience, and destitute of everything that could render success certain or even probable. This weighed heavily with me ... for that there should be carnage at all, was much to be lamented, but that it should be entirely on one side, and especially on the side of a poor and oppressed population, with whom all my sympathies were enlisted and with whom I in every way identified, was an idea from which I recoiled instinctively.[25]

After the collapse of the rebellion Michael Doheny reported that Young Irelanders who had fled to America alleged 'that the entire failure was attributable to the Catholic priests, and that in opposing the liberation of Ireland they acted in accordance with some recognised radical principle of the Church'. While not accepting these complaints uncritically, Doheny felt that they had some foundation and disclosed how the priests in Mullinahone and in Ballingarry advised against continuing in arms and also alleged that Fr Patrick Laffan, curate in Fethard, had 'read the names of the proscribed traitors for whose persons a reward was offered'.[26] Smith O'Brien unreservedly blamed the bishops for the people's failure to rebel. While the collapse of the rebellion was mainly due to the rebels' incompetent leadership, the intervention of Murray, Kennedy and priests on the spot played a major part in

---

25. Philip Fitzgerald, *Personal recollections of the insurrection at Ballingarry in July 1848* (London, 1861), p. 34.
26. Michael Doheny, *The felon's track* (New York, 1849; repr. Dublin, 1951) pp xxviii–xxix, 184.

preventing the rebellion from becoming more serious. As a result the loss of life was minimal and the government decided against executing any of the rebels. Most clerics acted for practical reasons – reaction against the sheer folly of pike-armed peasants confronting the might of the British Empire and the suffering that would follow. Questions of the inviolability of the social order or obedience to papal decrees were not to the fore in their arguments. A few years after the rebellion, the question was examined by Patrick Murray, professor of theology at Maynooth College, who had denounced the state trials of the Young Irelanders in 1848 and had become a close friend of Charles Gavan Duffy.[27] Obedience to the legitimate civil power in all things lawful, was, he argued, 'the defined and solemn teaching of the Church' and prescription made the British government legitimate. On the right to rebel, he maintained that it was lawful to resist by force a tyrannical ruler but only if stringent conditions were verified: the tyranny must be unbearable and manifest to men of good sense and not just to the revolutionaries; the evils following from submission must be greater than those resulting from rebellion; there must be no other means of shaking off the tyranny; there must be a moral certainty of success and the rebellion must be approved by the community at large. By and large, what Murray advanced in this article represented the general outlook of the Catholic theologians in Ireland and abroad. The first part of Brendan Behan's claim as regards the clergy and the 1848 rebellion was, then, substantially correct. The second part of Behan's claim, however, that the clergy told the people to give up their crops and die of hunger in the ditches cannot be sustained. The bishops, at their annual meetings in 1847, 1848 and at the national Synod of Thurles in 1850, insisted that the right to life must take precedence over property rights. The poor, they wrote, made in the image of the living God and purchased by the blood of Calvary, were victims of the most ruthless oppression that ever disgraced the annals of humanity. 'Exterminator' was the terrible name the Synod fastened on to describe those who carried out the evictions.[28]

Some of the 1848 rebels did not abandon their desire to end British rule by force and from the 1850s on their new organisation in the United States and Ireland, the Fenians, began to speak of rebellion.[29] Again church leaders opposed them, for some saw in the Fenians a recrudescence of the secret agrarian societies of pre-Famine Ireland which they had hoped that

---

27. 'The right to resistance to the supreme civil power: is it in any case allowable?' in P.A. Murray, *Essays chiefly theological*, (Dublin, 1852), iv, pp 379–407.
28. Kerr, *'Nation of beggars'?*, pp 82–3, 168, 229–30.
29. Larkin, *R. C. Ch. 1860–70*.

O'Connell had exorcised for ever, while others like Paul Cullen, now archbishop of Dublin, regarded them as on a par with European secret societies of the type encouraged by Mazzini. Cullen, the acknowledged leader of the hierarchy, led the attack. Like Troy eighty years before, Cullen brought the international dimension of the church into the question. For Cullen, a devout ultramontane reforming bishop who had trained in Rome and had spent many years there as rector of the Irish College, it was perfectly normal then that he should base his condemnation of fenianism on the popes' teaching. In 1821, Pius VII had reissued the condemnations of Clement XII and Benedict XIV, in a new apostolic constitution, *Ecclesiam*, adding specifically the Carbonari (who like the Fenians had claimed that the condemnation of the Freemasons did not apply to them) to the list of condemned secret societies. In 1825, Leo XII had repeated the previous condemnations in the apostolic constitution *Quo Graviora* and extended it to all existing and future secret societies which set themselves against the church and governments.[30] Cullen had been through the Roman revolution and republic in 1848–49 during which he had both developed a deep distaste for the revolutionaries and shown considerable courage and foresight in resisting them. The Fenian society, he believed, was no different from that of the arch-revolutionary, Mazzini, and so he condemned it as opposed to Catholic teaching. He was also motivated by the same practical pastoral reason that had influenced Troy, Philip Fitzgerald of Ballingarry, and Murray, whose timid and 'anti-national' stance he had too easily criticised. Pleading with Archbishop Martin Spalding of Baltimore to check the influence of the Fenians, he wrote: 'if the Fenians of America drive the people here to revolt, the massacres of Cromwell will be renewed and all gained by religion in a century will be lost'. Cullen, despite his own strong nationalistic feelings, had come to accept the Union as the framework within which much good could be achieved for Ireland and the Catholic church. He saw the Fenian agitation for an Irish republic as a chimera and an irritant because it distracted the people, 'with impractical madness', as he explained to Barnabò, so 'that they no longer think about education and the conditions of the poor and ... other ... necessary things'.[31]

To his chagrin, Cullen was challenged by Fr Patrick Lavelle, parish priest of Partry, who boldly accused him of falsely applying papal decisions on

---

30. 'societates occultas omnes tam quae nunc sunt tamque deinceps erumpent et quae ea sibi adversus Ecclesiam et supremas Civiles potestates proparunt'. The best study of the implications of these constitutions for the condemnation of the Fenians is the unpublished work of James O'Brien, 'The Irish hierarchy and the Fenian movement 1858–1870: a study of the right to rebel'.
31. Cullen to Barnabò, 16 Nov. 1861, quoted in Larkin, *R. C. Ch. 1860–1870*, p. 75.

secret societies to the Fenians. Lavelle made three points. The first was that the continental societies were condemned because they opposed both legitimate civil authority and the church. The Fenians, Lavelle argued, while they opposed the civil authority, did not oppose the church and so did not fall under the terms of the apostolic constitution. His second and major argument concerned the legitimacy of government. The opponents of rebellion, (particularly the Maynooth theologians such as Renehan and Patrick Murray) invoked 'prescription' or legitimisation through long-continued and unchallenged use, to justify English rule, a line of argument which Cullen and most churchmen accepted. Lavelle, however, and his ally in Philadelphia, Fr Philip Moriarty, an Augustinian friar, rector of St Augustine's church, Philadelphia, a fiery nationalist, challenged that argument, contending that Ireland had never given consent to England's rule; it was a rule of 700 years of misery, whose aim was that of exterminating those whom England unceasingly named aliens in blood, language and religion. This bold assertion of a widespread and continuous rejection of English rule was to become the classic nationalist justification of rebellion. Last, Lavelle adopted the social contract theory, which Doyle and the 1848 priests had introduced. All power came from God to the people, he claimed, who in turn bestowed it on the ruler. If the ruler is tyrannical, the people could and should overthrow him.

The ruler in question at the time he wrote was Lord John Russell and his Liberal government, and, as Cullen bitterly complained to Cardinal Antonelli, Pius IX's secretary for state, Russell was playing straight into Lavelle's hands. Russell and his government were foremost in seeking to overthrow the oldest legitimate state in Europe, the Papal States, on the ground of real or alleged popular discontent. Lavelle, in his memorial to the pope in 1864, was able to accuse Cullen of being the efficacious cause of the spoliation of the Papal States by his indirect support of the Liberal government, through the Independent Irish members.[32] Cullen, scandalised by Lavelle's audacity in challenging his authority and even more so by his continuous propaganda in favour of a secret oath-bound society, condemned him. For a decade, however, the resourceful Lavelle successfully defied him. He was protected by MacHale who indeed condemned fenianism but had no intention of allowing Cullen to dictate to priests in his province. When Cullen asked Rome for an explicit condemnation of the Fenians, the matter went before the Holy Office which referred back to its earlier statements. This was of no use to Cullen for it was precisely the interpretation of those statements as

---

32. Ibid., pp 248–9.

applicable to the Fenians that Lavelle had challenged. Rome's reticence lay partly in the Curia's normal reluctance to condemn by name, preferring implicit condemnation. But principally Rome was reticent because Lavelle and his supporters had raised a serious doubt, a *dubium iuris,* concerning the interpretation of the earlier apostolic decree.[33] That doubt would first have to be solved.

A new dimension to the problem emerged which was thenceforth to remain an integral part of all Irish nationalist problems – the impact on the Irish abroad. Since the Fenians had begun in America, the attitude of the American bishops and of their large Irish communities, had to be taken into account. The first bishops to condemn the Fenians were James Duggan of Chicago, and James Wood of Philadelphia. Other bishops were reluctant to follow their example and when they appealed to Rome for a decision Rome again referred to earlier documents. The Holy Office's position after these first appeals from Cullen and the American bishops was not as static as might appear for, in its reply, it added that if this did not have the desired effect, the matter was to be referred back. Furthermore, according to Odo Russell, the English envoy in Rome, Pius IX and Cardinal Antonelli, the secretary for state, not only opposed fenianism, but both also believed that the condemnations of the freemasons and secret societies in the Syllabus of Errors had implicitly condemned the Fenians.[34] Nevertheless, it still left Lavelle free to exploit the loopholes.

Cullen did his best to convince Rome that the Fenians were indeed anti-church and extreme statements in the Fenian press provided him with ample material to prove his case. Pius was convinced and, according to Odo Russell, he expressed his sympathy for the bishops who 'were constantly exposed to a bastonata from the Fenians who were the Garibaldians of England'.[35] Yet when the rebellion did break out in 1867, Cullen's own description of the pathetic failure of the rebellion in Kerry bears out to some extent Lavelle's claim that the Fenians, while they pilloried Cullen and other bishops, were not opposed to the church. 'It appears there were only 35 armed men to overthrow the British government' he told his confidant, Tobias Kirby, rector of the Irish College in Rome.

> One poor Catholic policeman was shot. The Fenians hearing he was a Catholic sent two men to call the priest. After he had attended the wounded

---

33. O'Brien 'The Irish hierarchy and the Fenian movement'.
34. Odo Russell to Clarendon, 6 Apr., 15 May 1866; 26 Mar. 1868; Noel Blakiston, *The Roman question; extracts from the despatches of Odo Russell from Rome, 1858–1870* (London, 1962), pp 325, 327, 351.
35. Russell to Clarendon, 13 Jan. 1870, Blakiston, *Roman Question*, p. 381.

man, the priest went to the police barracks and told the policemen to be on their guard. He then told the Fenians not to attack the police as he had give them notice that they were to be attacked. You never heard of so peaceful a revolution as this.

It was on this occasion that Bishop Moriarty preached those words never forgotten or forgiven by republicans: 'hell is not hot enough nor eternity long enough to punish those miscreants'. Yet his attack was directed not at the ordinary rank and file of the Fenians but at the Fenian godfathers in America whom he perceived as ultimately responsible for the sorry fate of the captured rebels. Cullen sharply criticised Moriarty for 'so foolish an exaggeration' and wished he could be called to account for it. Lavelle had written a fierce letter against Moriarty, Cullen added, and 'the worst of the letter is that it tells a good deal of truth'.[36] Cullen was also incensed at the 'godfathers', the Fenian instigators, and concerned about their 'dupes'. 'It is just the same as in Italy', he lamented to Kirby, 'the unfortunate agents suffered but the leaders, the Mazzinis and Garibaldis, all remain safe'.[37] Cullen regarded the Fenians as 'excommunicate' and, with manifest unhappiness, told Kirby in Rome, that 'The unfortunate Fenians generally attempted to go to confession – but they are always told that unless they gave up their insane projects, they could not get absolution'.[38]

After the failure of the 1867 rebellion, the amnesty movement for the Fenian prisoners found strong support even among the clergy. Cullen made one of his rare visits to the vice-regal lodge to plead for the life of Colonel Thomas P. Bourke and other Fenians. The condemned Fenians were reprieved at the eleventh hour. Yet Cullen feared that the many priests who sympathised with the aims of the Fenians, even if they disapproved of their means, might get out of control. He therefore pressed for firm and concerted episcopal action. The Vatican Council provided him with the opportunity, for the Irish bishops were thrown together for a number of months in Rome. Waverers like Bishop Keane of Cloyne were won over and a common policy formulated. Two weeks later the Holy Office came to a decision which, effectively, gave the bishops what they wanted – an inclusion of the Fenians in the category of condemned secret societies. Yet although this condemnation may have been due in part to a desire to meet the hierarchy's request, it is unlikely that it rushed the Holy Office into a decision a mere two weeks

---

36. Larkin, *R. C. Ch. 1860–70*, pp 421–7.
37. Cullen to Kirby, 12 Mar. 1867 (Irish College, Rome, Kirby Papers), cited in Larkin, *R. C. Ch. 1860–70*, p. 425.
38. Cullen to Kirby, 8 Mar. 1867, Kirby Papers, cited ibid., p. 423.

later. It is far more likely, as James O'Brien argues, that it was the end of the process initiated earlier.[39]

The case had been re-activated at the Holy Office in October 1869. By January 1870 it had resolved the doubt in law which Lavelle's interpretation had raised. The Holy Office did not issue a condemnation of the Fenians; it merely decided a dispute on a point of law which Lavelle's statement raised – were the Fenians included in the earlier apostolic constitutions or not. The result, however, was the same – the Fenians fell under the ban of the church. 'The American or Irish Society called the society of the Fenians, is included among the societies forbidden and condemned in the Constitutions of the Sovereign Pontiffs'.[40] The decision, dated 12 January 1870, could not have been more explicit.

The decision angered the American bishops who had not been consulted and it posed serious pastoral problems for them as Archbishop Spalding explained to Cullen.[41] Still, Cullen had gained his objective and had secured a common line on fenianism. The policy he put in place was to remain the consistent attitude of the Catholic church to the Fenians, to the Irish Republican Brotherhood and the post-Treaty Irish Republican Army – a secret oathbound society was subject to excommunication. Yet just as the Fenian rebellion persuaded Gladstone to promote concessions, it pushed Cullen to abandon his policy of keeping the clergy totally out of politics and convinced him to set up a political association for agrarian and other reforms.

How widespread was clerical support for the aims of the Fenians? There was disaffection with government and even Cullen told Archbishop Spalding that Britain had only itself to blame for the anger felt towards her by Irish-Americans. On 2 March 1868, Bishop Moriarty gloomily confided to his friend and supporter, Monsell, the MP for County Limerick, that 'the clergy will preach against rebellion on account of the evils it will bring on the people, but I am sure that their almost unanimous opinion [is, that] if there were a fair chance of success, it would be lawful, nay dulce et decorum'. This is probably an exaggeration. Yet some at least were sympathetic and for reasons not dissimilar to those put forward by Maginn and the priests in 1848 – a protest against the pitiful plight of their people. Lavelle's own fame came originally from his robust support of the peasants against what he saw as the rapacity and sectarianism of landlords. Others like Fr John O'Connor

---

39. O'Brien, 'Irish hierarchy and the Fenian movement'.
40. The original text is in *I.E.R.*, new ser., ii (1872), 240.
41. Cullen to George Conroy, bishop of Ardagh, 28 Jan. 1870, in Peadar Mac Suibhne, *Paul Cullen and his contemporaries* (Dublin, 1977), pp 47–8.

in Ballingarry, were sympathetic. In a revealing passage of his autobiography, Canon Peter O'Leary, An tAthair Peadar as he was affectionately known later, the founder of modern Irish language literature, recalls his sympathy with the Fenians. He believed that the Fenians were mistaken but he was as bitter as they were about what he perceived as English oppression of Ireland: 'I had a fierce hatred of the people of England because of that' [Ireland's oppression].[42] The parish priest of Doneraile in County Cork, William Croke, later declared that 'I could never bring myself to rank Fenians as a body with Freemasons…'. However, Croke (later a supporter of the Land League and home rule) prudently waited until he himself was an archbishop before telling Cullen so. Oliver MacDonagh wittily refers to 'recessional clerical ambivalence' which enabled the clergy, as particular manifestations of nationalistic violence receded in time, to sanction them more safely.[43] Yet if some clerics sympathised with the aims of the Fenians, Lavelle was alone in giving open support.[44]

A comparison with the Polish situation during the nineteenth century brings the Holy See's attitude to the right to rebel into greater relief. In 1830, the Poles, unwilling to co-operate in crushing the Belgians who had rebelled against the Dutch king, and hoping to regain their own independence, rose in revolt. Many of their priests preached insurrection, and the Poles appealed to the pope to call an urgent meeting of plenipotentiaries to resolve their difficulties with the tsar. The nuncio in Vienna approached the Austrian chancellor, Prince Metternich, but he refused to get involved. Pope Gregory XVI (1831–46) came under pressure from the tsar who insinuated that if the pope did not act he would be responsible for the repression that would follow. In the encyclical, *Cum Primum,* addressed to the Polish bishops, Gregory denounced revolutionary movements and condemned those who used religion as an excuse to revolt against the legitimate ruler. At the same time, he wrote to the tsar listing Polish grievances and called on him for better treatment. In an interview with Count Saint-Aulaire, French ambassador to the Holy See, he explained his conduct:

> The Pope said … that he was no politician, but had always performed what he felt to be his duty, and took the Bible as the Rule of his actions. Thus during the late revolution I remembered that Scripture enjoins men to be obedient to constituted authorities, and accordingly I endeavoured by means of letters which I addressed to the Catholic Clergy to recall the Emperor's

---

42. Peadar Ua Laoghaire, *Mo sgéal féin* (Dublin, 1915), pp 112–21.
43. Oliver MacDonagh, 'Ambiguity in nationalism: the case of Ireland' in Ciaran Brady (ed.), *Interpreting Irish history: the debate on historical revisionism* (Dublin, 1994), p. 115.
44. Larkin, *R. C. Ch. 1860–70*, p. 438.

Polish subjects to their allegiance. Now that the revolution has been put down, I call to mind that Princes are bound to be merciful to their subjects, and that my duty as Head of the Church obliges me to make the strongest representations in favour of those of our creed who are treated with over-severity ...[45]

This is as clear a statement of papal attitude as one can find. The tsar, however, was delighted with the pope's action. He made extensive use of the encyclical enjoining loyalty, but suppressed all mention of the other letters rebuking his own conduct. Further, the tsar ignored Gregory's repeated calls for better treatment for the Poles both in 1832, and again in 1842. It was a bitter time for Polish patriots who, in addition to Russian ill-treatment, felt abandoned and publicly rebuked by the head of their religion. By 1842, Gregory had learned a lesson and in that year vehemently charged the tsar with wholesale persecution. In 1844, when the Russian ambassador Count Butenev, and the tsar's special envoy, Count Struwe, suggested a concordat between Rome and Russia, which would mainly concern Polish Catholics, Gregory reprimanded the Russian envoys and declared that he would have no part in secret deals behind the backs of the people concerned and pointed to the Catholic Irish rejection of any such transactions. At the same time, he sought Metternich's support for his action towards the tsar. Gregory took a far more understanding attitude towards the Irish agitation for repeal of the Union, despite the misgivings of Metternich and the repeated efforts of Britain to extract a papal condemnation of O'Connell's agitation.[46] The probable reason is that Irish bishops and highly-placed clerics were able to persuade Gregory that the Irish agitation, however menacing, remained within constitutional limits. O'Connell, in the house of commons, had no hesitation in expressing his vigorous support for the Polish rebels.

The church's attitude during the Polish insurrection of 1863 was different. The Polish clergy, including an archbishop of Warsaw, took an active part in protests and rebellions against Russia and, in the insurrection, many priests and, particularly, very many religious supported the rebels. The rebellion brought savage reprisals against the church. Four-fifths of the religious houses and convents were suppressed; nine bishops and 400 clerics were deported to the interior of Russia. Pope Pius IX protested sharply and, in revenge, the tsar forbade the Polish bishops to attend the Vatican Council in 1869. In Ireland,

---

45. George Seymour to Lord Palmerston, 28 Aug. 1832, Foreign Office 79/65, cited in J. F. Broderick, *The Holy See and the Irish movement for the repeal of the union with England, 1829–1847* (Rome, 1951), p. 78. Seymour was Britain's special agent in Rome. Palmerston was British foreign secretary 1830–41.
46. Broderick, *Holy See and repeal.*

neither moderate nor advanced nationalists were sympathetic to the tsar, and Cullen, then involved in a campaign against the Fenians, publicly expressed strong sympathy with the Poles!

In the reaction of bishops and popes to the right to rebel, the personality of the prelates played a part. If, for all of the popes of this period, rebellion against the lawful authority was sinful unless the stringent conditions for a just revolt were fulfilled, in practice, interpretations could differ. Thus Troy and Murray, like Pius VI and Gregory XVI, belonged to the *ancien régime*. Doyle and Pius IX, before the Roman revolution, had sympathy with the new ideas. Pius VII, like Leo XIII later in the century, was quite willing to seek an accommodation with the revolution and its consequences.

In Ireland, the theology taught at Maynooth was not substantially different from that taught in Rome. In 1877, George Crolly, divinity professor at Maynooth College, restated the classic Catholic scholastic theory in his textbook for students of moral theology: rebellion was legitimate if it was the only means of redress from a grave oppressive tyranny, would not produce worse evils and had a well-founded hope of success. This view fitted the social background of the priests, who, for the most part, were sons of better-off farmers. Both clergy and people accepted, if not uncritically, the established social order at least up to the land war. The teaching which Patrick Murray and Crolly expounded remained the normal teaching of the church in the nineteenth and twentieth centuries and governed the attitude of the clergy to rebellion, whatever their inner sentiments might be. Whatever, too, the criticisms of British rule they may have secretly harboured, at no stage were the bishops, even Bishop Doyle, convinced that conditions existed which justified armed revolt.[47] There was, then, no widespread connivance at rebellion as Duigenan feared. Behan was closer to the mark but his categorisation of clerical attitudes is too stark and too generalised. The clergy, convinced that the conditions justifying revolt were absent, condemned rebellion, as a sin because it challenged lawfully constituted authority, as folly since it spelt catastrophe for its misguided perpetrators, and as an obstacle for it impeded constitutional action to achieve concessions, and put at risk those already acquired. Yet they were no less nationalist than their lay compatriots and, as

---

47. A possible exception was Bishop Edward Maginn of Derry, who, horrified by the suffering from famine and eviction in Ireland and the mortality among the emigrants, told George Poulet Scrope, MP for Stroud, in 1848 'that there is no means under heaven that I would not cheerfully resort to to redeem my people from their present misery: and sooner than allow it to continue, like the Archbishop of Milan, I would rather grasp the cross and the green flag of Ireland and rescue my country, or perish with its people.' He was accused of being implicated in the Young Ireland rebellion but strenuously denied it. Kerr, *'Nation of beggars'?*, pp 134–5, 155–6.

a result, their attitudes appeared ambivalent. A feeling persisted among most Irish nationalists, lay and clerical, that the root cause for many Irish ills was English rule. Musing on his Irish experience, John Henry Newman, a sympathetic and perceptive observer, wrote in 1859, a few months after leaving Ireland: 'one sentiment of hatred against the oppressor "manet alta mente repositum"'.[48] This antagonism may well have been at the root of that clerical ambivalence towards rebels which Oliver MacDonagh identified. Perhaps this is part of the reason why it was not the moderates like Troy or Murray but the colourful 'patriots priests' – Fr Sheehy of Clogheen, Fr Murphy of Boolavogue, Fr Lavelle of Partry – who retained the most enduring place in popular memory.

---

48. *Rambler*, May 1859, repr. in J.H. Newman, *Historical sketches* (London, 1872; repr. 1970), pp 257–60.

2

British Liberal Politics and Irish Liberalism after O'Connell

GEORGE L. BERNSTEIN*

THE SHADOW OF DANIEL O'CONNELL hung over Anglo-Irish Liberal politics between 1847 and 1865. From 1835–41 O'Connell had demonstrated that a reasonably disciplined Irish party could be a constructive partner for a Liberal government at Westminster. Both sides gained from such a relationship. The Irish got a government uniquely solicitous of the concerns of Catholic Ireland. There was also a serious though limited effort to legislate some of Ireland's grievances. The Whig government got a reliable block of Irish votes in the house of commons, which allowed it to retain power. It also got the assurance that its Irish supporters could win elections, so that Irish business could be conducted with minimum difficulty. Their relationship, however, imposed a cost on both sides. The Irish lost their independence and so their ability to press for more radical policies. The Whigs were tainted by their alliance with O'Connell, whom Tories portrayed as an unprincipled agitator who sought

---

* The author wishes to express his deep appreciation for the gracious permission of Her Majesty Queen Elizabeth II to use Lord Melbourne's Papers, for the permission of the Hon. Simon Howard to use the Castle Howard Archives, for the permission of the Earl of Clarendon to quote from the Clarendon Papers, and for the permission of the Trustees of the Broadlands Archives to quote from Lord Melbourne's and Lord Palmerston's Papers.

to destroy Britain. Since most of the Whig leaders accepted this view, they preferred an Irish liberalism purged of an independent nationalist party.

The Whigs got their wish following the split of the Repeal movement and the death of O'Connell in 1846–47. Yet for most of the period to 1865, Liberal governments missed that relatively reliable block of 35 Irish votes at a time when the house of commons was exceptionally fluid and Liberal MPs could be notoriously undisciplined. The MPs representing Catholic Ireland, whether professedly Liberals or Independents, were as unreliable as any, and their waywardness was a source of misery for Liberal chief secretaries and chief whips counting heads for close votes. Liberal governments also found it much more difficult to conduct their Irish business. Without O'Connell to manage a party machine in Ireland, Irish law officers or whips had difficulty winning Irish seats when Catholics were angry over government policies. In an ironic foreshadowing of later periods, when Liberals unable to win seats in England retreated to safe seats on the 'Celtic fringe', these Irish Liberals had to find seats in England to secure entry into the commons so that they could manage Irish legislation. Lord Palmerston finally had enough of what he perceived to be Irish Catholics' ingratitude, and from 1861 he sought to govern without them. While his action increased the difficulty for his government to administer Irish affairs, he could get away with it as long as Irish catholicism remained politically divided and he could garner Tory support. A liberalism that was not to rely on conservative votes, however, would have found life easier with the support of a well-organised Irish party.

Daniel O'Connell shared the central commitment of nineteenth-century British liberalism to civil and religious liberty. As a political radical, he supported an extension of the franchise, shorter parliaments, the ballot, and reform of the house of lords. As an economic radical, he was an opponent of the corn laws and an advocate of reduced public expenditure. On external matters, his opposition to the suspension of the Canadian constitution in 1838 and to Lord Palmerston's aggressively anti-French policy in 1840 also identified him with British radicals.[1] On only two major issues did he diverge from them: the extension of the poor law to Ireland and state support for sectarian education, both of which divided Irish Liberals.

O'Connell saw his movement as a part of liberalism. Like British Radicals and Whigs, Repealers could use the term 'liberal' sometimes to refer to their

---

1. Oliver MacDonagh, *The emancipist: Daniel O'Connell, 1830–47* (London, 1989), pp 19–27, 61. Angus Macintyre, *The liberator: Daniel O'Connell and the Irish party 1830–1847* (London, 1965), pp 164–5, 246–7. Lord Ebrington to Lord Morpeth, 24 Aug. 1840 (Castle Howard Archives, Papers of the 7th Earl of Carlisle [hereafter cited as C.H., C.P.], J19/1/28/22).

own group and sometimes to refer to all opponents of toryism.² From 1835, however, O'Connell's use of 'liberal' was most commonly in the inclusive sense that identified Repealers with the Whigs and Radicals as part of a Liberal party. O'Connell's strategy in the 1835 general election reflected this view, as he successfully worked to prevent Repealers and other Liberals from opposing each other in Ireland.³ That autumn O'Connell took another step toward Liberal fusion for electoral purposes, offering 'to withdraw from most of the Counties the persons he had put in at the last Election if Whig Country Gentlemen or Landed Proprietors could be got to stand instead'. Thereafter, O'Connell was effectively the broker of Irish Liberal politics. So when, in 1840, a Repeal candidate was threatened in Waterford county, Lord Carew reported to the prime minister Lord Melbourne, 'I have seen letters from O'Connell to Repealers in Waterford, stating his wish to strengthen the Government Candidate, that the Family of Carew deserved every support from the people …'.⁴

While O'Connell saw himself and his movement as part of a Liberal party, the Whigs never fully accepted that identification. Whig ambivalence was rooted in a contempt for O'Connell which made association with him difficult to accept. They constructed an O'Connell myth, based on claims that he was a demagogue who organised his agitations solely in order to get money.⁵ Even after the king dismissed Lord Melbourne's government in November 1834, the Whig leaders were reluctant to work with O'Connell. Lord Lansdowne, for example, protested against any communications with O'Connell 'should they in any degree assume the character of party concert & alliance', and Lord John Russell, Lord Grey, Lord Howick, and Thomas Spring Rice felt much the same way. With O'Connell effectively holding the balance after the

---

2. On the use of 'liberal' in Britain, see T.A. Jenkins, *The Liberal ascendancy, 1830–1886* (New York, 1994), pp 45–6; and G.L. Bernstein, 'The origins of Liberal politics, 1830–1874' in *Jn. Brit. Stud.*, xviii, no. 1 (Jan. 1989), pp 76–7. On its use in Ireland, see K. Theodore Hoppen, *Elections, politics, and society in Ireland 1832–1885* (Oxford, 1984), p 258; and J.H. Whyte, 'Daniel O'Connell and the Repeal party' in *I.H.S.*, xi, no. 44 (Sept. 1959), pp 304–6.
3. MacDonagh, *Emancipist*, pp 60, 117–19, 160. Abraham Kriegel, 'The politics of the Whigs in opposition, 1834–1835' in *Jn. Brit. Stud.*, vii, no. 2 (May 1968), p 74. Macintyre, *Liberator*, pp 52, 58–61.
4. Lord Mulgrave to Melbourne, 8 Oct. 1835 (quote); Carew to Melbourne, 12 Aug. [1840] (Windsor Castle, Melbourne Papers [hereafter W.C., M.P.], RA MP99/65, RA MP21/55). For discussions of O'Connell between 1837 and 1841, see Macintyre, *Liberator*, pp 62–71; MacDonagh, *Emancipist*, pp 159–61, 196–97; Diana Davids Olien, *Morpeth* (Washington, 1983), pp 179–80.
5. Lord Anglesey to Lord Melbourne, 2 Jan. 1831; E.J. Littleton to Melbourne, 19 Jan. 1834 (W.C., M.P., RA MP93/68, RA MP97/33). For examples of liberal claims that O'Connell's only concern was to get money, see *Leeds Mercury*, 2 Mar. 1833, p 4; Russell to Melbourne, 6 Sept. 1834, Lord Bessborough to Melbourne, 29 Dec. [1844] (W.C., M.P., RA MP13/37, RA MP3/131); Charles Villiers to John Bright, n.d. [29 Oct. 1846], (B.L., Bright Papers, Add. Ms 43386, f 18).

general election, however, the case for co-operation was irresistible.[6]

Relations between O'Connell and the new Irish government were generally harmonious. Most importantly, a real transformation occurred in the distribution of patronage. For the first time, Catholic law officers were appointed for Ireland, and wherever property and status were not criteria, most appointments were Catholics or liberal Protestants.[7] In return, O'Connell gave the government unswerving parliamentary support. Even when he became frustrated that the Whigs could not deliver the corporations or tithe bills he wanted, he always assured them that he would not turn them out on these issues, and he accepted the compromises they proposed. By 1839 Irish support was so reliable that Charles Greville, when estimating the government's strength, incorporated 'the Irish tail' into his 267, while reckoning separately the sixty-six Radicals.[8]

Yet Whig views of O'Connell had not changed. Melbourne thought his speeches in the autumn of 1835 showed that he was an 'irreclaimable Black guard, & that it is unfit for any gentleman to associate with him'. Liberals therefore sought to distance themselves from O'Connell, while the Tories used him to discredit the government with the British public. Following Liberal losses in the general election of 1837, Melbourne's steward told him 'that the real injury We have suffered in public opinion is from the Cry against O'Connell & the notion of England being governed by Irishmen & Roman Catholics'.[9] Part of the taint of O'Connell was the stigma attached to catholicism. Lord Duncannon told him in October 1836 that even among 'our own friends, there are many in England who will cry out if there is an appearance of preference to Catholics' in legal appointments. When the under-secretary Thomas Drummond died in 1840, Melbourne insisted that

---

6. Lansdowne to Russell, 1 Feb. 1835 (P.R.O., Russell Papers, [hereafter R.P.] PRO 30/22/1E, ff 19–21). Russell to Melbourne, 22 Sept. 1834; in Rollo Russell (ed.), *Early Correspondence of Lord John Russell, 1805–40* (London, 1913), ii, 47. Grey to Melbourne, 1 Feb. 1835 (W.C., M.P., RA MP5/128). Kriegel, 'Whigs in Opposition', pp 82–9.
7. Olien, *Morpeth*, pp 147–9. MacDonagh, *Emancipist*, pp 123, 127–31, 173. Oliver MacDonagh, 'Politics, 1830–45' in W.E. Vaughan (ed.), *A New History of Ireland*, Vol. V: *Ireland under the Union, I, 1801–70* (Oxford, 1989), pp 179–81. Macintyre, *Liberator*, pp 161–2.
8. O'Connell to Melbourne, 10 May 1838; to Lord Morpeth, 10 June 1838; to Lord Ebrington, 8 Aug. 1839; M.R. O'Connell, editor, *The Correspondence of Daniel O'Connell* (8 vols Dublin, 1972–80), vi, 160, 167, 269. (Hereafter cited as *O'Connell corr.*) Greville's diary, 10 Feb. 1839 quoted in, Jenkins, *Liberal ascendancy*, p. 36.
9. Melbourne to Lord Mulgrave, 16 Oct. 1835 (copy) (W.C., M.P., RA MP99/73). In other letters Melbourne called O'Connell 'the Beast' and referred to 'such coarse brutes as he is'. Melbourne to Mulgrave, 19, 23 Oct. 1835 (copies); ibid., RA MP99/72,76. Melbourne to Russell, 24 Aug. 1837; (Southampton University Library, Broadlands Archives, Melbourne Papers, MEL/RU/392). Lord William Russell to Lord Tavistock, n.d. [1839], agreed with Melbourne's steward; (P.R.O., R.P., PRO 30/22/3D, f 196).

the appointment of an Irish Catholic was politically impossible, so he vetoed the Irish Liberal, Richard More O'Ferrall.[10]

Another facet of the taint of O'Connell was his role as agitator. Melbourne's lord lieutenants worked tirelessly to end the Repeal agitation and render O'Connell's organisations harmless. O'Connell, however, could not fully co-operate without losing his popular influence.[11] While working with O'Connell, therefore, the Whigs also tried to marginalise him. Lord Mulgrave's goal as lord lieutenant after 1835 was to kill Repeal with kindness by using policy and patronage to undermine O'Connell's power. As he prepared to resign in January 1839, Normanby (formerly Mulgrave) claimed that he had 'been rather successful in detaching a large portion of the Liberal party from any active co-operation with him'. With O'Connell's organisation weakened by the alliance, the collapse of the Repeal party in the general election of 1841 apparently confirmed the success of Normanby's strategy.[12] Despite O'Connell's loyalty to the alliance, the lessons for British Liberals seemed clear: association with a nationalist and Catholic Irish party was a political liability, while a cautious reform policy which gave Catholics a share of patronage would consolidate a moderate liberal party in Ireland.

Nevertheless, with O'Connell still apparently strong in Ireland in 1845–46, Russell wanted 'to reintegrate the O'Connellites into the Liberal coalition'. So when he became prime minister in July 1846, Russell sought to return to the relationship of 1835–41, based on patronage for Catholics and moderate measures of reform for Ireland.[13] Yet even if O'Connell had not died in 1847, it would have been difficult to resurrect the old alliance. First, O'Connell no longer headed a united movement. Sir Robert Peel's 1845 bill creating non-sectarian Queen's Colleges divided Irish catholicism and Irish nationalism.

---

10. Lord Duncannon to O'Connell, 19 Oct. 1836; O'Connell, *O'Connell corr.*, v, p. 400. Ebrington to Melbourne, 26 Apr. 1840, 15 Oct. 1839, 18 June 1841 (W.C., M.P., RA MP101/55,35,87). Ebrington to Morpeth, 5 May 1840; Melbourne to Morpeth, 26 May 1840 (C.H., C.P., J19/1/26/88, J19/1/27/13.) Olien, *Morpeth*, pp 153, 157–9.
11. Mulgrave to Russell, 19 Aug. 1837; Ebrington to Russell, 8 Sept. 1839 (P.R.O., R.P., PRO 30/22/2F, ff 31–3; PRO 30/22/3D, ff 23–4). Mulgrave (Normanby) to Melbourne, 21 Aug., 27 Oct. 1838; Ebrington to Melbourne, 14 Sept. 1839 (W.C., M.P., RA MP100/86,90; RA MP101/34). Normanby to Morpeth, 18 Dec. [1838]; D.R. Pigot to Drummond, n.d. [April 1839]; Ebrington to Morpeth, 3 Apr. 1840; (C.H., C.P., J19/1/21/18, J19/1/22/92, J19/1/26/18). MacDonagh, *Emancipist*, pp 176–9.
12. Mulgrave (Normanby) to Melbourne, 1 Nov. 1835, 10 Jan. [1839] (W.C., M.P., RA MP99/81, RA MP101/3). Hoppen, *Elections, politics, and society*, pp 258–9. Olien, *Morpeth*, pp 179–80. MacDonagh, *Emancipist*, pp 189–90, 196–7.
13. Russell to Lansdowne, 27 Dec. 1845 (quote); Jenkins, *Liberal ascendancy*, p. 54. Bessborough to Russell, 11 Sept. 1846; Russell to Bessborough, 15 Sept. 1846 (copy) (P.R.O., R.P., PRO 30/22/5C, ff 116–19, 162–66). Macintyre, *Liberator*, pp 89–91. MacDonagh, *Emancipist*, pp 293–8.

Furthermore, the Young Irelanders were determined that the party should retain its independence and so broke with O'Connell in the summer of 1846. The death of the lord lieutenant, Lord Bessborough, in 1847 also undermined the liberal-nationalist alliance. Bessborough believed that peace in Ireland required co-operation with O'Connell. His successor Lord Clarendon told Russell's brother, the duke of Bedford, that the policy of 'dallying with a pestilent system of agitation ... for nearly 20 years' had laid the groundwork for the Young Ireland rebellion of 1848. So Clarendon would give no patronage to agitators or those who attacked the government. Clarendon's view of Catholic Ireland was transformed by the Young Ireland and Chartist crises of 1848. He believed most Irish Liberals had sat on the fence until they saw the outcome and told Bedford, 'rely upon it, in the event of real trouble, domestic or foreign, we shall find that the Protestants constitute the only link between this country & Eng'd'.[14]

Finally, the Famine undermined liberal-nationalist cooperation. It killed the reform programme that Bessborough and Russell were devising in 1846, as the government became absorbed in the debate over relief policy. While the Irish government continued to press for policies of amelioration in 1847 and 1848, its proposals divided British Liberals and so got nowhere. At the same time, British Liberal resistance to relief measures which required British money increased. With a divided Irish liberalism unable to mobilise effective pressure for either relief or reform, by 1848 the government was delivering neither. The inevitable effect was to alienate Ireland and Irish nationalism from British liberalism.[15]

This shift in Irish opinion was evident during the general election of 1847. Thomas Redington, the under-secretary, warned Clarendon in June that there was 'a total want of cordiality towards the Government', while three weeks later Lord Clanricarde told him, 'there are not a dozen out of the 100 Candidates who dare stand upon the declared ground of being a thoro'-going friend of the Ministry! are there 6?' Russell thought that if O'Connell were alive, seventy Repealers would have been returned. A year later, the government's standing remained abysmal. In such an environment, it could not return either

---

14. Ibid., pp 259–70, 278–89. James S. Donnelly, Jr., 'A famine in Irish politics' in *N.H.I.*, v, 359–64. Bessborough to Russell, 20 Feb. 1847 (P.R.O., R.P., PRO 30/22/6B, f 105). Clarendon to Bedford, 8 May, 17 Sept. 1848; to Russell, 23 Aug. 1847 (copy); (Bodleian Library, Ms Clarendon Deposit Irish [hereafter cited as Ms Clar Dep Ir.], Boxes 81 and 80, vol. 1, p. 30).

15. K.B. Nowlan, 'The political background' in R.D. Edwards and T.D. Williams (ed.), *The Great Famine: studies in Irish history 1845–52* (Dublin, 1956), pp 158–68. G.L. Bernstein, 'Liberals, the Irish Famine and the role of the state' in *I.H.S.*, xxix, no. 16 (Nov. 1995), pp 523–33. For the ambitious programmes that Russell considered, see Russell to Bessborough, 8 Dec. 1846 (copy) and Russell memo, 30 Mar. 1848 (P.R.O., R.P., PRO 30/22/5F, ff 102–3; 30/22/7B, ff 158–61).

Irish law officer for an Irish constituency. Finally in 1850, the Protestant solicitor general found a refuge at Windsor! Redington pressed the chief whip Henry Tufnell not to create a by-election for any Irish 'County as it wd. be next to impossible to return a voter who would steadily support [the] Govt'.[16]

This unpopularity of the Liberals in Ireland was only one result of the Famine. Britain's growing unwillingness to provide famine relief turned the Irish Liberal MPs into beggars, trying to persuade government and parliament of the imperative need to provide more. British Liberals developed a contempt for Irish MPs as, in the words of George Cornewall Lewis, 'nothing more than a set of ill conditioned growlers, who will extract all they can from England, & then abuse us for not doing more'. J.A. Roebuck was notorious for expressing his scorn for the Irish members in the commons, and he always provoked an outraged response from them. By 1849 Clarendon, anticipating another obstructive debate from the Irish MPs, hoped for some blunt talk from 'Citizen Roebuck'.[17]

By 1848, government disdain of the Irish Liberal MPs and Irish resentment of the government's Irish policies was leading to a low-level guerrilla warfare that would characterise their relationship to 1865. As they had with O'Connell, liberal leaders constructed a myth about the Irish MPs, claiming they were opportunistic and obstructionist, with no principles. The Irish, they believed, saw the need of the government's measures but opposed them for political reasons. For example, in 1849 Clarendon told Russell that Irish opposition to the suspension of habeas corpus 'will be dishonest, for they know as well as I do that it is indispensable for the peace & the future prospects of the country …'. In 1850 Sir Charles Wood, the chancellor of the exchequer, contended that, while the Irish blocked progress on an amendment of the Irish poor law, 'they admitted that they had nothing to find fault with, but they had letters from their constituents & must complain'.[18]

However much the government disliked the behaviour of Irish Liberal MPs, it still needed their votes. By 1849, the chief secretary Sir William Somerville

---

16. Redington to Clarendon, 19 June 1847, 14 Nov. 1848; Clanricarde to Clarendon, 3 July 1847; Russell to Clarendon, 9 Aug. 1847, 19 Oct. 1849, 13 Jan. 1850; Redington to Tufnell, 14 Mar. 1850 (Ms Clar Dep Ir, Boxes 24/1 and 24/2, 9, 43 and 26, 70).
17. Lewis to Clarendon, 22 Aug. 1847; (Bodleian Library, Ms Clarendon Deposit [hereafter cited as Ms Clar Dep], c.530). Roebuck to his wife, 21, 27 Jan., 11 Feb. 1847; 15 May, 20, 22 June 1849; R.E. Leader, *Life and letters of John Arthur Roebuck* (London and New York, 1897), pp 169–72, 223–4, 229. Clarendon to Grey (copy), 19 July 1849 (Ms Clar Dep Ir, vol. 4, p. 90). Lewis was disgusted by a scene between Roebuck and the Irish MPs, which he blamed on the former. Lewis to Clarendon, 20 June 1849 (Ms Clar Dep, c.530).
18. Clarendon to Russell, 6 Feb. 1849 (P.R.O., R.P., PRO 30/22/7E, f 269). Wood to Clarendon, 7 Apr. 1850 (Ms Clar Dep Ir, Box 32). See also Russell to Clarendon, 13 Mar., 29 July 1849 (ibid., Box 26). These criticisms show how Whigs could not accept the Irish view that the MP was answerable to his constituents. See Larkin, *R. C. Ch. 1860–70*, pp 344–5.

had no doubt 'that if any question turns up, involving the existence of the Govt. they will not lend a hand to save us'. At the end of 1849 the government feared that the Irish MPs, who claimed to be ruined by the cost of poor relief, would look to protection. Clarendon quickly determined that the Irish people would reject protection as a 'Landlord dodge' to push up rents, but a relieved Tufnell told Russell that Irish votes 'might have placed Free trade in jeopardy even in this Parliament'. The danger recurred in June 1850 when, during the Don Pacifico debate, a frantic Somerville claimed there were negotiations between the Irish and the Protectionists in an effort (which quickly collapsed) to establish an anti-government alliance.[19]

There was some truth in the British liberal picture of an unruly and unreliable group of Irish Liberal MPs hostile to the government.[20] Yet there was also a paradox. Despite much government hysteria about Repeal, Whigs tended to view Repealers as reliable supporters. For example, during the general election of 1847, Lord Carew drew a sinister picture for Clarendon of a Repeal party, seeking to establish a monopoly by intimidation of all elected office in the south and west, which had forced the withdrawal of the former Whig MPs for Waterford. Yet he concluded, 'The present Members for Waterford will however support the Ministers'. Similarly, during an 1850 by-election at Mayo, Clarendon told Tufnell that the Repeal candidate would be 'an unfailing supporter of the Government' while the Tory landlord 'will be always dead agst. us'. Again, while Clarendon disliked the Irish Liberal MPs, he wanted to use patronage and hospitality to consolidate an Irish Liberal Party. He pressed ministers to show some attention to potential supporters like William Monsell and John Sadleir, and at his urging Palmerston gave O'Connell's son Daniel a consulship in Brazil.[21]

Thus, relations between British and Irish Liberals were not as hostile as the comments of the liberal leadership imply. Yet clearly the crisis over 'papal aggression' in 1850–51 did not so much transform those relations as accentuate

---

19. Somerville to Clarendon, 26 Feb. 1849, 12, 27 June 1850; Clarendon to Wood, 14 Dec. 1849, 4 Jan. 1850 (copies) (Ms Clar Dep Ir, Boxes 27, 28; vol. 5, pp 61, 80). Sir John Young to Peel, 14 Dec. 1849 (B.L., Peel Papers, Add. MSS 40602, f 345). Tufnell to Russell, 9 Jan. 1850 (P.R.O., R.P., PRO 30/22/8C, f 243). Tufnell never mentioned a possible Irish–Protectionist alliance in his letters to Clarendon at the time of the Don Pacifico debate.
20. For the voting of Irish Liberal MPs prior to the Papal aggression controversy, see J.H. Whyte, *The independent Irish party, 1850–9* (London, 1958), p. 16.
21. Carew to Clarendon, n.d. [Aug. 1847]; Clarendon to Tufnell, 3 July 1850; Clarendon to Sir George Grey, 2 Feb. 1848 (copy) (Ms Clar Dep Ir, Boxes 8, 70; vol. 2). On the need to cultivate friendly MPs, see Wood to Clarendon, 1 Dec. 1847; Clarendon to Russell, 4 Dec. 1847, to Grey, 7 July 1848, to Wood, 8 Dec. 1849 (copies); ibid., Box 31; vol. 2, p. 6; vol. 3, p. 26; vol. 5, p. 57. Palmerston to Clarendon, 2 June 1850 (Ms Clar Dep, c.524).

existing trends. Irish hostility to the government, its consequent difficulty winning seats in Ireland with avowed supporters, the perceived unreliability of Irish Liberal MPs in the commons which could threaten the existence of the government, and the contempt of ministers toward those MPs all shaped the relationship between British and Irish liberalism in the years of the Famine. Nevertheless, Tufnell's judgement in May 1850 was, 'Nothing can *materially* injure the Govt. but its own imprudence or want of tact …'.[22] This was what Russell's letter to the bishop of Durham supplied.

Russell's letter and the bill that followed were a political catastrophe for the Whigs, especially for Russell himself. Yet all his friends in the government agreed that the pope's re-establishment of the English hierarchy was an aggression that required a response. It was the climax of a series of papal actions which they saw as hostile to British liberalism: the appointment of the conservative and ultramontane Paul Cullen as archbishop of Armagh, the convocation of the Synod of Thurles, and most importantly the refusal to withdraw papal condemnation of the Queen's Colleges. Thus, the Whigs already were convinced that the authority claimed by the pope was not merely spiritual, but a political right to interfere in the internal affairs of the United Kingdom. Russell complained to Clarendon on 13 November that thirty years of Whig sacrifices for Catholics had been met with ingratitude, as 'the Pope applies himself to thwart the English Govt. in every way he can imagine …'. Clarendon also saw papal ingratitude and told Russell on 23 November that the pope never would have acted contrary to the wishes of the government of a Catholic country. The other target of the Durham letter besides the pope was tractarianism. Russell's friends thought the letter a good one for the dual purposes of rejecting the secular pretensions of the papacy and attacking crypto-Catholics in the English church. It had been ruined, they believed, only by Russell's phrase 'mummeries of superstition', which had outraged Catholic opinion and alienated moderate Catholics who would have supported his attack on ultramontanism. It was this phrase, they concluded, that killed them in Ireland, not the Ecclesiastical Titles Bill.[23]

The political damage in Ireland was immediate. Catholic moderates were radicalised, making possible the revival of a Catholic nationalist movement which sought to be independent of British liberalism. More than ever, it was

---

22. Tufnell to Clarendon, 27 May 1850 (Ms Clar Dep Ir, Box 29). (Emphasis is Tufnell's.)
23. See Clarendon's correspondence for Oct.–Dec. 1850, as follows: in Ms Clar Dep Ir, see Clarendon to Bedford, Boxes 81, 82; Wood to Clarendon, Box 32; Russell to Clarendon, Box 26; Clarendon's Letterbooks, vol. 6. See also, Grey to Clarendon, 21 Feb. 1851; Somerville to Clarendon, 30 Sept. 1851; Redington to Clarendon, 2 Oct. 1851; Boxes 15, 28, 25. In Ms Clar Dep, see Lewis to Clarendon, c.530; Clarendon to Lewis, c.532/2.

futile for the government to contest an election in Ireland, while even 'moderate Tories like Ld. Haas & Peelites like Sir John Young', Clarendon reported to Bedford on 13 November, 'say it is all up with them at the elections ... or with any one who will not go all lengths with the most ultra Priest in hostility to Eng'd & Protest'm'. Irish members of the Irish government, like Somerville and Redington (himself a Catholic), found that loyalty to the Whigs meant rejection by their Catholic supporters and ultimately the end of their careers in Ireland.[24]

The Ecclesiastical Titles Bill made a bad situation worse. It smacked of religious persecution, and Clarendon told Bedford that the Irish bishops were justified in organising against it. The most offensive clauses finally were dropped, but the damage was done. Clarendon wrote Russell on 23 February that it 'has lowered Whig popularity 20 fathoms deep, & we shall not live to see it dry up again'.[25] Irish Liberals returned to Westminster determined to see the ministry thrown out, opposing it on all measures. Some long-standing supporters like Richard More O'Ferrall were bitterly hostile, while many others felt compelled to oppose it or risk defeat at the next election. Those who voted against the government on a protectionist amendment to the address were not invited to a meeting of Liberal MPs in early March, effectively expelling them from the party. Somerville and Clarendon both anticipated defeat on some issue before it came on Locke King's motion on the ballot in late February. Although the Whigs ultimately retained office, Irish hostility remained unrelenting for the rest of the session.[26]

Clarendon became increasingly cynical about their behaviour. With the odious parts of the bill deleted, he thought the Irish once more were playing to the mob for electoral purposes. Echoing Melbourne, he told the home secretary Sir George Grey on 25 May that 'the [Irish] Brigade are really not fit company for gentlemen'. Clarendon nevertheless understood that Irish behaviour was rooted in public opinion at home. It took Russell longer to

---

24. Clarendon to Bedford, 13, 16 Nov. 1850; Somerville to Clarendon, 11 Feb. 1851; Clarendon to Russell, 12 Nov. 1850, to Grey, 16 Dec. 1850 (copies); Ms Clar Dep Ir, Boxes 82, 81, 28; vol. 6, pp 57, 89. Larkin, *R. C. Ch. 1850–60*, pp 85–6. On 23 Dec. 1857 Clarendon wrote to Palmerston of the continued persecution in Ireland of Redington and Henry Hughes, the solicitor general in 1851 and also a Catholic, for their loyalty to the government during the crisis. (Southampton University Library, Broadlands Archives, Palmerston Papers, [hereafter S.U.L., Palm. P.] GC/CL/1127).
25. Clarendon to Grey, 16 Jan., 20 Feb. 1851 (copies); to Russell, 19 Jan., 23 Feb., 7 Mar. 1851 (copies); Clarendon to Bedford, 18 Feb. 1851; (Ms Clar Dep Ir, vol. 6, pp 107, 136–7, 108, 142, 149, Box 81). Somerville to Russell, 4 Mar. 1851 (P.R.O., R.P., PRO 30/22/9B, ff 213–14).
26. Somerville to Clarendon, 12, 14 Feb., 30 June, 17 July 1851; Clarendon to Bedford, 18 Feb., 27 Apr. 1851; Clarendon to Russell, 21 Feb. 1851 (copy); (Ms Clar Dep Ir, Boxes 28, 81 and 80; vol. 6, p. 140). Cobden to Bright, 6 Mar. 1851, reported on the party meeting; (B.L., Cobden Papers, Add. MSS 43649, ff 189–90).

figure it out. In April he wrote Clarendon about finding a seat for the Irish solicitor general. He did not grasp, as Redington told the lord chancellor, that 'a member of the Govt. wd. have no earthly chance now any where in Ireland'. In June he thought Irish anger must die soon, as the bill no longer applied there. Only upon visiting Ireland in August did he see 'that a most intense feeling exists on the part of the mass of the Roman Catholics against the Govt. & all who were the promoters of the Ecclesiastical Titles Bill'.[27]

In February 1852 Russell paid the political price when Irish votes were decisive in defeating the government. Irish Liberal MPs who had been leading the campaign against the bill also organised an Independent Irish Party, pledged to opposing any government that would not pass measures for tenant right and the removal of Catholic disabilities. Independence proved to be an excellent short-term election strategy, for it enabled many Irish Liberals to escape the taint of association with the fallen government. As a result, the balance within Irish liberalism was apparently transformed by the general election, which returned some forty-eight MPs committed to independence and only fifteen other Liberals. These independent Irish votes held the balance after the election.[28]

As a medium-term parliamentary strategy, however, independence had limitations, since Irish Catholics could expect little from the party of the Protestant ascendancy, while they could influence developments on the liberal side. Irish opposition helped assure that Russell could not return as prime minister, but with the Peelites and many in his own party equally opposed, Russell's leadership already was doomed. The need to get Irish support weakened the Whigs in negotiating with the Peelites, whose cultivation of Irish Catholic opinion had given rise to an Irish perception of Peelite sympathy for their causes. So a government with the Peelites Lord Aberdeen as prime minister, Lord St Germans as lord lieutenant, and Sir John Young as chief secretary suited the Irish. The Irish also were able to block the reappointment of old bogeymen like Redington to Irish positions. The appointment of two leaders of the independence movement, William Keogh

---

27. Clarendon to Grey, 25 May 1851 (copy) (Ms Clar Dep Ir, vol. 7, p. 22). For other examples of irritation, see Clarendon to Russell, 16 May, 12 June 1851 (copies) (ibid., pp 16, 26). Russell to Clarendon, 8 Apr., 10 June, 25 Aug. 1851; Redington to the lord chancellor, n.d. [April 1851] (ibid., Boxes 44, 25). Clarendon passed Redington's judgement on to Russell, 11 Apr. 1851 (copy) (ibid., vol. 6, p. 170).
28. Whyte, *Independent Irish party*, pp 40, 51–2, 82–91. R.V. Comerford, 'Churchmen, tenants, and independent opposition, 1850–56' in *N.H.I.*, v, 401–3. (Hereafter cited as 'Churchmen, tenants.') Lewis told Russell, 1 Oct. 1852, that the Chief Whip calculated that the Liberals had 275 seats in Britain as against 274 for the Tories (P.R.O., R.P., PRO 30/22/10E, f 140).

as Irish solicitor general and John Sadleir as a whip, confirmed the short-term nature of the independence strategy for around half of the Irish MPs who had taken the pledge.[29]

This left an Independent Irish Party of roughly twenty-five MPs in 1853 whose voting behaviour was distinguishable from that of other Irish Liberals. By 1858, their number had declined to about twelve, as had the distinctness of their voting behaviour. Independence did not mean that they always opposed the Liberal governments; on the contrary, at their most distinct they diverged from other Irish Liberals on between 15 and 20 per cent of their votes.[30] This was enough to make the security of Liberal governments uncertain if the Irish could join forces with the Tories and dissident British Radicals. The situation was different from 1835–41 when the Repeal vote was reliable in supporting the government, and from 1859–65 when Palmerston as prime minister often could win Tory votes. It was different from 1847–50 because the potential anti-government Irish vote was now better organised. Since the possible defection of British Radicals was a constant in all periods, the Irish vote (as well as the behaviour of the Tories and divisions among the Whigs) was crucial in determining the survival of Liberal governments and making the 1850s much less stable.

If the Independent Irish Party was to be viable, it needed to coalesce with British Radicals and to have some prospect of getting its policies enacted. Irish-Radical cooperation seemed possible because the Independent leader Frederick Lucas was related to John Bright by marriage. Bright was sympathetic to land reform, but not to the Tenant League. Other Radicals were more hostile to the Irish MPs and more indifferent to Irish concerns following the Famine, so Bright found no interest when he tried to promote an Irish alliance in 1852.[31] Radical indifference was symptomatic of a broader problem: the Independents' two principal policy demands, religious equality and tenant

---

29. John Prest, *Lord John Russell* (Columbia, SC, 1972), p. 351. Comerford, 'Churchmen, tenants', pp 405–7. J.B. Conacher, *The Aberdeen coalition 1852–1855: a study in mid-nineteenth-century party politics* (Cambridge, 1968), pp 23, 31. Wood to Russell, 13 Aug. 1851, argued that they must secure the Peelites if they were to get Irish support (P.R.O., R.P., PRO 30/22/10D, ff 103–5). For perceptions of Peelite cultivation of the Irish, see Grey to Clarendon, 3 Mar. 1848; Carew to Clarendon, 20 June [1848]; Somerville to Clarendon, 9 Mar. 1849 (Ms Clar Dep Ir, Boxes 12, 8, 27); and Clarendon to Lewis, 7 Mar. 1851 (Ms Clar Dep, c.532/2).

30. Whyte, *Independent Irish party*, pp 143–5. Steven R. Knowlton, 'The voting behaviour of the independent Irish party, 1850–59' in *Éire-Ireland*, xxvi, no. 1 (Spring 1991), pp 67–9.

31. Bright to Cobden, 17 Sept. 1849, 12 Oct. 1850; Charles Villiers to Bright, 25 Sept. 1852; (B.L., Bright Papers, Add. MSS 43383, ff 189–92, 202; 43386, f 96). Hume to Cobden, 9 Oct. 1852; (B.L., Cobden Papers, Add. MSS 43668, f 174). Diary of Sir John Trelawny, MP, 27 Feb. 1865 (commenting on Roebuck); T.A. Jenkins (ed.), *The parliamentary diaries of Sir John Trelawny, 1858–1865* (London, 1990), pp 307–8.

right, could command no significant support from British liberalism as it was constituted between 1848 and 1865. For the Catholic hierarchy, religious equality now meant state support for Catholic schools. British Liberals of all shades, however, were committed to keeping the national schools and the Queen's Colleges non-sectarian. Militant non-conformists in Britain were interested in Irish church disestablishment, but the larger body was divided over cooperating with Catholics, while they still had little influence with the Liberal leadership. Tenant right also commanded no support in Britain. Most Liberals agreed with the Peelite Edward Cardwell in 1860 when he equated tenant right with 'Landlord wrong'. While Liberal governments annually discussed bills to give tenants compensation for improvements, the leadership thought this too was an interference with property rights.[32]

The difficulty of getting a land bill passed was illustrated in 1855. A key issue since 1848 was whether compensation should apply to improvements undertaken prior to passage of a bill. The opposition of Palmerston and Lansdowne, both Irish landlords, had assured that no Whig bill would apply retrospectively. In 1855, Aberdeen's government introduced a bill with a retrospective clause before it fell. Palmerston's chief secretary Edward Horsman believed the new government must retain the clause or risk losing the support of fifteen to twenty Irish Liberal MPs. Horsman devised a compromise which Palmerston and Lansdowne reluctantly accepted. Both bills, however, were deemed inadequate by the Independent Irish. They joined the Tories and Whigs, who disliked the principle, to get the retrospective clause removed in committee, and the bill collapsed. Horsman was satisfied, however, that the exercise had drawn the Irish Liberal MPs closer to the government and further from the Independent party. Thus, on 24 July he assured the lord lieutenant Lord Carlisle, who as Lord Morpeth had been chief secretary from 1835–41, 'we are now honourably emancipated from the necessity of ever touching the Question again'.[33]

Thus, while key O'Connell policies like tithe and corporation reform were consistent with the principles of the British liberalism of his day, those of the Independents of the 1850s were not. At the same time, independence meant

---

32. G.I.T. Machin, *Politics and the churches in Great Britain, 1832–1868* (Oxford, 1977), pp 277–8. Larkin. *R. C. Ch. 1850–60*, pp 464–5. Palmerston memo, 31 Mar. 1848 (P.R.O., R.P., PRO 30/22/7B, ff 181–82). Clarendon to Grey, 21 Nov. 1850 (copy) (Ms Clar Dep Ir, vol. 6). Grey to Palmerston, 23 June 1857; (S.U.L., Palm. P., GC/GR/2492). Cardwell to Carlisle, 30 March 1860; (C.H., C.P., J19/1/88/5).
33. This narrative is based on Horsman's letters to Carlisle, 20 Apr., 3 May, 30 June, 3, 6, 24 July 1855; and to James Wilson, 4 Dec. 1855 (copy) (ibid., J19/1/57/27,47; J19/1/58/54,61,66; J19/1/59/16; J19/1/62/14). See also Lansdowne to Russell, 27 Jan. 1848 (P.R.O., R.P., PRO 30/22/7A, ff 214–14a).

that the Irish party was cut off from patronage in a way that O'Connell was not. Patronage was subject to familiar considerations. There was still a preoccupation with maintaining some religious balance so that the government did not seem excessively favourable to Catholics. With O'Connell's successor and son John now receiving an appointment as a reward for his loyalty, Carlisle also was subject to criticism that too much patronage was going to Radicals rather than moderate Liberals.[34]

As had been the case in the Clarendon era, the problem of holding a seat when faced with independent opposition could affect appointments. For example, when Sadleir resigned in January 1854, both Young and St Germans emphasised the difficulty of finding an Irish MP who could get re-elected to replace him in the whip's office. They finally appointed Chichester Fortescue of County Louth, who was able to squeeze out a victory despite Independent opposition. By 1856 the Independents were supporting Tories in by-elections where they did not have a viable candidate of their own, which allowed the Tories to win three seats. The Independents continued this policy in the 1857 general election, while, as in 1852, many government sympathisers adopted an independent line in deference to their constituents. Tory-Independent co-operation, however, had only a marginal effect on the balance of the parties.[35]

The Irish government still dreamed of consolidating a moderate liberal party that would be more reliable than the mixture of Whigs, Liberals, and Independents that constituted Irish liberalism. Yet the problem of Westminster indifference to Irish affairs bedevilled such efforts. When the government lost a vote in June 1856 on a Tory challenge to the national schools, the Irish attorney general J.D. Fitzgerald told Carlisle that 'were more members of the Govt. absent at the Queens [sic] Ball than would have been sufficient to turn the division the other way'. Nor could Horsman get the government to give any time to Irish bills. That October, he wrote to Carlisle complaining of cabinet indifference, bureaucratic hostility, and treasury parsimony toward Ireland. He saw a real danger from an apathetic cabinet '& not one Irishman

---

34. Carlisle to Palmerston, 1 Apr. 1856; (S.U.L., Palm. P., GC/CA/468). Palmerston to Carlisle, 2 Apr. 1856; O'Connell to Carlisle, 13 Aug. 1856; Grey to Carlisle, 5 Jan. 1858; Clanricarde to Carlisle, 2 June 1859; Felton Hervey to Carlisle, 20 Feb. 1860; (C.H., C.P., J19/1/64/12, J19/1/67/21, J19/1/77/39, J19/1/83/40, J19/1/87/12).

35. Young to Aberdeen, 4 Jan. 1854; St Germans to Aberdeen, 6 Jan. 1854; (B.L., Aberdeen Papers, Add. MSS 43251, ff 326–8; 43208, ff 43–5). Larkin, *R. C. Ch. 1850–60*, pp 226–7, 371–3, 381–2. Olien, *Morpeth*, pp 423–6. Whyte, *Independent Irish party*, pp 164–5. Olien claims a Liberal gain of three at the general election, Larkin a Conservative gain of three. She seems to be using the figures sent to Carlisle, which he forwarded to Palmerston; (C.H., C.P., J19/1/72/96; S.U.L., Palm. P., GC/CA/492).

of any position with a voice to secure common attention to any Irish Question'.[36] He needed an O'Connell!

Given the unremarkable record of the governments of the 1850s in dealing with Irish affairs, they were lucky that the Independents could not mobilise a more effective threat in the commons. They were able to inflict small defeats on the Aberdeen government early in 1853. Divisions among Irish Liberals, however, and Tory unwillingness to support them, assured that all motions against William Gladstone's proposal to extend the income tax to Ireland failed. Thereafter, the Crimean war created alignments that rendered the Irish vote less decisive. After the war, their potential as a swing vote returned if other Liberals were prepared to abandon the government. Thus, the nine Irish Independents who voted against Palmerston's China policy in 1857 were crucial because thirteen Peelites and thirty-six other Liberals also supported the motion.[37] Liberal support for Italian unification from 1859 offered the Independents a new opportunity. The immediate effect was to sustain their cooperation with the Tories in the 1859 general election, this time reinforced by the intervention of Cardinal Wiseman, the archbishop of Westminster. As a result, the Tories gained eight seats in Ireland, and the Liberal representation was reduced to forty-seven, roughly ten of whom were Independents. With an overall Liberal majority of about thirty, however, the Independents did not hold the balance in the commons.[38]

More importantly, the threat which Italian unification posed to the papacy, and the support given to Italian nationalism by British foreign policy under the hated Russell provided the most powerful issue for mobilising Irish Catholics against British liberalism since the Ecclesiastical Titles Act. One observer claimed that Catholic priests told their parishioners that Garibaldi was subsidised by the British and had English volunteers sent by the government to destroy the Catholic religion. By November 1860 Cardwell, the

---

36. Olien, *Morpeth*, pp 421–3. Fitzgerald to Carlisle, 18 June 1856; Horsman to Carlisle, 18, 13 June, 3 Oct. 1856; (C.H., C.P., J19/1/66/7,10; J19/1/65/95; J19/1/67/85). For the vision of a moderate Liberal party in Ireland, see above letter of 3 Oct. 1856, plus Horsman to James Wilson, 4 Dec. 1855 (copy); and Alexander Macdonnell to Carlisle, 12 Mar. 1855 (ibid., J19/1/62/14, J19/1/56/57).
37. Conacher, *Aberdeen Coalition*, pp 67–74, 124–5. Lady Clarendon's journal, 13 Apr. 1853; Sir Herbert Maxwell, *The life and letters of George William Frederick fourth earl of Clarendon* (London, 1913), ii, 10. Horsman to Carlisle, 4 Mar. 1857 (C.H., C.P., J19/1/71/19).
38. Larkin, *R. C. Ch. 1850–60*, p. 462. Whyte, *Independent Irish party*, pp 153–4. R.V. Comerford puts the number of Tory MPs at fifty-five (leaving fifty Liberals); 'Conspiring brotherhoods and contending elites, 1857–63' in *N.H.I.*, v, 417. Joseph Parkes estimated the government majority at thirty-four over Tories and Irish Independents; Wood estimated it at twenty-three, but it is unclear whether he included the Independents in the opposition. Parkes to Bright, 27 May 1859, (B.L., Bright Papers, Add. MSS 43388, f 244); Wood to Russell, 16 May 1859 (P.R.O., R.P., PRO 30/22/13G, f 214).

chief secretary, told Palmerston that 'our position in Ireland was that we had no reliable support' and 'that the Italian questions wd. continue to exercise an adverse influence ...'. The stationing of French soldiers in Rome to defend the papacy kept the issue alive. In 1864 Palmerston wrote the chief whip Henry Brand, 'until the Roman Question ... is finally settled and hopelessly for the Pope, we shall have the Irish Catholics against us ...'.[39]

Italian policy was not the only reason for Irish Liberal disenchantment with Palmerston's second government. While he reached out to British Radicals by including Charles Villiers and Thomas Milner Gibson in the cabinet, there was no such gesture to an Irishman. '[T]here can be no small hope for the Whigs', More O'Ferrall wrote to Carlisle on 26 June, 'if the leaders neglect to place the Irish representatives on a par with other Sections of the House not more numerous'. Education policy was another source of difficulty. In similar letters to Carlisle in June 1859, Monsell and More O'Ferrall, already alienated by Italian policy, urged concessions on Catholic education which reflected the views of Cullen and the Independents. Cardwell devised a compromise that temporarily satisfied Irish Liberals, but support of the national system became a prerequisite for Palmerston's appointments to Irish bishoprics.[40]

In the spring of 1861, a new crisis marked a turning point in the attitude of the government to the Irish Liberal MPs. When the cabinet cancelled a contract granted by the Conservatives providing a subsidy for a packet line between Galway and North America, there was an uproar which confirmed all that British Liberals disliked about the Irish. They believed that Lord Derby had granted the contract to buy political favour in Ireland, that the company which won the contract was unable to provide a satisfactory service, and that jobs in Galway were the cause of Irish anger over its cancellation. Public opinion drove the Irish whip to resign his position, while John Hatchell, Carlisle's secretary, told him on 30 May, all the 'Irish MPs are in great tribulation and are terribly scared by visions of angry constituents'. Thus, once again Irish MPs were driven by popular pressure rather than what was right. They threatened to vote against the repeal of the paper duties, an issue on which Conservative opposition seemed assured, unless they got some

---

39. Larkin, *R. C. Ch. 1860–70*, pp 3–19. Felton Hervey to Carlisle, 30 June 1860 (on the Catholic clergy); Cardwell to Carlisle, 11 Nov. 1860 (C.H., C.P., J19/1/89/37; J19/1/91/1). Palmerston to Brand, 8 Sept. 1864; quoted in Jenkins, *Liberal ascendancy*, p. 97. Palmerston added that the Irish would not support Derby either.
40. Monsell to Carlisle, n.d. [June 1859]; More O'Ferrall to Carlisle, 26 June 1859; J.D. Fitzgerald to Carlisle, 6 Jan. 1860; Cardwell to Carlisle, 15 Aug. 1860 (C.H., C.P., J19/1/83/76,77; J19/1/86/40; J19/1/90/6). Carlisle to Palmerston, 25 July 1862 (two letters on a clerical nominee) (S.U.L., Palm. P., GC/CA/516,517). Olien, *Morpeth*, pp 461–2.

promise of a new contract. As a result, Brand feared that the government's majority could disappear. The cabinet, however, would not give in to what it saw as Irish blackmail, and Palmerston refused to see a deputation of Irish MPs on the subject. In the end, Irish Liberals divided on the vote, while some Tories supported the government rather than see it turned out by Irish votes.[41]

After the vote, Brand insisted that there must be a new contract to conciliate Ireland. Otherwise, he wrote Palmerston on 31 July, 'you will not be able to reckon next Session upon *ten* Irish supporters upon any Question affecting the Stability of the Govt.' Palmerston admitted that the service would be beneficial. The real issue, he claimed in a note to the cabinet accompanying Brand's letter, was 'whether we Shall have Ireland with us or against us; whether we Shall conciliate a Third Part of the United Kingdom, or make the Same Mistake about it which Austria' was making in Hungary. In fact, it was two more years before there was a new contract. Furthermore, the real lessons of the crisis were that the Irish Liberals already could not be relied on and with Tory support the government did not need them. 'Independent opposition *pure et simple* was tried ... under the most favourable of circumstances', Hatchell wrote Carlisle, 'and miserably was it found wanting!'[42] So even as Palmerston wrote in favour of conciliating Ireland, he chose confrontation by appointing Sir Robert Peel his new chief secretary.

Palmerston knew what he was getting when he appointed Peel. He had written Carlisle in 1857, after Horsman's resignation, that Peel had 'neither Temper, Tact, nor discretion suitable for the office'. He told Russell in July 1861 that he hoped Peel's temper had improved with age, but Lord Bessborough told Carlisle, 'I cannot imagine any one worse'. Why, then, did Palmerston go ahead? His first choice, the Irish MP Chichester Fortescue, could not get re-elected. He needed more debating strength in the Commons and hoped Peel could provide it. He also told Russell that Carlisle was weak and dominated by a Castle clique, so he may have hoped that Peel could counter this.[43] If so, it was because Carlisle and his advisers were too Catholic in their sympathies.

---

41. Cardwell to Carlisle, 4, 21, 29 May 1861; Hatchell to Carlisle, 30 May, 1 June 1861; C.H., C.P., J19/1/93/42,52,78,100,102. Palmerston to Russell, 25, 26 May 1861 (P.R.O., R.P., PRO 30/22/21, ff 482–87). Trelawny's diary, 26–30 May 1861; Jenkins, *Diaries of Trelawny*, pp 172–4.
42. Brand to Palmerston, 1 June, 31 July 1861 (emphasis is Brand's); Palmerston Cabinet note, 2 Aug. 1861 (S.U.L., Palm. P., GC/BR/10,12 and enclosure). Hatchell to Carlisle, 1 June 1861 (C.H., C.P., J19/1/93/102). Olien, *Morpeth*, p. 466.
43. Palmerston to Carlisle, 11 Apr. 1857; quoted in Olien, *Morpeth*, p. 427; see also pp 467–8. Palmerston to Russell, 21 July 1861 (P.R.O., R.P., PRO 30/22/21, ff 512–13). Palmerston to Carlisle, 24 July 1861; Bessborough to Carlisle, 26 July 1861 (C.H., C.P., J19/1/94/48,52).

Palmerston had long believed in Irish ingratitude and the subversive influence of the Catholic clergy. On 19 August 1847, following the general election, he had written Russell, 'I see that almost all the Irish Elections have gone in Favour of Repeal Candidates; and this just after Two or Three Millions of Irish have been saved from Famine & Pestilence by Money which if the Union had not existed their own Parliament would never have been able to raise. This is not natural; but Effects must have Causes, and I should say that the Catholic Priests are the Cause of this Feeling'.

He thought the clergy encouraged popular violence and told Clarendon (presumably in jest), 'if you *could* hang the Priest of the Parish whenever a Murder Such as these last, was committed, I have a notion that Lay Protestant Life would be much more Secure'. Such cynicism about the Irish remained constant. Six years later, he asked Gladstone as chancellor of the exchequer to find money for an Irish project. 'The Expense would probably not be large, and Irish Gratitude would no Doubt last at least a Fortnight.'[44] The advent of Cullen and ultramontanism merely increased his distaste for Irish catholicism.

The appointment of Peel was Palmerston's response to one instance too many of Catholic ingratitude. As he wrote to Carlisle on 28 July, 'Now we the English Government have heaped Benefits and Favours on the Irish Catholics. We have relieved them from all their civil and political disabilities. We have given them their full Share ... of Patronage and Power and Places. Dead to every proper Sense of gratitude they turn against us as a Body at the Bidding of a Foreign Authority ...'.

Peel's brief would be 'to draw a little closer to the liberal Protestant Gentry of Ireland upon whom alone we can really depend'. For the next eighteen months, Carlisle and Peel waged a war over patronage. In January 1862 Palmerston himself returned to the fray. He called the Orangemen 'the Descendants of Whigs and the Inheritors of Whig Principles in Ireland' and insisted on a policy favouring Protestants 'when there are Two Candidates with nearly equal Pretensions ...'. Brand also weighed in, writing Carlisle in May, 'We shall get no good from the Ultramontane party ... We have no more bitter enemies in the H. of C. than M. O'Ferrall, Monsell & Co.' He urged Carlisle to use his patronage to 'sow Liberal seed' in the north. Carlisle, however, told Palmerston that Liberal Protestants were not 'very abundant products of the soil', and increasingly he went his own way on patronage, despite ever

---

44. Palmerston to Russell, 19 Aug. 1847 (P.R.O., R.P., PRO 30/22/6E, f 141). Palmerston to Clarendon, 13 Nov. 1847 (Ms Clar Dep, c.524). (Emphasis is Palmerston's.) Palmerston to Gladstone, 14 Mar. 1853 (B.L., Gladstone Papers, Add. MSS 44271, f 19). For similar sentiments expressed later, see Palmerston to Carlisle, 21 Aug. 1861, 21 Aug. 1863 (C.H., C.P., J19/1/94/107, J19/1/103/118).

shriller protests from Peel. He had no intention, he told Peel, of repudiating the Liberal party in Ireland in order 'to lean on Conservative support'.[45]

In other respects, Peel made Carlisle's life a misery, offending the Catholics at every turn. He challenged Cullen by launching a campaign to raise money to endow scholarships for the Queen's Colleges (Palmerston and Clarendon both contributed), while opposing a charter for the Catholic University at Dublin. When Cullen and the Catholic clergy denounced him, he assured Palmerston that 'liberal minded & independent R. Catholics of all classes' supported him in '"the setting down" I gave the Legate in answer to his unwarranteable [sic] & uncivil attacks'. When the session opened in 1862, Peel further offended Catholic MPs by insulting The O'Donoghue in a Commons debate. Through it all, Palmerston was well satisfied with his performance.[46]

The Irish people, however, were not satisfied, and so once more a Liberal government was unable to secure the return of its Irish officers. Following two promotions to the judicial bench, neither law officer sat in the commons. Brand tried to get the solicitor general returned for Coleraine, which would give them a toehold in the north. He had to abandon the contest, Carlisle told Palmerston, because he would get at most sixty out of 240 votes. The government had had no Irish whip since the cancellation of the Galway contract. All candidates faced clerical opposition, so Brand tried Luke White of Longford, whose family long had been the paramount influence in the county. White was defeated and had to retreat to an English constituency. An Irish supporter sadly told Carlisle, 'we are much in the same position that we were in, in 1852 [sic, 1851] after Lord Johns [sic] mild capers'. They finally were able to return the attorney general Thomas O'Hagan for Tralee, an O'Connellite seat, in the spring of 1863. Brand still urged the Duke of Devonshire, however, not to oppose a 'champion of independence' if he did not profess open hostility to the government.[47]

---

45. Palmerston to Carlisle, 28 July 1861, 7 Jan. 1861 [sic, 1862]; Peel to Carlisle, 20, 22 Dec. 1861, 1 Oct. 1862; Brand to Carlisle, 24 May 1862; Carlisle draft [reply to Peel's of 1 Oct. 1862] (ibid., J19/1/94/49, J19/1/96/111; J19/1/96/65,128, J19/1/100/65; J19/1/106/18; J19/1/100/66). Carlisle to Palmerston, 30 July 1861, 11 Jan. 1862; (S.U.L., Palm. P., GC/CA/510, 513). Olien, *Morpeth*, pp 475–8, 482, 503 (n85). Palmerston understood that the Liberals would not win Orange support, while Brand believed gains in the north would take time.
46. Larkin, *R. C. Ch. 1860–70*, pp 142–6. Olien, *Morpeth*, pp 473, 479–80. Peel to Palmerston, 26 Nov. (quote), 6, 10 Dec. 1861, 5 July 1862 (S.U.L., Palm. P., GC/PE/18–20, 25 enclosure). [Henry?] Ellis to Carlisle, 5 June 1862, cites a cabinet minister on Palmerston's satisfaction with Peel (C.H., C.P., J19/1/98/115).
47. Carlisle to Palmerston, 11 Jan. 1862 (S.U.L., Palm. P., GC/CA/513). Brand to Carlisle, 23 Nov., 22 Dec. 1861; 3 Feb., 22 May 1862, 10 Feb. 1863 (C.H., C.P., J19/1/95/113, J19/1/96/121, J19/1/97/85,97, J19/1/101/91). Ellis to Carlisle, 11 Mar. 1862 (quote); White to Carlisle, 5 Mar. 1862; ibid., J19/1/97/43,51. Palmerston to Gladstone, 8 Apr. 1863 (B.L., Gladstone Papers, Add. MSS 44272, ff 230–31).

Peel was undismayed. 'God forbid', he wrote Carlisle before White's defeat, 'any further concessions to the R. Catholics in Ireland until they manifest a disposition to appreciate the favours of the past'. When the Irish MPs forced him to abandon his legislative programme for 1862, Peel proposed no new legislation in 1863. The Irish also obstructed other liberal measures. After the defeat of the Deceased Wife's Sister Bill in March 1862, Sir John Trelawny noted in his diary, 'the Irish would, at present, seize any pretext for thwarting a measure supported by the bulk of the liberal party'. There was no danger of defeat, however, because, as Hatchell told Carlisle in June 1862, 'the Tory country gentlemen are not at all ambitious of so ill-starred an alliance'.[48] The best chance came in July 1864 on a Tory motion condemning the government's Danish policy. O'Hagan told Carlisle that More O'Ferrall was mobilising Irish Liberals against the government in revenge for Peel. Trelawny claimed that twenty-one Irish Liberals voted for the motion, but the government won handily because Radicals would not vote against a policy that had preserved peace.[49]

The cost of this success was the alienation of Irish liberalism. Upon the appointment of a new archbishop of Armagh in 1862, Bessborough told Carlisle, 'I cannot help feeling personally insulted at the Primacy, & if we had any remnant of a party left here I think this would alienate them'. The following year, when Arthur Stanley was rumoured as the new archbishop of Dublin, Hatchell wrote Carlisle that 'Lord Palmerston has ceased to care much about what poor Ireland wills or wills not'. Alexander Macdonnell urged Carlisle not to resign, whoever was appointed. Macdonnell speculated that Palmerston might be looking to appoint an evangelical like Lord Shaftesbury as lord lieutenant so he could try to carry the Protestant constituencies on an Orange cry. 'As to the Catholic ones they are all irretrievably gone already.'[50]

The years following the death of O'Connell were replete with cries of the end of Irish Catholic support for British liberalism. When general elections came, however, a substantial amount of Liberal support remained. The

---

48. Peel to Carlisle, 5 Mar. (quote), 18 June 1862; Hatchell to Carlisle, 2 June 1862 (C.H., C.P., J19/1/97/60, J19/1/99/35, J19/1/98/118). Trelawny diary, 12 Mar. 1862, 23 Apr. 1863, 24 June 1864; Jenkins, *Diaries of Trelawny*, pp 195, 242, 291. Olien, *Morpeth*, pp 478, 482–3.

49. O'Hagan to Carlisle, 6 [1?] July 1864 (C.H., C.P., J19/1/109/95). Trelawny diary, 9 July 1864; Jenkins, *Diaries of Trelawny*, p. 300. D.F. Krein, *The last Palmerston government: foreign policy, domestic politics, and the genesis of 'splendid isolation'* (Ames, IA, 1978), pp 168, 221 (note 36). Krein identified sixteen Irish Catholics who voted with the Tories in 1864 and twelve who voted with the Liberals. The difference between his and Trelawny's estimate may be accounted for by Protestant Liberals.

50. Bessborough to Carlisle, 20 Aug. 1862; Hatchell to Carlisle, 19 Oct. 1863; Macdonnell to Carlisle, 24 Oct. 1863 (C.H., C.P., J19/1/99/147, J19/1/104/29,46). Stanley was not appointed, but neither was Carlisle's recommendation. Olien, *Morpeth*, pp 482–3.

general election of 1865 was no different. The Independents won roughly a dozen seats, about the same as the eleven that Brand had counted in 1863. Brand was very pleased with the result.[51] The Palmerstonian solution could work as long as the Irish Catholics could not mobilise an effective independent party, and as long as British liberalism did not mind being alienated from liberal Ireland and relying on Tory support in the commons. It was not a long-term solution.

The Whigs of 1830–65 were not comfortable with any of their Radical allies in the Liberal party. Palmerston thought Bright and Cobden were just as dangerous as Grey thought O'Connell to be. Clarendon's constant use of the term 'Citizen Roebuck' reflected the Jacobin views he attributed to that tormentor. Thus, it is not surprising that they were contemptuous of the Irish Radicals and apprehensive about being associated with them. Yet during this period no Radical group gave them the reliable support that O'Connell and the Repealers did from 1835–41, and Irish behaviour contributed to the perception of many in the late 1830s that there *was* a Liberal party. Furthermore, it is questionable whether the Liberals by the 1850s had progressed much beyond the 1830s in their cohesion or sense of identification, and their more contentious relationship with Irish liberalism contributed to that failure.[52] Obvious changes had occurred to make the relationship more difficult. The advent of ultramontane catholicism and the emergence of sectarian education and tenant right as test issues for Catholic Radicals meant that British Liberals would be much less sympathetic to Irish concerns after 1850. The grievances of the 1830s were more susceptible to the kind of partial redress that was central to whiggism as a philosophy. The most significant change, however, was the presence of O'Connell from 1830–47 to assert an essential identity of Irish and British liberalism despite their many differences, and to broker an arrangement which, in providing benefits to both sides, embodied their common principles and interests.

The Whigs, however, could never accept that identity. Even when co-operating with him, they sought to weaken O'Connell, and they welcomed his movement's collapse. Yet many of the tensions that emerged after 1847 were there before, or would have been had it not been for O'Connell. Whig

---

51. Brand's division summary, 2 July 1863; (S.U.L., Palm. P., GC/BR/19, enclosure). Brand to Gladstone, 15, 17 July 1865 (B.L., Gladstone Papers, Add. MSS 44193, ff 120–25). Larkin, *R. C. Ch. 1860–70*, pp 348–9.
52. For evidence of no significant change between the 1830s and 1850s, see G.W. Cox, *The efficient secret: the cabinet and the development of political parties in victorian England* (Cambridge, 1987), pp 21–7, 97–112, and my interpretation of his evidence in Bernstein, 'Origins of Liberal politics', pp 77–8.

contempt for Irish nationalists and for their willingness to kow-tow to their electorate were constants from 1830–65. So was their suspicion of the sinister influence of the Catholic clergy, answerable to Rome, who wanted to keep the peasants ignorant in order to consolidate their own power. The baneful effect of the Famine, as well as the new policies and church influence of the 1850s, meant that British Radicals' attitudes toward the Irish were closer to their Whig leaders' after 1847 then before.

These views of Irish nationalism and Roman catholicism assured that any association with them would be an embarrassment to the Whig leaders. They constantly had to defend themselves from charges of favouring Catholics excessively in their appointments, and they constantly hankered after an alternative base of support in a moderate secular Catholic liberalism or in a liberal protestantism. In their more sober moments, however, the Whigs knew that protestantism was irretrievably Tory, while moderate catholicism was getting squeezed out, partly by the advent of Cullen, but partly also by their own policies that were dictated by British politics, such as famine relief, the Ecclesiastical Titles Act, and the support of Italian unification. Irish responses to these policies were dictated by Irish politics – O'Connell's Repeal agitation, the formation of successor Independent parties, opposition to avowed government supporters in the constituencies that at times made it impossible for them to win an Irish election, and church defence organisation. All this merely reinforced British impressions of the weakness of Irish Liberal MPs and the malevolent influence of the Catholic clergy.

Thus, while there were clear and broad bases for identification between British and Irish liberalism, and this would remain so up to 1914, there were also bases for divergence. O'Connell had been able to emphasise the former and limit the adverse effects of the latter; however, without strong Irish leadership that could make independence viable and assure that British Liberals took Irish Liberals and their concerns seriously, the points of difference increasingly became a source of friction, and the relationship broke down. The irony is that, even as British Liberals tried to ignore their Irish counterparts, British liberalism often was weakened in the house of commons without reliable Irish support.

3

1875: Faith or Fatherland?
The Contested Symbolism of Irish Nationalism

HUGH F. KEARNEY

EMMET LARKIN WAS THE FIRST HISTORIAN to draw attention to the significance of the Roman Catholic church in 'the making of modern Ireland'. His massive multi-volume history is now recognised as an essential starting point for future scholars.[1] Thanks to his formidable researches, it is now necessary to place Paul Cullen, archbishop of Dublin, John MacHale, archbishop of Tuam, Thomas Croke, archbishop of Cashel, and W.J. Walsh, archbishop of Dublin, alongside the figures of Peel, O'Connell, Gladstone, Parnell and Balfour. These bishops were able men of considerable political power with whom successive British governments had to deal in the second half of the nineteenth century and the early decades of the twentieth. Indeed, the Catholic hierarchy saw themselves as leaders of the Irish nation, as much as, if not more than, politicians like Parnell, Redmond and Dillon. In making sense of Irish nationalism, it is necessary to follow Larkin's lead and keep the Catholic hierarchy at the centre of the picture.

Larkin's work may be said to have introduced a new dimension into the study of Irish nationalism. However, it is not the only source of innovation.

---

1. Emmet Larkin, *R. C. Ch. 1850–60*, *R. C. Ch. 1860–70*, *R. C. Ch. 1870–74*, *R. C. Ch. 1878–86*, *R. C. Ch. 1886–88*, *R. C. Ch. 1888–91*. Professor Larkin's own account of the O'Connell celebrations is now available in his recent published volume, *R. C. Ch. 1874–78*, pp 401–20.

We may mention in particular a new level of sophistication in the study of nationalism associated with the work of Eric Hobsbawm, Terence Ranger, Ernest Gellner and many others.[2] It is now possible to place Irish nationalism in a comparative context. For these scholars the main concern is uncovering the problematic aspects of the concept 'nation'. In contrast nationalists, and nationalist historians, look upon their own nation and nationhood as in some sense 'God-given' or 'natural'. They see their national identity as resting upon 'language' or 'race' or 'religion' or 'territory' on a primordial basis. For them such signs of national identity are not the accidental product of historical change but part of a deeper providential pattern. In contrast, the new generation of scholars use such terms as 'the invention of tradition' or 'an imagined community' as the key to understanding the phenomenon of nationalism.

An article by Ashutosh Varshney 'Contested meanings: India's national identity, Hindu nationalism and the politics of anxiety' provides a good example of this approach.[3] Varshney shows how a formerly dominant Indian secular nationalism, the creation of Gandhi and Nehru, is today being challenged by an increasingly powerful Hindu nationalism. Allowing for obvious differences of scale, there are illuminating parallels here with Ireland. Throughout the nineteenth and much of the twentieth century there was continuous tension within Ireland between two images of the Irish nation, a secular image looking back to Wolfe Tone, Robert Emmet and the French Revolution, and a religious image deriving from the experience of a persecuted people during the Reformation and the post-Reformation period. The situation was complicated further by the incorporation of Ireland within the United Kingdom in

---

2. Ernest Gellner, *Nations and nationalism* (Oxford, 1983). Benedict Anderson, *Imagined communities: reflections on the origin and spread of nationalism* (London, 1983). Eric Hobsbawm, *Nations and nationalism since 1780: programme, myth, reality* (Cambridge, 1990). Eric Hobsbawm and Terence Ranger (ed.), *The invention of tradition*, (Cambridge, 1983). Peter Alter's article 'Symbols of Irish nationalism' in Alan O'Day (ed.), *Reactions to Irish nationalism 1865–1914* (London, 1987) provides an excellent introduction to the topic discussed in this paper. See especially his comments on the Manchester Martyrs and on the O'Connell Monument, pp 9–12. Recent literature making use of processions and commemorations as means by which communities define themselves includes Mona Ozouf, *La fête révolutionnaire, 1789–1799* (Paris, 1976), translated by Alan Sheridan as *Festivals and the French revolution* (Cambridge, MA, 1988), and George Mosse, *The nationalization of the masses: political symbolism and mass movements in Germany from the Napoleonic wars through the Third Reich* (New York, 1975). See also Jonathan Sperber's excellent article 'Festivals of national unity in the German revolution of 1848–1849' in *Past and Present*, no. 136 (Aug. 1992), pp 114–38; Timothy O'Keeffe, 'The 1898 efforts to celebrate the United Irishmen: the '98 centennial' in *Éire-Ireland*, xxiii, no. 2 (Summer 1988), pp 51–73, and 'Who fears to speak of '98? the rhetoric and rituals of the United Irishmen centennial, 1898' ibid., xxvii, no. 3 (Fall 1992), pp 67–91.
3. *Daedalus*, cxxii, no. 3 (Summer 1993), pp 227–62

1800 by the Act of Union and by the later rise of a powerful 'Orange' ethnic consciousness within the province of Ulster (the Irish equivalent of the Kashmir or the Punjab).

In the wake of new interpretations, historians and anthropologists have become increasingly aware of the ambiguities and tensions which lie at the heart of most, perhaps one should say all, nationalist movements. Since it is impossible to define 'nation' in such a way as to make it immediately and self-evidently acceptable to all possible members of a specific nation, disputes inevitably arise as to what constitutes the essential signs of the nation. 'Contested symbols' thus seem to form part of the histories of various nationalist movements, not least Irish nationalism.

This paper is concerned with the commemoration of the centenary of O'Connell's birth, which was celebrated over three days (5–7 August) in Dublin during the summer of 1875. As such it is clearly limited in scope. In my view, however, following Varshney's lead, it illustrates long-lasting divisions among Irish political activists about the meaning of the 'nation'. A struggle took place during the centenary celebrations of O'Connell's birth about interpretation of a national symbol – in this case, the figure of Daniel O'Connell himself. The question at issue was whether O'Connell was to be seen primarily as a figure sponsoring Catholic emancipation or as an advocate of the repeal of the Union. What was at stake was the nature of Irish identity. Was it religious or secular? The symbolism of O'Connell's memory became a critical issue as each side sought to annex it for its own purposes.

But O'Connell, while alive, had been an ambiguous figure and after his death did not become less so. Before 1829 O'Connell had successfully played the role of the liberator in the campaign for Catholic emancipation. During the 1830s he oscillated between Repeal and a policy of pragmatic alliance with the Whigs. After his death, the memory of O'Connell assumed great importance as a symbol of non-violent political agitation, particularly in reaction to the rise of the fenian movement in the 1860s. O'Connell's commitment to peaceful methods was undoubted. Where ambiguity arose was about the nature of his political aims. Was he prepared to accept the place of Ireland within the United Kingdom or was Repeal his long-term objective? It was this issue which divided the forces of constitutional nationalism during the early 1870s.[4] What was also at stake was the meaning of 'nation' and 'nationalism'. Was Ireland a Catholic nation as popular preachers such as

---

4. L.J. McCaffrey, *Irish federalism in the 1870s: a study in conservative nationalism* (Philadelphia, 1962). David Thornley, *Isaac Butt and home rule* (London, 1964). P. J. Corish, 'Political problems, 1860–1878' in P.J. Corish (ed.), *A history of Irish catholicism* (Dublin, 1967).

Tom Burke believed, or was it a nation defined by its historic territorial basis? The question had implications beyond the Irish Sea for Britain, the dominions of Canada, Australia and New Zealand and not least for the United States.

The Dominican preacher Fr Tom Burke had declared in 1872: 'Take an average Irishman – I don't care where you find him – and you will find that the very first principle in his mind is "I am not an Englishman because I am a Catholic". Take an Irishman wherever he is found all over the earth and any casual observer will at once come to the conclusion "Oh he is an Irishman, he is a Catholic. The two go together"'.[5]

The non-sectarian Home Rule League challenged this assumption head on. The three days of the O'Connell centenary thus became a contest between the two nationalist political groupings over the nature of Irish national identity.

The contest was focused largely upon two men, the Catholic prelate Paul Cullen and the Protestant lawyer Isaac Butt. In the preceding decade, Paul Cullen, archbishop of Dublin from 1850 and the most powerful prelate in Ireland, saw his role as that of combating fenianism and by implication what Fenian success might bring with it, socialism and secularism. Cullen's answer to fenianism was to encourage the development of a religious-based nationalism which could concentrate its aims upon the disestablishment of the Church of Ireland and the reform of higher education in the interests of the Catholics, with land reform as a third issue.[6]

In the election of 1874, however, Cullen's religious nationalism lost ground dramatically to the newly-founded Home Rule League led by Isaac Butt, who had shown sympathy to fenianism to the extent of defending them in court. Butt was a secular nationalist for whom the Irish nation rested upon the uniting of Catholic and Protestant. Butt saw his aim as the restoration of the historic Irish nation of 1782, under the British crown, but with its own lords and commons. He was not a Republican, but he showed himself willing to use the issue of 'amnesty' for Fenian prisoners as a means of increasing popular support for home rule. Cullen, in contrast, was bitterly opposed to home rule. In 1873 he wrote 'my opinion is that if we had a little parliament here, half Protestant or more than half and perhaps less than half Catholic, the MPs in order to give themselves something to do, would begin to make laws for priests and bishops and to fetter the action of the Church'. It seems more

---

5. Quoted in Hugh Kearney, *The British isles: a history of four nations*, (Cambridge, 1989), p. 184.
6. See Emmet Larkin, *R. C. Ch. 1870–74*, pp 192–9. Chapter iv of this volume provides an illuminating account of ecclesiastical politics prior to the O'Connell centenary.

than likely that in the aftermath of electoral defeat in 1874, Cullen and his political allies led by Peter Paul McSwiney, lord mayor of Dublin, seized upon the forthcoming centenary of O'Connell's birth (6 August 1875) as a way of restoring their fortunes. The religious card was to be played as a response to the challenge of Butt's secular nationalism.

The first day of the centenary celebration began with the celebration of high mass in the Catholic cathedral, followed in the evening by a formal dinner given at the Mansion House by the lord mayor, Peter Paul McSwiney.[7] On both occasions the tone was that of an embattled but confident catholicism. Representatives were present from the Catholic hierarchies throughout the British Empire as well as France and Germany. The 'Kulturkampf' was a major theme of the speeches with references being made to Bismarckian persecution in Poland and the Catholic Rhineland. The organisers of the celebrations claimed that their aims were non-sectarian. The tone of the speeches, however, was unmistakably Catholic. Indeed, later comments were made in the press about the ultramontane tone of the celebrations.

The high point of the celebrations in the cathedral was the sermon by Thomas Croke, the newly appointed archbishop of Cashel.[8] Croke's theme was O'Connell's role as a great Catholic. He left consideration of O'Connell 'the statesman' to 'an Irish nobleman of ancient lineage and well established fame, glowing Irish genius, instinct with Irish feeling' by whom he meant Thomas O'Hagan, lord chancellor of Ireland under Gladstone. There was no hint here that O'Hagan was a controversial figure in the eyes of the home rule party, as a man who had taken office in a British government

Croke drew a sharp contrast between English and Irish views of history. He expected an Englishman to speak of King Alfred, of the tyrant John and 'the struggle for the Charter of British freedom' and of the battles of Crecy, Agincourt and Poitiers. An Irishman however would refer to Ireland's 'once famous schools and Universities' and to Brian's defeat of the Danes, and to 'how the fruitful mother of so many saints and scholars was made to suffer for many a long and dreary age'. Ireland 'always held on to the faith of Patrick and was prepared to die in its defence'. 'If I say', Croke declared, 'such themes as these are touched on, I recognise forthwith in the speaker an Irishman

---

7. My main source is *O'Connell centenary record 1875* (Dublin, 1878). A less laudatory account is provided in the pages of pro-Butt periodical *The Nation* (Aug.–Sept., 1875), which is discussed by R.W. Warden in 'The interaction of Protestants and Catholics in the Home Rule League, as portrayed in the pages of *The Nation* during the O'Connell Centenary of 1875' (unpublished paper produced for the seminar on Nationalism, Department of History, University of Pittsburgh, Oct. 1994.)
8. *Centenary record*, pp 96–102.

born, or one in heart and sympathy and affection'. In this opening speech of the centenary celebration, Croke thus stressed the interlinkage of catholicism and Irish identity.

But what was 'the faith of Patrick'? Croke stated that a true Catholic should 'accept with a ready and unwavering assent every doctrine decree and decision that emanates from the Holy See'. He stressed that education should be under the control 'of the commissioned teachers and guardians of the Faith'. He praised France where, after the vicissitudes of the French Revolution, 'a new and bright educational era' had just begun thanks to the efforts of Felix Dupanloup, bishop of Orleans.[9] 'Thus you see, brethren', Croke declared, 'when France was infidel education was irreligious; and as it became Christian education became Christian also!' Croke went on to state that in Ireland, to be a Catholic was no longer contemptible. 'In rank and station, in intelligence not less than in integrity, in commercial enterprise and professional skill, in all the virtues that create social respectability or tend to ennoble it – I had almost said in wealth – we are equal to, as in numbers we immeasurably surpass any and all other denominations of Christians in our country'.

Croke praised O'Connell's character and career. O'Connell 'was thoroughly convinced of the necessity of having education for Catholic children and I believe he was one of the first who applied the term "Godless" to those Colleges which the late Sir Robert Peel founded for us in 1845'. Had O'Connell not been a devout Catholic – 'he could never have acquired that magic influence over his religious countrymen without which all his efforts would have been available: the great work of National regeneration, now so largely associated with his name could never have been achieved by him!'

Croke then went on to refer to O'Connell's criticism of violence in politics. 'He [O'Connell] thought much over and appreciated properly the very peculiar and indeed inflammable character of the materials with which he had to deal. He knew and no man knew it better that the Irish Celt is from nature ardent and excitable, highly sympathetic, daring devoted and generous!' In O'Connell, 'there was the righteous instinct of the just and religious man warning him to beware and suggesting to him, the awful responsibility of those who unite a struggling people to throw away the scabbard and to seek by

---

9. Felix Dupanloup (1802–78), bishop of Orleans from 1849, was involved in the passing of the Falloux Law of 1850, which removed discrimination against church schools. He was a defender of the temporal of the papacy but openly protested, like MacHale, against the doctrine of papal infallibility at Vatican I (1870), though he accepted it once promulgated. The references to Dupanloup in Croke's speech raise questions about the extent to which the French was seen as a model for Ireland in such areas as education. The 'devotional revolution' itself needs to be placed in a European context.

the naked sword what in time they are sure to get by conciliation!' O'Connell was 'the father of the salutary doctrine that there is no amount of national liberty that a people cannot win from their rulers without the shedding of one drop of blood or the desolation of one solitary hearth!' Moving towards his final peroration, Croke appealed to his audience 'as Irishmen and as Catholics'. 'We are fast working ourselves into that position of equality and independence under the protection of what I am not afraid to designate as the best balanced constitution in the world! ... As Catholics we have every reason to be proud! ... For all this social, civic and ecclesiastical progress', Croke concluded, 'we have every reason to be thankful'. He looked forward to acquiring by peaceful means 'our full complement of constitutional freedom'.

In the course of this speech Croke was highly critical of 'the Heathen Maxims' of the French Revolution and of 'the evil influence of the Encyclopedists!' He attacked in particular the republican view that religion should be excluded from the schools. For Croke, O'Connell was a symbol of 'the great work of national regeneration' in a peaceful manner, opposing those who sought to win 'by naked sword what in time they are sure to get by conciliation'. Surprisingly, in view of Croke's later reputation as an extreme nationalist, he seemed largely content with the position of the church. 'While persecution rages elsewhere, the sky is serene over our heads here and we can meet in Synod, and in every other way, advance the interest of our Church without let or hindrance, without State licence or State control!' Croke saw O'Connell as the source of these 'sound principles of political action'. Whether or not O'Connell was as unswervingly orthodox on educational issues as Croke implied is open to question. What is clear is the attempt by religious nationalists to seize upon O'Connell as a symbol of policies. From this point of view O'Connell the Liberator, advocate of Catholic emancipation, was the 'real O'Connell'. O'Connell the advocate of Repeal was to be tacitly ignored or played down. Within the confines of the cathedral this was easy enough. Once the organisers moved into a less controlled environment, however, difficulties began to arise.

After the celebration of high mass in the cathedral, the next event was the lord mayor's banquet in the Mansion House.[10] After a splendid dinner, Lord Mayor McSwiney proposed the first toast to 'His Holiness the Pope'. He referred to the support of the Irish nation, the Catholics of England, Scotland, France, Germany, and Italy and two hundred million Catholics who looked to the Holy Father as the infallible expounder of the word of God. McSwiney

---

10. *Centenary record*, pp 103–15. The menu is printed on p. 107.

thus followed Croke's lead earlier in the day in stressing the Catholic identity of the Irish nation.

He followed this toast with toasts first to the Queen, then the Prince and Princess of Wales and other members of the royal family. The lord lieutenant of Ireland was toasted next. McSwiney praised the lord lieutenant for pointing out 'the advantages of ... a resident proprietary in contradistinction to the disadvantages of absenteeism'. There was no hint here of the attack on 'landlordism' which was to characterise the Land League only three years later.

The moment now arrived which Cullen and McSwiney were probably dreading, the speech by John MacHale, archbishop of Tuam. Throughout the middle decades of the century MacHale and Cullen had been at odds, with MacHale consistently supporting a more nationalist line. For MacHale, O'Connell the Repealer took precedence over O'Connell the liberator. In his short speech he did not disappoint his supporters, referring to 'presages of the approaching autonomy exercising the right of self government which no people ever lost, to any extent, without being in a corresponding degree treated as slaves'.

He praised O'Connell's heroic exertions to realise the blessings of self-government. He referred to 'the Irish people', 'the Irish nation' and 'exalted patriotism'. He deplored 'the disastrous Famine' but expressed his hopes for the people's prosperity when the goal of legislative autonomy was reached.

McSwiney's and Cullen's response was once more to stress the role of the church. McSwiney in proposing the toast of 'the Cardinal Archbishop of Dublin and the hierarchy of Ireland' pointed to the leadership of the hierarchy under whose fostering care 'innumerable churches, educational establishments, hospitals and asylums have everywhere sprung up and been erected without State aid', and he also referred directly to the three aims of the National Association – religious equality, tenant compensation, and denominational education – of which two had been achieved.

In his reply to this toast, Cullen spoke of O'Connell as a 'second Moses'. He outlined what he saw as O'Connell's doctrines – 'his determination to obey the law, his determination to maintain the authority of the Church and State, and his hatred of bloody revolution'. He stressed O'Connell's loyalty to the pope and his influence outside Ireland. Cullen's O'Connell was clearly an anti-Fenian symbol.

There was thus a clear difference of emphasis in the speeches of MacHale on the one hand and those of McSwiney and Cullen on the other. MacHale's theme was self-government and his hopes of raising up a 'host of young men animated with ardent desire of treading in [O'Connell's] footsteps'. He argued that Ireland in seeking self-government was merely following England's example in asserting 'the uncontrolled expression of her native insular freedom'. In contrast, McSwiney and Cullen stressed what had been achieved under the leadership of the hierarchy. MacHale had ignored the hierarchy in his appeal for 'a succession of genuine and sterling patriotism'. For McSwiney and Cullen, the hierarchy were the natural leaders of the Irish people, under the leadership of the pope (unmentioned by MacHale). In McSwiney's final speech, however, there was a surprising shift, when he announced that 'the salvation of Ireland demanded nothing less that the Repeal of the Union'. The dinner at the Mansion House revealed what observers of Irish politics already knew – that Cullen and MacHale differed radically in their view of the Irish nation and its future. On the whole these tensions had been kept within bounds. On the following day, however, Cullen's opponents were able to mount a more open challenge.

The second day, Friday 6 August, 'the hundredth birthday of O'Connell' began with the marshalling of the procession at 10 a.m.[11] The starting point was the south-west corner of St Stephen's Green where middle-class catholicism had begun to make its mark. In this area was the Catholic University at 85–86 Stephen's Green, St Vincent's Hospital, the Loreto Convent and the Jesuit House of Studies at 35 Lower Leeson Street. The procession itself required a great deal of organising, made more difficult by the vast crowds, including many from Glasgow, Liverpool and Manchester. The organisers had given a great deal of thought to the route, which was largely based upon key sites connected with O'Connell's career – his house in Merrion Square, his role at City Hall as lord mayor, his imprisonment at Richmond Gaol, his early emancipation meetings in Capel Street and finally the site of his still unfinished statue at the south end of Sackville Street (now O'Connell Street.)

The procession was headed by contingents of over forty different groups representing the skilled and unskilled workmen of Dublin. The largest group were the bakers (1000) and the grocers' assistants (1500). Others included various groups associated with metal working, wood working, leather, shipbuilding, barrel making, silk weaving, boot and shoe-making, printing, hairdressing, chimney sweeping and various food trades. There was some 'modern' industry, represented by the United Machine Workers, but Dublin was clearly a pre-industrial city, contrasting in its structure with the factories of Belfast and the Lagan Valley. It was the traditional labouring orders of

---

11. Ibid., pp 143 ff.

Dublin who were most threatened by the industrial changes of the nineteenth century.

But the nationalism revealed by the banners of the trades groups were largely cultural in character. The symbols of Erin (a female figure), a harp, a wolfhound, a round tower and shamrocks were most common. Banners with explicit political references were exceptional. The horseshoe workers referred to Grattan, Emmet and Fitzgerald along with O'Connell. The Dublin Mariners, 600 in number, carried a banner with the names of Emmet, Hugh O'Neill and Brian Boru as well as that of O'Connell. The banners of hairdressers and bakers referred to 'amnesty' i.e. the demand for clemency for Fenian prisoners. In contrast, the stationary engine drivers carried a banner with medallion portraits of Stephenson and Watts, along with the slogan 'Encourage Irish manufacturers'. The United Machine Workers had borrowed their banner from Manchester. On this the names of the British engineers Sir Joseph Whitworth and Sir William Fairbairn were displayed. The Skinners' banner included the rose and thistle, along with the shamrock. Thus, although the tone of the trades procession was 'national', it can hardly be termed 'nationalist' in the sense of aiming at 'Repeal'. Indeed the banner of the foresters, who marched later in the procession, illustrated Robin Hood's last shot along with the figure of little John, symbols from English, not Irish, folklore.

The remaining part of the procession, which was numerically much stronger, stressed the religious identity of the Irish. The sodalities of the Sacred Heart alone numbered 6000 men. The contingents were organised on the basis of their parishes, led by their spiritual directors. National symbols such as the wolfhound and the shamrock appeared on the banners together with references to O'Connell and slogans such as 'God save Ireland' but in general the overall effect was religious in character. Among the most common motifs were the Sacred Heart, our Lady of Lourdes, St Joseph and 'the infant Saviour'. St Patrick and St Bridget appeared on some banners but not all. 'The devotional revolution' of mid century had clearly left its mark.[12]

The organisers of the centenary had clearly aimed to present a united Catholic front, in alliance with groups from Liverpool, Manchester and Glasgow. So far they had been largely successful. The unity of the proceedings, however, was deliberately challenged by a procession organised by the Home Rule League with the aim of arousing support for 'amnesty'. This procession began from a different starting point, the Customs House, and

---

12. One of Emmet Larkin's most fruitful concepts has been that of 'the devotional revolution.' See *A.H.R.*, lxxvii, no. 3 (June 1972) pp 625–52.

had its own black banner with the words 'Amnesty Association' on one side and 'Remember the prisoners still in chains' and 'God save Ireland' on the other. From another banneret were suspended a pair of prison anklets and chains. This rhetoric was Fenian in tone, clearly designed to recall 'the Manchester Martyrs' of 1867 as well as Fenian activists still imprisoned.[13]

In the procession were delegates from a large number of towns in England and Scotland, as well as from Ireland. The Liverpool home rulers in particular were strongly represented. Among the political leaders present were Isaac Butt and John O'Leary, who drove up in a carriage, and a number of home rule MPs in a two-horse brake. Their object was to hijack the leadership of the grand procession by moving ahead of it at a convenient point, Kingsbridge station. But the manoeuvre did not succeed. For the moment Amnesty men had to be content with joining the main procession at a point some way from the leading marchers.

The two processions illustrated the profound division which lay at the centre of Irish nationalism. The organisers of the main procession stressed the progress which Catholics had made since O'Connell's death. The official account of the proceedings drew attention to the fact that 'the great majority of the Judges of the Superior Courts, several of the Privy Councillors and many of the Judges of the County Courts' were Catholic. It also referred to the prominent place of Catholics among the high sheriffs and magistrates and the municipal governments of three of the provinces, and to the fact that fifty of the 103 MPs were Catholics. Stress was also laid upon the advances which Catholics had made in the professions, in the possession of landed property and in legislatures of the leading British colonies. There was clear middle-class thrust to this rhetoric together with a strongly ethno-cultural dimension, in the sense that the emphasis was upon Catholic advancement.

Thomas O'Hagan, first baron O'Hagan (1812–85), the organiser's choice as keynote speaker, appropriately symbolised this point of view. After studying at the King's Inns, Dublin and Gray's Inn, London, he was summoned to the Irish bar in 1835. He became a supporter of O'Connell, but drew back over Repeal. In 1861 he was appointed solicitor-general in Palmerston's government and in 1863 was returned as member for Tralee despite opposition from conservatives and nationalists. In 1868, on the formation of Gladstone's first ministry he was appointed lord chancellor of Ireland, the first Catholic to hold that office since the revolution of 1688. O'Hagan was an enthusiastic advocate of the national system of education in Ireland and was also actively

---

13. *Centenary record*, p. 173.

involved in plans to make university education more accessible to Catholics. He was thus a symbol of the success of constitutional gradualist reform in Ireland. Though an opponent of Repeal, he was in favour of the establishment of a local Irish legislature for local purposes. For the Home Rule Association, however, O'Hagan represented a system which they were determined to attack.[14]

Isaac Butt (1813–79) leader president of the Amnesty Association (1869) and founder of Home Government Association (1870) was a more ambiguous figure.[15] Originally a Tory, a committed Orangeman, and an opponent of O'Connell over Repeal, he later defended Fenians in court (1865–68). His political career was thus marked by extraordinary shifts. At this period, however, there is little doubt that he espoused a civic national identity for Ireland which would include Protestants as well as Catholics. His home rule party included MPs from varied religious backgrounds. Thus, where Cullen's National Association pointed to the election of fifty Catholic MPs as evidence of Catholic progress, the home rulers played down religious affiliation. Another difference between the two parties lay in the home rulers' demand for the extension of the franchise.

The first O'Connell dinner, on Thursday 5 August, had been a 'private' event given by personal invitation of the lord mayor, at his own expense. The second dinner on Friday 6 August was a much larger affair, held by invitation in the vast exhibition hall in Earlsfort Terrace, near the Catholic University.[16] One hundred distinguished guests sat at a dais at one end while several hundred more were accommodated at four tables stretching the length of the hall. (Ladies had a separate area in the galleries.) As it was a Friday the cardinal archbishop issued a dispensation from the obligation of avoiding flesh meat, thus earning 'the gratitude of the Irish race at home and abroad'. (As with Croke's sermon earlier, it was assumed that the 'Irish race' was Catholic.) Members of the hierarchy headed by the Catholic archbishop of Armagh, and members of parliament, including Isaac Butt, constituted the majority of guests at the high table. At the lower tables the clergy were strongly represented.

The proceedings began with a toast to Queen Victoria, described by McSwiney as 'one of the best sovereigns'. McSwiney then proposed a toast to 'the memory of O'Connell' whose name he declared 'symbolised Ireland'. Sir Colman O'Loghlen, Bart, QC, MP, a friend of O'Connell, spoke to the toast,

---

14. The text of O'Hagan's speech was printed later in ibid., pp 362–72.
15. For the text of Butt's speech see *The Nation* (21 Aug. 1875).
16. *O'Connell cent. rec.*, pp 375 ff.

claiming that when O'Connell 'sought to open the portals of the constitution to Catholics, when he sought for them the privilege of citizens, he did so in no sectarian spirit'. O'Loghlen associated himself with MacHale in claiming that O'Connell was not simply 'the Liberator of Catholics'. 'We should regard him', he declared, 'as the greatest patriot Ireland ever saw' though 'there may be men in this room who do not agree in the plan he adopted in the latter course of his life'. O'Loghlen thus again brought into the open the division among the admirers of O'Connell between the 'Liberator' and the 'Repealer' groups, a division which corresponded to a large extent to that between 'ethnic' and 'civic' nationalism. The next toast was to 'the French nation', which McSwiney described as 'the land of the Montalemberts, the McMahons, and the Dupanloups!' A note of religious nationalism had been sounded, which was taken further by the bishop of Nantes who declared that 'if a country is great, it is by religion that greatness is acquired'. 'In the religious order and in the political order', he added, 'France and Ireland had grouped hands' (a reference to the French president Marshall McMahon). A letter from Dupanloup was now read out praising O'Connell as the 'indefatigable champion of Emancipation'. The Viscount O'Neill De Tyrone, sub-prefect of the Seine, also spoke at length.

The toasts were beginning to take a European course, linking Ireland with Catholic Europe. This direction was continued with the next toast, 'Our foreign Guests', to which Prince Radziwill, member of the German Reichstag and representative of the imprisoned Cardinal Ledóchiwski, responded. He lamented the lack in Poland of a man like O'Connell and then went on to condemn revolutionary methods.

The lord mayor now proposed the toast of 'Legislative Independence', coupling with it the name of Sir Charles Gavan Duffy. Duffy was the first editor of *The Nation* and had been imprisoned along with O'Connell in 1844. It was, however, as the official representative of Victoria, the Australian state to which he had emigrated in 1855, that he was called upon to speak. As a former prime minister of Victoria 1871–72, who had been knighted in 1873, Duffy symbolised the possibility of Irish progress within the Empire. At this point, however, cries of 'Butt' were heard throughout the hall from those who had demonstrated at the platform in Sackville Street earlier in the day. Duffy could not make himself heard and when Butt rose to address the company, the lord mayor condemned the proceedings for being 'irregular and disorderly'. He withdrew from the chair, and the gaslights were lowered, about midnight.

Thus, the O'Connell centenary did not go entirely as its organisers hoped. They had demonstrated the emotional power of Irish catholicism and, despite their assertions of non-sectarianism, had underlined a link between Irish national and religious identity. But the organisers had not succeeded in dominating secular nationalism by sheer force of numbers. The supporters of Butt had been able to make their presence felt during the centenary procession, at the platform in Sackville Street and at the conclusion of the Earlsfort Terrace dinner. More significantly, they also controlled the proceedings at the trades grand banquet held north of the river Liffey at the Rotunda.[17] Five hundred representatives of 'the different operative classes' were present, many of them wearing the home rule medal. The two main guests were the pro-Fenian John O'Leary, who had been imprisoned from 1865–74, and T.D. Sullivan, brother of A.M. Sullivan, editor of *The Nation*. Once the toasts had begun, it was clear that the tone of the Rotunda dinner was to be very different from that of Earlsfort Terrace. The first toast was not to 'the Queen' but to 'The Queen, Lords and Commons of Ireland' – for the reason, the chairman explained, 'that the Irish people claimed to be a nation'. The nationalist note was continued by T.D. Sullivan, who in fact referred in the toast to 'Ireland a Nation'. Sullivan spoke of the noble bearing of working men of Dublin and Ireland. He then went on to call for the restitution of the rights and powers of a nation to Ireland. In words echoing those of Robert Emmet, he spoke of 'the determination to elevate Ireland to her right place in the full radiance of independence and freedom among the nations of the earth'.

The next toast was 'The People, the legitimate Source of Power'. The speaker was Thomas Mooney, who referred to O'Connell's demand for Repeal of the Union and to MacHale's support for Repeal on the previous night. John O'Leary followed, with the toast of 'the Restoration of Irish Independence'. A new note was struck by the next speaker, Charles Dawson, who proposed a toast to 'The Memory of Daniel O'Connell, the Man of the Irish People'. Dawson called for the removal of 'the shameful inequalities of the Parliamentary Franchise in Ireland and in England'. He claimed that 'the political rights of the middle and upper classes were won after many a struggle ... To complete the idea of O'Connell, we have yet to win for the working men of Ireland in field and factory, their political rights and for the country at large its political independence. This is our work. This is the legacy of O'Connell.'

In contrast to the Earlsfort Terrace banquet, that held in the Rotunda was working class in character. The toasts made no mention of Catholic

---

17. *The Nation* (18 Sept. 1875).

emancipation. On the contrary the emphasis throughout was on Repeal. There was clearly a whiff of popular radicalism about the proceedings. The nationalist rhetoric of O'Leary and Sullivan was consciously non-sectarian. Their emphasis was on 'the Irish people' not Irish Catholics. Sullivan referred to 'the long night of slavery and suffering' not to Catholic progress within the Union which had been the theme of Croke's sermon and of McSwiney's speech at the Mansion House on the previous day. It remains to mention the third day, Saturday 7 August, which because of bad weather was something of an anti-climax when judged by the vast throngs of Friday. A relatively small crowd assembled at Glasnevin cemetery near the O'Connell monument to hear a speech by Butt calling for 'the same franchise for Ireland that the English people enjoy'.

This final meeting was not the end of the affair. Throughout the next few weeks, articles and letters in *The Nation* complained that Butt and the home rule party had been badly treated. One letter for example declared that 'the man who leads the national party was either not to speak at all or to be shunted to the small hours of the morning!' O'Neill Daunt, the veteran home ruler, argued that it was 'enormously wrong' to restrict public recognition of O'Connell to his services in the cause of Catholic emancipation. Daunt stated that O'Connell 'repeatedly expressed his desire that if Repeal were not carried in his lifetime it might be recorded on his tomb that he died a Repealer!' A committee of enquiry under the Amnesty Association was presided over by Charles Stewart Parnell MP, as yet a relatively minor figure, but a future leader who would unite at least temporarily the forces of civic and religious nationalism.

The split within Irish nationalism, exposed by the O'Connell centenary celebrations, was between two groups of activists for control of a powerful political symbol. In his own lifetime O'Connell's own political position had shifted remarkably from time to time. At one period, that of the 'Lichfield House Compact' he had worked openly with the Whig government of the day. On other occasions he openly espoused Repeal as an issue which would best unite Catholics and Liberal Protestants.[18] The groups who fought over his memory in the 1870s were thus guilty of trying to use the past for their own purposes. O'Connell, who read Gibbon avidly in his youth and was a close friend of Bentham, was clearly not a single-minded ultramontane. What he would have made of the Syllabus of Errors must be a matter of speculation.

---

18. Jacqueline Hill, 'The response to repeal: the case of the Dublin working class' in Lyons & Hawkins, *Ireland*, pp 35–68.

In 1862 when plans for a national monument to O'Connell were first proposed, under the auspices of the *Freeman's Journal*, the image of O'Connell the liberator was dominant. John MacHale protested at that time about 'honouring the Emancipator only and ignoring the Repealer'. By 1882, however, when the O'Connell monument was unveiled, the Home Rule Party dominated the proceedings and the main theme of the speeches by Parnell and Charles Dawson, who was now lord mayor of Dublin, was 'O'Connell the Repealer'. The political pendulum had swung considerably since the centenary commemoration in 1872. It was to swing back towards the church during the Parnellite split of 1890–91. In the long run the church succeeded in establishing a firm grip on the memory of O'Connell. It was O'Connell the liberator, the Catholic nationalist, not O'Connell the Repealer, the civic nationalist, which became the dominant image. Two statues now dominate O'Connell Street, those of O'Connell and Parnell.[19] They may be seen as representing two traditions of Irish nationalism, civic and religious. They also illustrate tensions which at the end of the twentieth century remain to be resolved.

---

19. Oliver MacDonagh, *The hereditary bondsman: Daniel O'Connell, 1775–1829* (London, 1988), and MacDonagh, *Emancipist*, constitute the standard modern work but W.E.H. Lecky's analysis in *Leaders of Public Opinion in Ireland*, (new ed., London, 1903), vol. ii, is still well worth reading. See also Macintyre, *Liberator*. On Parnell, see Frank Callanan, *The Parnell Split, 1890–91* (Cork,1992), C.J. Woods 'The general election of 1892: the Catholic clergy and the defeat of the Parnellites' in Lyons & Hawkins, *Ireland*, pp 289–319.

4

Imagining the Nation in Irish Historical Fiction,
c.1870–c.1925

LAWRENCE W. MCBRIDE

THE HISTORICAL FICTION written by Irish novelists during the late nineteenth and early twentieth centuries had both aim and purpose. The authors aimed to entertain their readers with tales of romance and adventure. Their purpose was to use the stories to affect their readers' understanding of contemporary political and social issues. The Irish historical fiction of this era can be defined further – if not completely differentiated from the fiction which preceded and followed it – by analysing the authors' descriptions of Irish space, their concepts of Irish time, and their insights into the behaviour of the Irish people.[1] That is, the authors described the geographic features of

---

1. The eighty works of fiction written between 1870 and 1925 that inform this essay differ in literary style from the novels produced by Maria Edgeworth, John and Michael Banim, John Gamble, Charles Lever, Samuel Lover, William Carleton, Anthony Trollope, Somerville and Ross, and others who wrote before 1870. The earlier novels centre on questions of moral development and tend toward melancholic or comic plot developments. The use of the English language by the earlier writers may also presuppose a different reading audience in Ireland (and England and abroad) for the historical fiction than that which appeared in English later in the nineteenth and twentieth centuries. The selection of 1925 for this essay is somewhat arbitrary. Several of the authors who enjoyed initial success before 1925 – Birmingham, O'Grady, Pender, and Sheehan – have continued to have a readership in both English and Irish. Three works of literary criticism which take up the issues of categorisation and periodisation of the Irish historical novel are: John Cronin, *The Anglo-Irish novel*, vol. 1, 'The nineteenth century' (Totowa, NJ, 1980); Thomas Flanagan, *The Irish novelists, 1800–1850* (New York, 1958); and J.M. Cahalan, *Great hatred, little room: the Irish historical novel* (Dublin, 1983).

Ireland in ways that distinguished Irish places from all other places; they kept the past alive in Ireland by recalling historic events and processes and by explaining how those episodes affected the present and might shape the future; and they depicted the Irish as a unique race of people. This chapter examines each of the defining characteristics of Irish historical fiction before reaching some conclusions about how the novels collectively and imaginatively portrayed the Irish nation.

During the nineteenth century, Irish people who wanted to know about their national past could draw on a number of sources for information. Historical fiction occupied a niche alongside many other print sources, including newspapers, pamphlets, and formal narrative histories. A sense of the past was also communicated through the aural transmission of folkhistory, folklore, and folkmusic as well as through the visual stimulus of mass meetings, the built environment, and material culture.[2] These sources of information contributed to the social and political education of the people by filling the void in the national and intermediate school curriculum, which failed to provide much knowledge about Irish history. The schools' poorly trained teachers largely avoided history as a course of study until the early years of the twentieth century, and then the study of Irish history and culture held a minor place in the curriculum until it was revolutionised by the Provisional Government and Irish Free State in 1922–23.[3] As great as its failings were in the teaching of history, however, by the end of the nineteenth century the Irish schools had successfully taught the people how to read.[4] The publishing houses of Ireland and Britain responded to this potential market, which extended from Ireland to include the Irish diaspora in Britain, the continent, and the rest of the English-speaking world, by proffering thousands of titles, hundreds of which dealt with Irish topics.[5]

---

2. Among the books and articles that discuss some means of developing a historical consciousness are: Henry Glassie, *Irish folk history* (Philadelphia, 1982); M.H. Thuente, 'The folklore of Irish nationalism' in T.E. Hachey and L.J. McCaffrey (ed.), *Perspectives on Irish nationalism* (Lexington, 1989), pp 42–60; Thomas Flanagan, 'Nationalism: the literary tradition', ibid., pp 61–78; J.R.R. Adams, *The printed word and the common man* (Belfast, 1987); T.J. O'Keefe, 'The 1898 efforts to celebrate the United Irishmen: the '98 centennial' in *Éire-Ireland*, xxiii, no. 2 (Summer 1988), pp 51–74; and his 'Who fears to speak of '98?': the rhetoric and rituals of the United Irishmen centennial, 1898', ibid., xxvii, no. 3 (fall 1992), pp 67–91.
3. David Fitzpatrick, 'The futility of history: a failed experiment in Irish primary education' in Ciaran Brady (ed.), *Ideology and the historians* (Dublin, 1991), pp 168–83.
4. Donald Akenson, *The Irish education experiment: the national system of education in the nineteenth century* (London, 1970).
5. The scope of the market raises questions about the motives of the authors: were they writing nostalgic novels for an Irish emigrant audience? Were they trying to educate a non-Irish readership about Irish issues? Was financial gain a possible motive? Were the authors concerned about making a serious contribution to literature? Each of these questions can be answered in the affirmative; more exact answers would depend on an author-by-author analysis, which lies beyond the scope of this essay. A larger research project on Irish historical fiction during this period is currently being conducted by Eileen Reilly of Hertford College, Oxford. I am grateful to her for suggestions on some of the novels that provide the basis for this essay.

The books were often inexpensive; some editions cost as little as one penny. Many novels first appeared as serials in weekly or monthly periodicals, thereby expanding the accessibility of this kind of fiction. Publishers also used mail order marketing techniques to put their multi-volume 'Popular History Series' and 'Penny Libraries' into Irish homes at home and abroad. Well-read critics like the bibliographer Fr Stephen J. Brown contributed to the *Irish Booklover*, while anonymous reviewers for newspapers and journals heralded the publication of books that told the story of the triumphs and tragedies of Irish history.

Tales of Ireland's mythological figures and early heroes, its wars with the Danes, its rebellious seventeenth-century earls, the rising of 1798, and the land agitation, among dozens of other episodes, inspired the political enthusiasm of nationalist authors. Only the Great Famine – too horrifying, perhaps, even for fiction – was omitted as a source of ideas for a story. James Murphy, the author of several novels, was typical of those who drew inspiration from the story of the national struggle. In the preface to *Convict No. 25: or The clearances of Westmeath* (1913) he asked his readers: 'Now, I should like to know where an Irish novelist is to look for the lights and shadows necessary to a novel – where to look for the story of human hopes and sorrows and passions – if not in the strife waged for many years between one faction seeking the extermination of the people and the latter equally sturdily resolved to hold their homes' (p. ii).[6] The criteria for excellence demanded by nationalist critics were explicit in reviews like the one M.L. O'Byrne received for *Leixlip Castle: an historical romance of the penal days of 1690*, which her publisher appended to the end-pages of a new edition of a novel about the passage of the Act of Union in 1801, *Ill-won peerages or an unhallowed union* (1884). 'Independently of its historical character and warm Catholic and national feelings which pervade it', *The Nation*'s critic wrote, 'there are reflections and arguments put into Irish mouths to which Irishmen of the present day, and Englishmen, too, might harken with advantage' (pp 723–4). An individual's course of action in public life, it was hoped, might be affected by the messages found in the writer's art.

Imagining Irish spaces

The authors' descriptions of the physical and cultural features of the Irish landscape and their detailed descriptions of the interior spaces of Irish homes

---

6. The full bibliographic citations for the novels mentioned in this essay are located at the conclusion of the essay. The page number(s) of the quotations from the novels are provided in the parentheses at the end of the excerpt.

are a fundamental feature of the nationalist fiction of this period. Charles Kickham, the first important nationalist author of historical fiction after 1870, combined descriptions of the landscape with an examination of the social intercourse within the big house and the cabin.[7] His *Knocknagow, or the homes of Tipperary* (1873) provided an empathetic description of the domestic life of the inhabitants of a village in the years after the Great Famine. The story struck a powerful chord with Irish readers; *Knocknagow* was in its twenty-sixth edition in 1887 when it was reissued in a more 'popular' edition. Kickham laid bare all the physical and cultural features of the area for his readers: the fields and hills; roads and pathways; the parish church and the public house; the more substantial homes and out-buildings of the strong farmers and the modest cabins of labourers, small tenant farmers and artisans. Hospitality and friendship are the dominant moods in Kickham's interior spaces, until, about halfway through the text, the readers realise that Knocknagow is doomed. Its people will be cleared from the land by landlords who intend to increase the amount of grazing land for their cattle. Unable to pay the increase in rent demanded by the landlords and their agents, the ensuing evictions have a devastating effect on the tenant farmers. The novel concludes with a painful description of the decaying homes and empty spaces on the landscape. The novel's final two sentences – 'Thank God there are happy homes in Tipperary still! But ... but Knocknagow is gone!' – are terrifying because of the dispirited mental picture of negative space that they convey.

The prolific author and parish priest from County Cork, Canon Patrick A. Sheehan, DD, is perhaps the only novelist of the period who approached Kickham's celebration of Irish country people.[8] In his description of an archetypal small tenant farmer's cabin in *Lisheen or, the test of the wills* (1906), Sheehan primed his readers for his romantic portrayal of an heroic Irish peasantry. *Lisheen*'s main character is Robert Maxwell, a young Irish landlord who hopes to bring culture to the peasantry. Maxwell's initial encounter with the environment reveals the enormity of the task he has undertaken, but the setting also belies the dignity of the people who live there.

> He had no trouble in finding the wretched cabin; but if he had been told that it was a pig-sty, he would have readily believed it. Four mud-walls, about five

---

7. Kickham, a native of County Tipperary, is the appropriate place to begin a narrative on nationalist writers after 1870 because he was a member of the supreme executive of the Fenians in the 1860s and was a respected nationalist leader until his death in 1882. J.D. Nealon, Jr, 'Charles Kickham and *Knocknagow* (1873)' in *Éire-Ireland* xxiii, no. 2 (Summer 1988), pp 39–50; R.V. Comerford, *Charles J. Kickham* (Dublin, 1979), pp 197–203.
8. H.J. Heuser, *Canon Sheehan of Doneraile* (London, 1917).

or six feet high, pierced by a window not quite a foot square, and a door so low one had to bend oneself double to enter, supported a ragged roof of thatch and thistles, broken here and there where long leaves of grass grew, and held down by straw-ropes, or sugans, weighted with heavy stones. There was a pool of slimy, fetid water before the door, where four or five ducks cackled proudly; and from a neighbouring recess, so like the habitation of men that it seemed but a cabin in miniature, came the low gruntings of a pig. All was poor, lowly squalid ...

Maxwell looked at the place for a while, doubtful whether he would pursue his investigation further. The place was thoroughly uninviting; but the deeper the degradation, he reflected, the higher the resurrection (pp 20–1).

A description of an interior space outside of Ireland demonstrates the fundamental importance of the native environment for the Irish characters who populate these novels. In *A daughter of kings* (1905), Katherine Tynan Hinkson contrasted interior spaces in Ireland and England, thereby identifying the values of the story's heroine, Anne Daly. Anne is an Irish gentlewoman who is forced by financial circumstances to leave her ancestral Donegal home, Witch's Castle, to take up work as a tutor in a great English country house. Here is her reaction as she surveys her well-appointed new rooms:

She went hither and thither, touching one thing after another, feeling the cold fineness of the satiny linen, observing dimly the lace on sheet and counterpane, her feet sinking in the velvety carpets, every sense awake to the gratifications wealth had provided. Then, all of a sudden, she sat down in the hardest chair the room contained, and hid her face in her hands. She was hungry, sharply hungry, for the keen sweet air, the nakedness, the barrenness of Witch's Castle. She wanted to hear the wind pipe along the corridors, to lean from an open window and bathe her face in it while she heard the great assault and retreat of the Atlantic upon the crags below.

How was she ever to live in these heavily-carpeted rooms, the luxury of which stifled her? Even an open window brought no relief. (p. 48)

While the description of interior spaces proved to be a useful way both to reveal their characters' personalities and to offer a glimpse of the face of Irish national character, authors used exterior spaces to support the idea that the Irish enjoyed a special relationship with nature. Two types of exterior spaces were standard features in the Irish historical fiction of this period. The first type was the panoramic description of the Irish countryside and coastline – literary equivalents of the broad canvases of the nineteenth-century romantic landscape painters. Like those graphic artists, the writers of historical fiction included significant details that reminded readers of times in Ireland long since past. The second type, which has long been a standard convention in fiction, was the secret or remote place which played the utilitarian role of serving as the site for key plot developments. Because these hidden places could not be known to outsiders (unless they obtained directions to them from an Irish character), they function as spiritual sanctuaries for the main characters. There, in communion with the landscape, the heroes and heroines enjoy the peace and tranquillity they need to meditate on Ireland's history, its current troubles, and their role in determining its future direction.

M.E. Francis used both the sweeping landscape of County Down and a secret place in a passage in *Miss Erin* (1898) to establish the patriotic ardour of the novel's young heroine, Erin Fitzgerald. Imagining she is an Irish Joan of Arc, Erin surveys the countryside from her citadel:

> It was a very beautiful spot, rock-strewn and wild, and intensely, unspeakably lonely; but Erin loved it for its very loneliness. From her post of vantage she could see a very wilderness of hills of every shape and every hue, from distant, ethereal blue, floating as it would seem on the confines of an opalescent heaven, to the giant guardian of the valley, Beanagh-mor, the Golden spear, cone-shaped, rugged, resplendent, in purple and yellow and green, changing in aspect with every shifting cloud; its deep hollows and unexpected clefts appearing and vanishing as though by magic, its stony apex now glancing in the sun, like some crystal mountain of fairy lore, now frowning darkly down upon a landscape livid with stormy light, anon misty, shadowy, unreal, leaning as it seemed to her against a veiled, mysterious sky ...
>
> These very mountain fastnesses on which she gazed had from all time afforded protection to Irish rebels; the valley beneath her had been the scene of more than one engagement. Erin's imagination peopled it again with shadowy figures; warlike music sounded in the breeze – the clash of arms, the dull thunder of advancing feet, and then a mighty cry – the cry of triumph. (pp 89–90)

Canon Sheehan also used the Irish landscape to signal his characters' patriotism and to connect his characters to past – and future – events. His eleventh and final novel, *The graves at Kilmorna: a story of '67* (1915), tells the story of two Fenian officers, James Halpin, a mild-mannered school teacher, and his friend, Myles Cogan, a prospective lawyer. Sheehan included scenes where each character connected the landscape with the history of Ireland. In the scene involving Halpin, the teacher takes his surprised students outside for an impromptu history lesson. Pointing out the nearby sites that were occupied in 1690 by Dutch and English encampments and the places opposite held by the Irish brigades and their French allies, the local landscape slowly began to take on a life of its own for the young scholars. 'It is a beautiful view,' he said at length, 'and ours is the most lovely country on the face of the earth. We ought to love every blade of grass in its fields, every stone in its hollows, every leaf on its trees, every stream that runs, every hill that begets the streams'; he lowered his voice, 'every man that has shed his blood for Ireland ...' (pp 5–7).

In a dreamy scene involving Cogan, the young revolutionary describes how his vision of the landscape – personified as a woman – fostered his understanding of Irish history and foreshadowed his destiny.

> And I thought of that motherland, this Ireland of ours, with all her magic beauty – beauty of mountain and lake, of brown bog, and sandy seashore, of her seas and her rivers – of all these things that grow into our lives and become a part of our being; and then I thought of her long night of sorrow, of how she has been trampled and shamed and degraded, and then held up by her iron masters as an object of derision to the world – her masters who laughed at the hunger and ignorance they caused; her masters, who held up her rags and fluttered them in the face of the nations, who never knew, or cared that it was these very masters who cut every weal into her body, and took the bread from her mouth, and snipped her garments into fragments, until I grew mad with the thought, that perhaps the one chance of my life would escape me – to wreak vengeance on her foes, or save that motherland from further humiliation. (pp 24–5)

The importance of the landscape as an element that reflected a shared identity among the native Irish was re-emphasised by Daniel Corkery in his famous essay, *The hidden Ireland* (1924). He explained:

> Those O'Connells, O'Connors, O'Callaghans, O'Donoghues – all the Gaels – were one ... with the very landscape itself. To run off their names ... was to call to vision certain districts – hills, rivers and plains; while contrarywise, to recollect the place-names in certain regions was to remember the ancient tribes and their memorable deeds. How different it was with the Planters round about them. For them, all that Gaelic background of myth, literature and history had no existence ... the landscape they looked upon was indeed but rocks and stones and trees.[9]

Like Corkery, all of the writers of Irish historical fiction of this period understood that descriptions of the physical landscape would fire their readers'

---

9. Daniel Corkery, *The hidden Ireland* (Dublin, 1924), p. 64. See Emmet Larkin, 'A reconsideration: Daniel Corkery and his ideas on Irish cultural nationalism' in *Éire-Ireland*, viii, no. 1 (Spring 1973), pp 42–51.

imagination of the past and define the Irish nation and its communities in terms of place.

Imagining Irish time

The temporal dimensions of the past, the present, and the future provide a second defining feature of Irish historical fiction. Irish novelists of this period were concerned with the specific events in the past which provided the historical context for the tales, with the continuity of historical processes across time, from the past up to the time in which the story took place, and with the future, as the characters tried to fulfil their destinies – if fate permitted that option.

The first matter – selecting a historical event – was straightforward. Authors placed characters in specific historic situations that interested them and which they believed would provide the best setting for a tale of love and adventure. The historical setting, however, did more than provide a picturesque backdrop. Readers' memories or knowledge of the past were reconfigured in at least two important ways: first, through the authors' recreation – whether sanitised, idealised, or otherwise – of real historical characters and events, and second, by the narrative that placed fictional characters in the company of the historical figures.

Few authors were as obsessed with accurately portraying the past as the historian and novelist, Standish James O'Grady.[10] In the preface to *The flight of the eagle* (1897), O'Grady explained that his writing was an experiment in composition that blended the science and art of history. He researched early modern sources, including the *Annals of the four masters*, Philip O'Sullivan's *Historic Hibernia*, O'Clery's *Bardic life of Hugh Roe O'Donnell*, and the *Calendar of state papers, Ireland*, to supply the evidence he believed would help readers draw the proper conclusions from his narratives of Irish history. If most of the novelists were less specific than O'Grady about their sources of historical information, particularly on the details of Irish social history, they none the less understood the importance of maintaining a semblance of historical accuracy to make a plot ring true. Novelist Patrick Smyth, for example, understood the importance of historical research in writing irresistible historical fiction, although he made it clear that his principal task in employing the past was polemical. In the preface to *The wild rose of Lough Gill: a tale of the Irish war in the seventeenth century* (1883), Smyth explained:

---

10. P.L. Marcus, *Standish O'Grady* (Louisburg, 1970); David Cairns and Shaun Richards, *Writing Ireland: colonialism, nationalism and culture* (Manchester, 1988), pp 51–57.

'there is a due dash of fiction – and where it ends, and fact begins, and vice versa, is left to the inquiring reader to distinguish – but the exigencies of the past have been laid to accord with the truths of history, and in very rare or trifling instances has this principle been departed from'. He then added, 'However ... there must ever be a solid, intrinsic interest, thrilling and fascinating, in the bold and valiant exploits of the chivalry of Ireland in their struggle for homes and altars. With these brief premises the author invites the reader to accompany him under the national flag of green in its progress, surrounded by guardian swords, throughout Ireland.' (pp vii–viii)

The second temporal matter – presenting evidence of the continuity between the Irish past and the Irish present – could be accomplished in several ways. To highlight the survival of vestiges of Ireland's ancient civilisation, some authors added cultural features to their descriptions of the physical landscape when they set the geographical context for the stories. Druidic ruins, early Christian abbeys, round towers, and the crumbling walls of abandoned castles wrapped the novels' characters in romantic images of the distant past. Authors also placed characters in situations where Irish customs, place-names, or the use of the Irish language affected the plot; footnotes provided translations or explanations for the readers' edification. In these instances, the fictional Irish character's, and now the reader's, awareness of his or her cultural heritage underscored the difference between knowledgeable natives and ignorant outsiders who could not interpret what they heard or understand what they saw.[11]

The link between past and present might also be accomplished through scenes in which a knowledgeable character teaches an eager hero or heroine lessons from Irish history. The cramped rooms – secret places – of the tutor are invariably filled with ancient manuscripts and artefacts. A final technique used to connect the past and the present was to endow characters with a long family history. Virtually every main character in this period's historical fiction could trace their descent from an ancient Gaelic clan and identify the family heroes and their heroic deeds. 'I can trace my genealogies back to the time of "Con of the Hundred Battles"', declares Cormac Flattery, the main character in Rev. Joseph Guinan's *Annamore, or the tenant-at-will* (1924). Referring to his evicting landlord, and linking time, place, and social class in the process, Con chaffs, 'he can go back no further than a common Cromwellian drummer, who got the broad acres owned by my forefathers' (p. 15). Noble family, petty gentry, or peasant ancestry notwithstanding, a standard plot

---

11. A.C. Partridge, *Language and society in Anglo-Irish literature* (Dublin, 1984), pp 236–83.

involved Irish characters engaged in a struggle to keep the family bloodline vibrant and their lands whole, that is, to preserve the past in the present.

Fate's guiding hand over the future was the third dimension of Irish time that concerned the novelists. Will the hero and heroine live happily ever after? What will happen to the evicted tenants? Will the Irish National Party's constitutional methods win home rule for Ireland; or will physical force be necessary?

The characters find happiness in most of the love stories where the historic events, however vividly described, serve mainly to complicate the romance. In these stories, one of the characters typically experiences an eleventh hour catharsis that causes her to modify her behaviour. *Miss Erin*'s climactic scene provides an example. Erin Fitzgerald rushes to the site of an eviction to rally the tenants with her patriotic poetry. In the ensuing mayhem, her skull is cracked by a flying shovel. She recovers and the novel closes with Erin in the embrace of her English suitor, who finally understands her nationalist sympathies. Miss L. McManus's *The silk of the kine* (1896) opens with Margery Ny Guire, the last surviving member of the family of Connor, Earl of Fermanagh, being force-marched to Connaught by loathsome Cromwellian soldiers. Margery escapes, is recaptured, escapes again, and is again recaptured. Eventually, a persistent English major who had fallen in love with her at first sight spirits her out of the country. Indomitably proud and morally superior to her English captors in every way, she comes to feel a sense of gratitude and realises, on the last page, that she is in love with him. Exile with a renegade Englishman, however, does not bode well as a metaphor for the future of Anglo-Irish relations.

Fate deals particularly harsh blows when political issues, as opposed to affairs of the heart, are at the centre of the plot. In George A. Birmingham's *The bad times* (1908) a minor character who is described as 'a Celt and dreamer, child of a beaten race', observes, 'Sadness comes down like a cloud in the end for the lover of Ireland' (p. 52). *The graves at Kilmorna* concludes with the old Fenian, Myles Cogan, making his first political speech in public since his stirring speech from the dock some forty years earlier. He is fatally struck in the head by a rock thrown by a member of a drunken election eve crowd. Near the end of Sidney Royce Lysaght's *Her Majesty's rebels* (1907), the character Michael Desmond, leader of the National Party, is unexpectedly killed by a minor character whom he had successfully defended in court against a charge of murder. Michael's younger brother, Connor, reflects on Michael's destiny and the ambiguous Irish future: 'Memories of his brother, and reflection on the careers of others who, like him, had devoted their lives to the service of Ireland, absorbed him. "They went out to battle and they always fell." Failure seemed to be their destiny: hope sprung perennially from their defeats. The wrongs that kindled the revolt were still unforgotten: the ideals remained undimmed.' (p. 468)

Idealism may remain 'undimmed', but Irish heroes 'always fell'. Novels set before 1798 narrate stories of political corruption, conquest, colonisation, land expropriation, and exile. Novels set after 1798, during episodes of either constitutional agitation or physical force activity, do not end on optimistic notes. Given their chronicle in fiction of seven centuries of grief and broken dreams – the central interpretation of history in nineteenth-century Irish nationalist ideology – who could expect nationalist authors to be anything but wary of predicting the future? Unionist authors like Birmingham and O'Grady never hinted that home rule would lead to either a prosperous or harmonious future. Unionist writer Shan Bullock's look into Ireland's future under a republican government in *The red leaguers* (1904) reveals an anarchic country and a corrupt government whose leaders drive the story's idealistic revolutionary hero into exile.

Imagining the Irish people

The authors of historical fiction depicted the Irish people in two ways: implicitly, by generalising about the behaviour of both individual characters and social groups; and explicitly, by identifying the racial traits of the Irish people.

Two major character types are found in nearly every novel: a handsome male and a beautiful female, both usually of the gentry class. There is also a standard cast of minor characters: the family members or guardians of the hero and heroine; close friends; a Catholic priest and a Protestant clergyman; a local eccentric; and servants or labourers. Antagonists were usually English soldiers and absentee landlords or their administrative representatives. They could be broadly sketched, but the stereotypical, stage-Irish character so well developed by British writers was largely avoided by Irish writers. In the better novels of this period, therefore, major and minor characters were created slightly against type. That is, an individual landlord who played an important role in a story could not simply be a rapacious rent collector. Important female characters tended to be independent individuals who could assume traditional male roles to seize victory in a dangerous situation. Priests could not simply be either radical patriots or pious clerics. An English soldier could not simply be a monster, unless he was cast as a particularly odious villain. Irish policemen could not simply be the cold arm of Dublin Castle authorities. And individual country people could not simply be either boorish or heroic, although in some novels, authors used group scenes to put these characteristics on display. Above all, heroic Irish characters could not share British attitudes or manners.

Contact between individual members of the two ethnic groups was uneasy at best, but it was especially traumatic in the novels in which Irish land was being taken from the tenants. Perhaps Irish antagonism toward English characters has to be expected, given the polemical orientation of nationalist fiction and the thrust of the nationalist histories of the era.[12] The literary critic of the leading nationalist newspaper, the *Freeman's Journal*, praised M.L. O'Byrne's *The pale and the septs; or, the baron of Belgard and the chiefs of Glenmalure: an Irish romance of the sixteenth century* (1876) precisely because the novel's design 'illustrate[d] in all its cruelty, treachery, greed, and unscrupulousness, the steady advance of the English settlement on the possessions of the Irish people. To accomplish this purpose and to get hold of the Irish land was the real desire and object of the Englishmen; and to accomplish this object every conceivable expedient was adopted: religion, war, treachery, burnings, murderings, devastations, laws, and bribes were used without remorse'.[13] Religion was also a critical factor in differentiating between the English and the Irish. For Annie M.P. Smithson, a popular romantic novelist of the twentieth century, catholicism was the fundamental defining characteristic of her Irish characters, beginning with her early work in *Her Irish heritage* (1917). Tales describing the terrorism of the penal laws, when officials hunted Catholic priests and teachers down like wolves, clearly established an invasive English protestantism as the diabolical enemy of the native Catholic population.

Applying this general historical interpretation of religious and political antipathy to their particular stories, nationalist authors created Irish characters who approached social relationships with English characters with caution. Even when 'love conquers all' in the end, as it did in romances like *Miss Erin* and *The silk of the kine*, the Irish women put their English suitors through hell. In other stories, ethnicity and religious differences placed a permanent bar across the road to romance. In Sidney Royce Lysaght's *The marplot* (1893), for example, Elsinora Chillingham, the Irish Catholic heroine, drowns

---

12. Roy Foster, 'The lovely magic of its dawn. Reading Irish history as a story', *Times Literary Supplement*, 16 December 1994: 4–6.
13. This undated review is appended to the back pages of O'Byrne's *Ill-won Peerages*.

before Dick Malory, her English Protestant suitor, can communicate either his new-found sympathy with the Irish tenantry or his freedom to marry. The extreme case – the unequivocal rejection of an English suitor's interest – was illustrated with brutal forcefulness in Margaret Pender's *The last of the Irish chiefs* (1920). The following passage describes the reaction of Irene Magennis, one of the novel's two main female characters, to a proposal of marriage from Sir Arthur Chichester, the English Lord Deputy of Ireland:

> Standing before him, in the light of her fair young beauty, her delicate neck slightly bent, her shimmering amber robes trailing about her like a sunset cloud, Irene looked down from her graceful height at the kneeling figure, with its freakish knots and gnarls; its huge joints, and spindle limbs; the great, round, black head, the evil eyes, the wry mouth, and square, cruel jaw; the whole features now darkly flushed, and wearing their vilest and most hateful expression – she looked down at him for a single instant, listening to his croaking voice beseeching her to love him – him – this creature in all his ugliness and meanness; his complaisant villainy and cool audacity, and for an answer – she could form no other – a little maddening peal of mocking laughter – wildly musical, wildly mocking, burst from her scarlet lips.
>
> … In no other way could she have touched so keenly, stung so deeply, the little venomous soul of the man before her.…
>
> Then Irene turned from him, and with another burst of laughter, more musical, more scornful, more maddening than before, she swept across the turret-room towards the door. (pp 36–37)

Nevertheless, the ability of individual Irish characters to put aside differences in matters of religion, class, lineage, and political orientation and to live peacefully with one another provides the central focus of the plot in several novels of this era. Canon Sheehan's *The intellectuals: an experiment in Irish club life* (1911) was 'an attempt to describe a possibility which the author hopes lies latent in the future that is before the country; when, under the influences of wider and more rational systems of education, the barriers of racial and sectarian prejudices may be broken down, and the higher humanities accepted as an integral portion of social and domestic life'. (p. v) The novelist placed characters from England, Scotland, and Ireland in 'The Sunetoi' Club in Cork. With an Irish priest serving as a moderator, they begin a communal search – which concludes in the wilds of County Kerry – for common ground through convivial dialogue. Lysaght's *Her Majesty's rebels* provides another example for nationalist, and perhaps unionist, readers of how Irish people might learn to accept their differences. The story features

Michael and Connor Desmond, brothers in a largely dispossessed Irish Catholic gentry family. For a time, they appear to be rivals for the affection of their neighbour, Elizabeth O'Brien, whose ancestors had saved their land and taken Desmond land by converting to protestantism. Michael, the charismatic older brother, becomes the leader of the Nationalist Party in parliament; but like Charles Stewart Parnell, he falls in love with another man's wife. In the end, the jealous husband murders him. Connor's life-long romantic interest in Elizabeth is eventually rewarded and even the crusty parents of both families resolve their estrangement.

Through characters like Connor and Elizabeth and the members of 'The Sunetoi' Club, Lysaght and Sheehan and other authors of historical fiction posed some interesting questions for their readers about who, exactly, were the members of the Irish nation. Had, for example, the passage of time blurred the distinctions among the descendants of the ancient Irish Gaels, the Anglo-Normans, the later English settlers, the Scots in Ulster, and the descendants of Cromwell's soldiers? Could all these newcomers ever become natives? To explore these questions, the authors created situations that forced their readers to consider the leadership of the nation: which Irishmen had the political acumen that was necessary to settle the land and national questions, and perhaps more important, the civic competency to make the nation whole?

Novels set before the Act of Union focus on characters from the Irish nobility who are portrayed as the natural leaders of the Irish people. Standish O'Grady's *The flight of the eagle*, which was also published in a special school edition, tells the heroic tale of bravery associated with the O'Neill saga. Yet, the composite picture of the elite that emerges in other novels does not inspire much confidence. For example, in novels set during the period of active colonisation, Irish armies are defeated by the English. It is cold comfort that victory is snatched from Irish chieftains because they are betrayed by traitorous members of their own caste. The fact that the 'wild geese' confound the English enemy on foreign battlefields at a later date is only a bit more consoling. The hope authors hold out for readers is that the émigré might return sometime in the future to avenge past wrongs.

In novels set in the nineteenth century, Irish gentry families are in desperate financial straits, barely able to help themselves; little seemed to have changed for this class since the publication of Maria Edgeworth's morality tale of ascendancy ruin, *Castle Rackrent* (1800). In novels written a century later, the gentry are riven by dissension caused by land expropriation, religious sectarianism, and rival political allegiances. In Lysaght's *Her*

Majesty's rebels, Michael Desmond gives his younger brother, and the readers, a history lesson about the division among the Irish gentry and the effects it has had on the home rule movement:

> They all know each other – they're like one family, and I wish to God they were on our side instead of against us and the country,' said Michael as they drew near. 'We ought to be fighting side by side and they compel us to fight against them. And they're Irish at heart. Is there a man amongst them cares a thrawneen whether his neighbour is rich or poor?'
>
> 'And they're Protestants, [referring to the Irish gentry] when they ought to be Catholics, and that's another barrier between them and their country. But their forefathers were compelled to change by the English Government. Those, like ourselves, who did not turn were ruined. They were not like that fellow of our family who turned traitor; they did it to hold their lands and for the sake of their families, and begad, Connor, I respect them more than those English Dissenters' sons and daughters who are turning Church of England as they get rich all over the country, not because they're compelled to it, but because they want to belong to a more respectable religion.' (p. 25)

After Michael's murder, Connor considers the gentry's role in providing political leadership, but he is not optimistic about their ability to fulfil their destiny.

> … if it be found possible to settle the land question finally, so that patriotic men of the class for which the people still retain their instinctive respect, no longer fearing spoliation, may identify themselves with the national spirit from which they have hidden themselves, and take their proper place in the national councils – when these men, and those who have led the attack against them may unite in the common cause of their country's welfare – then the day will have dawned when self-government shall be the voice of the national life. But the hour is not yet: its adventure is a duty left for a new generation. (p. 469)

Canon Sheehan, in *Lisheen; or a test of the wills*, placed the blame for Ireland's social and political problems squarely on the gentry. The novel's quixotic main character, Robert Maxwell, understands his responsibilities toward Irish tenant farmers who work largely for his welfare. Maxwell explains to some other landlords that their own class and religion has stood in the way of ameliorating Ireland's condition:

> How could I speak of such things [cultural enrichment] to a people sunk in all kinds of abject poverty, with the hand of the bailiff ever on their doors,

> and the awful shadow of landlordism glooming over all? ... Where's the use of talking about the resurrection of a people until you remove the stone from the door of their sepulchre? You cannot have a nation without manhood; you cannot have manhood without education, you cannot have education without leisure and freedom from sordid cares, and you cannot have the latter until landlordism is removed wholly and entirely from the land. (p. 273)

But the reforming landlord also fails in his attempt to bridge the gap between gentry and peasantry. Maxwell takes a job as a labourer on Owen McAuliffe's farm and lives with the family. When the McAulliffes are evicted, it appears to the local farmers that Maxwell is in collusion with the authorities. He finds another job, but is boycotted by the other labourers. Maxwell then secretly purchases, remodels, and returns the farm to Owen, yet when the secret is revealed, neither the McAuliffes nor their neighbours are enthusiastic. When Maxwell returns for a visit, the family members refuse to recognise him. They knew from the outset that he was not one of them; they could never overcome their suspicion that he was somehow responsible for their problems.

The professional classes occupy the social space between the gentry and the tenantry. Like the members of the gentry, representatives of the professional classes are divided politically and are generally corrupt to boot. In her novel about the passage of the Act of Union, *Ill-won peerages or an unhallowed Union* (1884), M.L. O'Byrne laid out the differences in the character between the outnumbered patriotic nationalists and the loyalist lawyers and clerks who were 'smuggled' into the Irish parliament by Lord Castlereagh and the British government to wrest away Irish liberty. Several other novels feature courtroom scenes in which honest lawyers defend nationalists in cases of sedition after a rising or felony stemming from actions in the land agitation. The prosecutors are place-hunting creatures of the Dublin Castle ascendancy. Occasionally, a judge will empathise with the defendant's plea but, inevitably, he will either don the black cap or deliver a harsh sentence.

Nor do other members of the professional or business classes exhibit leadership qualities. Teachers are ciphers. Land agents have few redeeming social graces. Publicans are unsavoury. Irish policemen just do their duty. Indeed, the entire middle class receives a thorough thrashing from D.P. Moran in *Tom O'Kelly* (1905). Best known as the author of the essay, 'The battle of two civilizations' (1898) and as editor of the nationalist magazine, *The Leader*, Moran's novel is set in Ballytown, where no one has any true understanding of the Irish past and, worse, none has a vision of Ireland's future as an independent nation-state. The characters shout anti-English slogans at political rallies and then adjourn to enjoy English entertainment at the local theatre.

Members of the clergy fare much better. Although protestantism is often blamed for Irish discontent by an author serving as narrator or by a particular character, Protestant clergymen are nearly always portrayed as respected figures in the eyes of all the people of a locality. The exception to this general rule is found in novels set during the Reformation when Protestant bishops enter into dark collusion with evil English politicians in Ireland to subvert and convert the native Irish Catholics. Catholic priests occupy a more important role in the stories, particularly in works by Canon Sheehan. His *My new curate, a story gathered from the stray leaves of an old diary* (1899) was one of the most popular novels in the genre. *Luke Delmege* (1901) and *The blindness of Dr Gray or the final law* (1909) completed Sheehan's trilogy about contemporary clerical life in rural Ireland. Each of these novels addresses the generational differences that exist among the Catholic clergy: the oldest generation that was educated on the Continent and which was welcomed in the landlord's big house; the generation that was educated at Maynooth and which stood with Daniel O'Connell and survived the Famine; and the new generation from Maynooth, that was just as patriotic, but which took a more casual approach to their responsibilities. Whatever historical era provided the setting for nationalist authors, however, the priests invariably stand side-by-side with the people during times of trouble, taking direct action, administering the sacraments and offering wise counsel in domestic matters. There is virtually no anticlericalism in these novels, although Gerald O'Donovan's *Father Ralph* (1913) bitterly attacked the education of the Catholic clergy and Edward McNulty's *Misther O'Ryan* (1894) and Ernest Temple Thurston's *May Eve, or the Tinker of Ballinatray* (1924) contained passages about priests' social life that could have offended some Catholic readers.[14]

The priests are at their most heroic in stories set during the seventeenth or eighteenth centuries. The famous patriot priest, Fr John Murphy, is featured in several novels about the rising of 1798. Here is how M.L. O'Byrne described an esteemed sixteenth-century prelate, Dermod O'Hurley, in *The pale and the septs*:

> His furrowed cheek seemed less worn by the time than by ascetic mortification, and there was a tremor in his step of dignity that told of

---

14. Catholic priests do not fare as well in Irish-American fiction produced in this same time period. See Charles Fanning, *The Irish in America: Irish-American fiction from the 1760s to the 1980s* (Lexington, 1990), pp 153–97.

declining strength; but when, with mitre blazing on his lofty brow, and with pastoral staff, he stood on the altar steps, to raise his hand in benediction over the bowed-down heads of the assemblage, in the deep tones of his earnest voice there was no quiver, in the strong light of the warm, kindly eye, that looked upon his prostrate flock, and with soul-like power seemed to individualise each one, there was no sign of weakness; and yet eyes that looked upon that saintly form grew dim with tears, hearts that yearned to him with hallowed impulse throbbed with unwonted emotion. Was it presage or was it vision of the martyr's crown, shining over the mitre on his brow, that convulsed with hysterical sensation each bosom that heaved in his presence? (p. 74)

Nationalist priests acted forcefully in novels set during the land war. An older priest's conflict with his radical young curate was the subject of a subplot in Birmingham's *The bad times*. In that novel, a wise old priest curbs his naive young curate, whose fiery speeches have roused the local tenants to resist eviction, but the discipline comes too late to save the novel's main characters from disaster. Sheehan's title character, Luke Demelge, summons up seven hundred years of Celtic rage to attack an armed policeman at a painful eviction scene, and then pays the price by going to gaol. Scottish author Annie S. Swan's *A son of Erin* (1899) nears its climax when tenant farmers in County Wexford are stirred up by an outside agitator. In an effort to stave off potential violence, the parish priest, Fr O'Hagan, enters the local pub and effectively takes the heart out of the meeting:

Don't listen to him, friends – sedition and poison drop from his tongue. I am an old man. I have gone in and out among you for over forty years, sharing in your joys and sympathising with your griefs. I have seen the night closing in upon your homes – but all hope is not extinguished yet. If you act upon the wicked advice given you by this man, who, believe me, has no end to serve by it but his own, you will regret it to the last day of your life. The arm of the law is like a vice, and the man who has been in prison is never the same man again. Therefore, I say, listen to him no more, but rather to me, who have your best interests at heart. (p. 171)

Could the answers to Ireland's problems come from below, from the men of little or no property – the small tenant farmers and labourers? Novels set during the land war present numerous examples of individuals of humble origin who possess the potential for leadership. Birmingham presented an extraordinary example of the power of one tenant farmer's presence in *The bad times*. Sheridan, the youthful leader of the local Land League, stands before the rent agent just after his family was turned out of house and home:

> Sheridan was a young man, probably not more than five-and-twenty years of age. He was of more than ordinary height, and looked even taller than he was because he was slightly built and was besides extremely thin, almost emaciated. His skin was dark; his clean-shaved face sallow and dusky. He had long, straight black hair, locks of which hung over his forehead and gave him a wild, unkempt appearance. He had large, dark eyes – eyes capable of expressing, and accustomed to express, an extraordinary range of emotions. They were the eyes of a dreamer, of one for whom old romantic things might be plainly visible, who might see the fairy cavalry sweep across the country on stormy nights; who might, under certain conditions, see the Son of God walking in beggar man's attire through the fields of Ireland. He was the best man in the whole county at playing the fiddle, and the people said that when he played his face was wonderful to look at. They saw in his eyes then the passion of love at its highest, love that was pure of all sensual feeling, the supreme desire for some ideal perfection. But those great eyes of his were capable also of letting white-hot anger, fury, and an unquenchable desire for revenge shine through them. (pp 203–4)

Canon Sheehan idealised the tenant farmers and the labouring classes and in his last novel he left no doubt about their ability to act collectively to redress grievances. He described the revolutionary solidarity of the Irish working class in *The graves at Kilmorna* when forty Fenian soldier-workers meet the evening before the battle:

> The men, about forty in number, crept close together around their young Captain. They were strong, sinewy fellows, accustomed to bend their backs to their daily toil, and go through life without pillows beneath their elbows. There were masons, carpenters, bricklayers, shoemakers – representatives of every kind of trade amongst them; and, strange to say, many of them, who had been ploughing through life in a broken-backed, weary manner, were suddenly stiffened and strengthened into some kind of unnatural vigour, when they became soldiers of the Republic. And in their eyes, gleaming with expectancy, as they stood there in the dim light shed by the smoky stable-lamp above their heads, there shone a steady light of determination, as of men who had deliberately staked all on some desperate issue, and were fully prepared to abide by the result. (p. 20)

Other writers, however, offered readers an alternative assessment of the political philosophy of the Irish country people. In *Her Majesty's rebels*, Lysaght depicted the uncritical political discourse of farm labourers in a scene, written for comic relief, in which several drunken men debate the relative merits of either using 'the dinnamite' or maintaining unity behind the

Nationalist Party and its leader. After another scene, which includes the narration of a friendly brawl that breaks out after mass and before a political rally, Lysaght concludes, 'The majority of the people took far less interest in the political question which they were called together to hear discussed than might be supposed. They had no personal enmity to the landlords, no private conviction on the subject of rent; but perhaps in no other country in the world could a crowd have been collected which was so united by the bond of national sentiment.'

> The political questions of the hour [Lysaght continued] were unimportant details; they were agreed on these because their leaders were agreed; but the true bond of their union was the love of their country – the inborn national spirit which had been nursed in the memory of old wrongs and old honour....
> If the landlords were unpopular it was not because they were unjust in their dealings, but because they stood aloof and looked coldly on the national aspirations; and if the Crown was little loved, it was not because it represented the oppression of England, but because it was an absentee power un-identified with the hopes of Ireland. This is the feeling of the Irish people. (p. 308)

Ultimately, however, the fate of the tenants and labourers resembles that of the gentry. The potential leadership ability of the heroic tenant farmer who takes the initiative is nullified by the superior force of the police and the law. As with the people of Knocknagow, the tenant farmers in story after story watch as their neighbours are cleared from the landscape. Only Standish O'Grady foreshadowed the triumph of the peasantry, but the prospect of life under the dictatorship of the proletariat did not please him. In *Ulrick the ready* (1896), a novel about the landing of the Spanish army at Kinsale in 1601, he explained:

> This wretched, servile commonality was, in fact, the one class in Elizabethan Ireland that was to rise and rise, to become the people, the nation, and the depository of power. Aristocracy after aristocracy has been all but ground away in those slow revolving mills of God, but the plebs, then treated as of little more than the mud on the highway, will endure and flourish, growing to be, perhaps, itself a tyranny upon whose reduction the brave men of the future must spend themselves. (p. 140)

If the authors did not provide readers with much reason to believe in the problem-solving ability of Irish social groups, they still held out hope for the victory of the Irish nation over an alien foe. They grounded that hope in the inherited traits of the Irish race – the second way in which the authors depicted the Irish people. The authors either described an inherited behavioural trait that was common to all Irish people and which sprang into action to save a hero or heroine from an unhappy fate; or they described aspects of a particular character's personality and then generalised about the national character of Irish people from that example.

In *Miss Erin,* M.E. Francis used the former method. The orphan child, Erin Fitzgerald, is the product of a combination of Irish gentry and Irish peasant blood. This genetic blend was designed to permit readers to understand any action that Erin might take during the course of the novel.

> She had, to begin with, inherited very opposite qualities from her parents – her father having endowed her with much of his dreaminess and impracticableness; and the peasant blood of her mother carrying with it certain characteristics of its own. The child could love passionately, and idealize the object of her love – she could hate and resent savagely.... She was absolutely undisciplined, and, at the same time, curiously reserved. (p. 105)

Annie S. Swan's *A son of Erin* provides another example. Her main character, Robert Burns Fletcher, is also an Irish orphan whose Scottish foster-parents notice his ethnic temperament from an early age: 'While the child had much that was lovable and sweet in his disposition, he at times revealed a terrible and passionate temper, and a vindictive disposition which occasioned them both the greatest concern' (p. 21). Both Francis and Swan include passages in which adults attempt to acculturate Irish children through reading regimens, history lessons, and old fashioned discipline – all to no avail. The children's genes overcome their best efforts.

While some authors developed individual Irish characters who personified Irish racial characteristics, others portrayed the Irish people in ways which made it impossible for readers to confuse them with other ethnic groups, including other Celts. In an early scene in *The last of the Irish chiefs,* Margaret Pender described the difference between the native Irish and the alien newcomers, the English and the Scots:

> The hall was filled by a brilliant and varied assemblage, including many high-born and gallant Scots; some in ruffs and velvets, but not a few in their picturesque national gear, with gay tartans, and tufted sporrans, and jeweled dirks in their embroidered girdles.
>
> There, too, were many noble dames and gentlemen of the English Pale, all gorgeous in the magnificent fashions and fopperies of the day; all tricked out

> in silks and velvets, and cloth of gold and silver, and all stiff, haughty, and ceremonious.
>
> A striking contrast to all these, in dress, language, look, and manner, were the Irish chiefs and ladies, in their distinctive Celtic costumes.
>
> The Irish, secretly scorning the mushroom noblesse of the Pale, with a scorn begotten in an ancient land, of uncounted centuries of noble blood, and looking on them as nameless and penniless adventurers who had fattened on the fields of Ireland, regarded their haughty airs with covert contempt, wonder, or amusement; while a few looked on them with good-tempered indulgence, as merely some of the pardonable eccentricities of their queer foreign breeding. (pp 17–18)

Nature or nurture notwithstanding, avid readers of Irish historical fiction were confronted with a staggering list of Irish racial characteristics as they moved from novel to novel. The Irish were described as being as proud as Spaniards, from whom they trace their blood. They were anguished, moody Celts who touched so often, by the curse and blessing of the race, the depths and the heights of life. If in one novel they were too ready to forgive and forget, in the next one they were a fighting, stubborn, and courageous race. They were people who loved the wildness of the wind and the rains and the storms. They had instinctively delicate minds which prevented them from prying into other people's business; in other stories, they were as nosy as could be. They had infallible instincts. They had a free, open-hearted spirit that made them so loveable. They were all these, and much, much more. Whatever the sum of these often contradictory yet fundamentally human traits amounted to, Myles Cogan, the hero in Canon Sheehan's *The graves at Kilmorna*, concluded that the Irish were: 'a *race apart*; that so surely as Jehovah of old selected the Jews as his people – the chosen nation – so we, by God's design or destiny, stand aloof from the nations around us. Their ways are not our ways, their God is not our God'. (p. 336)

Given the wide genetic parameters, to say nothing of the special relationship with the Almighty, the Irish in fiction were not only capable of experiencing any mood; ultimately, they were invincible. Standish O'Grady, perhaps more than any other author, was determined to impress his readers with the enduring power of their national character. In his retelling of ancient tales in *The gates of the north* (1901) O'Grady explained that 'the mighty destiny, the cosmic significance, the daring and indomitable, far-reaching, and far-aspiring spirit of the Gael' (p. 9) could never be extinguished. He wanted readers to take heart from his retelling of the ancient tales and learn from the example set by the characters in his historical fiction. These individuals, he explained:

> ... give us the imagination of the race, they give us that kind of history which it intends to exhibit, and therefore, whether semi-historical or mythical, are prophetic. They unveil, if obscurely, the ideals and aspirations of the land and race which gave them birth; and so possess a value far beyond that of actual events, and duly recorded deeds. Our heroic literature is bound to repeat itself in action and within the constraining laws of time and space.... For that prophecy has been always, and will be always, fulfilled. The heroes are coming, of that you may be sure; their advent is as certain as time. Listen well and you may hear them, hear their glad talk and their sounding war songs, and the music and thunder of their motion. The heroes are coming; they are on the road. (pp 9–10)

Conclusion

The authors of historical fiction used their imaginations to write romantic love stories and exciting adventure tales. Perhaps that is all some of them intended and all that some readers at home and abroad demanded. On that level, the books are as effective for us as they were for those earlier readers. On another level, however, these stories deliver more than excitement and romance. As the reader encounters one Irish community after another while proceeding from book to book, the themes of Irish space, Irish time, and Irish people combine to present a composite picture of the Irish nation as it was imagined by the authors.

In most of the Irish historical fiction written by nationalists during this period, the Irish nation was fundamentally Gaelic and Catholic. Characters of Norman-Irish or Anglo-Irish or Scots-Irish lineage are tolerated, however, regardless of their role or class. That is, each community member, including those who lived on its cultural or political periphery, was given the opportunity somewhere during the narrative to express his or her point of view on the issues of the day. These fictional scenes depicting the social discourse of average Irish characters pose a fundamental question for the reader: who are the members of the Irish nation? The answers that the authors implicitly provide often parallel the conclusions Emmet Larkin reached in his essay, 'The Irish political tradition', when he explored the relationship among religion, nationality, and the Irish idea of freedom.[15] Larkin observed that the

---

15. Emmet Larkin, 'The Irish political tradition' in Hachey and McCaffrey, *Perspectives*, pp 99–120.

Irish political tradition was communitarian rather than individualistic, and that in its practical workings, the political system functioned by consensus rather than by majority. The system of communalism, he added, was sustained by a cultural homogeneity that allowed Irish society to absorb an endless variety of peoples and traditions in a way that is virtually unknown elsewhere in the world. The political and social systems survived because those occupying the centre could not ignore those on the periphery. Popular novelists from two traditions, P.A. Sheehan and George A. Birmingham, are prime examples of writers from the period 1870–1921 whose work idealised the second factor in this equation: the open Irish community, and by extension, an adaptable Irish nation. These authors, as well as others who wrote in this vein, ran counter to the claims of the Irish cultural nationalists like D.P. Moran who restricted membership in the Irish nation to the racially pure descendants of the ancient Gaelic people.

The nationalist and unionist novelists' idealised view of the Irish nation also contrasts with the historical fiction of regional novelists who wrote about the north of Ireland from a unionist and sectarian perspective. Readers of May de la Cherois Crommelin, for example, encountered an exclusive and aggressive Protestant culture in her *Orange lily* (1880). Likewise, Shan Bullock's salt-of-the-earth Protestant communities near the 'Thrasna River' were populated by proud – but parochial – descendants of English Puritans and Scottish covenanters. The novels of nationalist writers of County Down, however, largely resembled those of nationalists whose stories were characterised by their representations of life in the southern and western counties. For example, W.G. Lyttle, who was best known for his regional view of the revolution of 1798 in *Betsy Gray* (1888) included a deadly eviction scene that cut across religious lines in *Sons of the sod: a tale of County Down* (1886).

In all Irish historical fiction, however, the civic virtues of order and justice were the levers which activated the social mechanics of the imagined Irish community. Order rested on the ownership or possession of land. Justice regulated the social relationships between individuals. When order was maintained, the community remained stable. When social relationships were in a state of disequilibrium – which they always were, otherwise one would not have much of a story – justice was meted out through such social sanctions as ridicule, intimidation, boycott, assault, and in extreme cases, assassination. As for the two spiritual virtues that are corollaries of order and justice: there was plenty of room for charity in the Irish community, but there was little mercy.

Ireland as defined by the large cohort of nationalist and unionist authors who worked between 1870 and 1921 was, then, a beautiful place populated by generations of people who had endured an unhappy past, who lived in a troubled present, and who faced an uncertain future. Yet what reader could put down one of these books late at night and drift off to sleep without imagining the muffled sound of the steps of the next redeemer of the Irish nation pounding ever harder on the footpath beneath the window?

Select list of the historical fiction examined in this chapter

BANIM, Michael, *The croppy; a tale of 1798* (London, 1828) D.&J. Sadlier & Co., 1885.
BERTHOLDS, W.M., *Connor D'Arcy's struggles* (New York, 1913) Benziger Brothers.
BIRMINGHAM, George A., *The bad times* (London, 1908) Methuen & Co.
—, *The northern iron* (London, n.d.) Everett & Co., Ltd.
BODKIN, Matthew McDonald, *True man and traitor, or the rising of Emmet* (Dublin, 1910) J. Duffy and Co. Ltd.
BULLOCK, Shan, *The squireen* (London, 1903) Methuen.
—, *The red leaguers* (New York, 1904) McClure, Phillips & Co.
—, *The loughsiders* (London, 1924) Harrap and Co.
BUTLER, A., *Shamrock leaves* (Dublin, 1886) Sealy, Bryers & Walker.
CARLETON, William, *The black prophet*, (1847) (Shannon, 1972) Irish University Press.
—, *The tithe proctor* (1849) (New York, 1979) Garland Press.
CROMMELIN, May de la Cherois, *Orange lily* (London, 1880) George Routledge and Sons.
—, *'Divil-may-care' alias Richard Burke, sometime adjutant of the black northerners* (London, 1899) F.V. White & Co.
DOYLE, Lynn, *Ballygullion* (Dublin, 1918) Maunsel & Company, Ltd.
EDGEWORTH, Maria, *Castle Rackrent* (1800) (New York, 1965) W.W. Norton.
FITZPATRICK, Thomas, *Jabez Murdock: poetaster and 'adjuint'* (Dublin, n.d.) James Duffy.
FRANCIS, M.E. [Mrs. Francis Sweetman Blundell], *Miss Erin* (New York, 1898) Benzinger Brothers.
GUINAN, Rev. Joseph, *Annamore or the tenant-at-will* (London, 1924) Burns Oates & Washbourne Ltd.
—, *The soggarth aroon* (Dublin, 1905) James Duffy and Co., Ltd.
HINKSON, Katharine Tynan, *A daughter of kings* (New York, 1905) Benziger Brothers.
—, *Countrymen all* (London and Dublin, 1915) Maunsel and Company, Ltd.
—, *Lord Edward: a study in romance* (London, 1916) Smith, Elder & Co.
KENNY, Louise M. Stacpoole, *Mary: a romance of the west county* (London, 1915) R.&T. Washbourne, Ltd.

KICKHAM, Charles, *Knocknagow, or the homes of Tipperary* (1873) (Dublin, 1886) James Duffy & Co., Ltd.

LAWLESS, Emily, *The race of Castlebar* (London, 1913) Murray.

LYTTLE, W.G., *Sons of the sod: a tale of County Down* (Belfast, 1886) R. Carswell & Son, Ltd.

—, *Betsy Grey; or Hearts of Down: a tale of ninety-eight* (Bangor, 1888) The Mourne Observer.

LYSAGHT, Sidney Royse, *Her Majesty's rebels* (London, 1907) Macmillan and Co., Ltd.

—, *The Marplot* (London, 1893) Macmillan and Co.

McCRAITH, L.M., *The romance of Irish heroines* (London, 1913) Longmans, Green, and Co.

MACMAHON, Ella, *Fancy O'Brien* (London, 1909) Chapman & Hall, Ltd.

McMANUS, L., *The silk of the kine* (New York, 1896) Harper & Brothers, 1896.

McNULTY, Edward, *Misther O'Ryan* (London, 1894) Edward Arnold, 1894.

MORAN, D.P., *Tom O'Kelly* (Dublin, 1905) Cahill, J. Duffy, 1905.

MULHOLLAND, Rosa, *The return of Mary O'Murrough* (London, 1910) Sands & Co.

MURPHY, James, *Convict no. 25: or the clearances of Westmeath* (Dublin, 1913) James Duffy & Co.

O'BRIEN, William, *When we were boys* (London, 1890) Longmans, Green, and Co.

—, *A queen of men* (London, 1898) T. Fisher Unwin.

O'BYRNE, M.L. [Emelobie de Celtis], *The Pale and the septs; or, the baron of Belgard and the chiefs of Glenmalure: a romance of the sixteenth century* (Dublin, 1876) M.H. Gill & Son.

—, *Ill-won peerages or an unhallowed union* (Dublin, 1884) M.H. Gill and Son.

O'DONOVAN, Gerald, *Father Ralph* (London, 1913) Macmillan.

O'GRADY, Standish James, *The coming of Cuculain* (London, 1894) Methuen & Co.

—, *Ulrick the Ready* (1896) (Dublin, 1921) The Talbot Press, Ltd.

—, *In the gates of the north* (Kilkenny, 1901) printed and published by Standish O'Grady.

—, *The flight of the eagle* (1897) (Dublin, 1910[?]) The Educational Company School Edition.

PENDER, Margaret T., *The bog of lilies* (Dublin, 1927) Talbot Press Ltd.

—, *The last of the Irish chiefs*, (Dublin, n.d.) Martin Lester, Ltd.

—, *The green cockade: a tale of Ulster in 'ninety-eight* (1900) (Dublin, 1920) Martin Lester Ltd., 1920.

SHEEHAN, Canon P.A., *My new curate, a story gathered from the stray leaves of an old diary* (1899) (Boston, 1916) Marlier Publishing Co.

—, *Luke Delmege* (London, 1901) Longmans, Green, and Co.

—, *Glenanaar: a story of Irish life* (London, 1905) Longmans, Green, and Co.

—, *The blindness of Dr Gray or the final law* (London, 1909) Longmans, Green, and Co.

—, *The intellectuals: a story of Irish club-life* (London, 1911) Longmans, Green, and Co.

—, *Lisheen or, the test of the spirits* (1907) (London, 1916) Longmans, Green, and Co.

—, *The graves at Kilmorna, a story of '67* (New York, 1915) Longmans, Green, and Co.

SMITHSON, Annie M.P., *Her Irish heritage* (1917) (Cork, 1988) Mercier Press.

SMYTH, P.J., *King and viking or the ravens of Lochlan* (Dublin, 1899) Sealy, Bryers & Walker.

—, *The wild rose of Lough Gill: a tale of the Irish war in the seventeenth century* (Dublin, 1883) M.H. Gill & Son, Ltd.

SWAN, Annie S., *A son of Erin* (London, 1899) Hutchinson & Co.

THURSTON, E. Temple, *The greatest wish in the world* (New York, 1910) Mitchell Kennerley.

—, *June Carroll* (London and New York, 1927) A.P. Putnam's Sons.

—, *May eve, or the tinker of Ballinatray: a novel* (London, 1924) Hutchinson & Co.

THYNNE, Robert, *A story of a campaign estate; or, the turn of the tide* (1896) Roxburghe Press.

TROLLOPE, Anthony, *The Kellys and the O'Kellys* (1848) (London, 1929) Oxford University Press.

—, *The Macdermots of Ballycloran* (1847) (New York, 1981) Arno Press.

—, *The Land Leaguers* (London, 1884) Chatto & Windus.

WALSH, A.T., *Casey of the IRA* (Dublin, 1923) Talbot Press.

WALSH, Louis J., *The next time: a story of 'forty-eight* (Dublin, 1919) M.H. Gill & Son.

5

The *Irish Peasant* and the Conflict between Irish-Ireland and the Catholic Bishops, 1903–10

FRANK A. BILETZ

THE INCREASING PROMINENCE of a cultural, rather than political, definition of the Irish national question created unexpected tensions after the turn of the century between some proponents of the new cultural nationalism, which promoted an 'Irish-Ireland' ideal, and members of the Catholic hierarchy and clergy. In a sense this was paradoxical, because the cultural revival tended to strengthen the identification of the Catholic faith with Irish nationality. Most priests, moreover, considered themselves sympathetic to the national cause in general and many actively participated in the Gaelic League and other organisations of the new nationalism. As Larkin has argued, however, the Irish church as an institution had committed itself during the 1880s to the political nationalism of the Parliamentary Party.[1] By challenging the primacy of constitutional politics, the cultural nationalists also necessarily questioned the role the church had assumed in the emerging Irish political system. It was not only, however, the political approach of the church that the cultural nationalists disputed, but its perceived resistance to the new cultural priorities.

---

1. See Larkin, *R. C. Ch. 1878–86*; *R. C. Ch. 1886–88*; and *R. C. Ch. 1888–91*

The Conflict between Irish-Ireland and the Catholic Bishops, 1903-10

Originating as a term used by the journalist D.P. Moran, 'Irish-Ireland' encompassed all aspirations for a national identity that was Irish in language and Gaelic in culture.[2] By implication, Moran also insisted that Irish identity was inevitably Catholic as well, simply because the indigenous language and cultural traditions had been preserved in the countryside by Irish-speaking people of Catholic background. Although many in the Irish-Ireland movement repudiated the sectarian aspect of Moran's thought, all agreed that achieving cultural self-reliance was of greater importance than acquiring mere political independence, and that Irish national identity could only be rooted in the distinctive traditions of early Gaelic civilisation. During the first decade of the twentieth century, these ideas found expression in a number of prominent Irish-Ireland newspapers, which included Moran's own *The Leader*, Arthur Griffith's *United Irishman*, and W.P. Ryan's *Irish Peasant*.

A curious episode at the end of 1906, which involved the temporary cessation of publication by the *Irish Peasant*, casts considerable light on the nature of the escalating tensions between the new cultural nationalists and the Catholic hierarchy. Each of the paper's two editors, Patrick D. Kenny and W.P. Ryan, became, in turn, involved in disputes with the church. These differences centred on the role of the priesthood in building a new, self-sufficient Ireland and the degree of control to be allowed the church in setting the curriculum in the national schools. The roots of the conflict between Irish-Ireland and the Catholic bishops, however, went back to the 1880s, when the church first achieved a formal role in the emerging Irish political system.

The 1880s was the crucial decade in determining the profound part the church would play in the founding of an independent Irish state.[3] At that time, Charles Stewart Parnell created in the house of commons an independent Irish party committed to achieving home rule. In building a disciplined party machine, Parnell relied to a much lesser extent than had Daniel O'Connell's emancipation movement of the 1820s and Repeal movement of the 1840s on the Catholic clergy to create his grass-roots organisation.[4] Parnell himself was a Protestant landowner and his constitutional movement espoused a non-sectarian ideal of the Irish nation. By providing a consultative role for the Catholic hierarchy, however, Parnell institutionalised a formal position for the church in the emerging Irish political system. According to

---

2. See D.P. Moran, *The philosophy of Irish Ireland* (Dublin, n.d. [1905]).
3. See Larkin, *R. C. Ch. 1886–88*, pp 314–22.
4. For a useful brief treatment of the general relationship between Parnell and the church, see C.J. Wood, 'Parnell and the Catholic Church' in D. George Boyce and Alan O'Day (ed.), *Parnell in perspective* (London and New York, 1991), pp 9–37.

Larkin, this distinctive system achieved a consensus for action by balancing the claims of three sources of authority: the leader, the party, and the Catholic bishops.[5] The resulting 'de facto Irish state' proved to be, in Larkin's analysis, strong enough to survive even its leader's fall.

The crystallisation of this distinctive Irish political system was made possible in October 1884, when a working arrangement was reached between the Irish bishops and the Parliamentary Party. 'The essence of the Clerical-Nationalist alliance', according to Larkin, 'was that the initiative and control of the Education Question at all levels was to remain with the Bishops, while the Bishops as a body signified that the Party was now *bona fide* as far as their own and their clergy's participation in politics was concerned'.[6] Over the next few years, as Larkin has depicted, the specific details of this alliance were worked out, including, most importantly, the extent to which on national issues the Irish church could be counted upon to remain independent from the dictates of Rome. In the final analysis, the presence of the bishops as an essential element in Parnell's political system demonstrated that by the end of the nineteenth century any viable national ideal had to incorporate the Catholic church.

The emergence of cultural nationalism as a major force in Irish society during the 1890s, however, complicated the relationship of church and nation. It is true that, to a considerable extent, the new nationalism confirmed the equation of Irishness with catholicism. By this time, virtually all Catholics were nationalist in political affiliation and most Protestants were unionist. Cultural nationalists like Moran maintained that these party affiliations did not represent mere transitory political allegiances, but immutable cultural facts. By defining national identity in terms of cultural tradition rather than political viewpoint, it was the inevitable tendency of cultural nationalism to harden further the lines of denominational difference. The consequences this might have for the inclusion of the Protestant Anglo-Irish, as well as Ulster's substantial Presbyterian community, in an independent Irish state remained still largely unforeseen. The participation of the church hierarchy in the governing consensus of a de facto Irish state did not, however, satisfy those who believed the primary task involved not state-building, but the revival of the national culture. Indeed, much of the tension between lay Catholics, such as Kenny and Ryan, and the church hierarchy that

---

5. See Emmet Larkin, 'Church, state, and nation in modern Ireland' in his *The historical dimensions of Irish catholicism* (Washington, DC, 1984), and 'The Irish political tradition' Hachey and McCaffrey, *Perspectives*, pp 99–120.
6. Larkin, *R. C. Ch. 1886–88*, p. xiii.

emerged during the first decade of the twentieth century resulted from the opposition of cultural nationalism to the fundamental assumptions, goals and methods of the political system that Parnell had created, and in which the bishops formed a key element.[7]

As debated in the pages of the *Irish Peasant* during both editorships between 1903 and 1910, the principal conflicts between the Irish-Irelanders and the Catholic church involved the general role of the clergy in deciding policy on social issues and the specific case of control over the educational system. Although the Catholic clergy had performed an essential role in organising movements for constitutional change since the days of Daniel O'Connell, Irish-Ireland expanded the scope of national concern to areas where the majority of clergy were significantly less enlightened in their attitudes than they were in their politics. From the standpoint of cultural nationalism, some of the social values inculcated by the priesthood tended to make the Irish people less, rather than more, self-reliant. The cultural nationalists complained, for instance, about the general resistance of the clergy to modern, scientific methods that could help provide Ireland with a more self-sufficient economy. By focusing overmuch on the spiritual realm, some Irish-Irelanders further charged, many priests encouraged their flocks toward acquiescence in secular affairs. Another major source of conflict involved sexual morality. Many lay Catholic intellectuals argued that the austere morality promoted by the priesthood contributed to the pervasive joylessness of life in rural Ireland and was a significant factor in continuing emigration. Whenever such lay-clerical conflicts arose, lay Catholics criticised clerical dictation on all matters not directly involving faith and morals. Underlying all of these particular conflicts was the struggle for social leadership in the new Ireland between lay Catholic intellectuals, who were increasingly secularised and receptive to modern ideas, and the Catholic clergy, who sought to preserve their traditional authority.

These differences over the role of the priesthood in building an Irish-Ireland were only exacerbated by increasing tensions over conflicting educational priorities. In the concordat achieved during the 1880s, the Irish Parliamentary Party had acknowledged the overriding interest of the church in all issues affecting the education of Irish Catholics. From the standpoint of the Catholic hierarchy, the educational system needed, above all, to provide Catholic children with suitable religious instruction free from Protestant proselytism and secular ideas. By the turn of the century, the cultural

---

7. For a perceptive analysis of the role of the bishops in the Irish political system between the fall of Parnell and the creation of the Free State, see Miller, *Church, state & nation*.

nationalists had come to regard a measure of control over the schools as essential to their aims. Their priority was that Irish children be taught the Irish language and national culture. In a society in which virtually all educational institutions were under denominational control, the failure of many clerical managers promptly to provide adequate instruction in these subjects led to inevitable and vociferous protests from the cultural nationalists.

All of these controversies found expression in the *Irish Peasant*, which soon became one of the liveliest of the new Irish-Ireland newspapers. The weekly was established in 1903 in Navan, County Meath, by James MacCann, who had been a successful businessman in Dublin until he became a convert to the cause of the national economic revival. MacCann initiated a number of improvement schemes, including both farms and factories, near the family home of Navan. In order to advance these agricultural and industrial activities, he launched the *Irish Peasant*. Shortly after the paper's founding, Patrick D. Kenny, better known as 'Pat', became its editor and also contributed a weekly column of personal reflections, 'Patriana'. Although MacCann died in February 1904, his widow and sons continued the enterprises he had begun, including the paper. Kenny continued to edit the *Peasant* until December of 1905, when, amid growing opposition from the local clergy, he was replaced by W.P. Ryan.

Kenny was a maverick and gadfly, who proved to be a formidable opponent to the authority of the Catholic clergy in political and social matters. He also provided the Irish-Ireland movement with one of its strongest internal critics. In certain respects, notably his scepticism about the revival of the language and about the usefulness of the Gaelic past as a model for the Irish present, Kenny hardly seemed to be an Irish-Irelander. Despite his many differences with other cultural nationalists, however, Kenny's overriding commitment was always to advancing the national revival, especially in the economic realm, and he remained critical of mere political solutions. In his cultural critiques, he echoed D.P. Moran by insisting that the reformation of the Irish national character was an essential step toward a truly independent Ireland. The cornerstone of Kenny's thought, however, was the assertion of individual liberty against clerical dominance. He believed that the country would remain economically backward until its people broke what he perceived as the church's stranglehold on intellectual activity. Throughout the many controversies in which he participated Kenny continued, without sacrificing his own avowed faith, to distinguish between catholicism as such and the opinions of its clergy.

Born in Ireland, Kenny had emigrated to England as a youth and worked as a journalist on a London paper, writing chiefly dramatic criticism. He lived in Britain for a total of seventeen years, settling at last in Brighton, a seaside resort on the southern coast, 'among classical concerts, church parades and lawn-tennis'. In 1901, learning that the family farm in County Mayo was in jeopardy, he returned to Ireland to assist his family of 'affectionate incapables'.[8] Knowing next to nothing about farming, Kenny was, according to his own account, apparently the only person in the family with any drive, energy or willingness to break established moulds. Thus, as something of 'an economic and sociological experiment', he gave up his secure life in Britain: '... solely to do something for Ireland, sacrificing half my income, most of my comfort, the whole of my material prospects and of my peace; exchanging pleasant drawing rooms, valued friends, and bright evenings for a solitary life in a tent among the misery of Mayo, crushed by undertakings beyond my means and still more by the enmity of the very people who ought to have understood and helped me'.[9]

Within a few years, Kenny's 'little farm' was reputedly so much more productive than neighbouring properties that people came from all over Ireland to examine its miraculous transformation. Although some questioned the flourishing state of the farm as described in his journalistic accounts, Kenny's interpretation of his agricultural achievements as an argument for greater efficiency and the use of modern scientific methods was tirelessly promulgated through numerous newspaper articles and several books. Kenny eventually became acquainted with MacCann, another improver, who recruited him to edit the new paper.

Throughout his writings, Kenny argued that liberty of thought was essential if Ireland was ever to flourish as a nation.[10] It was the first condition of social progress, far more important than any political separation from Britain. 'The Freedom of Ireland remains to be achieved among and between the Irish themselves', Kenny declared, referring specifically to the unfettered exchange of ideas, 'and the day they learn to tolerate each other, that day brings their

---

8. 'Pat' [P.D. Kenny], *The sorrows of Ireland* (Dublin, 1907), p. 8.
9. *Irish Peasant*, 21 April 1906; see also [Kenny], *Sorrows*, p. 9.
10. In considering Kenny's general views, his books as well as columns written after he relinquished the editorship will be used, because very few issues of the *Peasant* from its first three years of publication are extant. The microfilm copy available at the National Library of Ireland contains only one issue from 1903, two issues from 1904, and two issues from 1905 before Ryan became editor in December. There is also a significant gap during Ryan's editorship between the 22 Sept. 1906 and 15 Dec. 1906 numbers. In sum, only from 9 Dec. 1905 through 22 Sept. 1906 does the *Irish Peasant* survive reasonably intact, albeit with scattered missing pages and whole issues. Fortunately, its successors, the *Peasant and Irish Ireland* and the *Irish Nation and Peasant* survive virtually complete.

relief from tyrannies inflicted on them from outside'.[11] He believed that the subservience of the Irish people to the Catholic clergy was the major expression of this lack of due regard for individual liberty. 'Liberty is essential to character, and character is essential to progress, economic or otherwise', Kenny maintained, 'but progress of any kind is plainly impossible in so far as one class of men dictate their liberty, their character, and their conduct in all concerns to all the other classes'.[12] The particular 'class of men' he blamed for encouraging Ireland's economic lassitude and social inertia was the Catholic clergy. Still, Kenny always held the Irish people to be ultimately responsible for their own subservience.

According to Kenny, the priesthood in Ireland had been granted a degree of social authority beyond that in most other places and had gradually extended their dominion to cover areas outside their recognised spiritual province. It was time, he argued, for the Catholic laity to reclaim control over their own destinies from 'parochial terrorism'.[13] He insisted, however, that the problem was not with catholicism itself but with its ministers. He went so far as to assert that, to a significant extent, the Catholic clergy in Ireland would rather accept social and economic backwardness than risk diminishing their authority. 'Many of our priests', Kenny charged, 'see that wherever the growth of industry develops the economic faculties, a lay life grows up that will not accept their dictation outside their sphere'. As a result, 'they think it better to reign over ruin than to take their due and proper place in economic progress'. In the end, 'Ireland suffers not from "the Roman Catholic Religion", but rather from the want of it, and it remains for the Catholic people to make good the defect'.[14]

His opponents frequently accused Kenny of being anti-clerical, a charge he vigorously denied. Those called 'anti-clerical' in Ireland, he contended, were usually those who had discovered that a priest had 'no right to settle their opinions for them'. Religious doctrine rested ultimately 'on a higher authority than [the priest] can exercise'.[15] Kenny claimed the sanction of the pope and canon law for his view of catholicism. Interestingly, anti-clericalism scarcely existed in Ireland in the same sense that it did on the Continent. In France, for example, 'anti-clericalism' involved an assault by radical republicans on entrenched privilege, including the church. It was egalitarian, positivist,

---

11. *Irish Peasant*, 18 Nov. 1905.
12. Patrick Kenny, *Economics for Irishmen* (Dublin, 1907), pp 146–7.
13. Ibid., p. 164.
14. Ibid., p. 156.
15. [Kenny], *Sorrows*, p. 68.

often socialist, and definitely anti-Christian. In Ireland, on the other hand, the Catholic church had become identified with the tenant-farming class and their national aspirations. For his part, Kenny favoured equality of economic opportunity and espoused rational farming techniques, but he opposed the collectivist tendencies of socialism, or even co-operation, and was certainly not anti-Christian.

Kenny believed that the Catholic clergy, with their high level of education and considerable skills, could be, if properly reformed and stripped of their pretensions to infallibility on social issues, of enormous assistance in the economic development of Ireland. Complaining about the lack of a course in economics at Maynooth, Kenny declared that if 'our priests [were] but competent economists, the result would be of more value to Ireland than any number of free Parliaments'.[16] He also advocated agricultural education in the national schools, which were largely under clerical control.[17]

In addition, Kenny vehemently opposed the general tendency of the Catholic clergy to become entrenched in positions of authority in secular organisations. Virtually all organisations working for the national cause were, according to 'Pat', compromised by clerical involvement. As a result, rather than encouraging cultural vitality and economic growth, the national organisations stifled individual initiative and limited social development. The Parliamentary Party, for example, was constrained in the formulation of its agenda by the veto of the bishops. According to Kenny, by compromising with the priesthood, John Redmond and his associates in the party tacitly admitted that 'home rule, on the present footing, is a clerical affair, to be accepted in so far as the cleric may dominate it, and damned in so far as the people claim rights in it'. Kenny criticised both the party and the clergy for their collaboration in the Irish political system, which he regarded as a betrayal of both the nation and the church. 'This ugly thing known as Parliamentary Nationalism', Kenny charged, 'is no more national than the uglier thing corrupting and directing it is religion'.[18]

Sinn Féin, the extra-parliamentary political movement founded by Arthur Griffith in November 1905, fared no better in Kenny's estimation. Its membership, he insisted, remained under the domination of the priesthood, limiting the organisation's freedom of action. 'The Sinn Féin rebel who hurls defiance at the mightiest of all empires turns pale before the village curate and his sway over the territories of eternity.'[19] Despite its motto of 'Ourselves

---

16. [Kenny], *Economics*, p. 6.
17. *Irish Peasant*, 26 May 1906.
18. [Kenny], *Sorrows*, pp 81–2.
19. Ibid., p. 57.

Alone', its 'trembling leaders still pretend to be in earnest, ready enough to make Ireland Irish in so far as Britain is concerned, but still more ready to make her perfectly Italian at the first touch of the Ultramontane button'.[20]

The Gaelic League too, was, in Kenny's view, subjugated to the priesthood, with 'the boundaries of its influence carefully determined by clerical preference'.[21] He did, however, acknowledge the benefits brought about by the Gaelic League: 'Wherever I see the Gaelic League allowed to grow, encouraging normal interests of mind and body, there I see bright sobriety, a courage and character begotten of clear thought, a higher level of industrial efficiency, and a lower drink bill'.[22] Despite these gains, Kenny acknowledged the 'cruel truth' that, despite the best efforts of the language movement, the use of Irish continued to decline.[23] The League had failed to reach or influence the rural poor, who represented the vast majority of the population and its only surviving native speakers. In any case, Kenny considered the language revival useless if the people did not have food or jobs.[24] He applauded, in the end, the social values the movement encouraged, while remaining sceptical about its professed goals.

All of these national organisations revealed, Kenny believed, an inability of the Irish people to think independently. 'While other peoples', he complained, 'are brought up to develop mental initiative from the very cradle, we are brought up rather to fetter the individual mind under all manner of impositions dictated by organised authority, so that we reach manhood and womanhood, incompetent, inefficient, unenterprising'.[25] The Irish, 'not daring to think or act on their thought, start "organisations" as the alternative, and the priest gets control of every organisation in proportion as it becomes strong enough to be of use to him'. By controlling nationalist organisations, the priests, with their imposition of an intellectual tyranny, prevented the natural growth of the nation. Moreover, clerical control of education made certain, in Kenny's opinion, that new ideas were killed before they could even be born. Despite all his criticism of national organisations, however, Kenny was not opposed to collective action as such. 'We have not enough individualism', he declared, 'to be effective collectively'.[26] Any authentic collective effort could only emerge from the interplay of individual efforts.

---

20. Ibid., p. 59.
21. Ibid., p. 54.
22. *Irish Peasant*, 4 Nov. 1905.
23. [Kenny], *Sorrows*, p. 52.
24. *Irish Peasant*, 24 Mar. 1906.
25. Ibid., 19 May 1906.
26. [Kenny], *Sorrows*, p. 67.

Kenny's conception of the Irish nation was a rather idiosyncratic one. For him, the nation was founded on economic prosperity, not on the continuity of cultural traditions. Consequently, the principal focus of his writings remained economic development, which he believed could only occur if the native intellect broke the shackles of clericalism. By means of greater efficiency, Kenny sought greater productivity. In this, he had much in common with those cultural nationalists, including Moran, Griffith, and the co-operative movement propagandist George Russell, who concentrated on economic revival as a vital aspect of nation-building. Kenny's interests, however, were primarily agricultural, not industrial, and he opposed the protectionist measures advocated by Moran and Griffith. Although Kenny shared Russell's agrarian concerns, he remained too much an individualist to believe that agricultural co-operation could ever be a viable economic strategy. Co-operation involved, in Kenny's view, 'the mere transfer of the economic process, in Production and Exchange alike, from one set of hands to another'.[27]

With regard to the cultural aspects of national identity, Kenny remained totally uninterested in ancient Gaelic civilisation and he maintained that all efforts to save the language were doomed to fail. While a practising Catholic, he did not view religion to be a defining element of Irish identity. He condemned any sort of sectarianism, because he always judged people as individuals, not as members of a group. In reviewing the novel *Hyacinth*, for instance, Kenny praised its Protestant author, 'George Birmingham' for his 'superiority to bigotry of any kind, which enables him to see Ireland and her conditions from the national and comprehensive standpoint'.[28] On several occasions, he denounced anti-Semitism, which infected the views of some Irish-Irelanders, including most notably Griffith. Kenny also refused to dislike the English or to disdain their culture. He pointed out that his life in England had been relatively happy, and that the people had been 'very kind and just to me during my seventeen years among them'.[29] 'It is easy to abuse the British behind their backs', he observed, 'but it is better for the Irish to be told the truth about themselves before their faces'.[30]

In political terms, Kenny's conception of Irish national aspirations was also unusual for an Irish-Ireland journalist, in that he opposed republican separatism. Although he criticised the Parliamentary Party for being too much under the sway of the bishops, he expressed a willingness to accept

---

27. *Irish Peasant*, 9 Dec. 1905.
28. Ibid., 31 Mar. 1906.
29. Ibid., 21 Apr. 1906.
30. Ibid., 7 Apr. 1906.

some sort of home rule. Breaking the imperial bonds was not, for Kenny, essential for national well-being. Indeed, he thought the Irish nation, if granted appropriate rights, might best flourish within the Empire and would be ruined as a fully independent entity. In *The sorrows of Ireland*, Kenny envisioned a 'new order of Nationalism', in which liberty of thought had broken the grip of both 'the rebel and the priest'.

> Nationalism, free and informed, wants to be in the empire, but neither confiscated nor coerced under the terms. My ideal of an empire is an association of nationalities for the common good, in which the nation gives up the liberty to harm the empire, in which the empire gives up the liberty to harm the nation, and in which all give up to their joint authority the liberty to harm one another. On the other hand separation means the end of Irish nationality.[31]

Although he never spelled out beyond this what sort of imperial order he advocated, Kenny seemed to favour a federation of nationalities, in which each nation would be assured its cultural integrity. In his view, 'the definition of an Empire implies nations within it, free to grow in the essentials of their nationality'.[32]

In one of his 'Patriana' columns, Kenny explained why he believed Ireland might be better able to realise its nationhood within, rather than outside, the British Empire. Although 'theoretically', he was for total separation, he also acknowledged that, in practice, 'Ireland cannot hope to grow as a totally separate nation hostile to Britain'. If Ireland were to become independent, Kenny maintained that further conflicts with Britain were inevitable, because the stronger neighbour could not help but treat the smaller country as part of its sphere of influence. 'On the other hand, assuming a state of good feeling between the two peoples, there is no reason why Ireland should not prosper as part of the Empire, not only in her material condition, but also in her nationhood.'[33] Furthermore, he hoped that the growth of democracy in both countries would, in the long run, improve relations by fostering a sense of common interests.

Kenny had no patience with those revolutionaries who wanted to sacrifice themselves for their country. 'I find, too, as a rule, that those who want to die for Ireland do not know how to live for Ireland, or even for themselves, which would obviously be a greater service to a country that suffers so much

---

31. [Kenny], *Sorrows*, p. 71.
32. *Irish Peasant*, 10 Feb. 1906.
33. Ibid.

from death already. I wish heartily that those who want to die for Ireland would go at once and do it, so that those who want to live for Ireland and for themselves might do so in a saner atmosphere'.[34]

In 'living for Ireland', the essential first step was to reform the national character. A spirit of self-reliance was required if the Irish people were ever to overcome their past subservience and to create a prosperous future. Economic progress had to be based on more efficient techniques in both agriculture and industry. As part of this social transformation, the Irish people had to learn to depend on their own initiative, not on the guidance of their priests. Above all, liberty of thought was necessary to foster the emergence of new ideas to meet changing needs. The free play of ideas might even allow the emergence of a new framework for Anglo-Irish relations that would transcend the ideological rigidities of the past. Throughout the bitter disputes of his day, Kenny remained an idealist whose aspirations for his country were epitomised by what he achieved with his own individual efforts at his 'little farm' in Mayo.

Although its columns were devoted largely to local matters, the *Peasant* developed, under Kenny's editorship, a considerable national following. Kenny himself boasted that the circulation of the *Peasant* had increased five-fold under his editorship.[35] If true, this claim was somewhat deceptive, because the paper never circulated to more than a few thousand subscribers. Despite his successes, Kenny was replaced as editor at the end of 1905, though he continued to write his column. Evidently, he had antagonised the local priests. In noting the change in editors of the *Peasant*, the Gaelic Leaguer Mary Butler wrote in a letter to William Bulfin, who edited the *Southern Cross*, a nationalist paper for Irish emigrants in Argentina, that 'the former editor P.D. Kenny got into hot water with the priests over some things he wrote'.[36]

With Kenny's removal, Ryan was brought in as someone likely to be a '"safe" Irish-Irelander with regard to clerical questions'.[37] Kenny, meanwhile, continued to defend his editorship. 'More lies have been told about me in the last year than in all the other years of my life together', Kenny insisted, soon after his successor took over, 'but the more widely my wickedness was spread, the more curious were the public to read what I wrote, driving the circulation higher and higher'.[38] He courted controversy, and, with a persona later described by Ryan as one of 'agreeably whimsical egoism', he seemed to take

---

34. Ibid., 7 July 1906.
35. This claim was made in ibid., 30 Dec. 1905.
36. Quoted in Martin Waters, 'W.P. Ryan and the Irish Ireland Movement,' (Ph.D. thesis, Connecticut, 1970), p. 159, from N.L.I., Bulfin papers.
37. Ibid., p.152.
38. *Irish Peasant*, 23 Dec. 1905.

inordinate pleasure in the attacks made on him.[39] Kenny proudly called himself 'one of the most unpopular and most dangerous men in Ireland'.[40] After relinquishing the editorship of the *Peasant*, Kenny continued to write his weekly column until the paper relocated in Dublin at the beginning of 1907, as well as to manage his 'little farm'. He also expressed his opinions in several books, which included *The sorrows of Ireland* (1907), *Economics for Irishmen* (1907) and *My little farm* (1915).

In her letter to Bulfin, Butler described W.P. Ryan, the new editor of the *Peasant*, as 'a clever journalist and an ardent Gael'.[41] William Patrick Ryan was born on 26 October 1867 near Templemore, County Tipperary. His father worked as a farm labourer and many members of his extended family had been obliged to emigrate to America. Ryan was described by the historian Martin Waters, who has written the only full treatment of his career, as being bookish and 'something of a dreamer' in his youth.[42] Although he trained for five years to teach in the national schools, he ultimately decided against that profession in favour of journalism. Unable to find an opening on the Irish provincial papers, Ryan went to London in November 1886 when he was nineteen. He would spend only about five years of the remainder of his long life in residence in Ireland, making a total of only twenty-four out of his seventy-five years. His activities during his relatively brief return to his native country from 1905 to 1910 would prove, however, very significant in the development of Irish cultural nationalism.

Ryan's first position in London as a journalist was with the anti-Parnellite *Irish National Press*. He went on to write for a succession of newspapers, including most importantly T.P. O'Connor's *Evening Sun*, for which he worked for four years during the 1890s. Ryan often felt keenly the conflict between devoting time to writing ephemeral journalism as opposed to composing more lasting literary works. In 1893, he published a 'rather mediocre novel', *The heart of Tipperary*, which, in Waters' words, 'heartily endorsed the Land League and celebrated the virtues of the oppressed peasantry'.[43] In his personal life, Ryan had, during the previous year, married Elizabeth Boyd, a London-born Irishwoman of mixed religious background. The couple celebrated in 1893 the birth of a son, Desmond, who would himself become a prominent figure in Irish letters.

---

39. W.P. Ryan, *The Pope's green island* (London, 1912), p. 6.
40. *Irish Peasant*, 17 Mar. 1906.
41. Quoted in Waters, 'Ryan', p. 159; original source: N.L.I., Bulfin papers.
42. Waters, 'Ryan', p. 7.
43. Ibid., p. 25.

In London, Ryan became active in several organisations of Irish émigrés living in the imperial capital. As a supporter of land reform, he joined the Clapham branch of the Irish National League of Great Britain. As a man with literary interests as well, Ryan became acquainted with many Irish writers living in London through the Southwark Irish Literary Club. This group, which included W.B. Yeats, T.W. Rolleston, and Dr John Todhunter, was superseded in December 1891 by the Irish Literary Society. Ryan chronicled the early days of the burgeoning literary movement in his book *The Irish literary revival: its history, pioneers, and possibilities*, which he published privately in 1894.

For Ryan, the rampant jingoism of the British press during the Boer war, fought from 1899 to 1902, accentuated his alienation from what he considered the soulless, business-oriented culture of England and created the conditions for his conversion to Irish cultural nationalism. Working at this time for the *Sunday Special* as literary editor and chief reviewer, Ryan strongly criticised the pro-British books on the war that he was given to review. Ultimately exasperated, he quit the *Special* and took a reporting job with the *Morning Leader*, because it was the only daily in London sympathetic to the Boer cause. The imperialistic posturing that surrounded him in England made Ryan ever more aware of his communal identity as an Irishman. Early in 1899, Ryan joined the London branch of the Gaelic League.

While continuing to work as a journalist, moving to the *Daily Chronicle* after his stint with the *Morning Leader*, Ryan devoted most of his spare time to working as a propagandist and organiser for the League. In 1901, he became a member of the League Executive, or *Coiste Gnótha*; in 1902, he was elected secretary of the London branch and served in that capacity until 1905; and finally, in 1903, he was considered for the editorship of the League's newspaper, *An Claidheamh Soluis*, before that post was given to Padraic Pearse. On behalf of the League, he wrote a pamphlet, 'Lessons from modern language movements – what native speech has achieved for nationality', in which he surveyed the efforts to revive or preserve national languages among a number of European peoples, including the Czechs, Hungarians, Serbs, Danes, Belgians, and Poles, for the insights afforded into the Irish situation.

Ryan's opportunity to return to Ireland and to participate at first-hand in the revival of the national culture came late in 1905, when the MacCann family offered him the editorship of the *Irish Peasant*. The first issue under Ryan's editorship appeared on 9 December 1905. He altered the design and features of the paper, to make it 'more national in scope and Irish Ireland in tone'.⁴⁴ Among the new features were sections on 'People and Problems', which addressed social and economic issues of national importance, and 'Irish Pioneers', which consisted of a series of profiles of leaders of the Irish-Ireland movement, including the founders of the Gaelic League, Douglas Hyde and Eoin MacNeill, the prominent writer of stories and plays in the native language, Fr Peter O'Leary, as well as D.P. Moran and Mary Butler. The 'Patriana' column was retained. Both local and national editions were published, with the latter omitting such material as reports on the meetings of the Meath County Council. Major attention was given instead to events sponsored by the Gaelic League. The goal of the *Irish Peasant*, according to Ryan, would now be to 'represent and illustrate all sides of Irish-Ireland thought and activity'.⁴⁵ In his first editorial, Ryan asserted that though 'our most pressing problems may appear to be material, they are really intellectual and spiritual'.⁴⁶ In discussing the intellectual ramifications of Irish cultural nationalism, Ryan soon found himself in conflict with the established spiritual leaders of Ireland, the Catholic bishops.

The question of lay rights assumed particular prominence in Ireland during the first decade of the twentieth century, when people like Ryan, who regarded themselves as Catholics in good standing, found their activities on behalf of the Irish nation called into question by church authorities. As Waters has noted, the willingness of secular intellectuals like Ryan to set themselves up as alternative sources of authority to the clergy on social questions was a significant factor in the rising tensions.⁴⁷ So far as priests were concerned, Ryan acknowledged that 'we have of course a deep reverence for all men whose main concern is to inspire humanity with the sense of spiritual things'. At the same time, however, he insisted that 'we have also a very definite idea of the respect and consideration due to lay humanity. We respect and insist on the rights of all'.⁴⁸ In Ryan's opinion, one of the 'gravest dangers' was 'that laymen will break with the Church because of differences with her human ministers'. In regard to the fundamentals of religious faith, Ryan continually affirmed that 'there is not the remotest possibility of the slightest clash between the Church and Irish-Ireland; and if clergymen clash with Irish-Ireland or with Irish-Irelanders it is important to remember that the matter raises no question of Catholicity whatever'.⁴⁹

---

44. Ibid., p. 163.
45. *Irish Peasant*, 16 Dec. 1906.
46. Ibid., 9 Dec. 1905.
47. Waters, 'Ryan', p. 207.
48. *Irish Peasant*, 18 Aug. 1906.
49. Ibid., 12 May 1906.

Ryan's outspokenness about clerical control of education in Ireland eventually led to concerted pressure being brought on the MacCann family, the proprietors of the *Peasant*. During the course of his first year as editor of the paper, Ryan challenged the church's position on two noteworthy occasions. First, he opposed the church on the English education bill of 1906, which he regarded as irrelevant to the Irish national cause because it affected only English Catholics. Second, and more seriously, Ryan argued for a greater lay role in Irish primary education, which the priests treated as their sole preserve. The outspokenness of Ryan and several of his contributors on this latter issue was what, in the last analysis, incited the clerical 'campaign' against the *Irish Peasant*.

The English education bill was proposed in 1906 by the Liberal Party in order to redress the grievances of English non-conformists with regard to the provisions of earlier legislation. (The Act of 1902 had granted public funds directly to Anglican and Catholic schools, while the new bill would distribute such aid through local authorities.) Ryan criticised the Irish Parliamentary Party for supporting the legislation on the grounds that no Irish issue was involved and its votes were in any case not needed for the bill's passage. Ryan asked 'why it is we should interfere, and how we could effectively interfere, in a British domestic question, and on behalf of Catholic leaders in Britain?'[50] Moreover, the Irish hierarchy had made their initial mistake, Ryan believed, by siding with the established church in 1902, creating a situation which this new bill would only compound, not correct. As Ryan viewed the situation, the Irish Parliamentary Party, under pressure from the Irish bishops, was being forced to defend the position of Catholic religious schools in England. In opposing the legislation, the party would side with their usual enemies, the English Tories, the Church of England, and aristocratic English Catholics such as the duke of Norfolk, instead of with their old allies, the Liberals and non-conformists. The Liberals would, moreover, have the votes to pass the bill anyway with or without their support.[51] It was, for Ryan, a clear example of the bishops interfering in an issue on which their priorities were entirely different from those of the nation.

'The supreme education business for us today', Ryan argued, 'is the nationalising of our own school systems in Ireland'. This task 'will take all the energy we can give it, and we are afraid that this British business is being used

---

50. Ibid., 2 June 1906.
51. See Miller, *Church, state & nation*, pp 153–9 and 165–76, for a detailed account of the debates over the education bill of 1906. In the end, the bill passed the Commons, but the House of Lords killed it with amendments unacceptable to the government.

indirectly to draw off attention from this grievous problem of our own'.[52] Ryan perceived no benefit to be gained from antagonising the only forces in British politics sympathetic to Irish aspirations. He dismissed the Catholic schools in England as acting anyway largely as anglicising agents on those Irish Catholics forced by difficult circumstances at home to emigrate to England. In sum, for Ryan, 'the preservation, the uplifting, the strengthening of Ireland is an immeasurably bigger matter, from the broad Catholic point of view alone, than this school management business over in Britain'.[53] Ryan's views excited considerable negative responses from readers, both lay and clerical, which the *Peasant* duly printed in the interests of an open debate.

The more significant dispute concerned Ryan's challenge to what he believed was the overly prominent role the Catholic clergy had assumed in managing the Irish educational system. Ryan did not contest that priests had the right to supervise the religious education of Irish children, but he questioned whether that prerogative extended to secular subjects as well. The conservatives among the clergy asserted that such overall control was necessary to protect the faith and moral purity of Catholic children from the dangers of secularism and modern anti-religious attitudes. By contrast, Ryan firmly believed that Irish children needed to become familiar with contemporary intellectual developments if they were to take their place in the modern world. In his retrospective account of the controversies of this period in *The Pope's green island* (1912), Ryan criticised most of the clergy for being 'afraid of new ideas'. Compared with the priests, Ryan described the bishops as being, in general, even 'more formalistic, more fearful of human nature, more remote from social and intellectual realities; more inimical to nearly all things distinctively Irish'.[54]

Besides their lack of receptivity to modern ideas, the Irish clergy had also, in Ryan's view, acquiesced in a British system of education that was designed to advance imperial designs. Ryan argued frequently in his editorials in the *Irish Peasant* that the Irish Catholic priests were not only subservient to Rome, but that Rome was concerned much more with appeasing British diplomacy than with aiding the aspirations of the Irish people for national independence. The priorities of both Rome and the British Empire were global in scope, whereas Irish problems were of merely local import. Ryan concluded that the clerical managers of Irish schools served, in effect, as instruments of the British for maintaining control over the Irish people.

---

52. *Irish Peasant*, 5 May 1906.
53. Ibid.
54. Ryan, *Pope's green island*, p. 23.

In *The Pope's green island*, Ryan charged that the Catholic clergy 'were not managers in their priestly capacity, as many had innocently imagined, but were there by virtue of English legislation'.[55] The underlying purpose of this could only be, for Ryan, to keep the Irish relatively docile politically by means of the moral strictures promoted by clerical teachers. Ryan considered it to be highly ironic that the English had mandated Rome to cultivate good morals among the people by 'putting the priest in pride of place over the schools and the teachers of our youth', while, at the same time, 'inveighing against Rome rule, and calling us a priest-ridden people'.[56] Ryan sought a larger role for lay teachers because he believed they would be both more receptive to modern ideas and more devoted to the national cause. In response to the complaints of those, like Michael Davitt, who asserted that lay teaching of religion was inadequate, Ryan maintained in a February 1906 *Peasant* editorial that the 'vital and immediate question' was not the place of Catholic instruction in the schools, but rather the nationalisation of the educational system.[57]

A campaign in opposition to these editorial positions was directed at the MacCann family, culminating in a letter from Cardinal Logue to the eldest son, John MacCann. Michael Logue (1840–1924) was the son of a Donegal innkeeper who had become bishop of Raphoe in 1879, archbishop of Armagh in 1887, and had been appointed a cardinal in 1893. Although he favoured home rule, he was not considered to be an ardent nationalist. The historian David W. Miller has contrasted him with the scholarly, politically astute archbishop of Dublin, William Walsh (1841–1921). Logue 'enjoyed waiting upon royalty, delighted in entertaining British dignitaries with champagne and oysters, and, in short, possessed none of that political sensitivity which enabled Walsh to lead the hierarchy in such a creative fashion'.[58] Despite this portrait, however, Logue was far from being completely anglicised. As a native Irish-speaker, he had always generally supported the Gaelic League.

Logue acted against the *Peasant*, according to a later account by Ryan, 'on the strength of articles which it is now understood he had not read and in regard to which he took the partial report of others'.[59] As a result of the cardinal's objections, the widow MacCann, described by Ryan as 'a pious and kindly lady', decided to shut down the paper. The final issue of the *Irish*

---

55. Ibid., p. 40.
56. Ibid., p. 41.
57. *Irish Peasant*, 10 Feb. 1906.
58. Miller, *Church, state & nation*, p. 12.
59. *Peasant and Irish Ireland*, 16 May 1908.

Peasant published under the auspices of the MacCann family appeared on 22 December 1906. Ryan rushed out a single-sheet emergency edition on 29 December with the headline: '"SUPPRESSED"??? The Campaign Against the "Irish Peasant"'. He explained that clerical interference had forced the 'suppression' of the *Peasant* in Navan and announced that publication would resume from Dublin as soon as financing could be arranged. In this emergency edition, Ryan published the letter from Cardinal Logue to John MacCann, as well as his own exchange of correspondence over the previous week with the Cardinal. The letter (dated 12 December) to MacCann read:

> My Dear Mr McCann:
>
> I find your paper, the *Irish Peasant*, is becoming a most pernicious anti-Catholic print. Its columns are open to all kinds of characters to vent their anti-clerical views. As it is published on the borders of my archdiocese, to guard the people for whom I am responsible from its poisonous influence I shall be obliged to denounce it publicly and prohibit the reading of it in this archdiocese.
>
> I am, Dear Mr McCann
>
> Yours faithfully
>
> Michael Cardinal Logue

In a letter to the cardinal dated 17 December, Ryan stated that he and his staff were all Catholics, 'loyally accepting the doctrines and teaching of the Church', and that therefore they were 'naturally pained and amazed at the charges made by your Eminence'. He requested specific instances in which the *Irish Peasant* had demonstrated that it was 'anti-Catholic'. In his initial response, Logue doubted that he had used that particular epithet, while in a subsequent letter he acknowledged that 'I suppose anti-clerical would have better expressed what I had in mind'. In his final letter on 22 December, Ryan denied that the paper was either anti-Catholic or anti-clerical, stating that 'we have stood consistently for the ideal of harmony and comradeship between clergy and laity in social and National affairs – a harmony and comradeship founded on sympathy, understanding, and due recognition of each other's rights'.[60]

On 9 February 1907, Ryan's paper began to appear from Dublin as the *Peasant and Irish Ireland*. It continued to publish under that name until the end of the following year. In October 1907, shares were offered in the Irish

---

60. Logue's letter to MacCann and the ensuing correspondence with Ryan were all published in *Irish Peasant*, 29 Dec. 1906.

Ireland Publishing Works, the company that had been formed to print the paper. The Dublin-based *Peasant* claimed, at that time, that its circulation had tripled since it had left Navan, though, even if true, the total numbers surely remained quite low.[61] In January 1909, in the interests of emphasising its national perspective over its rural origins, the name was changed to the *Irish Nation and Peasant*, and in that incarnation it continued to be published until the end of December 1910. The primary reason for its eventual failure was the inability to raise further capital to continue its subsidised existence. Whatever its name, the paper experienced, according to Ryan's subsequent account, 'an acute financial crisis about once every three months'.[62] Waters has suggested that the paper's lack of 'regular ties with any sustaining group' contributed to its uncertain finances.[63]

During his few remaining years in Ireland following the 'suppression' of the Navan-based *Peasant*, Ryan became more openly critical of the Catholic hierarchy. Under the sway of Eastern mysticism, then popular among some Dublin intellectuals, he apparently also lost his Christian faith. Ryan's contribution to the debates during 1908–9 about whether the Irish language should be made mandatory for matriculation at the new National University may serve to summarise his later views. Writing in February 1909 in the *Irish Nation and Peasant*, he re-affirmed his commitment to the language movement and took issue once again with what he regarded as the pretensions of the bishops to pronounce *ex cathedra* on social and political questions. By this time, Ryan had become totally disillusioned with the Catholic hierarchy:

> It becomes plainer every day that the saving of Ireland will have to be accomplished without the help or sympathy of the bishops. For the Irish nation as a whole, and democracy in particular, they have little friendliness and less feeling. In truth unless the Irish nation is very determined about the saving of itself, and very emphatic in the manifestation of its spirit, it must count not on sympathy but on the hostility, open or covert, of the majority of the hierarchy, all of whose appointments are political as well as religious appointments, and whose danger to nationality is that ill-informed people take their political ordering as if it were religious.[64]

As this passage indicates, Ryan had come to believe that episcopal appointments for Ireland were often motivated by a hidden political agenda. Ryan

---

61. See *Peasant and Irish Ireland*, 19 and 26 Oct. 1907. This claim, like Kenny's earlier assertion that the paper's circulation had increased five-fold under his editorship, should be treated with considerable scepticism.
62. Ryan, *Pope's green island*, p. 12.
63. Waters, p. 432.
64. *Irish Nation and Peasant*, 27 Feb. 1909.

particularly suspected Propaganda Fide, the congregation of cardinals in Rome which had ecclesiastical jurisdiction over Ireland. He had earlier charged in a *Peasant* editorial in July 1907 that, because of diplomatic pressure exerted by the British, Propaganda nominated men were 'not always the choice of the pastors of the diocese'. When bishops unsympathetic to the ideology of Irish-Ireland or the language movement were chosen, Ryan insisted that 'the English influence at Rome is at the back of it'.[65]

In making these larger claims about the subservience of the Irish church to Roman dictation on issues affecting national aspirations, however, Ryan displayed a fundamental misunderstanding of the terms of the alliance between the Irish bishops and the Parliamentary Party. As Larkin has illustrated in his volumes on the history of the church, the viability of the concordat depended on a measure of demonstrated resistance on the part of the bishops to attempted Roman interventions in Irish affairs. This had first been manifested in the independent course pursued by the Irish bishops during the plan of campaign of 1886–88 against the expressed wishes of Rome. At that time, the bishops' approach served both to maintain the devotion of the people to the church and to validate the terms of the clerical-nationalist alliance.[66]

When he became editor of the *Irish Peasant* in late 1905, W.P. Ryan was a believing Catholic, who thought there could be no possible conflict between his religious faith and his nationalist activities. By the end of the decade, his views had evolved to the point where he asserted that there was a fundamental incompatibility between the priorities of institutional catholicism and the aspirations of Irish cultural nationalism. Although Ryan's writings focused on the tensions between the clergy and lay Catholic nationalists, they also implicitly attacked Moran's linkage of catholicism with Irish identity. Moran had no qualms about incorporating the socially conservative values of the church into the mores of the nation, because he shared those values. Ryan, however, was socially progressive and eager to explore modern ideas. As a consequence, he chose to sacrifice his Catholic faith, rather than to limit his hopes for the nation. After the demise of the *Peasant* in 1910, Ryan decided to leave Ireland and resume his journalistic career in London.

In conclusion, although the relationship between the Catholic faith and the Irish nation has long stood at the centre of debates over Irish identity, the terms of that relationship have shifted over time. There have always been

---

65. *Peasant and Irish Ireland*, 27 July 1907.
66. See Larkin, *R. C. Ch., 1886–88*, pp 314–22.

inherent tensions between the universalist values of the church and a particular allegiance to the Irish nation. The tensions that arose in the 1890s and 1900s, however, were of a substantially different kind than those that had arisen earlier, for instance, between the strict teachings of the church and the secret plottings of the Fenians. By making cultural activity the focus of the national effort, the Irish-Ireland movement legitimised a closer connection between the Catholic religion and Irish identity than any that had existed previously, while at the same time it challenged the place of the institutional church in the established constitutional system. The basic problem in all the disputes that have been recounted in this essay was not so much that the Irish hierarchy opposed an independent Ireland, but that the independent Ireland they favoured was, in effect, the home rule state of the constitutional tradition, not the authentic Irish nation as conceived by the cultural nationalists.

6

On The Birth of the Modern Irish State:
The Larkin Thesis

J.J. LEE*

Many a student of Irish history will, like myself, doubtless recall the exhilarating shock on first reading that 'in the seven short years between his taking up the combined leadership of the Land League and the home rule movements in 1879 and the introduction of Gladstone's first home rule bill in 1886, Parnell created the modern Irish state'.[1] The article from which this quotation is taken, 'Church, state, and nation in modern Ireland', as subtle as it is seminal, must count as one of the most powerful analytical contributions ever made to the study of Irish history.

So pungent are the formulations that it is impossible to paraphrase without oversimplifying the argument. It is safer to cite directly, even if at some length, Larkin's own exposition, according to which Parnell, through his control of the Land League from 1879 to 1881

---

*I am grateful to the editors for their careful critique of an earlier version of this chapter. They are not to be implicated in the remaining inadequacies from which they have striven to rescue me. I am also grateful to the President's Fund of University College Cork, for financial support.

1. Emmet Larkin, 'Church, state, and nation in modern Ireland' in *A.H.R.*, lxxx, no. 5 (Dec. 1975), p. 1263. For a slightly different formulation see Emmet Larkin, *R. C. Ch. 1878–86*, xxi.

> ... successfully focused a national political consciousness by creating a genuine national grass-roots organisation that made every Catholic tenant farmer and shop keeper realise that they not only had something to defend together as farmers and shop keepers, but something to aspire to as Irishmen. Between 1882 and 1885, furthermore, Parnell structured and contained that consciousness he had focused in the Land League by creating a national and local political apparatus that gave both substance and coherence to the idea of a de facto Irish state. Through the Irish National League, which he founded in 1882 after the suppression of the Land League and which rapidly established branches in nearly every parish in Ireland, Parnell eventually made himself and his party responsible for the administration of law and the maintenance of order ... finally, in the general elections of 1885 and 1886, Parnell crystallised in his person as leader and institutionalised in the Irish Parliamentary Party the deep conviction among Irishmen that their state would soon be as legal as it was then real. The conversion of the Irish clergy in this great political revival was perhaps, after the containment of land agitation, the most significant factor in the creation of the Irish state.[2]

As a result of this accommodation between the three decisive sources of influence on Irish politics – leader, party and clergy – an accommodation originally attempted, but with only fleeting success, by O'Connell, the British state by 1886:

> ... had lost the great game it had played for so many centuries in Ireland. An Irish state had not only been created in the minds of most Irishmen, but the national and local political apparatus necessary to the functioning of that state was operative. The apparatus, moreover, was entirely in the hands of Parnell and his party. When Gladstone proceeded to give those executive, legislative, and judicial functions form in the first Home Rule Bill final notice was given that the ratification of the substance of that state by the British Parliament was really only a matter of time. After 1886, therefore, to talk about a solution to the Irish question, other than self-government, was not to face up to the realities of Irish political life.[3]

The further elaboration of the thesis lost nothing in either excitement or ambition.[4]

> Between 1878 and 1891, Parnell both created and consolidated the modern Irish state. In the creating of that state between 1879 and 1886, he structured

---

2. Larkin, 'Church, state, and nation', pp 1263–4.
3. Ibid., p. 1266.
4. Larkin, *R. C. Ch. 1888–91*, p. 289.

an effective governing consensus of Leader, Party and Bishops, which acquired a formidable de facto control in maintaining law and order in the country. This effective control was then consolidated in two distinct phases. In the first phase, between 1886 and 1888, the governing consensus was transformed from an informal working political arrangement into a constitutional system. In the second phase, between 1888 and 1891, that constitutional system was so strengthened and hardened that it survived the supreme political crisis in modern Irish history, the fall and death of Parnell. This crystallisation of a political system ... has survived virtually intact almost down to the present day ...

In addition to advancing this thesis on the birth of the modern Irish state, Larkin asserted the importance of the Parnellite accommodation for the nature of that state. In particular, he stressed the crucial role of the clergy, arguing:

... that the Irish state could not have been made stable before 1886 if the Irish clergy had not been accommodated. If the clergy, moreover, had not accepted the accommodation when it did, the character of the Irish state would have been a great deal different from what it eventually became.

In early accepting its place in the Irish state, the Church, for example, prevented that state from being eventually turned into the worst kind of autocracy by either the leader or the party.[5]

All this was tantamount to lobbing a grenade into the conventional conceptual categories with which historians of modern Ireland were accustomed to operate. The Irish historiographical tradition at the time, still largely anchored in the empiricist ideology of English historiography of inter-war vintage, had scarcely begun to contemplate the concept of the modern Irish state after 1921, much less before then. Its conceptual capacity might extend to incorporate the idea of a state within a state, but the idea of a state before a state was, for most, just stretching the imagination too far.

Even Conor Cruise O'Brien, whom no one could suspect of a deficiency of conceptual imagination, and to whose *Parnell and his party 1880–1890* Larkin pays richly deserved tribute as 'a basic book, which no scholar or student of the period can do without',[6] had not ventured so daring a hypothesis. Nor had another conceptually challenging mind among the historians who pondered the period, Nicholas Mansergh, in *The Irish question 1840–1921*.

---

5. Larkin, 'Church, state, and nation', 1266–7. For a similar formulation, see Larkin, *R. C. Ch. 1888–91*, p. 394.
6. Larkin, *R. C. Ch. 1878–86*, p. 396.

The audacity of the thesis is breathtaking. Not only does it inject the concept of the Irish state explicitly into the mainstream of Irish historical interpretation, but it purports to find that state fully formed, de facto, more than thirty years before it came into formal existence. It confidently identifies the date of conception, the date of birth, and the date of self-sustainable life. No wonder the thesis simultaneously excites and incites. It compels us to ponder our assumptions – often our silent assumptions – about what we mean when we refer to the state in Ireland, and to review systematically what we regard as essential, and what as accidental, what as enduring, and what as ephemeral, in the emergence of the polity that became the Irish Free State in 1922, and its rechristened successors in 1937 and 1949.

So concentrated is the power of Larkin's presentation that one is in danger of being swept along by the sheer momentum of the exposition. Even if one were to finally reject the entire argument – and I will express some reservations – it is clear that it has made a crucial contribution to our understanding of modern Ireland by raising the level of analysis of a crucial concept to a new plane.

The first and fundamental question concerns the issue of inevitability. There is a danger that the thesis can be interpreted as shrivelling the subsequent history of the emergence of the de jure Irish state to a footnote to the events of 1878–91. All that has happened subsequently, or so the argument could be interpreted, is largely the working out in detail of the imperatives inherent in the Parnellite creation of the de facto state. The claim that 'after 1886 ... to talk about a solution to the Irish question, other than self-government, was not to face up to the realities of Irish political life' seems to me, however, to exclude prematurely the possibility of alternative outcomes at any time between 1891 and 1921, or indeed well beyond 1921, an exclusion which makes inadequate allowance for the variety of outcomes that I believe remained possible throughout the entire period. The Larkin thesis does not, of course, imply the precise trajectory of subsequent events, but it does strongly imply the answer lay in the stars glittering in the Parnellite galaxy, however temporarily obscured by passing clouds. That is an ambitious thesis indeed.

It may be retorted that, ambitious or not, the thesis remains valid. Was not the framework firmly and finally set by 1886, and the detail only – detail? I would suggest, however, that in a period of such rapid and unpredictable flux, the detail, however closely it must be incorporated into the analytical framework, itself helped structure and shape the framework into which it has to be incorporated. I am not, in short, convinced of the inevitability of Irish self-government after 1886. A strong case can indeed be made for the likelihood of home rule, but even that would depend on the balance of probabilities at Westminster. The case for dominion status, much less a republic, seems to me far more problematical. I think it quite possible that a home rule Ireland might have, but for the development of an alternative concept of nationalism after the fall of Parnell, settled comfortably enough into the role of an imperial acolyte, not entirely unlike the Scotland of the time. Whether that would have been for better or for worse is a matter of opinion. But I do not believe it to have been at all inconceivable with its huge implications for the ethos of subsequent Irish public life. That it would not do so could not, in my opinion, have been predicted in 1886, or even 1891. While I would not wish to deny for a moment the magnitude of Parnell's achievement, or the incisiveness of Larkin's analysis, Irish history still had many futures after 1886. Much depended on timing, and timing was determined by a host of factors beyond Irish, or even British control. There are, in short, several plausible virtual histories of post-1886 Ireland.[7]

It would be intriguing to structure a series of virtual histories around not only such indigenous themes as if Parnell hadn't died in 1891, or the Easter Rising had occurred as planned, and not merely as improvised, but around such extraneous themes as if the Boer war hadn't occurred, or if Asquith had a Liberal majority in 1910, or if the First World War hadn't broken out, or hadn't broken out when it did, or if it had been over by Christmas, or if its outcome had been different, or if Lloyd George hadn't ousted Asquith, or if unionists hadn't dominated the post-war government, or if the British hadn't insisted on the oath in the Treaty negotiations, etc. etc.

Larkin, of course, knows all this. His model is sufficiently flexible to incorporate varieties of ways in which the drama could unfold. But it has to unfold to a preordained climax, even if the details of that climax remain to be determined in the future. Here we must begin delving into the detail of Larkin's concept of state and nation. Larkin is loath to define the nation in unhistorically narrow or rigid terms. But his solution, although highly ingenious, and leading to many fruitful insights, does not really answer the question. 'In order to escape the dilemma of defining the nation so broadly as to make the term virtually meaningless, I propose to define it here as that class of Irish Roman Catholic tenant farmers who since 1750 have occupied more than 30 acres. They are, in effect, the critical nation forming class.'[8]

---

7. For an interesting exercise in disciplined speculation, see Alvin Jackson, 'British Ireland: what if home rule had been enacted in 1912?' in Niall Ferguson (ed.), *Virtual history: alternatives and counter-factuals* (London, 1997), pp 175–227.
8. Larkin, 'Church, state, and nation', p. 1245.

This, illuminatingly though Larkin develops the theme, does not leave us much wiser as to what the nation is. It seems to be whatever the nation-forming class wants it to be at any given moment.

In his exhilarating iconoclastic essay, 'The Irish political tradition',[9] Larkin does indeed weave together with inimitable deftness a number of threads that go into the making of the texture of Irish political culture. But even this has less to do with nationalism than with defining 'the Irish idea of freedom'. The concept of the nation therefore remains rather elusive.[10]

Larkin's main criterion for the existence of the state, on the other hand, is quite concrete. Did it enjoy a monopoly of power – of law making and law enforcing – on a particular territory? Thus the de facto Parnellite state was a state because it enjoyed 'de facto control in maintaining law and order in the country'.[11] One question that immediately suggests itself is: what country?

Even allowing for Parnellite control of law and order over much of Ireland, Parnell certainly did not enjoy de facto control over all of Ireland. Parnellite control, whatever its level, and whatever its duration, never extended to all parts of the country. The writ of the de facto Parnellite state never ran over those parts of Ulster which had either a unionist majority, or came under unionist control.

Larkin himself recognises that control existed only 'outside of Protestant Ulster'. But where did 'Protestant Ulster' begin and end? Territory is a major constituent of the identity of any state. Boundaries matter. 'Not an inch' was to become a powerful assertion of Ulster unionist identity. And it would be the British government that determined the boundary of the Irish state, even if it did not determine it entirely in accordance with its own wishes. It purported to want a nine-county Northern Ireland. But it conceded the argument of Ulster unionists that a six-county border would allow them surer control over the Catholics within the gates. Irrespective of the decisions actually taken, or the manner in which the decisions were taken, it was the British who imposed the six county boundary in the Government of Ireland Act of 1920. The Ulster Volunteer Force and the Specials could probably have successfully defied any IRA attempts to coerce the areas of unionist majority into a united Ireland. It is much more problematical whether they could have compelled the areas of nationalist majority close to the border, running from south Down and south Armagh through much of Fermanagh

---

9. Larkin, 'The Irish political tradition' in Hachey and McCaffrey, *Perspectives*, pp 99–120.
10. For an alternative approach to this problematical issue, see the 'Introduction' to the classic study by a Larkin student, Miller, *Church, state & nation*.
11. Larkin, *R. C. Ch. 1888–91*, p. 289.

and Tyrone and up to Derry city, into a unionist-controlled Northern Ireland. It was the certainty of sufficient support from superior British power which enabled a six county border to be imposed and held.

Likewise, the various stages by which the Free State came to accept the line of partition between 1921 and 1925 reflected its recognition of the reality of superior British power. The manner in which British policy evolved, in terms not only of what it conceded, but of what it refused to concede, has to remain an integral part of any study of the emergence of the de jure Irish state. It wasn't all over, bar the rhetoric of retreat, in 1891.[12]

Far from 'the power of the British to coerce the Irish'[13] therefore ceasing in 1891, coercion or the threat of coercion, remained a trump card in the British hand, and not only in the context of defining the line of partition. The very terms of the Treaty of 1921, after all, were accepted by the Irish delegation, and by the Dáil, only under the threat of British resumption of the war. The implication of claiming that 'the power of the British to coerce the Irish' ended in 1891 is that Lloyd George was bluffing in threatening a resumption of the war in the Treaty negotiations, and that Britain would not have reverted to war if the Dáil had rejected the Treaty in January 1922. We can never know if the threat would have been implemented. But it was made, and made in the knowledge that Britain still disposed of overwhelming military force to coerce Ireland. It was invoked again when Collins and Griffith sought to smuggle a de facto republican constitution through the British monitors in May 1922.[14]

George Boyce has pithily summarised the situation in 1921. British public opinion had come to the conclusion that 'if home rule would not do, then something else must be found. But the British people were determined that any new solution must be set firmly in the British political tradition; there was no room for a republic'.[15] Of course it would not matter in the slightest what 'the British people were determined' should or should not be the case unless they possessed, or were believed to possess, superior military power to enforce their determination in the last resort. However lightly later generations would treat the alternatives of empire or republic, they loomed large for contemporaries, and the conflict between them was determined by the

---

12. For a scholarly study of the entire partition issue, see Nicholas Mansergh, *The unresolved question* (London, 1992).
13. Larkin, *R. C. Ch. 1888–91*, p. 296.
14. D.G. Boyce, *Englishmen and Irish troubles: British public opinion and the making of Irish policy 1918–22* (London, 1972), pp 174 ff.
15. Ibid., p. 14.

reality, or perception, of superior British control of military force. One cannot therefore claim that the influence of British military force in Ireland ended in 1891. On the contrary, the shadow of superior British force lay over all Irish affairs far into the twentieth century. In one sense, it still hovers over them, because it is unlikely, for all the rhetoric of peace processes, that either the boundary, or the politics, of Northern Ireland would be what they have been, or are, but for the fact that British force underpinned the Government of Ireland Act.

It is ironic that the Larkin volumes contain so little reference to Ulster unionism. Even the handful of references turn out to involve little sustained discussion of the Ulster situation, being mostly glancing allusions in the course of enquiries into other issues. References to Ulster, Belfast, Protestant, Presbyterian, Church of Ireland, Orangemen, etc. are scanty indeed. It would seem that the Larkin thesis imposes a large measure of probability, if not inevitability, not only on the emergence of the de jure Irish state, but on the emergence of the de jure Northern Ireland state, as if this too was 'only a matter of time' after 1891, or even 1886. In the event, there is a certain irony attaching to the fact that a Northern Ireland state emerged before the Irish Free State, which turned out to be the residual legatee of the Government of Ireland Act.

Unless partition, and not only partition in principle, but the actual border of 1920, be deemed to have been inherent in the de facto situation from 1886 onwards, then subsequent events obviously did significantly influence the nature of the de jure Irish state. For partition was much more than a territorial matter. It is inconceivable that the history of a thirty-two-county Ireland could have been simply that of a twenty-six-county state writ large. Whether it would have been better or worse, and for whom, is a matter of opinion. That it would have been different seems incontrovertible. It even seems possible that a Northern Ireland state with a boundary corresponding to Parnell's perception of 'Ulster' might have had significant implications for the internal history of both states, and thus possibly for their relations with each other, although this is more debatable.

The reluctance to recognise the reality of the essence of Anglo-Irish relations, which was the disparity in military power between British unionism and Irish nationalism, which pervades almost all the historiography of home rule, is curiously reminiscent of the assumptions of home rulers themselves. Redmond refused to take at anything like face value the Bismarckian resonances of the rhetoric of Bonar Law and Carson between 1912 and 1914.

Home rulers and British Liberals chose to consider the Curragh mutiny a deplorable aberration. But the rhetoric and the mutiny reflected an underlying reality, which would not simply go away because it was a bit awkward for Liberal constitutional theory. It would have been fascinating to see how the mutiny mindset would have been resolved in British political practice had the First World War not intervened.

In short, whether in determining the line of the border, or in obliging Sinn Féin to accept the oath of fidelity to the king in the Treaty negotiations, which would in turn provoke the split in Sinn Féin out of which the civil war emerged, it is difficult to accept that 'the power of the British to coerce the Irish was ended with the final consolidation of the de facto Irish state' in 1891. Of course Larkin is right to stress the growing marginalisation of military force in British policy for a generation after the fall of Parnell. But when he argues that 'when it was tried, after 1916, it only signified the last gasp of de jure British power in Ireland ... the reality of British power in Ireland had been rendered marginal by 1890, and it became increasingly marginal until 1921, when it was finally liquidated', he seems to me to press the case too far. After all, 'the last gasp' left a major mark on the future configuration of both Irish territory and Irish politics.[16] It left the south with much more of a bang than a whimper, and in so far as it left the north, including the Catholic border areas of the north, it was in circumstances which did not preclude the possibility of its return.

This almost fatalistic attitude towards the role of military power, whether in the war of independence, or in the Ulster situation, contrasts strikingly with the scholarship and skill Larkin devotes to probing the nature of the interrelationships between leader, party and bishops. Yet even here, despite the admiration, indeed the envy, one feels for the manner in which such a master of archival research can soar above the mass of detail to draw so vivid a map of the wider landscape, one may wonder how far the Parnell years do fix the mould of Irish politics in succeeding generations.

For there would be no second coming for the Parnell model of leadership. The Parnell model died with Parnell himself. Individual features of his leadership style could, of course, be replicated. But the full leadership experience, from the manner of his emergence, and the manner in which he consolidated his authority, to the manner of his fall, would never be repeated.

Larkin demonstrates with surgical skill the manner in which Parnell emerged as leader of the home rule party. But, however much he changed the

---

16. Larkin, *R. C. Ch. 1888–91*, pp 296–7.

nature of that party, he had a party whose nature he could change. Even if he transformed it into what was in many ways a new type of party, his leadership nevertheless emerged within the movement created by Butt, not outside of it, and the system he created, as Larkin perceptively insists, was strong enough to survive him.

Redmond too emerged as leader in 1900 within the parameters of the existing party system, even if he emerged from a fusion process. But he never towered above his party in the manner of Parnell, and he died as still leader, if of a disintegrating movement. The next nationally recognised leader, de Valera, achieved his eminence outside the home rule party, through the leadership of a rival party which, although nominally in existence for a dozen years, had little more than a name in common with the original Sinn Féin.

Even when Sinn Féin decisively superseded the home rule party, however, de Valera never dominated it in the manner of Parnell. His fall from national leadership, and his fall as party leader, on the Treaty issue, occurred in very different circumstances indeed from the fall of Parnell. De Valera brought it on himself through a political miscalculation, not through the eruption of his private life into the public arena. The Treaty split, however much his enemies may wish to blame him for it, is not popularly known as the de Valera split in the way that the conflict within the home rule party is known as the Parnell split.

In contrast to Parnell, de Valera was immediately superseded by a leader of comparable popular stature in Michael Collins, who came to dominate the country in the eight short but action-packed months from January to August 1922, in a manner which none of Parnell's critics had succeeded in achieving during the ten-month struggle between Committee Room 15 and his death. Whatever permutations one may choose to contemplate as the causes of the civil war, it cannot be fully, or even mainly, understood in terms of the leader versus the party. It has to be understood much more in terms of one leader versus another leader, at least as far as popular perception went.

Popular perception must be qualified in one way, however. It is true that the Sinn Féin parliamentary party was crucial on only two occasions. But they were crucial occasions, the vote on the treaty on 7 January 1922 and the vote on the presidency of the Dáil on 10 January. Four votes could have changed the result on the treaty, carried by 64–57. Two votes could have changed the presidency, carried for Griffith against de Valera by 60–58. The implications of either vote having gone the other way are almost unimaginable. Several scenarios are plausible. After the vote on the presidency, however, the pro-Treaty deputies, as a party, seem to have exerted little influence. On 14 January they rubber-stamped on the key decision that Collins rather than Griffith should become chairman of the provisional government, a decision taken apparently at very short notice by Griffith and Collins themselves.[17] But it then became just one more piece, and not necessarily the most important one, in the coalition of interests supporting the provisional government. Collins seems to have more or less taken the party for granted as he wrestled with more pressing challenges to the new regime.

It was, ironically enough, on the more militant anti-Treaty side that the party played a more prominent role, but the party was increasingly dominated by the militarist element, to the extent that de Valera found himself marginalised within anti-Treaty Sinn Féin, and could only regain some authority when the main military leaders, Rory O'Connor, Liam Mellowes and Liam Lynch were dead. Even then, de Valera never acquired a Parnell-type command of his own nominal post-split followers. As late as 1926, he still could not bring 'his' anti-Treaty Sinn Féin with him on the question of the oath, and had to split off from his own party in order to found Fianna Fáil and establish a party more loyal to his leadership. It beggars belief to conceive of Parnell having to split from the Parnellites.

Once de Valera did found Fianna Fáil, moreover, he spent a great deal of time making sure to bring his followers with him rather than adopting a high-handed attitude, however much his public persona was that of the charismatic chief. For all that he was widely revered, he sought to lead his cabinet by consensus, often by the consensus of attrition, as Brian Farrell has shown.[18] Having twice been at the centre of great splits, in 1922 and 1926, he never played with his party as imperiously as Parnell chose to do at times. However much he wrapped himself in his cloak, both literally and metaphorically, however much he might seek to cultivate a Parnellian aura of authority, even of mystery, he also made sure to stay close to the roots once he had founded Fianna Fáil. One can certainly detect similarities of personality and of style between the two leaders, but de Valera's model after 1926, especially on what *not* to do, was less Parnell than his own earlier self.

In the nature of their office, bishops were not subject to the same type of political pressure as leaders and parties. The originality and assiduity Larkin has brought to his great enterprise has made it possible to establish the

---

17. See J. Lee, 'The challenge of a Collins biography' in Gabriel Doherty and Dermot Keogh (ed.), *Michael Collins and the making of the Irish state* (Cork, 1998), p. 35. See the revealingly unrevealing reports in the *Freeman's Journal*, *Irish Independent* and *Irish Times*, 16 Jan. 1922.
18. Brian Farrell, *Chairman or chief* (Dublin, 1971), pp 26–41.

striking degree of continuity in the role of bishops once they acquired effective control over the lower clergy in the 1860s. Personalities made a difference, with Cullen, Croke, Walsh, and McQuaid having very different profiles from McCabe and Byrne. Nevertheless, while the corporate structure of the episcopacy might bend beneath the impact of powerful personalities, it did not break.[19] Potential splits were contained, and degrees of continuity sustained, through the modalities of appointment and the nature of the appointees, with the *dramatis personae* changing only gradually over time, the sense of continuity further reinforced by the remarkable longevity of so many of their lordships, one of the neglected but important continuities of Irish history. Without labouring the point, for even more striking examples can be cited elsewhere, the four archbishops in office in 1900 enjoyed reigns of twenty-one years in the case of MacEvilly of Tuam, twenty-seven years in the case of Croke of Cashel, thirty-six years in the case of Walsh of Dublin, and thirty-seven in the case of Logue of Armagh. The average tenure of the thirty-six bishops holding office in 1886 was twenty-three years.[20]

The main institutional innovation to disturb the serenity of episcopal enjoyment of office was the appointment of a papal nuncio from 1929 onwards, which caused a certain discomfiture to their Hibernian lordships, some of whom much preferred papal eyes to be exercised at a discreet distance.[21] Nevertheless, the episcopal experience was continuity personified compared with the changing fortunes of leaders and parties. However strained their relations with the politicians, or with themselves, might be at times, it was much easier for them to sustain a sense of seamless continuity in their own corporate character.

The bishops, and the clergy more generally, enjoyed immense authority. But it is important to understand the limits, as well as the nature, of that authority. Irish history is prone to be hopelessly misunderstood by interpreting it solely, or even primarily, in terms of clerical influence.

The influence of the Catholic church was virtually all-powerful in the area of sexual morality. Deviants from the idealised self-image were liable to be cruelly punished by the society, no less than by the church. Protestant Ireland was also characterised by a degree of sexual restraint that was exceptional

---

19. Larkin has traced the emergence of an episcopal corporate structure with immense assiduity and skill in his multi-volume study of the Catholic church in post-Famine Ireland. Students of the twentieth century will detect numerous resonances in the standard works of Miller, *Church, state & nation*; Whyte, *Church & state*; and Keogh, *Vatican, bishops, Irish politics*, and *Ireland & Vatican*.
20. Emmet Larkin, *R. C. Ch. 1886–88*, x–xi.
21. Keogh, *Vatican, bishops, Irish politics*, 136–8.

compared with that in many other areas of the United Kingdom, or of Europe, whether Protestant or Catholic. The Protestant marriage rate in Ireland was low by international standards, and Protestant behaviour within marriage apparently very similar to that of Catholics.[22] Only from a truly insular perspective can Protestant Ireland be deemed 'promiscuous', or 'liberal', depending on one's ideological perspective. It was as deeply marked, in its own way, as was the Catholic church, by the nature of the society in which it found itself.

The bishops also acquired, through a process which Larkin has delineated with consummate skill, controlling influence over Catholic education. Or rather, it was not so much education, as the politics of education, that the bishops came to control. Bitter though battles over the content of some individual subjects, not least history, could be,[23] the vast bulk of what was taught at every educational level would have been taught anyway, irrespective of who 'controlled' education. In the history of education, the similarities between what was taught are far more striking than the differences between who taught what. Nevertheless, given that education was a crucial arena of political conflict, episcopal success in securing substantial control in this sphere, as much against other Catholics, clerical or lay, as against a Protestant-dominated state, was one of major political significance. Outside these two areas, however, the bishops exerted little direct influence.

The Parnell split has of course been adduced as evidence to the contrary. The split certainly provides a dramatic example of direct episcopal intervention in party political conflict. But it did so, and could do so, only because the issue involved the question of sexual morality. It would be otiose to regurgitate here the details of the well-known story, which Larkin himself has probed so incisively, beyond observing that the episcopal response was a carefully calibrated one. It would have been fascinating to have seen how they would have handled the issue, in either the shorter or longer term, if the *saevo indignatio* of the nonconformist conscience hadn't snatched the initiative away from Gladstone.

Although episcopal political influence did indeed remain dominant in these two main areas in the following generation, what is striking about the next great split, the Treaty split, is how marginal episcopal influence turned out to be. However skilfully the bishops manoeuvred between 1916 and 1922

---

22. D.H. Akenson, *Small differences: Irish Catholics and Irish Protestants 1815–1922. An international perspective* (Kingston, 1988), 25–6.
23. See, for instance, G. Doherty, 'National identity and the study of Irish history' *English historical review*, cxi, (Apr., 1996), pp 441, 324–49.

to sustain their influence in their areas of prime concern,[24] they had to adapt far more to leader and party than either had to adapt to them. The bishops backed the winning side in the civil war. But it wasn't the winning side because the bishops backed it. They were effectively neutered, as they had largely been during the war of independence, the most decisive years of Irish politics in the twentieth century. The issues involved were simply deemed to lie outside their jurisdiction. Episcopal condemnation appears to have had little influence on attitudes towards political revolt, or indeed political killing. However, often such killings were condemned as murder during the war of independence, or the civil war, by the bishops, and by many priests, such denunciation seems to have had little effect on those responsible.

De Valera might be Satan incarnate in the eyes of a number of bishops. He might be demonised. But he could not be demonised as unsound on either education – he had taken care not to rock the episcopal boat on the education issue, carefully avoiding the appointment of a minister for education in his Sinn Féin cabinets – much less on sex. There was no sex in the civil war! Both sides shared the same sexual morality. It is not indeed inconceivable that in practice champions of the Treaty may have been rather more sexually active in the wrong beds than their anti-Treaty counterparts. Whatever about that, de Valera was impeccably monogamous. So indeed was Parnell – but he was monogamous with another man's wife. De Valera gave no hostage to fortune on that score. And once he was safe in that respect, episcopal denunciation mattered little in the world of *realpolitik*. The antagonists in the civil war, as in the war of independence, naturally wanted to have the bishops on their side rather than against them. But they did not conduct their policies primarily to secure episcopal sanction, however tortuous the theology with which de Valera justified his position to John Hagan at the Irish College in Rome.[25]

More generally, it is fashionable to argue that the Catholic church controlled all Irish life in the decades after independence, citing the case of censorship, or the constitution of 1937, as evidence of the allegedly credulous Catholic Irish as victims of Rome rule. The church certainly sustained its influence over the conventions of sexual morality, and over the management of schools for Catholics. Outside the two areas of sex and education, once again, episcopal thinking had little direct influence on the constitution. Of course, the mindsets of the drafters of the constitution, and the public, were

---

24. See Miller, *Church, state, & nation*.
25. Keogh, *Vatican, bishops, Irish politics*.

influenced by Catholic values. But many of those values were not explicitly Catholic values at all. On issues like property rights, or indeed church control of the management of the education of their own members, they were just as much 'Protestant' as 'Catholic' values. And even for Catholics, 'Catholic' values were influential only in those areas where the politicians and the public happened to find them congenial.

Where they did not find Catholic teaching convenient, they largely ignored it. Indeed, in virtually every other area of life, outside educational politics and sexual morality, bishops were, at least directly, either irrelevant or ineffectual, when their views deviated from those of the dominant elements in the body politic. Episcopal influence, or the lack of it, became clearer once the de jure state emerged. The de facto state did not need policies on a wide range of issues. The de jure state had to have policies in everyday areas of agriculture, trade, industry, fisheries, justice, defence, foreign affairs, to say nothing of fiscal and monetary policies. There were no episcopal policies in most of these areas. The dual purpose cow was not a regular item on episcopal agendas.

The limits of episcopal influence, as enjoyed in the post-Parnell years, were not incompatible with the ground rules identified by Larkin. For Larkin is undoubtedly right to insist on the long-term political implications of the Persico mission and the Roman decree, or rather of the handling of it by the bishops, who found themselves obliged to tell Rome where to draw the line, not only in order to protect the Vatican, but to protect themselves.[26] Nevertheless, while this provided a pointer to where the demarcation lines would be drawn in a de jure state, it did not decisively establish the limits of episcopal influence on socio-economic policy in a subsequent era of a rapidly changing role for the state, or indeed for the development of Catholic socio-economic teaching that could scarcely be visualised in the 1880s.

But even in areas on which a body of Catholic thought subsequently developed, however, the politicians simply ignored inconvenient implications. The classic case was vocationalism. The Catholic credentials of corporatism, or vocationalism, as it tended to be called in Ireland, were impeccable. Pius XI's 1931 encyclical, *Quadragesimo Anno,* sketched the ideal organisation of society according to Catholic values. Fine Gael adopted the rhetoric to some extent, little though the Cosgrave government had done to implement the vague vocational sentiments contained in the 1922 constitution during its decade in office. If Fine Gael's adoption of vocationalist rhetoric was largely a tactic with which to embarrass Fianna Fáil, de Valera was not one to allow

---

26. Larkin, *R. C. Ch. 1886–88*, especially ch. VIII.

himself to be embarrassed. He made a genuflection in the vocational direction in the 1937 constitution by making formal provision for vocational representation in his new Seanad, the weaker of the two legislative houses.[27] But he immediately devised an electoral system which made a mockery of the vocational principle and ensured complete sway to professional politicians.

De Valera would also throw a sop to church teaching by appointing a commission on vocational organisation which reported enthusiastically in favour of the idea in 1943. Although chaired by Bishop Browne of Galway, a formidable member of the hierarchy, this did not suffice to save the report from brusque dismissal by Seán Lemass, minister for supplies, and for industry and commerce, who simply brushed it aside. Neither did his episcopal dignity protect Bishop Dignan of Clonfert from an equally brusque dismissal by the relevant minister, Seán MacEntee, when he advocated a national insurance policy in 1946. In short, bishops who presumed to pronounce on topics outside sex and the political control of education, could find themselves briskly repudiated by strong ministers. Nor was this simply the unrepresentative reaction of a small number of powerful, but ideologically isolated, politicians. Vocationalism received short shrift not because of the reaction of an individual minister, but because it threatened the primacy of political parties, and of the bureaucracy. Had the Sacred Heart of Jesus and the Blessed Virgin appeared in person to them, they might have received a more respectful response than Dr Browne and Dr Dignan, but they would have returned to Paradise just as empty-handed.[28]

The occasions on which politicians choose to ignore episcopal pronouncements have been disguised by the furore over the Mother and Child Scheme involving the then minister for health, Dr Noel Browne, in 1950. This row, highly romanticised in retrospect by champions of Browne, or by anti-Catholic commentators seizing on a golden opportunity, emerged in the guise of an issue of sexual morality, whatever the real basis for it, which had much to do with medical earnings and with tensions between Browne and his own party leader Seán MacBride. What is interesting from the perspective of episcopal influence, however, is that Dr Browne's enemies had to turn it into an issue of sexual morality, knowing that this was the only safe ground for their response in going for his jugular, irrespective of the influence

---

27. Bunreacht na hÉireann (Constitution of Ireland), Art. 19.
28. J.J. Lee, *Ireland 1912–1985* (Cambridge, 1989), pp 271–7, and 'Aspects of corporatist thought in Ireland: the commission on vocational organisation 1939–43' in Art Cosgrove and Donal McCartney (ed.), *Studies in Irish history presented to R. Dudley Edwards* (Dublin, 1979), pp 324–46. Larkin rightly adverts to this issue ('Church, state and nation', pp 1274–5), but it seems to me to deserve greater emphasis in the discussion of the limits of episcopal power.

Archbishop McQuaid, Browne's chief episcopal antagonist, was presumed to enjoy. In the event, although MacBride, and the taoiseach, John A. Costello, manoeuvred Browne's resignation, the public response at the following general election was more supportive of Browne than of his party critics, for all the furore on the implications for sexual morality.[29]

Far more important as an index of the irrelevance of the church to most areas of material life than the outcome of specific clashes between church and state, was the absence of clash over most areas, particularly relating to economic policy, simply because there was no church policy in those areas. Individual bishops might pen minority reports to commissions of enquiry into particular areas of economic activity, like the banking commission of 1938, or the emigration commission of 1956, but government simply ignored them.

Larkin makes a powerful case for the vital role of his trinity of leader, party and bishops in the Parnell years. But the translation of the de facto state, to the extent that it existed, into the de jure state, involved a further crucial variable. For the military played so significant a role in the war of independence, and in the civil war, in a manner far more central than the modest physical force activity of the Parnell period, that excluding them from the analysis could not conceivably capture the reality of the 1919–23 period. Just as the role of British or unionist physical force in this period can be underestimated, so can the role of Irish nationalist physical force.

A study of the manner in which the Free State either emerged, or consolidated itself, which ignored the IRA, or the Free State army, would be a curious history indeed. Some would argue that broadly the same results would have emerged from a purely constitutional process, or through the activity of the home rule party, had it never been superseded by Sinn Féin. Apart from the highly debatable, and inevitably ideological, nature of that proposition, the fact remains that it was through Sinn Féin, through a struggle for independence against a British regime based on superior military force, and through a civil war, that the Free State emerged. And the nature of that state was itself significantly influenced by the manner of its emergence.

The Larkin model requires the co-option of the military movement into the political movement, as Parnell largely co-opted the Fenians into Parnellism in 1879–81, and again in 1891. The balance was much more finely struck in Sinn Féin-IRA relations in 1919–21.[30] It could be argued, as has already been

---

29. Lee, *Ireland*, pp 319–20.
30. Valuable studies include Charles Townshend, *Political violence in Ireland: government and resistance since 1848* (Oxford, 1983), especially chs. 7 and 8, and Joost Augusteijn, *From public defiance to guerrilla warfare: the radicalisation of the Irish Republican Army – a comparative analysis 1916–1921* (Amsterdam, 1994).

suggested, that it was the militarists on the anti-Treaty side who co-opted the politicians, more than vice-versa, in 1922–23. There was in truth a great deal of uncertainty, on both sides, in 1922 about the precise relationship of political to military, a question that only gradually began to be answered in the course of the civil war itself. On the pro-Treaty side it carried down, partly through IRB activity, to the army 'mutiny' of 1924. On the anti-Treaty side, it has carried right down to the present day through various manifestations of IRA activity which have left some mark on the southern state and a deeper one on the northern state.

The most striking feature of the 1922–23 period is the manner in which Collins, the military leader, acquired control over the political process of the provisional government, and the manner in which de Valera, the political leader, lost control to the military element on the anti-Treaty side in the spring and summer of 1922, and recovered it, in so far as he did, only in the spring of 1923, following the death of Liam Lynch. The manner in which the gun was taken out of the politics of the de jure state was very different indeed from what might have been presumed on the basis of 1879–91 experience. When Kevin O'Higgins claimed that the provisional government was merely eight young men trapped inside the city hall with the bullets flying about them, he was guilty of some rhetorical exaggeration. But it may be surmised that he would have found scant consolation in the thesis that this was merely a detail in the emergence of the de jure state from the already long existing de facto one. W.K. Hancock's tribute to W.T. Cosgrave, 'and other steadfast men who had been faithful to the Treaty, who had defied … all the romantics, living and dead, in order to achieve a new thing in Irish history, a well-ordered prosaic Irish state', came close to capturing a prevailing sense of a defining moment in Irish history.[31]

Nor should we allow inevitability to cloud our judgement about the military outcome of the civil war. If there is any one 'inevitability' which subverts historical understanding, it tends to be the assumption that the outcome of wars, both in manner and in timing, can be taken as given, and that we need mainly busy ourselves with the consequences of inevitable results. The warning is pertinent not only with regard to the First World War, but with regard to the civil war. For it was quite possible that had the anti-Treaty military leaders taken advantage of their presumed superiority in numbers immediately after the Treaty debate in January 1922, they could have staged a successful coup against the Dáil, with incalculable consequences. However

---

31. W.K. Hancock, *Country and calling* (London, 1954), p. 153.

much it means rejecting the knowledge of hindsight, it cannot be insisted too often that it was not inevitable that the Treaty forces would either win the civil war at all, or would win it as and when they did. Who knows what might then have happened, either within Ireland, or in terms of Anglo-Irish relations?

The introduction of the military element in the 1912–23 period cannot be treated simply as a marginal modification of the primacy of leader, party and bishops. Its presence in nationalist Ireland by definition affected the relations of the other three to itself. But it also affected the relations between the other three. Collins enjoyed his degree of influence during the Treaty negotiations, for instance, and in particular as chairman of the provisional government, less because he was minister for finance than because of his military reputation. Military calculations about the likely outcome of future conflict were possibly crucial in his decision to accept the Treaty, and in the decision of Richard Mulcahy, and many others, to support him. Whether these calculations were correct or not may be debated. But they certainly affected attitudes, just as the desire for peace was undoubtedly a major influence on public opinion. The civil war likewise derived at least partly from calculations about the likely outcome of a resumption of conflict with the British, and the character of that war in turn fundamentally influenced the politics of the independent Irish state for long afterwards.

Although military influences played a leading role for only a brief period, before being banished back into the wings, they significantly influenced the script of the play not only while they occupied centre stage, but for much longer, given that the careers of so many of the senior figures in the first half-century of independent Ireland derived from their participation in the military struggle, whether in 1916 or later. And it was of course a 'military influence' that left the biggest question of all behind – the 'what might have been' if Michael Collins had lived. One might of course apply the same question to some of the executed leaders of 1916, or indeed might ask what if de Valera had not lived. But the Collins case is the most relevant, given the indisputable evidence of his energy and ability. Who knows what, assuming Collins lived out his biblical span, the next forty years would have brought? Whether relations between leader, party and bishops would have been better or worse in the Ireland of Collins than in the Ireland of Cosgrave or de Valera is a subject conducive to endless speculation. But that it might have been different is certainly conceivable.

In short, it seems to me that the Sinn Féin leaders, whether de Valera, Collins, Cosgrave, Mulcahy or O'Higgins, faced a far more formidable challenge in riding the political and military horses than anything that confronted Parnell. Parnell had of course shown superb gymnastic ability, as Larkin persuasively argues, in harnessing the two tendencies. But there is really no comparison between the role of the Fenians, whether during the land war, or during the constitutional civil war that raged during the fall of Parnell, and the role of the IRA during the war of independence and the actual civil war of 1922–23. 'Quicklime in Parnell's eye' reflected the bitterness of the earlier conflict. But quicklime was still a far cry from the bullet behind Collins' ear, the assassination of Seán Hales, the retaliatory executions of 'Rory and Dick and Liam and Joe', or the horrors of Ballyseedy. It was the higher stakes being played for, not only in relation to the terms of the Treaty, but in terms of the price of defeat, that makes the civil war, rather than 'the fall and death of Parnell', at least for me, 'the supreme political crisis in modern Irish history'.

One further variable, more elusive and diffuse, must be addressed before we can be confident that we have covered the relevant factors involved in the emergence of the de jure state. Leader, party and bishops, even military to some extent, offer an example of high politics with a vengeance. But precisely because of the *popular* basis of Irish nationalism, and the success of Parnell in both broadening and harnessing popular support, it is artificial to limit our discussion to the relationships between these three or four, as if they operated in a hermetically-sealed world of their own. Of course, much high politics did operate in its own closed world. But ultimately 'high politicians' were subject to public sanction in nationalist Ireland, just as they were in Ulster unionism. This may seem a contradiction in terms in the case of the bishops, immune as they were to electoral hazards. But the bishops' political authority ultimately derived from the willingness of their flock to accept their authority.

That willingness was by no means unconditional. As we have already suggested, while it acknowledged the legitimacy of episcopal authority in given areas, it also insisted on confining that legitimacy to those particular spheres. Episcopal writ could run only as far as the votes they presumed to mobilise. It is therefore essential to integrate the role of public opinion, however defined, and however determined, into any comprehensive analysis of the creation of either the de facto or the de jure state.

Larkin himself provides intriguing hints of this. We learn that in the late 1880s, 'the agrarian wing continued to force the pace[32] – against the bishops, against Parnell, and against more than half the party'. We are told that the

---

32. Larkin, *R. C. Ch. 1888–91*, p. 290.

bishops lost out to 'the agrarian wing after Persico, even if they recovered what they then lost during the Parnell split'.[33] Parnell's own de facto control of the country, we learn, depended on the tenantry.[34] And it was this tenantry he unavailingly sought to mobilise against the party when he lost control of his own parliamentary followers.[35] Public opinion therefore seems to play a far more active role than merely providing the chorus to the three lead actors of leader, party and bishops. It is a major actor in its own right. This is crucially important for the nature of Irish politics, and for the type of southern state that was to emerge. Ironically, it is in this respect, more than any other, that a degree of continuity can be traced from the de facto to the de jure state. For it was the decision of the electors in 1890–92, and again in 1918–22, whether at general elections or at by-elections, that determined the outcome of conflicts involving leaders and parties. In the first instance, the electorate was absolutely decisive, because there was no other court of appeal. In the second instance, the anti-Treaty IRA chose to defy the electorate, and might have done so successfully with better leadership. Nevertheless, the clearest continuity of all between the Parnell split and the Treaty split was that the result was what the electorate intimated it wanted, perhaps reluctantly, but decisively. However, there was no causal connection between the two. The electorate of 1922 did not make its decisions on the basis of the precedent of 1890–91.

The linkage between 'high' and 'low' politics must therefore be explored further. A model dominated by leader, party and bishops cannot explain why the country divided the way it did during the Parnell split. What decreed that 'the Bishops and the Party', of Yeatsian formulation, together would win either the number of votes or the number of seats that they did? Why did the electorate apparently split about 2:1 against Parnell, rather than in some other ratio? Had John Dillon and William O'Brien stood with Parnell, rather than against him, would this have made a significant difference? For that matter, how susceptible was the electorate of 1922 to the appeal of different Sinn Féin leaders? Had the roles of Collins and de Valera been reversed, for instance, would this have made a significant difference to the outcome of the June election, assuming that matters had reached that stage? Or was the electorate so desperate for peace that it would have supported any agreement, virtually independently of which leader stood on which side?

The Larkin model allows for division within the home rule party, for the great split, but not for the decline and fall of the party. Yet the party did not

---

33. Ibid., p. 292.
34. Ibid., p. 291.
35. Ibid., p. 296.

vanish after 1918 because of a split. The party fell despite the continuing unity of leader and party. The problem was that the followers dwindled away. The party did not collapse from the top down, but from the bottom up. It could not hold its support. Members who abandoned the party did not proceed along the lines of a split, but to transfer to Sinn Féin, even though many may have done so to sustain the same aspirations.[36] The fact remains, however, that it was through a change of allegiance to a rival party that they now sought to achieve those aspirations. Concentrating on leader and party alone can't explain the ultimate fall of Parnell's party.

Nor does the model allow any prediction of how the Sinn Féin split on the Treaty would be reflected in the country. The Sinn Féin split was much more evenly balanced than the split in Committee Room 15, which appears to have been roughly reflected in the ratio among the electorate. In contrast, the June election of 1922 reflected a much larger majority in the country than in the party for the Treaty.

The limits on the power of leader, party and bishops were therefore set not only by relations between themselves, but by the ability, or the assumed ability, of any of them to mobilise public opinion. Larkin would have no difficulty accepting this, it seems to me, for no-one has done more than himself, in his later article on the Irish political tradition, to illuminate the role of popular opinion in the Irish political system.[37] Nor is this hindsight on his part. The final pages of his *Fall of Parnell* contain a powerful statement of this very case. But his insights in this respect do not seem to me to be integrated into his filigreed analysis at the level of high politics. They need to be meshed more closely into the model of leader, party and bishops in analysing the actual emergence of not only the de facto but the de jure state.

This assumes added importance once we turn from the issue of sovereignty – the transition from de facto to de jure statehood – to the second major issue addressed by Larkin, the nature of the de jure regime. Larkin's reflections on this vitally important topic have attracted less attention than they deserve, as readers have grappled with the boldness of his approach to the sovereignty issue. The implications deserve to be pondered at far greater depth than can be attempted here. Even though my own emphasis differs somewhat from his, Larkin has identified an issue that will not go away.

The essence of this second part of the Larkin thesis is that 'in early accepting its place in the Irish state, the church ... prevented that state from

36. The classic study is David Fitzpatrick, *Politics and Irish life 1913–1921: provincial experience of war and revolution* (Dublin, 1977).
37. Larkin, 'Irish political tradition', pp 111 ff.

being eventually turned into the worst kind of autocracy by either the leader or the party'. What saved the Irish state 'both during and after the fall and death of Parnell, from the tyranny of either the leader, the party, or even the majority was that in the last analysis the bishops had enough real power and influence in the country to resist effectively any attempt by either the party or the leader to impose their will unilaterally on the others in the consensus'.[38] As a corollary, the thesis suggests that not only did church power contribute to the emergence of a democratic rather than an autocratic state, but that it was also crucial in ensuring the stability of the new state. There can obviously be no definitive way of testing hypotheses of this type, absolutely central though they be to our understanding of Irish history. All one can do here is establish as far as possible the balance of probabilities.

In what way, then, did church influence, and especially episcopal influence, enhance the prospects of democratic stability? This could arise, presumably, only where leader and party would have been inclined to autocracy in the first place, and the system the politicians devised among themselves would have suffered from inherent instability. 'The worst kind of autocracy' seems to me somewhat of an overstatement here. Irish political culture doubtless had the potential to indulge, or foster, autocratic tendency. But by the standards of much of European political culture at the time, to say nothing of European dictatorships of the twentieth century, or indeed many third world regimes, 'the worst kind of autocracy' seems an excessively pessimistic prognosis. But let us assume the probability of this. How could the bishops – or rather the existence of an independent episcopal power base, irrespective of the intentions of the bishops themselves – have held out against these tendencies in a manner conducive to both democracy and stability? It could only have done this where the public was prepared to follow, however intense episcopal resistance to instability or autocracy might be. And we have suggested that the incontestable authority of the church was confined to quite specific areas. Important though their control of the politics of education was for providing citizens with some independent rights over and against the state, their authority did not extend into most areas of daily life.

A crucial challenge to democratic stability – the militarist mindset of the anti-Treaty activists – was crushed not by the power of the church, but by the military power of the provisional government. It can certainly be argued that the hierarchy's condemnation of the anti-Treaty forces helped legitimate the provisional government's prosecution of the civil war in the eyes of public

---

38. Larkin, 'Church, state, and nation', p. 1267. See also, Larkin, *R. C. Ch. 1878–86*, p. 396.

opinion. But I remain sceptical of the real impact of this. I am more impressed by the rise in the anti-Treaty vote in the 1923 general election than by the response to the condemnation, or even excommunication, of anti-Treaty activists. In any event, once the military issue was decided in the civil war, the key factor in the consolidation of democratic stability was the emergence of a de facto two-party system in place of the one-party system of the nationalist Ireland of Parnell's day. Conflicts concerning the power and structure of government in the de jure state, not least in the Blueshirt period of 1932–34, were fought out not mainly between church and state, but between parties and within parties, making all allowance for the varying contributions of the bureaucracy, and the judiciary. Of course church teaching on the morality of power, and on the abuse of power, influenced the views of the protagonists at all levels. But so did many other factors, including not least the entire constitutional inheritance, much of it of English provenance, as Larkin himself recognises.[39]

The formal English inheritance was not enough by itself to ensure democratic stability. What would subsequently distinguish the character of the two states that emerged on Irish soil was less the role of the Catholic church in one compared with the other, than the emergence of a working democracy in the Free State, which essentially depended on the possibility of the government being replaced by an opposition. It was the prospect of an alternative government emerging that offered the best hope of restraining the abuse of power by any government in office, much more than the strictures of the church, except in the very specific areas in which politicians either accepted church authority or shared church views. The institutions of Northern Ireland were as formally democratic as those of the south. But the north did not achieve democratic stability because of the de facto impossibility of changing the government.

The emergence of a competitive party system was probably the single most important element in establishing the de jure state as a working democracy. And it had to devise this system for itself. However closely parliamentary procedure was modelled on the Westminster example, an example made familiar by the long home rule experience in the house of commons, there were no precedents for the party system of the de jure state. Parnell's Ireland had no real competitive party system. Instead, it had in effect two parallel one-party systems, nationalist and unionist. If the systems did not exactly correspond to the line of the later border, the territories of the two party systems were clearly delimited on ethno-religious grounds.

---

39. Larkin, 'Irish political tradition', p. 115.

If one were to project this system forward, one would have had to anticipate either a united home rule Ireland with two antagonistic parties, largely mutually exclusive territorially, or, if one postulates partition of some sort, then two one-party states. For practical purposes, that was what happened in Northern Ireland during the Stormont era. There was an Irish nationalist opposition, but it was effectively neutered in power terms, and kept outside the decision-making process, with no hope of ever attaining office. Northern Ireland was de facto a one-party regime.

There is no reason why the same shouldn't have happened in the south. But it didn't. What did happen was not predictable from the experience of the 1880s, indeed was not predictable as late as December 1921. The Parnell split provided no precedent, in party political terms, for the Treaty split. Relations between winners and losers in the civil war did not develop in a manner analogous to those between Parnellites and anti-Parnellites. Had Sinn Féin followed the precedent of Parnell's party, it would have come together again as a national front, as the home rulers did in 1900, rather than sustaining the rivalry which would still, seventy-five years later, provide the main basis of party competition in the Irish Republic. The Parnell split did, as Larkin shrewdly observes, provide a learning experience in containing divisions within nationalist Ireland in an institutionalised manner. But that didn't prove sufficient to contain the differences on the Treaty within constitutional channels.

Larkin's later elaboration of his model posits the Irish Parliamentary Party (1885–1918) as a precursor, in the sense of reflecting a one-party system, of both Sinn Féin (1918–32) and Fianna Fáil (1932–86).[40] However, to me, 1918–32, and 1932–86 seem to be very different types of party systems from that of the Irish Parliamentary Party. Sinn Féin could indeed be deemed a 'one-party system' until the great split of 1922, but not subsequently. The party system of independent Ireland does not carry over from pre-Treaty Sinn Féin. Nor was the system fundamentally changed in 1932, even if Fianna Fáil superseded Cumann na nGael as the biggest party. And while it is quite true that Fianna Fáil dominated the following fifty years, the realistic prospect of a change of government existed over most of that period. Fianna Fáil has indeed been the only party with any prospect of forming a single-party government. But a one-party government is not identical with a one-party system. A one-party system is one where only one party has a prospect of power, the Northern Ireland situation, but not the southern Ireland one.

---

40. Larkin, 'Irish political tradition', p. 113.

None of that was foreordained, not even by the events of 1922–23, much less by those of 1891. A prognosticator of the likely party political system of a de jure home rule Ireland following the assumed implementation of the Third Home Rule Bill, and allowing for partition, might have anticipated a continuation of the existing structure, with a dominant single home rule party, sniped at by largely localised movements of the type that clustered around William O'Brien, or family factions of the Tim Healy variety, with a Labour Party, founded in 1912, acquiring a modest degree of support, and a 'Gaelic Ireland' party of uncertain size and influence, all offering criticism, but hardly effective opposition, given both their size and the differences among themselves. That sort of alignment did emerge in some other new independent states. An alternative, which occurred in most emerging states of eastern Europe after the First World War, was to move rapidly into multi-party systems, to the point of party anarchy.[41]

The de jure Irish state did neither. That it did not do so seems to me to owe far more to immediate short-term circumstances than to anything relating to the de facto institutional inheritance from the Parnell era.

The civil war was of course a major factor in shaping party loyalties. But the issue was more complicated than that. Even in the boiler house atmosphere of 1922 and 1923, there were distinct intimations that a substantial proportion of the Free State electorate did not feel fully at home in either of the two main Treaty parties. In the 1922 election, Labour secured 21.1 per cent of the valid poll. Other parties, mainly farmers, as well as a sprinkling of independents, won 18.3 per cent of the vote. In the next election, August 1923, three months after the end of the civil war, the combined vote for Labour and 'other' came to more than 30 per cent of the total. That election is even more notable, however, for the fact that the anti-Treaty party held its percentage share, and substantially increased its absolute vote. At a time when everything seemed to conspire to marginalise the anti-Treaty party – decisive defeat in the civil war, episcopal condemnation, a degree of repression that made electioneering virtually impossible – the vote of the anti-Treaty party increased almost as much as the pro-Treaty vote, by 155,000 compared with 164,000. Anti-Treaty Sinn Féin had spectacularly not gone away, much to the chagrin, and surprise, of the victorious Free Staters. The 1923 election was decisive in the sense that it ensured that nationalist Ireland would have at least two main nationalist parties, and not simply drift overwhelmingly to the side of the victors of the civil war. Victory in that war turned out to be far more decisive militarily than politically.

---

41. Lee, *Ireland*, p. 80.

It might indeed seem that the impressive performance of Fianna Fáil after de Valera split from Sinn Féin in 1926, at the first subsequent general election of June 1927, definitely consolidated the party system around the Treaty issue. Nevertheless, it can also be argued that the most striking feature of this election was that, despite the intensity of the rivalry, to put it mildly, between the two civil war parties, they garnered between them only 54 per cent of the total vote, compared with nearly 67 per cent in 1923. Nearly half the electorate seemed to be trying to break away from the straitjacket of the Treaty inheritance. Three months later, however, in the September 1927 election, nearly 75 per cent now rallied to the Treaty parties, on an almost evenly-divided basis. It was now, and only now, that they established their dominance of the party system. The significant shift over so short a period in 1927 must presumably be attributed to the fears and feelings aroused by the assassination of Kevin O'Higgins in July, which drove voters one way or the other towards the two Treaty parties.

These two parties managed to increase their share of the vote until the 1943 election, when they won 85 per cent of the total between them. It would take us beyond our brief to follow subsequent party fortunes. But it is not going beyond our brief to stress that the party system remained in a state of fluidity, with the outcome uncertain, until at least 1927. The system that then emerged bore little relation to the party system of Parnell's day, or to the manner in which Parnell's party divided, or reunited, between 1890 and 1900.

The point of this litany of election results is to stress how much the party system of the de jure state arose directly from the circumstances of the time, none of which were inevitable, and many of whose consequences were unexpected, even in the very short term. The political culture, in the broadest sense, was certainly conducive to the idea of party and of the central roles of parliament and of party, and in this respect the Parnellite inheritance was indubitably important. But the leaders and parties of the de jure state had to work extremely hard, and without any guiding model, on creating a party system conducive to both democracy and stability in the unprecedented circumstances in which they found themselves. The Catholic church in general had little direct influence on the outcome, however supportive of stability the advice of individual clergy might be on particular issues. No doubt, the values associated with the Catholic concept of the state themselves influenced political opinion and behaviour. But that influence expressed itself in a diffuse and general way, rather than through the explicit and direct political role of the episcopacy.

The Larkin thesis then, for all the daring of the conceptualisation, for all the searing insights, seems to me to imprison the Irish future after Parnell in too restrictive a grid because it was all 'only a matter of time'[42] until the essentially inescapable consequences of the manner in which Parnell had 'focussed, crystallised and institutionalised' Irish politics worked themselves out.

I prefer to think that the essential lesson of Larkin's riveting analysis of the seismic decade of 1879–91 is that nothing was predictable. For who could have anticipated in 1879 the extraordinary events of the next twelve years? Certainly not the Mayo tenant farmers who crowded into Westport on 8 June to see and hear this strange aristocratic apparition from the other side of the island warning them to keep a firm grip on their homesteads. And certainly not Parnell himself. For what the Parnell years illustrate most of all is the power of personality. It is truly ironic that the conclusion drawn from so probing and perceptive an exploration of the role of personality is the almost impersonal 'inevitability' of the direction of subsequent developments.

The Parnell years opened up a wider range of possibilities for the future than could have been dreamed of in 1879. But which of these possibilities would be realised, and indeed what further possibilities would emerge from them, only time would tell. But time telling was not the same as 'only a matter of time'. For the succeeding generations would make their own history, strongly influenced, but not determined, by the legacy of Parnell. By analysing that legacy with great originality and insight, based on superb scholarship, Larkin renders an enduring service to Irish historiography.

Perhaps my main reservation derives more from temperament than scholarship. Larkin's model is not of course a rigidly determinist one. It allows for the play of the contingent and the unforeseen in influencing the detail of subsequent developments. But it is not, I hope, a misrepresentation to suggest that Larkin considers the direction of development, if not the detail, to be determined by 1891, whereas I'm inclined to see the contingent as influencing not only the detail, but the direction, of later events. This must, of course, remain a matter of opinion. Conscious though I am that this rapid overview has done nothing like full justice to the sweep and the majesty of Larkin's vision, I hope it does suggest that the inferences can, and should, be endlessly debated, the highest tribute that can be paid to the fertility of so invigorating a contribution to our historical understanding.

---

42. Larkin, 'Church, state, and nation', p. 1266.

7

Mass attendance in Ireland in 1834

DAVID W. MILLER

ARGUABLY, EMMET LARKIN'S MOST INFLUENTIAL CONTRIBUTION has been his 1972 'devotional revolution' thesis that Paul Cardinal Cullen presided over the making of 'practising Catholics of the Irish people in a generation'.[1] I well remember him discussing his early speculations on this matter when, as a doctoral student in about 1966, I showed him some of the church attendance figures in Fullarton's *Parliamentary gazetteer of Ireland* (1846), which I had been consulting simply to locate some parishes in Connaught. The low figures for many parishes which had piqued my interest became grist for a mill which was clearly already in operation as Larkin puzzled over the discrepancies between the almost universal fulfilment of canonical obligations in mid twentieth-century Catholic Ireland and evidence which he had been encountering of quite a different pattern in the early nineteenth century. A few years later, after finishing my dissertation, I did some preliminary work on the mass attendance data which the Fullarton gazetteer had reproduced from an 1835 blue book, the *First report of the commissioners of public instruction, Ireland*.[2] Larkin alluded to my unpublished findings in his

---

1. Emmet Larkin, 'The devotional revolution in Ireland, 1850–75' in *A.H.R.*, lxxvii, no. 3 (June 1972), p. 650.
2. H.C. 1835, xxxiii.

1972 article.[3] It was not until after I had completed my first book, however, that I found time to complete the analysis which resulted in my own 1975 article,[4] and which, by demonstrating that regular mass attendance was very uneven in pre-Famine Ireland, provided quantitative support for Larkin's thesis. In recent years, I have returned to these data with the benefit of more modern technology.

How and why the data were gathered

The Public Instruction Commission was an initiative undertaken in 1834 by a Whig government flushed with victory over the forces of reaction in the Irish Church Act of the previous year. To gain ammunition for further attacks upon the privileged position of the Protestant established Church of Ireland, Lord John Russell, paymaster-general, and E.J. Littleton (afterwards Lord Hatherton), chief secretary for Ireland, persuaded their cabinet colleagues to appoint a commission whose primary purpose would be 'to ascertain the proportion of Protestants and Roman Catholics in each parish in Ireland'.[5] One of the commissioners, the redoubtable reformer George Cornewall Lewis, quipped to a friend late in the year that for the past six months he had been in Dublin, 'demolishing the Church. Our proper style', he continued, 'is the Public *Instruction* Commission, which the friends of the Church in this country changed into Public *Destruction* Commission. It is a mere statistical inquiry, and proceeds very satisfactorily, but, as you say, proves only what everybody knows. Nevertheless it is something to establish disagreeable truths beyond the power of contradiction'. Richard Whately, the Protestant archbishop of Dublin and an independent liberal in politics, Lewis reported, 'is supposed to have said that the clergy had been long revelling in the Book of *Job*, but that now they were forced to take a spell in the Book of *Numbers*'.[6]

Lewis and his twenty-three fellow commissioners were charged with collecting certain information for each parish, including the number of Church of Ireland members, Roman Catholics, Presbyterians and other Protestant Dissenters, the 'periods at which Divine Service is performed' in each place

---

3. Larkin, 'Devotional revolution', p. 636.
4. D.W. Miller, 'Irish catholicism and the Great Famine' in *Journal of Social History*, ix, no. 1 (fall, 1975), pp 81–98.
5. Edward John Littleton, first Lord Hatherton, *Memoir and correspondence relating to political occurrences in June and July 1834*, ed. Henry Reeve (London, 1872), p. 8.
6. *Letters of the right hon. Sir George Cornewall Lewis, bart., to various friends*, ed. Rev. Sir Gilbert Frankland Lewis, Bart. (London, 1870). pp 38–9.

of worship, and 'the average number of persons usually attending the Service in each, and ... generally whether those numbers have been for the last five years increasing, stationary, or diminishing'.[7] To carry out this charge the commissioners, insofar as practicable, retained the same enumerators who had conducted the 1831 census, supplied them with copies of their own manuscript returns and directed them to ascertain the religion of each person returned. Questionnaires were sent to each clergyman asking for information on the various points in the commissioners' terms of reference, and encouraging him to conduct a census of his own. When the enumerator had completed his entries, his returns were made available for public inspection for a period of fourteen days, after which one or more of the commissioners would visit the locality to conduct a public inquiry.

In cases where there was no challenge to the enumerator's return, the commissioners generally projected his numbers forward from 1831 to 1834 on the sensible assumption that each denomination had continued to grow at the same rate that the whole population of the parish had grown between 1821 and 1831. In many cases, however, other adjustments were made on the strength of local censuses and other evidence received upon oath. Probably few of the inquiries were as contentious as that in Newport-Pratt, County Mayo, where the commissioners found themselves adjudicating an argument between the parish priest and the rector by sending the enumerator out to enquire of a certain Mrs Gordon whether she wished to be enumerated among the 12,000 Catholics or the 500 members of the established church.[8] However, the commissioners certainly took advantage of the adversarial character of the proceedings to try to obtain a reasonably accurate account of denominational affiliation.

Adversarial proceedings were also possible in the determination of church attendance. W.D. Killen, the Presbyterian historian who in 1834 was minister of Raphoe, County Donegal, alleged that attendance figures in his parish were obtained by a Catholic official actually counting the worshippers and that the Catholic priest was given advance notice and took steps to have an especially full attendance while Killen was kept in the dark until the official arrived in his meeting-house. In response to Killen's objection the commissioner 'asked the priest if he was prepared to swear that his return presented a fair average of his attendance. He demurred to make this

---

7. *First report*, iii–iv. They were also charged with obtaining certain information about clergy and about schools.
8. *Hansard*, 3rd ser., xxviii (Lords, 26 May 1835), pp 131–5.

deposition, and in the end the commissioner reduced this estimate considerably'.[9] The procedure recounted by Killen, however, seems to have been atypical: most of the attendance data in the report are given as round figures; few appear to be the result of actual head counts. The commissioners' main priority was to obtain accurate affiliation data, and they probably tended to accept the word of each clergyman as to the attendance in his own facility.

Interpreting the data

In addition to a number of minor anomalies, the data present several major difficulties to the student of religious practice.

1. While the attendance data were collected for each place of worship, the affiliation data were collected for the parishes of the established church. Problems arise, for example, in the case of many parishes which contained no Catholic chapel, and where it is not obvious from the Report how to allocate the Catholic population to nearby chapels.
2. For chapels which had more than one mass on Sundays the total attendance at all masses is sometimes unclear. The commissioners were instructed to report the attendance at the principal service and to use their own judgement as to whether to include information about attendance at other services.
3. For many chapels the entry under 'Periods at which Divine Service is performed' is 'On Sundays', or 'Every Sunday' or simply 'Sundays', and the number of services on each Sunday is not made explicit.
4. Neither the population returns nor the attendance figures draw any distinction between those required by canon law to attend mass each Sunday on the one hand, and children, the infirm and persons living at such a distance from a chapel that they may have been excused from this canonical obligation on the other.

In my 1975 article I dealt with each of these difficulties to the best of my ability given the means then at my disposal. To address the first difficulty I chose as the units for my analysis groups of adjacent parishes large enough to avoid major errors resulting from Catholics crossing Protestant parish boundaries to attend mass. To deal with difficulties 2 and 3 I generally avoided choosing areas having many entries with these ambiguities and I expressed the attendance rates which I reported as ranges from the lowest to the highest

---

9. W.D. Killen, *Reminiscences of a long life* (London, 1901), p. 75.

values which might reasonably be calculated from the raw data. I handled difficulty 4 by simply warning that the rates which I was reporting – mass attendance as a percent of Catholic population – were not comparable to the rates reported by investigators of current religious practice who have access to individual-level data.

Despite the limitations which were imposed by the four major difficulties, I was able to show that mass attendance in Ireland varied considerably – from nearly 100 per cent of Catholic population in certain towns and prosperous eastern rural areas to 30 per cent or even less in certain western districts. These findings were presented, however, in the form of a very crude and 'lumpy' map. Not only was this an unsatisfactory form of data visualisation, but the numeric findings for some twenty-three study areas were in no sense a random sample suitable to serve as observations in a more sophisticated statistical analysis. In the two decades since my original treatment of the problem the technology for addressing such problems has advanced considerably, and I have returned to it with the benefit of such advances and with the objective of remedying the deficiencies in the 1975 treatment of the problem. The present article offers substantially better data visualisation; I intend to carry out appropriate statistical analysis in a subsequent article.

Difficulty 1 was reconceptualised in terms familiar to the users of geographic information systems, which reduce spatial realities to three types of objects: points, lines and areas. The Commissioners' data characterise two different types of objects: points (the locations of Catholic chapels for which attendance data were collected) and areas (the Protestant parishes for which population data by religious affiliation were collected). When the problem was considered in these terms a solution suggested itself. All 2164 chapels at which mass was regularly celebrated in 1834 were located on a map. Where there was more than one chapel in a town they were grouped together and treated as a single mass location. A geometric construction known as a Voronoi tesselation of the points representing to the resulting 2049 mass locations was created (Figure 7.1). Each of the polygons in the tesselation (a 'catchment') corresponds to one mass location and includes all the territory which is closer to that location than to any other mass location. This map was overlaid on a map of Protestant parishes (Figure 7.2), and area of each fragment of territory resulting from the intersection of these two systems was calculated. The Catholic population of each catchment was then estimated by first assigning the Catholic population of each major town to the catchment of which it was the centre, and then allocating the rural Catholic

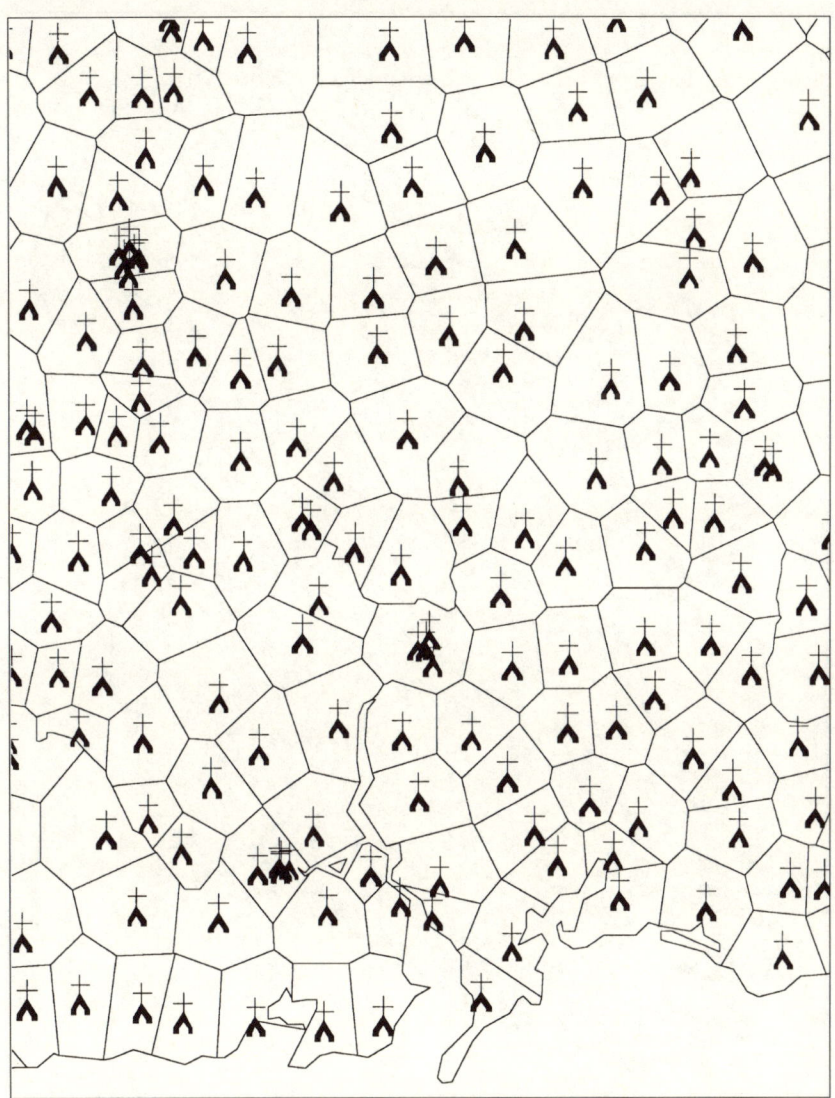

Figure 7.1
Example of Voronoi tesselation of mass locations

population of each parish according to the proportion of its land area falling in different catchments. This procedure meant that each of 2049 mass locations (as opposed to twenty-three study areas in the 1975 study) was potentially a valid observation for data visualisation and statistical analysis.

Figure 7.2
Civil (i.e. Church of Ireland) parishes, c. 1834

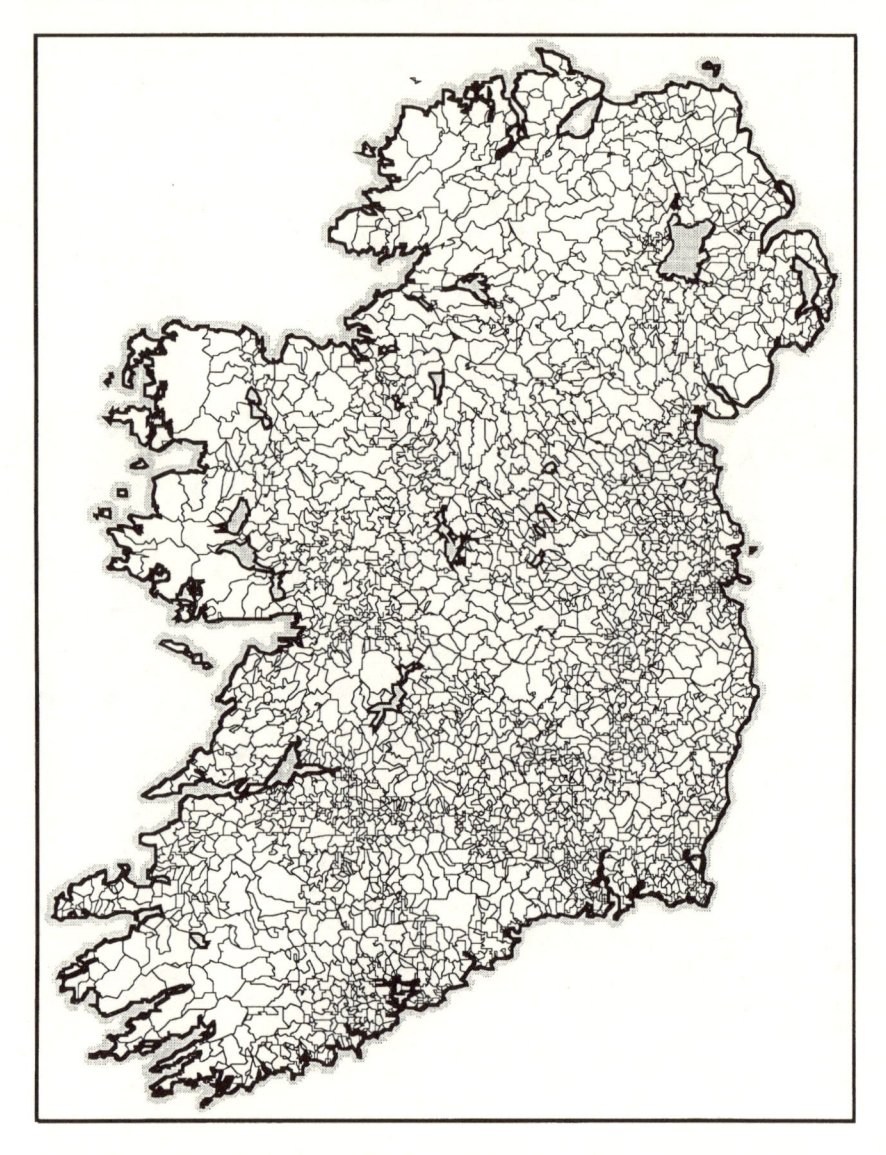

Table 7.1
Frequency of Sunday masses at Roman Catholic chapels, 1834

	ALL CHAPELS	TOWN CHAPELS	COUNTRY CHAPELS
Once	1027	21	1006
Twice	394	20	374
3 times	70	36	34
4 times	11	9	2
5 times	8	6	2
6 times	5	5	0
7 times	4	4	0
8 times	1	1	0
10 times	2	2	0
11 times	5	5	0
12 times	3	3	0
TOTAL with regular unambiguous frequency	1530	112	1418
AMBIGUOUS: 'Every Sunday', 'Each Sunday', 'On Sundays', 'Sundays'	500	6	494
MISCELLANEOUS: average of more than one service per Sunday	27	8	19
MISCELLANEOUS: average of less than one service per Sunday	45	0	45
MISSING DATA, frequency not stated and other missing data problems	62	2	60
TOTAL	2164	128	2036

To address difficulties 2 and 3 I considered the frequency of Sunday masses at the 2164 chapels. Table 7.1 summarises the stated frequency of Sunday masses at Catholic chapels as reported by the commissioners. How should we treat the chapels (nearly one-quarter of the total) with frequencies like 'Every Sunday' which, to escape difficulty 3, I mostly avoided using in my 1975

Figure 7.3
Major categories of ambiguous reporting of Sunday mass frequently in Catholic places of worship

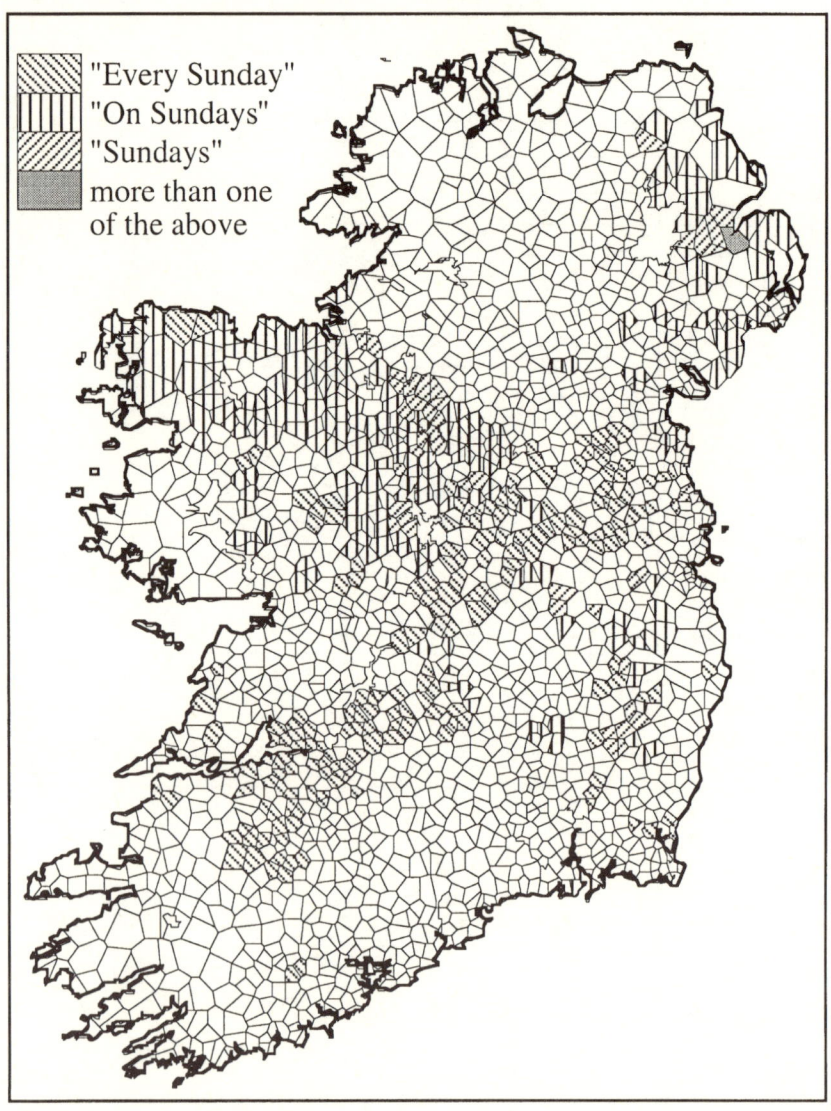

analysis? It turns out (Figure 7.3) that these seemingly ambiguous returns were highly concentrated in certain parts of the country and appear to reflect the scribal idiosyncrasies of one or more commissioners (or clerks) in recording the findings of the local inquiries. Did they reflect actual imprecision of the respondents over how many services were held on Sunday, or were they merely a shorthand way of writing 'Once each Sunday'? To answer that question I focused on the data for country chapels, since few of the ambiguous entries were for town chapels, but town chapels were substantially more likely to hold multiple services (only twenty-one out of 112, or 19 per cent, of town chapels held only one mass each Sunday, compared to 1006 out of 1418, or 71 per cent of country chapels). I also took advantage of the fact that in six of the thirty-two dioceses there were no ambiguous reports of Sunday frequency.[10] Table 7.2 rearranges the data in the final column of Table 7.1 (omitting the sixty cases with missing data problems). It treats the forty-five miscellaneous responses such as 'Alternate Sundays' as single mass reports and the contrasting twenty miscellaneous responses like 'Twice every Sunday in summer, once in winter' as reports of multiple masses.

How should the 494 ambiguous cases be redistributed between the single mass and multiple mass cells of their row? The group of twenty-six dioceses contains a substantially higher percentage of multiple-mass chapels (23 per cent) than does the group of six dioceses with no ambiguous reporting (14 per cent), and the twenty-six-diocese group shows a strikingly smaller percentage of single-mass chapels (48 per cent) than does the six-diocese group (86 per cent). It seems unlikely that the number of multiple-mass chapels in the twenty-six-diocese group is understated, or that we will go far wrong by reclassifying all 494 seemingly ambiguous cases as single-mass chapels. Accordingly I am treating the 500 reports of mass 'Every Sunday', 'On Sundays', etc. as meaning 'Once every Sunday'. For all single-mass chapels the stated attendance figure is used as the numerator of the attendance rate. In cases in which the attendance is given as a range (e.g. 'From 600 to 700' or '1200 in summer, 900 in winter') the midpoint of the range is used. Figures given as the upper or lower limit of an implicit range are adjusted by 5 per cent in the appropriate direction: 'Nearly 1000' would be treated as 950, 'Upwards of 1000' as 1050.

---

10. Lismore, Ross, Derry, Kilmore, Raphoe and Kilmacduagh.

DAVID W. MILLER

Table 7.2
Rural Catholic chapels by frequency of Sunday masses and by dioceses with and without reporting ambiguities

	ONE MASS PER SUNDAY	TWO OR MORE MASSES PER SUNDAY	AMBIGUOUS SUNDAY FREQUENCY	TOTAL
6 dioceses with no ambiguous reports of Sunday mass frequency	243 86%	41 14%	0 0%	284 100%
26 dioceses with at least one ambiguous report of Sunday mass frequency	808 48%	390 23%	494 29%	1692 100%
All dioceses	1051 53%	431 22%	494 25%	1976 100%

The problem of how to handle the cases in which multiple services are specified (difficulty 2) is more complicated. There is no problem, of course, where a single figure or range is given and explicitly described as the attendance for all the services or where the attendance is enumerated separately for each service (e.g. '500 at each service' or '500 at the first mass, 750 at the second, 1000 at the third'). Where a single figure or range is given and there is no explicit indication of its meaning, I begin with the hypothesis that the commissioners were following their instructions and recording average attendance at the 'principal' service. But how does that translate into total attendance at all services? Fortunately, for sixty-five of the 394 chapels with two Sunday services attendance is given separately for each service. Taking the service with the larger attendance to be the 'principal' one, the average principal service in these sixty-five cases had 62.84 per cent (standard deviation = 10.22 per cent) of the total attendance at both services. Similarly there were twelve chapels with three Sunday services whose attendance is listed separately. Attendance at principal services in these twelve chapels averaged 48.82 per cent (standard deviation = 11.02 per cent) of total attendance.

Mass Attendance in Ireland in 1834

For chapels with attendance given as a single figure (or range) for two services and no evidence in the return that the figure was a total for both masses, attendance was first estimated by dividing the figure by .6284. A provisional attendance rate was then calculated by dividing by the Catholic population of the catchment. If that rate did not exceed 140 per cent I used the estimate; otherwise I surmised that the commissioners had reported aggregate attendance without labelling it as such and I treated the reported figure as a total for both masses. The same procedure was followed with three-mass chapels, using a divisor of .4882.

Table 7.3
Summary of data recoding procedure by catchments

Catchments containing only chapels with straightforward reports of frequency and attendance	1137
Catchments containing chapels whose returns include ambiguities like 'On Sundays' which are easily resolved	487
Catchments containing two-mass and three-mass chapels whose total attendance was estimated on the assumption that the return is for the principal mass	270
Catchments with two-mass and three-mass chapels for which above assumption was rejected for leading to unrealistically high attendance rate	40
Catchments containing at least one chapel for which the investigator made an ad hoc inference concerning attendance	30
Catchments excluded from present analysis because of missing data problems or other data uncertainties	85
Total catchments	2049

A number of special problems arise in larger towns, which might have several chapels, each with multiple services. There seemed no sensible way to extend the rules for two-mass and three-mass chapels to those with more than three services. Inspection of cases with four or more separately reported services in major towns suggests that the pattern of a single principal service with more attendance than the others was not so marked in large towns, where a sequence of masses, each of which filled the chapel to capacity, was common. In a few town chapels it seemed obvious that the commissioners had made the error of reporting aggregate attendance without labelling it as such, but the presence of several chapels in one catchment confounded the use of such procedures as outlined above for automatically detecting such problems in two-mass and three-mass chapels. In some cases an anomaly in only one of several chapels – missing figures, for example, for a single nunnery chapel which obviously had small but not zero attendance – complicated the task of reporting an attendance rate for the whole town. Various anomalies and omissions in reports on country chapels were handled simply by excluding them from consideration. However, since the 1975 study established that towns might well have a very different pattern of mass attendance from the surrounding countryside, some heroic measures to salvage as many towns as possible for inclusion in our data visualisation seemed warranted.

Accordingly, I inspected a number of returns from town chapels (and from the country chapels with more than three services) and made some *ad hoc* judgements as to what the data probably meant. One guideline which I followed was based on the fact that the maximum number explicitly reported as the attendance for a single service anywhere in Ireland was 5000. Few Catholic chapels anywhere in Ireland would have accommodated 5000, and while there were certainly reports in this period of large numbers of mass-goers kneeling on the ground outside country and small town chapels, I am dubious that such spectacles occurred regularly in the crowded streets of major towns where sufficient masses were being said to serve the entire Catholic population in a more orderly fashion. In cases where attendance greater than 5000 was reported for a multiple-mass urban chapel I typically treated the report as reflecting total attendance rather than principal service attendance.[11]

Table 7.3 summarises the way in which the 2049 catchments, which are the units on which the data-visualisation will be based, were treated in the processes just described.

As for difficulty 4, I remain unrepentant over my decision in 1975 to report attendance rates as a percentage of Catholic population rather than of those canonically required to attend mass. As I indicated at that time, there

---

11. There are several towns for which I am not yet satisfied that I have correctly interpreted the data. Limerick is an especially problematic case in which it is difficult to apply consistent logic to the various chapel returns and get a plausible total attendance figure. My least defensible ad hoc judgement concerns the main chapel in Dundalk which had three Sunday services and for which the attendance was reported as follows: 'The number is not known; it is very large.' For the purpose of this exercise I assigned this chapel a total attendance of 11,000 – tantamount to a 100% attendance rate, which is indeed comparable to the experience of the neighbouring town of Drogheda. While I believe this action is justifiable for data-visualisation purposes, it would be hard to defend in any analysis carried out for rigorous hypothesis-testing.

is no reason to suppose that any children who did attend were excluded from the attendance estimates which form the numerator of the rates, so it would be erroneous to try to exclude them from the denominator. Patrick Corish argues that the rates which I reported in 1975 should be increased by one-fifth, citing the 1836 *Catholic Directory*, which enjoins mothers 'not to disturb the congregation by bringing children under the age required'.[12] But surely this rule appeared in what was the first edition of the *Catholic Directory*, and in a few subsequent editions, precisely to stamp out a practice which very much existed. It would, in any event have been a nonsensical instruction for Catholic mothers who were served by the 1500 chapels which had only one mass per Sunday: what were they supposed to do with their infants and toddlers? Leave them with the rector's wife? And we need only to reflect on the contretemps in Raphoe reported by Killen to realise that any such children who turned up in either Catholic or Protestant churches would certainly have been included in the estimates which their respective clergy reported to the commissioners.

More to the point, I am trying to construct a set of defensible entries into regression analyses. To adjust all of them by some percentage would only add noise to the data, complicating the problem of assessing the meaning of ambiguous multiple-service reports. I am interested in the behaviour of Catholics in this life, not their candidacy for eternal bliss in the next.

Visualising the data in space

Now the purpose of all this data preparation has been to enable us to get an overall picture of mass attendance in pre-Famine Ireland. Figure 7.4, a choropleth map showing the mass attendance rate in each catchment for which the data was judged usable, is not a really satisfactory way of visualising general patterns in the data, but it does make clear what we can and cannot expect to learn from this evidence. Often there are extreme variations between attendance rates for adjacent catchments, and in some cases attendance appears to exceed 100 per cent. These anomalies reflect the process by which the data were gathered as well as any failures of the Voronoi tesselation to capture actual contemporary walking patterns. In general, the data are not very helpful in trying to determine the level of religious practice among those served by any one chapel in isolation. However, the data can be quite useful in enabling us to see larger patterns of religious practice over the country as

---

12. *The Irish Catholic experience: a historical survey* (Dublin, 1985), p. 167.

a whole if we visualise them through a method which allows random errors in individual observations to cancel one another out.

Figure 7.5 is a contour map constructed by such a method from the same data as Figure 7.4. The data, however, were 'smoothed'. For each mass location having a usable attendance estimate, the attendance figures and Catholic

Figure 7.4
Choropleth map of estimated mass attendance as percent of Catholic population, 1834

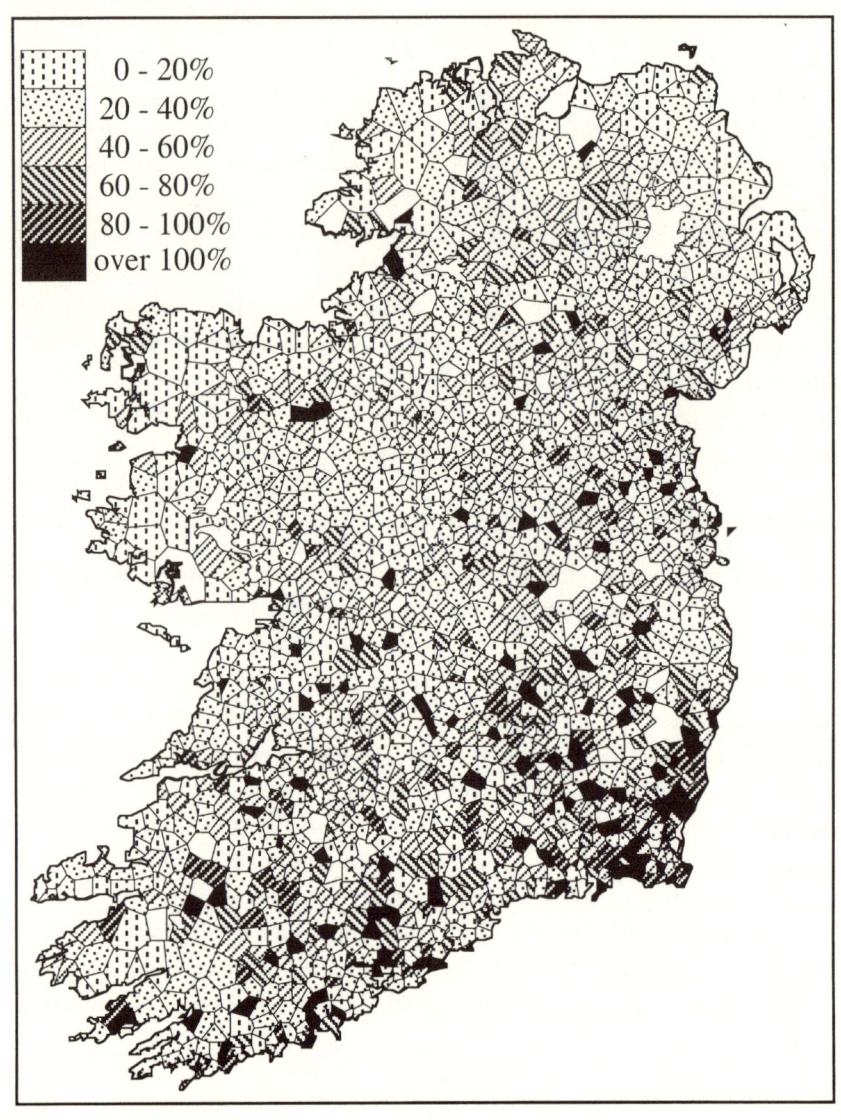

Mass Attendance in Ireland in 1834

Figure 7.5
Contour map of estimated mass attendance as percent of Catholic population, 1834

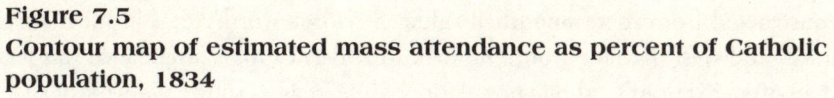

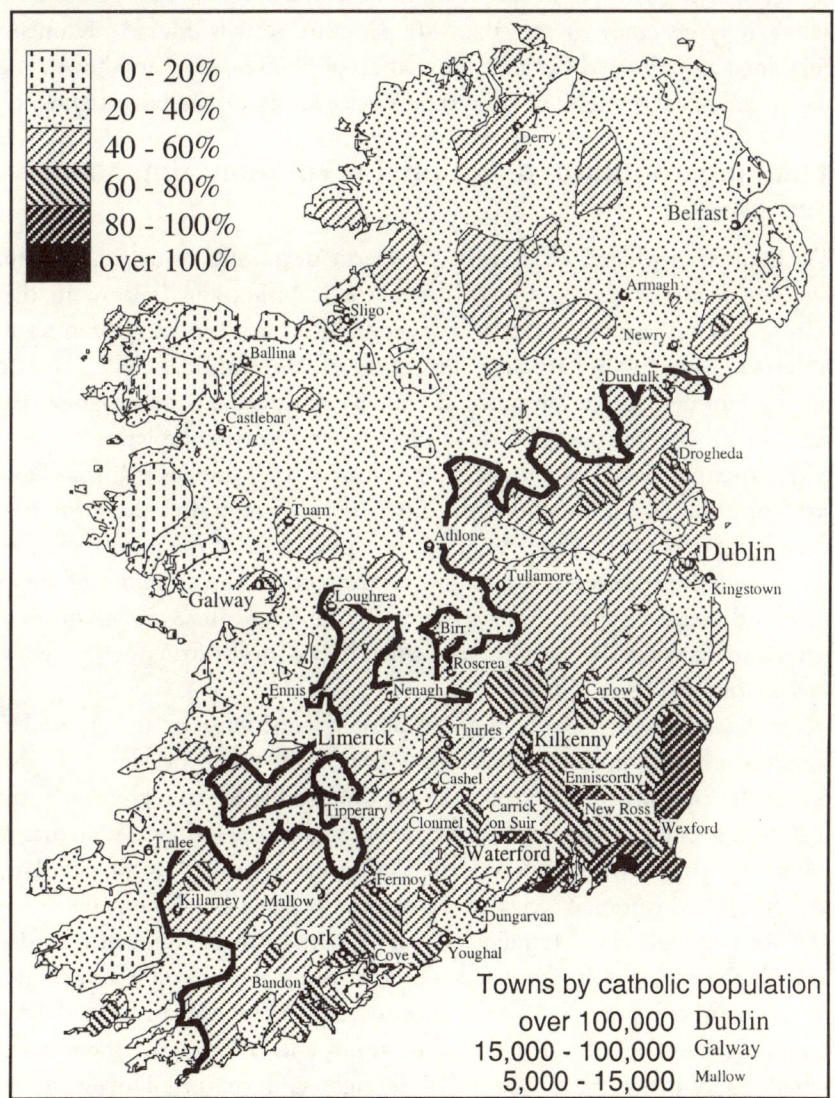

populations for that catchment and its neighbours were aggregated. A smoothed attendance rate was calculated from these aggregated totals. (Neighbouring catchments which appeared to lack convenient pedestrian routes to the mass location in question, e.g. because of unbridged major rivers or mountainous terrain, were excluded from this calculation.) Figure 7.5 is

173

constructed from these smoothed values. It is noteworthy that in most areas north and west of a line from Dundalk to Killarney mass attendance was less than 40 per cent of Catholic population while in areas south and west of such a line it is generally greater than 40 per cent. Towns whose catchments contained an estimated Catholic population of 5000 or more are shown, and they sometimes (though not always) produce a local peak in mass attendance.

Thinking about the devotional revolution: time, space and class

The context in which Larkin coined the term 'devotional revolution' was his life-long study of the politics of the Catholic bishops in Ireland. In that setting it is not surprising that he conceptualised his subject largely in terms of human agency – in particular the agency of Paul Cardinal Cullen. We do not have to deny the importance of Cullen's achievements to recognise that for a fuller understanding of these matters we should complement agency with structure. To be sure, the term 'revolution' itself implies that *time* has a structure: things are somehow fundamentally different after the revolution from what they were before. To grasp the significance of the information we are considering, however, we should also attend to the structure of time's partner dimension, space. Furthermore, we should of course pay attention to what historians usually have in mind when they contrast structure to agency: social structure.

Significantly, some of the most important contributions to our understanding of the devotional revolution have been made by someone professionally committed to thinking about time and space simultaneously, the historical geographer Kevin Whelan. It is therefore reassuring to note that in Figure 7.5 southern Leinster, which Whelan has identified as the heartland of Catholic institutional revival at the end of the penal era,[13] shows up clearly as a zone of high mass attendance. More generally, mass attendance tended to be higher in areas of Norman settlement, which were also the hinterlands of the southern ports in which dispossessed Catholic gentry could keep economically afloat through the penal times and be ready to support the rebuilding of the church at the end of the eighteenth century. This entire line of explanation for the situation in the mid nineteenth century stresses the working out in space of the Catholic community's political defeat two centuries earlier in time.

---

13. 'The regional impact of Irish catholicism, 1700–1850' in W.J. Smyth and Kevin Whelan (ed.), *Common ground: essays on the historical geography of Ireland: presented to T. Jones Hughes* (Cork, 1988), pp 253–76.

Another approach to understanding the 1834 mass attendance data was suggested some years ago by Eugene Hynes,[14] who argued that lax mass attendance was essentially a behaviour of the underclass of cottiers and labourers who loomed so large in pre-Famine Irish social structure. The devotional revolution, he suggested, was primarily a result of the elimination of this class by the Famine and subsequent emigration, leaving better-off farmers who were already regular mass attendees to dominate religious practice in post-Famine Ireland. One need only compare Figure 7.5 with Figure 7.6, which maps the percentage of families in 1841 classified as 'chiefly dependent on their own manual labour' (which the census operationalised in rural areas by the holding of less than five acres) to see that Hynes' hypothesis deserves serious attention. This line of argument stresses the working out of Ireland's peculiar history of class formation in the eighteenth and nineteenth centuries, which shows up in the spatial distribution of lax mass attendance on the eve of one large class's destruction.

Another line of explanation favoured by a number of scholars stresses the obstacles to regular mass attendance – long walking distances, bad roads, etc. A recent example of this reasoning is to be found in the examination of the public instruction commission data by Ambrose Macaulay in his excellent biography of Archbishop Crolly.[15] Certainly mass-going is a spatio-temporal phenomenon not only because we can map it in space and chart its rise and fall over time but also because at the most fundamental level, like many religious rituals, it entails a journey through space repeated at certain intervals of time. Now here it would be helpful to reflect upon the spatial structure of Ireland over a very long span of time.

One aspect of a country's spatial structure is a set of hierarchies of locations or 'centres' defining a commercial landscape, a military or administrative landscape, a sacred landscape and perhaps others. We should not expect the different landscapes to correspond exactly – in the nineteenth century Tuam, being the seat of an archbishop, was much more important in the sacred landscape of Ireland than in the commercial landscape within which it was a very minor market town. However, in the long run the most dynamic landscape can affect the shape of the others.

Now consider the landscape of Ireland over the course of the present millennium. A thousand or more years ago Ireland had both a military and a sacred landscape defined by centres on the high places which are still

---

14. 'The great hunger and Irish catholicism', *Societas*, viii, no. 2, (Spring 1978), p. 145.
15. *William Crolly, archbishop of Armagh, 1835–49* (Blackrock, 1994), pp 114–20.

Figure 7.6
Percent of families 'chiefly dependent on their own manual labour', 1841

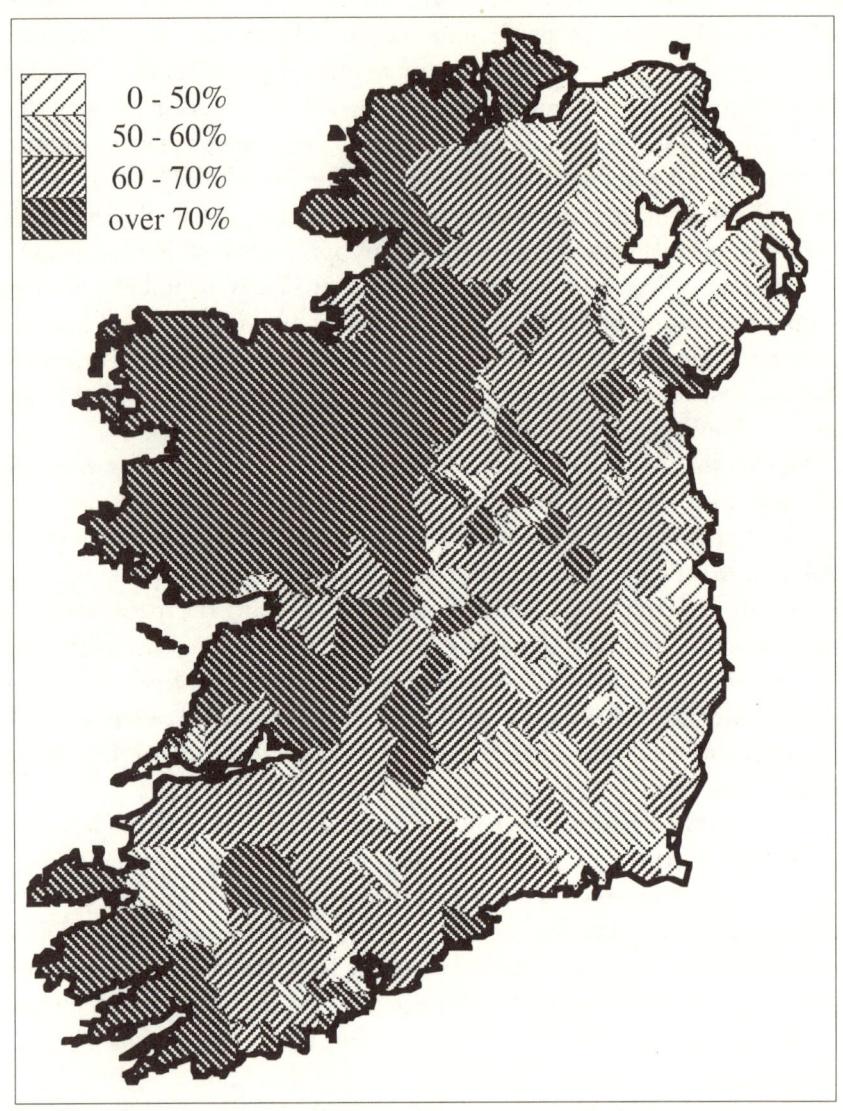

0 - 50%
50 - 60%
60 - 70%
over 70%

crowned today with cairns and other remains – including Cashel, Tara and many others. Nowadays, however, space in Ireland is structured predominantly by a hierarchy of commercial towns which tend to be located in lowland sites, either coastal or riverine, and the sacred landscape tends to conform much more to this modern commercial landscape than to its ancient sacred counterpart. Thus we can speak of a physical inversion of the landscape occurring during the millennium; a landscape structured around upland centres was supplanted by one focused on lowland centres.

Both ways of organising the space of Ireland coexisted from the late middle ages to the nineteenth century. We can understand how they could coexist when we see how each is related to time as an organising factor in people's lives. The new lowland-centred landscape is associated with weekly, or sometimes even daily, movement to and from markets; the older upland-focused landscape depends upon movement which is seasonal or annual or even less frequent. The fair, a phenomenon which is less frequent than weekly, but more than semi-annual, probably represents an intermediate stage, as suggested by some intriguing examples which Máire MacNeill reports of Celtic Lughnasa celebrations moving from upland to lowland sites to accommodate trading.[16]

In my 1975 article I did devote some attention to Celtic festivals like Lughnasa and to other extra-canonical rituals, such as patterns, wakes, bonfires, and celebrations at holy wells. I interpreted them as functional alternatives to canonical Catholic practice. Insofar as they were seasonal, I saw them as surviving because they functioned as a kind of predictive magic which may have allayed anxiety over potential harvest failure. The undeniable failure of such magic in several successive years of massive harvest failure in the 1840s, I argued, rendered the older non-canonical system dysfunctional and opened the way for the triumph of canonical practice which functioned to address other critical problems in an era in which physical starvation rapidly declined as a real threat.

While I still think it useful to reflect on the functions which alternative ritual systems may have performed, I now think that the most salient difference between the canonical and non-canonical system was spatial. Many of the older practices, such as pilgrimages, festivals and patterns, were associated with the old landscape in which the routine movement of persons in earlier centuries had typically been seasonal, for example, in the form of transhumance – i.e. semi-annual migration with herds between lowland and upland pastures. The regular discharge of canonical obligations is associated with the newer landscape of market towns in which routine movement to and from market proceeds on a weekly or even daily basis.

---

16. Máire MacNeill, *The festival of Lughnasa: a study of the survival of the Celtic festival of the beginning of harvest* (London, 1962), pp 287–9.

While some towns in Figure 7.5 had markedly higher mass attendance rates than the surrounding countryside, this tendency is not nearly so pronounced as I would have expected from my 1975 work. More notable is the disproportionate number of towns in the zone of higher attendance generally. What this may suggest is that indeed the development of a commercial central-place system may have fostered habits of routine movement to and from local towns (including many towns too small to be shown on Figure 7.5) consistent with massgoing as a regular behaviour. Of course the sparsity of towns in Ulster in Figure 7.5 results not from any underdevelopment of an urban hierarchy there but from the dominance of the town populations by Protestants, but this may also reflect some lack of participation by Catholics in the kinds of routine movement which go with both consumerism and massgoing.

So to return to Larkin's provocative claim, certainly there were many practising Catholics in Ireland in 1834, and equally there were many more lax participants in canonical rituals than would be the case by the mid twentieth century. Without question something dramatic happened in the aggregate to Catholic religious practice after 1834; how much of it happened during the primacy of Paul Cullen remains difficult to establish. But if we cannot with certainty establish the exact timing of the change, we can at least speculate about its meaning. Patrick Corish argues whatever low rates of mass attendance were reported in 1834 represented 'a deterioration over the previous fifty years'.[17] There are no data remotely comparable in comprehensiveness for the eighteenth century on which to base such a claim. Nevertheless, it is not preposterous to suggest that the growth of the agrarian underclass in that period had been difficult for the church to keep up with. It does not, however, follow that if we had comparable data for, say, 1784, they would show higher rates of mass attendance. During the century or so before the Famine there were some factors working in favour of more regular mass attendance – the growth of a market economy (which made massgoing an intelligible part of life's routine for middling farmers) and the recovery of a Catholic elite from the effects of the penal laws. There was also a massive change in the class structure which worked in the other direction. It may well be that regular massgoing and the conscious choice not to go to mass regularly were both new behaviours.

If we cannot answer with certainty all the questions about variation in religious practice over time, the preparation of the data reported in this

---

17. Corish, *Irish Catholic experience*, p. 167.

article makes it possible now at least to analyse the variation in mass attendance in 1834 itself. Many of the explanatory variables which have been suggested – the church's resources, class structure, walking distances – are quantifiable, and important hypotheses about the meaning of the evidence now become testable. To that task I now intend to turn.

8

The New Reformation Movement in the Church of Ireland, 1801-29

STEWART J. BROWN

A call to arms

ON 24 OCTOBER 1822, WILLIAM MAGEE, the newly appointed Protestant archbishop of Dublin, gave out his first charge to the clergy of his archdiocese in Dublin's St Patrick's Cathedral. He opened with references to the widespread attacks being made upon the clergy of the established church in Ireland. 'Irreligion, and false religion, abound', he observed, 'We have fallen on evil days, and evil tongues'. In one sense, he maintained, the attacks on the clergy of the establishment were unwarranted. Recent years had brought significant improvements in clerical discipline, residency and pastoral commitment; indeed, 'at no time within the memory of any now living, has the Established clergy, as a Body, been less deserving of reproach than at present'. In another sense, however, the clergy deserved criticism. They had, Magee believed, been too conciliatory, too anxious to maintain cordial relations with other churches, and not sufficiently zealous in their responsibilities as ministers of the one true church in Ireland. The time had now come for the established clergy to throw aside the cloak of compromise and accommodation and proclaim the truth to all those sunk in religious error.

They must boldly denounce the claims of both Roman Catholics on the one side and of Presbyterian Dissenters on the other:

> We, my Revd Brethren, are placed in a station, in which we are hemmed in by two opposite descriptions of professing Christians: the one, possessing a Church, without what *we* can properly call a Religion; and the other possessing a religion, without what *we* can properly call a Church: the one so blindly enslaved to a supposed infallible Ecclesiastical authority, as not to seek in the Word of God a reason for the faith they profess; the other, so confident in the infallibility of their individual judgement as to the reasons of their faith, that they deem it their duty to resist all authority in matters of religion.[1]

The clergy of the establishment must recover a sense of responsibility for the religious and moral instruction of the whole nation. They must continue working for an improved pastoral ministry. But more than that, they must adopt a more militant spirit, and strive to bring the entire Irish population into conformity with the church as by law established.

Magee's charge raised a storm of protest. Here was a leading figure in the hierarchy, one of the new bishops in the established church, openly renouncing the spirit of religious conciliation which had prevailed among leaders in the three major churches in Ireland for the past half century. His remarks seemed all the more deliberately provocative, coming, as they did, at a time of intensifying religious and political strife, when agricultural distress was fuelling violent anti-tithe agitation in Munster, and when growing demands for Catholic emancipation were contributing to confrontations between Orangemen and Catholics in Ulster. Although Magee had denounced both Presbyterians and Catholics, his charge gave most offence to Catholics. 'The Catholics have a Church, without a Religion!', thundered the liberal *Dublin Evening Post*, 'We do not remember any thing so thoroughly offensive to the people of Ireland … Such a charge, coming from such a man, must strike home, wound deeply, and rankle long'.[2] Catholic leaders, including James Doyle, bishop of Kildare and Leighlin, and Dr John MacHale of Maynooth College, rushed forward to answer Magee's attack.[3] When on 6 November a severed calf's head was thrown upon the altar of a Catholic chapel in Ardee, Patrick Curtis, the Catholic archbishop of Armagh, insisted in a public letter

---

1. William Magee, *A Charge delivered at his primary visitation, in St Patrick's Cathedral, Dublin, on Thursday, the 27th of October, 1822* (London, 1822), pp 13, 17, 25–6.
2. *Dublin Evening Post*, 29 Oct. 1822.
3. W.J. Fitzpatrick, *Life, times and correspondence of the Rt. Rev. Dr. Doyle, bishop of Kildare and Leighlin* (2 vols., Boston, 1869), i, 214–30; *Letters of John MacHale, archbishop of Tuam* (Dublin, 1893), pp 121–37.

that Magee's charge had incited the outrage.⁴ Magee became a hated figure among Catholics – so much so that he soon feared to leave his residence without being armed.⁵

Magee's charge of 1822 was an important expression of a movement in the established church in Ireland which would soon be called the 'new reformation' or 'second reformation' – a movement which aimed at succeeding where the sixteenth-century Reformation had failed. Magee expressed the growing mood of confidence in the established church in Ireland of the 1820s, a mood associated with increased levels of state support and a new religious zeal growing out of both the evangelical and high church revivals in anglicanism. In the years leading up to the watershed of Catholic emancipation in 1829, church leaders in both Ireland and England embraced the hope that the large majority of the Irish population could be brought into conformity with the Protestant establishment. This would, they trusted, not only benefit the cause of religious truth, but also help to integrate the Irish population into the British state. Recent work by Jonathan Clark, Linda Colley and others has drawn attention to the central importance of protestantism in shaping a British identity during the eighteenth and early nineteenth century. A shared belief that Providence guided the destinies of the British state, a commitment to the union of church and state, and a perception of Roman catholicism as the main threat to traditional British liberties had contributed significantly to the consolidation of the British state.⁶ The reformation movement in the Irish establishment in the first decades of the nineteenth century represented an attempt to integrate the Irish Catholic population into the British Protestant state, consolidating the Union of 1801 on the basis of common religious beliefs and values. Nor was this an unrealistic goal. The seminal work of Emmet Larkin on the 'devotional revolution' in Ireland has highlighted weaknesses in the institutional Roman Catholic church in early nineteenth-century Ireland.⁷ Suffering from a shortage of priests and nuns, a lack of church and school buildings, and serious problems of discipline among the clergy, the Catholic population seemed ready for a sustained missionary effort on the part of the Protestant establishment. At the same time, the established church in Ireland was being strengthened. The Union of 1801

---

4. *Dublin Evening Post*, 12, 16, 21 Nov. 1822.
5. W. Magee to J. Jebb, 29 May 1824, (Trinity College, Dublin, Jebb Papers, Ms 6396–7/196).
6. J.C.D. Clark, *English society 1688–1832* (Cambridge, 1985), ch. 4; L. Colley, *Britons: forging the nation 1707–1837* (London, 1992), especially ch. 1; Robert Hole, *Pulpits, politics and public order in England 1760–1832* (Cambridge, 1989), especially chs. 2, 13.
7. Emmet Larkin, 'The devotional revolution in Ireland, 1850–75' in *A.H.R.*, lxxvii, no. 3 (June 1972), esp. pp 625–39.

had joined the established churches of England and Ireland into a single religious establishment which in theory could draw upon the resources of the united parliamentary state in the work of achieving uniformity of belief and purpose among all the peoples of the Atlantic archipelago. The Protestant crusade in nineteenth-century Ireland has been ably explored in two important books by Desmond Bowen, and in a superb doctoral thesis by Irene Whelan, while David Hempton and Myrtle Hill have provided a broad survey of evangelical protestantism in Ulster.[8] The emphasis in these works, however, has been on Protestant proselytising activity in general, rather than the campaign to secure the conformity of the Irish people specifically to the established church as an agency for the consolidation of a Protestant United Kingdom. This essay will explore the 'new reformation' campaign of the first three decades of the nineteenth century as an effort to extend the influence and authority of the established church over Ireland's Catholic majority. The campaign was directed primarily at the Catholic population and did not directly seek conformity from Protestant Dissenters. The reformation movement in the established church as an exercise in cultural transformation and state building has been largely neglected, in part because the campaign was soundly defeated in the later 1820s, not least by the success of Daniel O'Connell's Catholic Association in mobilising Catholic communities in defence of their traditional faith.[9] The reformation campaign also revealed that those Catholic communities had a far more defined sense of their religious identity than leaders of the established church had imagined.[10] Yet for a brief period in the mid 1820s, there seemed a real possibility that the established church might finally achieve the ascendancy over the religious, moral and intellectual life of Ireland that had eluded it since the Reformation.

The United Church of England and Ireland, 1801–24

The failure of the Reformation to take hold in sixteenth-century Ireland has been the subject of lively debate in recent years, a debate which has suggested

---

8. Desmond Bowen, *Souperism: myth or reality? A study of Catholics and Protestants during the Great Famine* (Cork, 1970); Desmond Bowen, *The Protestant crusade in Ireland 1800–70* (Dublin, 1978); I.M. Whelan, 'Evangelical religion and the polarization of Protestant-Catholic relations in Ireland, 1780–1840', (University of Wisconsin-Madison Ph.D. dissertation, 1994); David Hempton and Myrtle Hill, *Evangelical protestantism in Ulster society 1740–1890* (London, 1992).
9. An argument advanced with great skill by Oliver MacDonagh, 'The politicisation of the Irish Catholic bishops, 1800–1850', *Historical Journal*, xviii, no. 1 (Jan. 1975), pp 37–53.
10. Emmet Larkin has recently explored the role of the Irish custom of stations in strengthening Irish Catholic identity in an important, and as yet unpublished paper on 'The rise and fall of stations in Ireland, 1750–1850'.

that there was nothing inevitable about the failure or the later connection of catholicism and Irish national identity.[11] Various reasons have been suggested for the limited impact of the Reformation in sixteenth-century Ireland – the divisions between the proponents of persuasion and of coercion during the crucial first decades of the Reformation, the frustrations of key elements of the Old English community in Ireland which felt neglected and undervalued by the Tudor state and therefore proved open to Counter-reformation missions, the paucity of resources available to the Irish Protestant establishment as a result of appropriations of church lands by the landed gentry and aristocracy. By the early seventeenth century, as the Protestant establishment finally gained control over a portion of the patrimony of the medieval church, it had developed an exclusionist mentality, restricting its ministry largely to the English settlers, those who might be regarded as among the 'elect' in a predestinarian theology, while leaving the Old English and Gaelic populations to traditional Catholic religion or counter-reformation missionaries, and the Lowland Scottish settlers in Ulster to Presbyterian Dissent.[12] The sixteenth-century Reformation had demonstrated the futility of attempting to impose a state reformation on a country in which there was not firm state control.

A second opportunity to extend the influence of the state reformation in Ireland had come in the aftermath of the revolution of 1688 and the defeat of the Jacobite military forces in 1691. For perhaps the first time, the London-based monarchical state exercised political control over the whole of Ireland, making the achievement of religious conformity a realistic goal. The Irish parliament embraced a policy of coercion, enacting the penal laws which subjected the non-conformist population, especially the Irish Catholics, to severe civil disabilities. Among these were the proscription of Catholic education, resulting in widespread illiteracy among the lower social orders. Such coercive measures might have proved effective, had they been accompanied by persuasive measures – that is, by decided efforts on the part of the established church to evangelise among the Catholic Gaelic and Old English

---

11. Brendan Bradshaw, 'Sword, word and strategy in the Reformation in Ireland' in *Historical Journal*, xxi, no. 3 (1978), pp 475–502; Nicholas Canny, 'Why the Reformation failed in Ireland: *une question mal posée*' in *Journal of Ecclesiastical History*, xxx, no. 4 (Oct. 1979), pp 423–50; Nicholas Canny, 'The formation of the Irish mind: religion, politics and Gaelic Irish literature' in *Past and Present*, no. 95 (May 1982), pp 91–116; Karl Bottigheimer, 'The failure of the Reformation in Ireland: *une question bien posée*' in *Journal of Ecclesiastical History*, xxxvi, no. 2 (Apr. 1985), pp 196–207; S.G. Ellis, 'Economic problems of the church: why the Reformation failed in Ireland' ibid., xli, no. 2 (Apr. 1990), pp 239–65. I am grateful to my colleague at the University of Edinburgh, Dr Jane Dawson, for these references.
12. Bradshaw, 'Sword, word and strategy in the Reformation in Ireland', p. 502.

population. Despite a few sporadic efforts, however, no sustained effort was made to expand the religious and educational influence of the established church. This was in part because the strong Jacobite sentiments among the high church group in the Irish establishment raised suspicions among the triumphant Irish Whigs.[13] Further, many Protestant landowners feared that a strengthened, missionary establishment would seek to reclaim the whole patrimony of the pre-Reformation church, including tithes and properties that had been appropriated by the landed classes.[14] This concern would fuel anti-clericalism among the landed classes throughout the eighteenth century.[15] The established church in Ireland thus remained the church of the Protestant minority, a church subordinate to the landed classes and at the same time dependent on tithes which imposed a heavy burden on probably the poorest peasantry in western Europe. In the 1770s, the Irish parliament, under pressure from the British imperial state, began a process of granting Irish Catholics relief from the penal laws. This reflected both the growing spirit of religious toleration associated with the enlightenment and the need of the empire for a loyal Irish population from which many would be willing to be recruited into the armed forces.[16] By the mid 1790s, Catholics had been granted relief from virtually all the penal laws relating to the leasing and ownership of land. Catholics, moreover, could hold many Crown offices, and those meeting the property requirements, including the large number of 40s freeholders in county electorates, had been given the right to vote in parliamentary elections. New liberal and radical groups emerged, calling for full emancipation of Catholics from the remaining political disabilities and the equality of all religious denominations under the law. By now, only about 10 per cent of the Irish population adhered to the established church. Its weakness was demonstrated by the unseemly haste with which many Protestant clergy fled from their parishes at the first reports of the rising in 1798.[17]

---

13. S.J. Connolly, 'Reformers and highflyers: the post-revolution church' in A. Ford, J. McGuire and K. Milne (ed.), *As by law established: the Church of Ireland since the Reformation* (Dublin, 1995), pp 152–63.
14. Thomas Bartlett, *The fall and rise of the Irish Nation: the Catholic question 1690–1830* (Dublin, 1992), pp 25–9; [S. O'Sullivan], 'Modern reformation in Ireland', *Blackwood's Magazine*, xxvi (July 1829), pp 85–6.
15. Edward Brynn, *The Church of Ireland in the age of Catholic emancipation* (New York, 1982), pp 18–20, 27–8. There is evidence that some Protestant landlords in Munster supported the violent anti-tithe campaign of the Rightboys, an agrarian secret society, during the later 1780s. See Jacqueline Hill, 'The meaning and significance of "Protestant ascendancy", 1781–1840' in *Ireland after the Union: proceedings of the second joint meeting of the Royal Irish Academy and the British Academy* (London, 1986), p. 6.
16. Bartlett, *Fall and rise*, pp 66–81.
17. Edward Brynn, 'Some repercussions of the Act of Union on the Church of Ireland, 1801–1820', *Church History*, lx, no.3 (Sept. 1971), p. 289.

The third major opportunity for a successful state reformation – and the subject of this essay – came in the aftermath of the parliamentary Union of Great Britain and Ireland in 1801. The Act of Union greatly strengthened the situation of the established church in Ireland by uniting it with the established Church of England to form a single united church of England and Ireland. It transformed the Protestant establishment in Ireland from being the church of a small minority in Ireland into the church of the majority in the United Kingdom. Further, it shifted responsibility for maintaining the Irish establishment from an Irish parliament of landowners who were largely adverse to strengthening clerical influence to a British parliament that was becoming increasingly supportive of the religious establishment as a bulwark against social unrest and political radicalism.[18] A few years after the passing of the Union, in 1807, a royal commission on the state of the Irish church revealed a scandalous state of affairs – including dilapidated churches and widespread clerical non-residence and pluralism. In the south and west, whole Protestant congregations had disappeared and many Protestant families had gone over to the Catholic church as a result of years of neglect by the established clergy. Rather than acquiesce in the manifest failures of the Irish church, the parliamentary state took steps to reform and strengthen the Irish establishment, treating it as a vital national institution which would have to be preserved.[19] This new commitment to the establishment in Ireland corresponded with similar efforts to reform the established church in England.[20]

The major thrust of the government's reform programme was to strengthen the parish system, including the improvement of clerical residency and pastoral work in the approximately 2500 parishes of the Irish establishment. After 1808, parliament began providing interest-free loans for building and repairing glebe houses and parish churches. Grants for these purposes averaged £10,000 per year in 1808 and 1809, £60,000 per year in 1810–16, and £30,000 per year in 1817–21.[21] Although much of this money was wasted or diverted to personal uses by unscrupulous clerics, there was also substantial construction. The number of glebe houses increased from 295 in 1800 to 768 in 1829; during the same period, 697 churches were built or

---

18. Brynn, *Church of Ireland*, pp 29–30; D.H. Akenson, *The Church of Ireland: ecclesiastical reform and revolution, 1800–1885* (New Haven, CT, 1971), pp 72–3. For the increased support for the establishment in England after the 1790s see especially G.F.A. Best, *Temporal pillars: Queen Anne's bounty, the ecclesiastical commissioners, and the Church of England* (Cambridge, 1964), pp 137–84.
19. Brynn, 'Some repercussions'.
20. Best, *Temporal pillars*, pp 213–38; W. Gibson, *Church, state and society, 1760–1850* (London, 1994), pp 32–6.
21. Akenson, *Church of Ireland*, pp 117–8.

enlarged.²² In 1808 and in 1824, parliament passed acts on clerical residence, which greatly strengthened the powers of bishops in enforcing residence on the clergy in their dioceses. The result of the bishops' new powers and the state investment in building glebe houses was a steady improvement in clerical residence. While in 1806 only 46.4 per cent of the clergy of the Irish establishment resided in their parishes, by 1819 this had increased to 65.2 per cent and by 1832 to 74.8 per cent. There was also a dramatic increase in the number of clergy, from 1253 in 1806 to 1977 in 1826, which allowed for a steady reduction in clerical pluralism.²³ Clerical discipline was improved through closer episcopal supervision. The Act of Union allowed only four Irish bishops to sit in the house of lords, which meant that most Irish bishops now resided more regularly in their dioceses. The office of rural dean was revived in the Irish establishment to improve diocesan administration, and by 1820, sixteen out of twenty-two dioceses had rural deans, with an average of six rural deans per diocese. Changes in the Irish bench in the early 1820s brought consecrations of new men of talent and energy, including Richard Laurence to the see of Cashel, John Jebb to Limerick, J.G. Beresford to Armagh and William Magee to Dublin.²⁴ The established church also began to take more seriously its educational responsibilities. The acts of the Irish parliament of 1537 and 1695 requiring the establishment of parish schools had been largely ignored, and such parish schools as existed in the eighteenth century were often poorly housed and staffed. After 1800, however, there was a steady increase in the numbers of parish schools, from 361 in 1788 to 549 in 1810 and 782 in 1823, while the numbers attending parish schools more than tripled during this period, from 11,000 in 1788 to 36,000 in 1823.²⁵ After 1800, moreover, parliament began making substantial grants to the Association for Discountenancing Vice and Promoting the Practice of the Christian Religion, which existed to encourage the development of schools in connection with the established church.²⁶

Contributing to the improved discipline and pastoral care within the established church in Ireland was a new commitment among the clergy, associated with the two early nineteenth-century movements to revive anglicanism

---

22. Ibid., p. 119; Brynn, *Church of Ireland*, pp 127–35; H. Newland, *An apology for the established church in Ireland* (Dublin, 1829), p. 155.
23. Akenson, *Church of Ireland*, pp 127–9.
24. Ibid., pp 131–2; Brynn, *Church of Ireland*, pp 77–81.
25. Akenson, *Church of Ireland*, p. 137.
26. D.H. Akenson, *The Irish education experiment: the national system of education in the nineteenth century* (London, 1970), pp 81–2; H.R. Clayton, 'Societies formed to educate the poor in Ireland in the late 18th and early 19th centuries' (Trinity College, Dublin, M.Litt. thesis, 1981), pp 104–21.

– the high church and evangelical movements. The high church group within the Irish church was connected with the high church party that had re-emerged in England in the late eighteenth century and which was represented by the philanthropic and educational activities of the 'Hackney Phalanx' in London. Prominent high churchmen in Ireland included John Jebb, bishop of Limerick, William Magee, archbishop of Dublin, Richard Mant, bishop of Down and Connor, and Thomas and Charles Elrington. The movement placed great emphasis on apostolic succession and a 'high' view of the clerical office, on due order and ceremony in worship, on sacramental grace, on the union of church and state, and on the character of the establishment as the one true catholic and apostolic church within the United Kingdom.[27] It gave particular attention to the pastoral ministry, and to the need for the parish clergy to embrace a sense of responsibility for the spiritual and moral welfare of all the inhabitants of their parishes.[28] The evangelical movement in Ireland was part of the larger British evangelical movement associated with the 'Clapham Sect', the parliamentary 'Saints' and a host of philanthropic, educational and missionary societies. Evangelicals embraced a strongly biblicist faith, with an emphasis on emotive preaching, the conversion experience, the doctrine of the atonement, 'serious' conversation and regular Bible reading. Less concerned than their high church brethren with the authority of the visible church, evangelicals were prepared to co-operate with Protestant Dissenters in missionary work.[29] Evangelicals in the Irish establishment often looked to extra-parochial societies for mutual support. Many formed clerical associations – that is, groups of ministers who met monthly for Bible study and serious conversation, such as the Ossory Clerical Association formed in 1800, or the clerical association in the Limerick district, formed about 1820.[30] In Power le Poer Trench, bishop of Waterford (1802–10), of Elphin (1810–19) and archbishop of Tuam (1819–39), the evangelical cause had an effective supporter on the episcopal bench.

After 1806, evangelicals in both Britain and Ireland increasingly embraced the cause of converting the whole people of Ireland, including the Catholics,

---

27. P.B. Nockles, 'Continuity and change in Anglican high churchmanship in Britain, 1792–1850' (2 vols., Oxford University Ph.D. thesis, 1982), ii, 344–9.
28. See, for example, John Jebb, *A charge, delivered to the clergy of the diocese of Limerick, at the primary visitation ... the 19th of June 1823* (Dublin, 1823), pp 37–54.
29. Hempton and Hill, *Evangelical protestantism*, pp 47–61; A.R. Acheson, *'A true and lively faith': evangelical revival in the Church of Ireland* (Belfast, 1992), pp 8–14.
30. Samuel Madden, *Memoir of the life of Rev. Peter Roe* (Dublin, 1842), pp 71–94; Dawson Massy, *Footprints of a faithful shepherd: a memoir of the Rev. Godfrey Massy, vicar of Bruff* (London, 1855), pp 60–70.

to their ideal of a biblical, heart-felt Christianity. This was inspired by the larger overseas British missionary impulse which in 1804 had led to the formation of the celebrated British and Foreign Bible Society, with its prodigious goal of translating the Bible into every language and providing a Bible to every inhabitant of the globe. The spread of Bibles and preachers, the evangelicals believed, would break through cultural barriers and unite the world in a common Christianity.[31] Not surprisingly, many evangelicals also began looking closer to home – to the millions of Irish Catholics who were, they believed, deprived of the saving influences of the gospel by a combination of illiteracy and the opposition of their priests to the free circulation of the Bible. In 1806, evangelicals in Britain and Ireland co-operated to form the Hibernian Bible Society on the model of the British and Foreign Bible Society. The aim was to distribute Bibles in both the English and Irish languages, and to encourage the use of the Bible in popular education. Receiving considerable support from England, the Hibernian Bible Society established branches in many Irish towns and by 1828 claimed to have distributed some 950,000 Bibles.[32] The work of the Hibernian Bible Society encouraged additional missionary efforts. The Irish Society for Promoting the Education of the Native Irish through the Medium of their own Language, founded in 1818, recruited, trained and supported Irish speakers to serve as scriptures readers, visiting homes in Irish-speaking communities to read the Bibles provided by the Hibernian Bible Society. By 1825, the Irish Society was also maintaining some 140 separate schools, mainly in Connaught and Munster.[33] Evangelicals embraced the cause of popular education, viewing it as a means of teaching the labouring poor to read the Bible for themselves. Soon evangelical societies were establishing hundreds of schools across Ireland to provide a scripture-based popular education to the mainly Catholic labouring poor. The Sunday School Society for Ireland, formed in 1809 to provide basic literacy as well as Bible knowledge, claimed to have more than 150,000 pupils by 1825. In the early 1820s, evangelicals gained control over the Kildare Place Society, which had been established in 1811 to provide non-denominational popular education to the Irish poor. With some 1100 schools by 1823, the Kildare Place Society now became a leading institution for the spread of scripture education.[34] In a country where the

---

31. For these hopes of a world Christianity through the British and Foreign Bible Society, see especially R.H. Martin, *Evangelicals united: ecumenical stirrings in Victorian Britain, 1795–1830* (London, 1983), pp 85–92.
32. 'The Irish Reformation', *British Critic* (January 1828), p. 22.
33. Whelan, 'Evangelical religion', pp 284–7; Clayton, 'Societies formed to educate the poor in Ireland', pp 222–31; Hempton and Hill, *Evangelical protestantism*, pp 56–7.
34. Akenson, *Irish education experiment*, pp 85–90.

legacy of the eighteenth-century penal laws meant there were few educational opportunities for the poor, Irish Catholics were often prepared to brave the censures of the priests and send their children to Sunday schools, Kildare Place schools or other scripture education schools.

The evangelical scripture education movement received support from a number of Irish landowning families, who had themselves come under the influence of heart-felt evangelical piety and felt called to communicate the gospel to the tenants on their estates.[35] Religious zeal was often combined with the belief that scripture education would help to alleviate poverty by encouraging greater thrift, temperance, hard work, delayed marriage, as well as teach tenants and labourers the duties of humility, respect for property and deference to social superiors. Among these evangelical landowners were such prominent names as Farnham, Roden, Powerscourt, Lorton, Mandeville, Mountcashel and Gosford. Frequently connected by ties of marriage and friendship, the evangelical landowners formed networks of considerable power and influence. Evangelical landowners served as patrons of local branches of the Bible society or scripture education societies, providing funds and chairing meetings. On taking control of the Kingscourt estate near Cavan in 1826, for example, the evangelical Lord Farnham began establishing schools for his tenants in connection with the Irish Society, and by 1826 he was maintaining at his own expense seven schools with some 700 pupils. The growth of the scripture education movement exceeded all expectations. The annual April meetings of the Bible and educational societies in the Rotunda of Dublin brought together hundreds of delegates and became major events in strengthening the confidence and cohesion of the Protestant community.[36] In 1825, the first report of a Parliamentary Irish Education Commission estimated that nearly 390,000 pupils were attending one of the Protestant scripture education schools, as compared with only about 20,000 in such schools in 1812.[37] These schools seemed destined to win the next generation of Irish Catholics to the Protestant faith. 'The progress of knowledge in Ireland', enthused one observer, 'through the circulation of the Holy Scriptures and education, is becoming daily more apparent. And perhaps in nothing does it appear more, than in the growing independence of the people in spiritual matters, and the declining influence of the priests'.[38]

---

35. I am indebted here to the important discussion of the evangelical gentry and aristocracy in Whelan, 'Evangelical religion', pp 390–418.
36. R.S. Brooke, *Recollections of the Irish church* (London, 1877), p. 35.
37. *Practical observations upon the views and tendency of the first report of the commissioners of Irish education Inquiry* (London, 1826), p. 35.
38. R. Steven, *Remarks on the present state of Ireland* (London, 1822), p. 16.

The high church group within the Irish establishment was initially hostile to the Bible Society. They criticised the Bible Society for opening its membership to Protestant Dissenters and for placing too much reliance on individual Bible reading, to the neglect of the guidance, authority and sacraments of the established church. Such an emphasis on the Bible alone, the high churchman William Phelan maintained, would fill individuals with over-confidence and lead to religious enthusiasm and sectarian divisions.[39] By the early 1820s, however, many in the high church group were reconsidering their position on the Bible Society and other scripture education societies, viewing them more as potential allies than rivals in the effort to expand the influence of the established church. They were responding both to the success of the scripture education movement and the growing strength of the established church. High church fears that scripture education would only strengthen dissent diminished. With the increased levels of state investment in churches and schools, and the improved discipline in the clergy, the established church was in a strong position to receive those Catholics who were expected to be drawn to protestantism through the agency of scripture education. Irish evangelicals, influenced by such figures as Charles Simeon of Cambridge and Thomas Chalmers of Glasgow, increasingly valued the established church, with its parish organisation and ideal of the united Christian commonwealth. By the early 1820s, high churchmen and evangelicals were overcoming their differences and uniting behind the combined aims of extending Scripture education and the influence of the established church.[40] They looked to both regular Bible reading and the development of close-knit parish communities as means to the religious and moral transformation of Ireland. The established church seemed poised for a breakthrough in its mission to the Irish people. It was this new confidence that William Magee had expressed in his controversial charge of October 1822. With the victory over Napoleonic France, the unprecedented levels of state investment in the Irish religious establishment, and a growing romantic celebration of the Anglican church's traditions and its missionary outreach – all things began to seem possible, even the final victory of the reformation in Ireland and the consolidation of the Union of 1801 on the basis of the Protestant constitution. The established church in Ireland, wrote one of her Irish apologists

---

39. William Phelan, *The Bible, not the Bible Society* (Dublin, 1817); Evidence of William Phelan, House of Lords committee on the state of Ireland, *Parliamentary Papers*, vol. viii (1825), pp 494–500; Nockles, 'Continuity and change', ii, 349–50.
40. T.C.F. Stunt, 'Evangelical cross-currents in the Church of Ireland, 1820–1833' in W.J. Sheils and Diana Wood (ed.), *The churches, Ireland and the Irish*, ('Studies in Church History', xxv, Oxford, 1989), p. 219.

in December 1823, was a force for transforming the Irish into 'Englishmen'. 'She has taught her followers', he maintained, 'to blend England with all their dearest, their holiest, their most ennobling recollections – to trace thither the pedigree of their blessings – to make it in heart and spirit, the country of their earthly affections, and the guide to that better country, whose foundation is in the Heavens'.[41]

At the same time, support for the goal of converting the Irish Catholic population to the protestantism of the established Church of England and Ireland was by no means universal. On the contrary, in Britain as well as Ireland, a growing number of Whigs and liberal Tories had become convinced of both the justice and the expediency of Catholic emancipation – that is, of admitting Irish Catholics into full political rights without requiring their conformity to protestantism. Supporters of emancipation were also gaining ground in parliament. In April 1821, the house of commons had passed a bill for Catholic emancipation. Although defeated in the lords, the bill nonetheless demonstrated the strength of the liberal, 'pro-Catholic' forces. For them, the Union of 1801 would be consolidated and Ireland integrated into the British state, not through the religious and moral influence of the established Church of England and Ireland, but through fundamental change in the Protestant constitution – not through the conformity of the Irish Catholic masses to the established faith, but through their political emancipation.

The 'Bible war', 1824–26

In Ireland, Catholic leaders were acutely aware of the new missionary zeal in the established church. With unprecedented state investment in the established church, and the desire of most Irish parents to educate their children, there was a serious possibility that the establishment might achieve a considerable increase in influence, or even gain the ascendancy over Irish religious life which had eluded it since the Reformation. The hold of the Catholic clergy on the Irish Catholic population at this time appeared less than secure. As Emmet Larkin has demonstrated, there was a serious shortage of priests for the rapidly growing population – less than 2000 for a Catholic population of over four-and-a-half million. Clerical discipline was often lax, with problems of sexual misconduct and alcoholism. There were, moreover, considerable inequalities of income among the clergy, widespread complaints among the impoverished peasantry about clerical avarice and often deep divisions

---

41. [William Phelan], *The case of the Church of Ireland stated, in a letter respectfully addressed to his excellency the Marquis Wellesley* (Dublin, 1823), p. 49.

between Catholics over such issues as state payment of the Catholic clergy.[42] While Catholic organisations, most notably the Christian Brothers, endeavoured to provide schools, they could not command anything near the resources of the established church and Protestant scripture education societies. One who recognised the urgency of the situation confronting the Catholic church was James Doyle, bishop of Kildare and Leighlin. 'Behold', he wrote in 1824 of the scripture education societies:

> ... the force with which these societies press on an impoverished and broken-hearted people. Funds to the amount of, or exceeding £200,000 a year, are at their disposal; the influence of the landlord, and influence paramount to every other, the zeal of the inspector, the power of the press, and of the tongue – calumnies incessantly repeated, the hallowed name of the word of God, the thirst of the people for education, their excessive poverty, all these form a moral phalanx more formidable than that of Macedon.

'We have' he added, 'borne many things, but we have never borne a persecution more bitter than that which now assails us'.[43]

The threat posed by the scripture education societies was important in helping to ensure that the majority of Irish Catholics, among them Doyle, came to support the Catholic Association – an organisation formed by Daniel O'Connell and several supporters in May 1823. The essential purpose of the association was to mobilise Irish popular opinion in support of Catholic emancipation. Early in 1824, however, the association broadened its activities, setting up a fund to subsidise pro-emancipation newspapers and to provide legal counsel for Catholic tenants victimised for their political views. The fund would also be used to support Catholic popular education, build churches and clerical residence houses, and improve the incomes of the priests – or in short to strengthen the religious and moral instruction of the Catholic church at the parish level, enabling it better to resist the forces being mobilised by the established church.[44] The challenge from the scripture education movement and revived established church helped convince many priests to give their active support to the Catholic Association. Before 1823, the Catholic clergy in Ireland, haunted by memories of the French Revolution and the rising of 1798, and under pressure from Rome to avoid involvement

---

42. Larkin, 'The devotional revolution in Ireland, 1850–75', pp 625–39; Bowen, *Souperism*, pp 51–4; S.J. Connolly, *Priests and people in pre-Famine Ireland 1780–1845* (Dublin, 1982), pp 58–73.
43. JKL [J.W. Doyle], *Letters on the state of education in Ireland; and on bible societies* (Dublin, 1824), pp 22–3.
44. Fergus O'Ferrall, *Catholic emancipation: Daniel O'Connell and the birth of Irish democracy 1820–30* (Dublin, 1985), pp 52–5.

in politics, had remained aloof from the O'Connellite agitation. By the spring of 1824, however, significant numbers of Catholic priests were assisting the Catholic Association in enrolling members, collecting subscriptions and drafting petitions.[45]

In the late summer of 1824, O'Connell found an opportunity to demonstrate the Catholic Association's readiness to combat the scripture education societies. On 9 September, he and Richard Sheil were in Cork to attend a dinner in honour of Sheil when they 'discovered by accident' that there was to be a meeting of the Ladies' Auxiliary of the Munster Hibernian Bible Society in the county court house, at which two British organisers from the London Hibernian Bible Society, Baptist Noel and James E. Gordon, were to speak. Accompanied by a crowd of supporters, O'Connell and Sheil entered the meeting hall and over the course of the next two days engaged Noel and Gordon in a spirited public debate over the value of scripture education. O'Connell was in his element, entertaining the crowd for over three hours on the second day. Bible societies, he warned, would lead to the spread of sectarian enthusiasm and turn good Irish Catholics into 'Muggletonians'. He reminded Gordon, a Scot, how the Scottish covenanters had resisted the imposition of an alien church, and he recommended that Noel and other English supporters of the London Hibernian Society should concentrate on alleviating widespread ignorance and irreligion in England, rather than sending missionaries to 'convert' Irish Catholics, who were already Christians, possessors of the pure catholic and apostolic faith. On the second day, the crowd grew raucous, Protestant speakers were shouted down and the meeting ended in confusion.[46]

The event marked the beginning of open warfare by the Catholic Association upon the scripture education societies. O'Connell's action in Cork encouraged local Catholics in the south and west of Ireland to adopt similar tactics. There were a number of incidents of Catholics breaking in upon the meetings of the scripture education societies, denouncing their proselytising aims and engaging the Protestant organisers in debate. On 21 September, for example, a Catholic crowd disrupted a meeting of the Church Missionary Society in Cork, and constables were called in to clear the hall. On the same day, Catholics broke into the meeting of the Hibernian Bible Society in

---

45. Ibid., pp 61–3; for the changing attitudes of the clergy to popular politics, see Oliver MacDonagh, 'Politicisation', pp 37–42.
46. *Constitution, or Cork Morning Post*, 10, 13, 15, 17 Sept. 1824; D. O'Connell to his wife, 11 Sept. 1824, in *O'Connell corr.*, iii, 77–8; John Wolffe, *The Protestant crusade in Great Britain 1829–1860* (Oxford, 1992), p. 35.

Clonmel. Catholic crowds interrupted bible society meetings at Waterford on 28 September and at Kilkenny on 14 October.[47] A crowd violently broke up the meeting of the Galway branch of the Hibernian Bible Society on 19 October, despite the presence of Power le Poer Trench, the evangelical archbishop of Tuam.[48] To avoid violent confrontations, local Catholic and Protestant leaders began organising formal debates, or 'biblical discussions', with admission limited to purchasers of tickets. Champions emerged out of the confrontations, including Richard Pope and Robert Daly for the established church, and Fr Eneas McDonnell and Fr Tom Maguire for the Catholic church. On 18–19 November 1824, a debate was held at Carlow, the episcopal seat of James Doyle, the bishop of Kildare and Leighlin, in which three Protestants engaged three Catholics. Despite efforts to restrict attendance to ticket-holders, the meeting ended in disorder and the Protestant speakers had to be brought out through a back door to avoid rough treatment by the excited crowd.[49]

The disruptions of bible society meetings and the subsequent 'biblical discussions' aroused considerable popular excitement, providing entertainment to local communities and receiving widespread coverage in the British and Irish press.[50] The 'Bible war', as it was dubbed, brought forward a new militancy on both sides.[51] The confrontations forced supporters of scripture education to admit openly that their aim was not simply to extend popular education, but to convert the Irish Catholic population. Many Protestants in both Ireland and Britain welcomed the confrontations, believing that the fundamental differences between Protestant and Catholic, played down by the educated classes in recent decades in the interests of peace and reconciliation, would now be clarified. The confrontations, they claimed, revealed the Catholic leadership to be opposed to both popular education and the free circulation of the scriptures.[52] As the Irish Catholics as a body came to see this, they would turn from the priests and the political agitators of the Catholic Association. The combination of scripture education and the 'Bible war' was preparing the ground for the coming of the reformation to

---

47. Bowen, *Protestant crusade*, pp 98–9.
48. J.D. Sirr, *A memoir of Power le Poer Trench, last archbishop of Tuam* (Dublin, 1845), pp 466–82.
49. Mrs Hamilton Madden, *Memoir of Robert Daly, lord bishop of Cashel* (London, 1875), pp 105–7; Fitzpatrick, *Life of Dr Doyle*, i, 374–6; evidence of John Rochfort, House of Lords committee on the state of Ireland, *Parliamentary Papers*, viii (1825), pp 445–6.
50. Including the English religious press: see, for example, *Christian Guardian* (Nov. 1824), p. 433; *Christian Observer* (Nov. 1824), pp 727–8.
51. *Constitution, or Cork Morning Post*, 25 Oct. 1824.
52. Ibid., 13, 17 Sept. 1824.

Ireland. 'When we advert also to the scenes which preceded the Reformation', noted the evangelical *Christian Observer* of London in November 1824, 'we find them so far at least analogous to those now passing in Ireland'. 'They called the attention of the mass of the laity', it continued, 'to the points in dispute, and thus secured that attention which is always useful to the cause of truth, and fatal to that of error'.[53]

For the high church archbishop of Dublin, William Magee, the spread of the 'biblical discussions' after September 1824 demonstrated a new openness to Protestant influence on the part of the Catholic population. In attending the debates, Catholics were listening to the arguments of the Protestant missionaries and it was only a matter of time before such arguments made their impact felt. In evidence given before a select committee of the house of lords on 'the state of Ireland' in April 1825, and published separately as a pamphlet, Magee argued that there was now a real possibility that the established church would gain the adherence of the majority of the Irish people, if only the church would give its support to and assert its authority over the scripture education movement.[54] Magee proceeded to argue that the numbers of Protestants in Ireland had never been so low as was commonly supposed. On the contrary, there was much 'latent' protestantism, especially among the lower social orders. Many Protestant families had drifted into catholicism because they had been neglected by the established clergy or because there was insufficient church accommodation in the established church. Such 'Catholics' were, at best, uncertain and often irregular attendees of Catholic chapels. Magee even argued that some attended Catholic chapels only out of the mistaken belief that the Catholic church was the legal establishment in Ireland, which the state expected them to attend.[55] The biblical confrontations, however, were at last clarifying the situation for many of these nominal Catholics. What they now needed, Magee maintained, was greater commitment on the part of both the state and upper social orders to extending the parish system of the established church. There were, he claimed, over 90,000 Protestants residing in Dublin but only twenty-five established churches, which made it impossible for many Protestants to join in public worship and thus contributed to the drift into catholicism. They

---

53. *Christian Observer* (Nov. 1824), p. 727.
54. William Magee, *The evidence of his grace, the archbishop of Dublin, before the select committee of the house of lords on the state of Ireland* (Dublin, 1825), pp 17–22.
55. Ibid., pp 14–5; a similar argument about the extent of latent protestantism in Ireland was made by the Belfast Presbyterian clergyman, Henry Cooke, in his evidence before the select committee. See House of Lords committee on the state of Ireland, *Parliamentary Papers*, vol. viii (1825), p. 360.

required more parish churches, with lower seat rents, to enable the poor to attend. Wealthy Protestants, moreover, must support the established church by giving preference in employment and leases to Protestants. Above all, parliament must cease considering Catholic emancipation. Any further concessions would be viewed as a victory for the Catholic Association and would signal to the Irish Catholics that their religion was a matter of indifference to the British state. It must be made clear to Irish Catholics that the British state was Protestant and that conformity to the established church was a requirement for full political rights. 'The constitution of this realm', he insisted, 'knows of one allegiance, ecclesiastical, as well as civil'.[56]

In the diocese of Limerick, one clergyman of the established church was beginning to achieve visible results through an aggressive pastorate as recommended by Magee. The evangelical Richard Murray arrived in October 1824 as the new vicar of Askeaton. He began regular visiting among all his parishioners, established parish schools with an emphasis on biblical teaching, conducted bible classes in his home, and distributed bibles and religious tracts. He made no effort to cultivate friendly relations with the Catholics in his parish, but on the contrary claimed all his privileges as a clergyman of the established church. He insisted, for example, on reading the Anglican burial service at every funeral in the Askeaton churchyard, including those for Catholics, often in the face of angry threats by outraged relatives. Soon his uncompromising ministry began gaining converts. In June 1825, two Catholic families conformed to the established church, and by the end of the year forty Catholics in the parish had conformed. Murray gained the confidence and support of his bishop, the high churchman John Jebb, and at the regular meetings of the Limerick clerical association he encouraged neighbouring clergy to adopt his aggressive pastoral methods.[57] His example indicated what could be accomplished through the parish ministry.

As well as encouraging more confrontational attitudes in the established church, the excitement aroused by the biblical confrontations also strengthened the Catholic Association as an organisation for the defence of Catholic identity. Indeed, the most dramatic expansion of the Catholic Association came in the autumn of 1824, at the same time that the 'Bible war' had broken out in the south and west.[58] O'Connell now insisted that as much as half the Catholic 'rent' be sent to the parishes to support Catholic education

---

56. Magee, *Evidence ... before the select committee*, p. 112.
57. Charles Forster, *The life of John Jebb* (2 vols., London, 1836), ii, 433–45; Massy, *Footprints*, pp 112–55; H. Hamilton to J. Jebb, 8 Dec. 1825, (Trinity College, Dublin, Jebb Papers, Ms 6396–7/240).
58. Wolffe, *Protestant crusade*, pp 34–5; O'Ferrall, *Catholic emancipation*, pp 56–85.

and the clergy in their struggle with the 'biblicals'.[59] According to Thomas Wyse, a leading figure in the Catholic Association, the confrontations played a major role in convincing the Catholic clergy not only to support the Catholic Association but also to take a leading role in recruitment and collecting the 'rent'. 'The Catholic clergy', Wyse observed in 1829, had been roused to a spirit of combination by the necessities of self-defence. Their repugnance to public exhibition was overcome; they stept out beyond the modesty of their habitual functions into the activity of public life; they began to feel the usual excitements of such scenes, to acknowledge the *gaudia certaminis* of such a warfare: the church became gradually militant.[60]

The Protestant 'phalanx' which in 1824 James Doyle had described as behind the scripture education movement was by 1825 being confronted by a Catholic 'phalanx' under the leadership of the Catholic Association.[61] O'Connell and the association offered Irish Catholics a radically different future from that represented by the established church – not entry into the full rights of British citizenship through conformity to the established church, but a radical change in the constitution of the British state so that Irish Catholics could gain full rights of citizenship without sacrificing their church and cultural identity.[62] Parliament, moreover, seemed to be moving closer to passing emancipation. In the spring of 1825, the house of commons passed another Catholic emancipation bill, though again it was defeated in the lords. Then, in the general election of June 1826, the Catholic Association gained a notable victory with the defeat of the powerful Beresford interest in the parliamentary contest for Waterford. In Waterford and several other constituencies, Catholic priests assumed a key role in encouraging Catholic 40s freeholders to vote against their Protestant landlords. This came as a profound shock to the Protestant landed class across Ireland. In recent years, Protestant landowners, and especially the 'Bible gentry', had been growing more favourably disposed to attempts to extend the influence of the established church to Catholics. The general election of 1826 convinced one prominent landowner that the Irish Protestant landed classes must now assume an even more active leadership role in the campaign for the reformation in Ireland – not only to preserve the Protestant constitution, but also to safeguard the union of Britain and Ireland.

---

59. Bartlett, *Fall and rise*, p. 332.
60. Thomas Wyse, *Historical sketch of the late Catholic Association of Ireland* (2 vols., London, 1829), i, pp 231–2.
61. For the argument that the Catholic Association was largely a response to the aggression of the established church, see 'The second reformation', *Dublin Evening Post*, 31 July 1827.
62. For an expression of this aim, see the letter of James Doyle, a prominent member of the Catholic Association, to Lord Farnham, *Dublin Evening Post*, 8 Feb. 1827.

The new reformation, 1826–27

In October 1826, the beginning of the long-awaited Irish reformation was heralded with a series of dramatic conversions to protestantism in Cavan, on the estate of John Maxwell, fifth baron Farnham, a devout Protestant landlord and a leading opponent of Catholic emancipation. Since assuming control over his 29,000-acre estate in 1823, Farnham had sought to make it a model of Christian 'moral management', emphasising the improvement of the tenants through moral supervision and the spread of bible-based, popular education. As we have seen, he was zealous in establishing scripture-education schools on his estate. In 1826, moreover, he appointed a 'moral agent', William Krause, who was to supervise the moral and religious life of the tenants and their families. With the local linen industry in a state of virtual collapse in the mid 1820s, many hard-pressed local inhabitants sought employment on Farnham's lands.[63] Then in September 1826 Farnham was approached by three Catholic school teachers who claimed to have been converted by teaching bible lessons to children. They asked for his support and protection to enable them to conform to the established church. Farnham agreed, and he let it be known that he would offer his protection to other Catholics wishing to conform. On 8 October seventeen Catholics conformed in Cavan. The news of these conversions spread, and Catholics who were prepared to conform made their way to Farnham's estate. By 4 November, forty-seven Catholics had conformed in Cavan. 'I can with truth assure you', Farnham wrote to Sir Robert Peel, the home secretary, on that day, 'that the Roman Catholic religion has already received a severe blow'. Farnham attributed the conversions to the new zeal in the established church, to the spread of scripture education and, above all, to the rancour that many Catholics felt over 'the recent conduct [of] the R.C. Clergy in mixing Politics and Religion'. If the parliamentary state would remain firm in support of the Protestant constitution and established church, he continued, 'we might hope that the light of reason would break in on the deluded people, and an explosive inroad be made upon the Roman Catholic church in this country'.[64]

A steady procession of Catholics made their way to Farnham's estate to be received into the United Church; by early December, over 250 were reported to have conformed.[65] The Dublin Protestant press reported that the Catholic

---

63. Whelan, 'Evangelical religion', pp 415–22; Hempton and Hill, *Evangelical protestantism*, pp 86–7; N.D. Emerson, 'Church life in the nineteenth century' in W.A. Phillips (ed.), *History of the Church of Ireland* (3 vols., Oxford, 1933), iii, p. 342.
64. Lord Farnham to Sir R. Peel, 4 Nov. 1826, (B.L., Peel Papers, Add. MSS 40389, fols. 254–7).
65. *Dublin Evening Mail*, 11 Dec. 1826.

populations of whole parishes in the county of Cavan were preparing to go over. 'So rapidly is the spirit of desertion spreading in this County', the *Dublin Evening Mail* wrote of Cavan on 4 December, 'that all we apprehend is a lack of shepherds to collect the straying flock and guide them to the fold'. 'Never, since the days of England's Reformation', it continued, 'has such a scene been presented to the Empire'.[66] Veteran evangelical champions of the 'Bible war', including Richard Pope and James Gordon, hurried to Cavan to assist in the work. Here, it seemed, was the culmination of the efforts to improve the parish system of the established church and expand scripture education to the Catholics.

The reports from Cavan were taken seriously by leaders of the Catholic church. In mid December a deputation of five Catholic bishops, led by Patrick Curtis, the archbishop of Armagh and Primate, travelled to Cavan to investigate. Brushing aside a challenge to engage with the Protestant champions in yet another biblical discussion, Curtis and his fellow bishops instead interviewed local Catholics about the conversions. The arrival of the bishops served to discourage waverers within the Catholic community. Further, the bishops soon claimed to have uncovered evidence of widespread bribery – with beggars, unwed mothers and unemployed teachers lured into conforming to protestantism by gifts of food and clothing, or promises of pensions or employment. Others, the deputation insisted, were caught up in the atmosphere of religious enthusiasm and fanaticism. They pressed the magistrates, without success, to take affidavits from those alleged to have been offered bribes.[67] One of the deputation, John MacHale, bishop of Killala, portrayed Cavan in a published letter as the scene of religious mayhem: 'the highways were covered with carts, conveying to the strong citadel of the Reformation, a precious cargo of vagrants'. Catholic children, he claimed, were abducted, their relatives were threatened when they interceded, while 'fanatical females' fell into trances and prophesied.[68] With national interest now fastened on Cavan, the crowds and excitement continued to grow.

On 26 January 1827, Farnham and other supporters held a public meeting in Cavan to publicise the achievements of the reformation movement and mobilise national support. By now there were over 450 converts in County Cavan, and conversions were being reported elsewhere in Ireland. In his opening speech, Farnham vehemently denied the allegations that bribery or threats were being used to gain conversions, or that the converts came only

---

66. Ibid., 4 Dec. 1826.
67. *Dublin Evening Post*, 19, 23, 30 Dec. 1826; Hempton and Hill, *Evangelical protestantism*, pp 89–90
68. *Letters of John MacHale*, pp 228–9.

from the lowest social ranks. On the contrary, he claimed, the converts were from all social orders, and were of respectable moral character. The real causes of the reformation breakthrough, he insisted, were not bribes but the spread of scripture education and gospel truth, and a desire among Catholics to be free of control and financial exactions by the Catholic clergy. Many Catholics, he maintained, had particularly resented the conduct of their priests in the recent general election, when they had pressured the Catholic 40s freeholders into voting against their landlords, thus disrupting the ties of paternalism and deference which should exist in rural society and leaving the tenants 'alienated from their landlords'. Now a great opportunity had come. An experiment had been made at Cavan, which had demonstrated that Catholics were prepared to conform in large numbers, if given proper encouragement by the natural leaders of society, the landowners and the established clergy. The United Church of England and Ireland, backed by 'the united efforts of the British Empire', was in position at last to achieve the reformation in Ireland. At the same time, he warned, were this reformation movement to fail, it would open the way for the passing of Catholic emancipation, which in turn would lead to the disestablishment of the Protestant church and the end of the Union. 'If something be not effected in this way', Farnham averred, 'and we are obliged to abandon our Church Establishment, which now stands in such manifest jeopardy, it requires not much foresight, and still less of the spirit of prophecy, to foretell, that many years will not elapse until a separation takes place between the two countries'. In response to Farnham's appeal, the meeting agreed to establish a Reformation Society that would co-ordinate a national movement to work for the final victory of the reformation.[69] 'In every point of view', enthused the *Dublin Evening Mail* on 29 January, 'this was the most important meeting that has ever been held in Ireland ... Cavan this day presents a grand spectacle to the world'.[70]

The movement continued to spread beyond Cavan, and by April 1827, 1340 conversions had been reported at different sites around Ireland.[71] Even the initially sceptical high church Bishop of Limerick, John Jebb, became convinced that a great religious transformation had begun.[72] In Dublin, bulletins of the numbers of converts were published in the newspapers and placarded on walls.[73] It was, the *Dublin Evening Mail* insisted with

---

69. *Dublin Evening Post*, 3 Feb. 1827.
70. *Dublin Evening Mail*, 29 Jan. 1827.
71. Sirr, *Memoir of Trench*, p. 539.
72. Wolffe, *Protestant crusade*, pp 38–9.
73. W.J. O'Neill Daunt, *Eighty-five years of Irish history 1800–1885* (2 vols., London, 1886), i, p. 93.

millenarian fervour in March 1827, a moment 'big with futurity': 'these are "signs and wonders" which must be taken as unerring harbingers – prophetic admonitions of events that must be'.[74] Opponents of Catholic emancipation, including the earl of Roden in a speech in the house of lords, seized on the reformation movement to call for an end to further concessions to Catholic claims.[75] Between 19 and 25 April, national attention focused on an extended public debate held in Dublin between Richard Pope, a leading Protestant preacher, and Tom Maguire, a Leitrim Catholic priest who had achieved local fame during the 'Bible war'. Presented as a major confrontation between supporters of the reformation and emancipation movements, the debate attracted large crowds and was extensively reported in the press. In the event, the outcome was unclear and both sides claimed victory.[76] Undaunted, supporters of the reformation movement organised for the expected national breakthrough. They began establishing local branches of the Reformation Society, intended to carry forward the work of the bible societies, and gather in the expected rich harvest of converts.[77] In England, many within the established church became convinced that the reformation had begun in Ireland. C.J. Blomfield, bishop of Chester, welcomed the movement and was 'very anxious that the sound and orthodox churchmen should take the lead'.[78] The liberal Anglican, Thomas Arnold, believed that the conversions 'afford certainly a most cheering prospect of future good for Ireland'.[79] English evangelicals brought the reformation movement to Britain, and in May 1827 the British Reformation Society was inaugurated at a large public meeting in the Freemason's Hall, London, at which Lord Farnham was a principal speaker. The British Reformation Society established branches in England and Scotland, working for the promotion of Protestant principles and the elimination of Roman catholicism from the British Isles.[80]

By the late spring of 1827, the reformation movement had made significant progress in Ireland. For many in the established church, the movement

---

74. *Dublin Evening Mail*, 26 Mar. 1827.
75. Earl of Roden, speech in House of Lords on 16 Mar. 1827, *Hansard*, new ser., vol. xvi, cols. 1232–3.
76. *Authenticated report of the discussion which took place between the Rev Richard T.P. Pope and the Rev Thomas Maguire* (Dublin, 1827); Bowen, *Protestant crusade*, pp 107–8; *Dublin Evening Mail*, 16 July 1827; *Dublin Evening Post*, 4 Aug. 1827.
77. For example, the *Dublin Evening Mail*, 9 Feb., 19, 22 Oct., 2, 9 Nov. 1827; see also Wolffe, *Protestant Crusade*, pp 38–9.
78. C.J. Blomfield to John Jebb, 27 Mar. 1827 (Trinity College, Dublin, Jebb Papers, Ms 6396–7/278).
79. T. Arnold to F.C. Blackstone, 2 Mar. 1827 (Bodleian Library, Oxford, MS Eng. Lett. d. 348, fols. 32–3).
80. *Dublin Evening Mail*, 25 May 1827; Wolffe, *Protestant crusade*, pp 36–7.

that began at Cavan in September 1826 marked the culmination of two decades of preparation, and was destined to bring Ireland at last into conformity with the religious and intellectual culture of Britain. The movement seemed to be gaining broad support within the United Church. At the same time, supporters felt a sense of urgency. As Farnham had warned at the inauguration of the Reformation Society in Cavan in January 1827, unless the established church could extend its influence among the Catholic majority in Ireland, there would be Catholic emancipation and, they feared, a growing religious and cultural divergence between Ireland and Britain. Thus, the reformation movement marked not only the culmination of extensive investment in the established church and scripture education; it was also perhaps the last chance to make the established church the predominant agency for the religious and moral instruction of the Irish people. There was certainly reason to believe that time was running short for the established church in Ireland. Political changes at Westminster in the late winter and spring of 1827 greatly advanced the cause of Catholic emancipation. In February 1827, the prime minister, Lord Liverpool, a leading opponent of Catholic emancipation, suffered a stroke which forced his retirement, and on 10 April 1827, the 'pro-Catholic' George Canning was called to form a government. The Catholic Association intensified its agitation for emancipation and grew confident that victory was close. English supporters of emancipation also felt confident that the reformation would not thwart victory. 'Can any man who has ... been out of Bedlam three weeks', asked the liberal Anglican, Sydney Smith, in the *Edinburgh Review* of March 1827, 'believe that the Catholic question will be set to rest by the conversion of the Irish Catholics to the Protestant religion?'[81] Nor was O'Connell much worried by the reformation movement. 'These conversions', he assured his anxious wife on 22 March 1827, 'are exceedingly foolish things. They are buying wretches in every direction who are a disgrace to them and no loss to the church they desert'. The extravagant claims of the reformation movement, he predicted, would very soon bring a reaction against the movement from the 'dispassionate'.[82]

The failure of the new reformation, 1827–29

'It is really a pity', wrote James MacHale, Catholic priest of Hollymount, in the *Dublin Evening Post* on 31 May 1827, 'that it was at the eleventh hour –

---

81. [S. Smith], 'The Catholic question', *Edinburgh Review*, 45 (Mar. 1827), p. 436.
82. D. O'Connell to his wife, 22 Mar. 1827, in *O'Connell corr.*, iii, 302; for O'Connell's anger toward the established church at this time, see O'Ferrall, *Catholic emancipation*, p. 152.

unfortunately for the Parson, later than the eleventh hour, that the Reformation began here. Unfortunately, when Liverpool and Eldon, and the other rewarders of bigoted and proselytising Parsons are out of office'. 'Had they but known the strange shifting of events', MacHale continued, 'they would not have thus striven to purchase public ridicule'.[83] The high expectations of the reformationists were soon dashed. By the late spring, within months of its inauguration at Cavan, the reformation movement was in serious difficulties. The number of new converts fell dramatically. The movement failed to make significant inroads into a Catholic population that was being organised by the Catholic Association and which could see Catholic emancipation approaching.[84] By mid 1827 there was a new confidence in the Catholic community, a growing feeling that Providence was on the side of Catholic Ireland in its struggle against an alien protestantism.[85] Catholics increasingly turned upon the scripture education societies. In some districts, night marauders burned the schools; in others, parents simply removed their children and left them empty shells.[86] In the face of renewed Catholic solidarity, the costs of conforming to the established church grew heavy. Catholics who conformed were denounced by priests, the Catholic Association and the liberal press for having sold their birthright – their church and community – for money or promises of employment. They found themselves cut off from their families and communities, and figures of contempt.[87] At the same time, Farnham and other wealthy supporters of the reformation movement, sensitive to the accusations of using bribery to obtain converts, became increasingly reluctant to provide financial support or employment for the converts.[88] Finding little help in the established church, many converts returned to the Catholic church and made peace with their families and communities. In late September 1827, the Irish Catholic primate, Patrick Curtis, described to Rome how, in the presence of a crowd of 5000, a large number of converts had renounced their defection amid tears of repentance.[89]

By the summer of 1827, the reformation had lost its momentum. 'The shocking mummery practised in Cavan', proclaimed the liberal *Dublin*

---

83. *Dublin Evening Post*, 31 May 1827.
84. Sirr, *Memoir of Trench*, p. 542.
85. Gearóid Ó Tuathaigh, 'Gaelic Ireland, popular politics and Daniel O'Connell', *Galway Archaeological and Historical Society*, xxxiv (1974–75), pp 21–34.
86. Wyse, *Historical sketch*, i, 234–5.
87. See, for example, *Dublin Evening Post*, 8 Feb., 27 Mar., 12 May, 31 July 1827; *Dublin Evening Mail*, 3 Aug. 1827, 4 Jan. 1828; 'The Irish Reformation', *British Critic*, iv (January 1828), pp 38–47; 'The second year of the Irish reformation', ibid., v (January 1829), pp 128–32.
88. *Christian Guardian* (Oct. 1828), pp 394–7.
89. Ambrose Macaulay, *William Crolly, archbishop of Armagh, 1835–49* (Dublin, 1994), p. 98.

Evening Post on 31 July 1827, 'where starving and half naked wretches were bribed with a dinner, a pair of trowsers, or a petticoat, to foreswear themselves … has come to a full stop'.[90] Local supporters continued to form branches of the Reformation Society, but the surrounding Catholic population was hostile or indifferent to the proceedings and there were no further mass conversions such as those at Cavan. It was not until December 1827 that a branch of the Reformation Society was formed in Dublin.[91] Most Irish landowners declined to follow Farnham's example and commit themselves to the movement.[92] In January 1828, the high church *British Critic* of London attempted to arouse British interest in the Irish reformation with a lengthy account of the movement. Since the autumn of 1826, it insisted, some 2400 Catholics had conformed to the established church in Ireland, and there was hope that the numbers would increase.[93] The *British Critic* appealed to English Christians to recognise the critical importance of the Irish reformation movement. In Ireland, it insisted, the United Church of England and Ireland was confronting the Roman Catholic church in its last stronghold in the United Kingdom. The struggle was one of life and death, that would end either in the conformity of the Irish people to the established church or in Catholic emancipation. If the latter, it would mean the eventual end of the Protestant constitution and the established church in England as well as Ireland: 'Either England must subdue the Papacy by reforming Ireland, or the Papacy will overthrow the Church and Constitution of England'.[94] Yet 2400 converts out of a Catholic population of over five-and-a-half millions was not a great number after so much investment of money and effort. Moreover, fewer and fewer new converts were being reported. 'There has been', the London *Eclectic Review* observed of the movement in January 1828, 'a long pause in the announcement of its progress, and we fear, it is a "pause prophetic of its end"'.[95] With the final stages in the struggle for Catholic emancipation, beginning with the County Clare election of July 1828, interest in the reformation movement rapidly faded.[96] Some leaders, like Lord Farnham, shifted their efforts from the reformation movement to political

---

90. *Dublin Evening Post*, 31 July 1827.
91. *Dublin Evening Mail*, 17 Dec. 1827.
92. *Dublin Evening Mail*, 17 Aug., 19 Sept. 1827; *Christian Guardian* (Aug. 1828), p. 316; Newland, *Apology*, pp 90, 212.
93. 'The Irish Reformation', *British Critic*, iv (Jan. 1828), pp 27–58.
94. Ibid., p. 55.
95. 'O'Driscoll's *History of Ireland*', *Eclectic Review*, xxix (Jan. 1828), p. 30.
96. It was reported in the Dublin press, for example, that the Reformation Society had been dissolved and the movement abandoned: *Dublin Evening Post*, 2 Aug. 1828; *Dublin Evening Mail*, 6 Aug. 1828.

resistance to emancipation through the Brunswick Clubs. Others, like the Rev. Robert Daly of Powerscourt, withdrew from the Reformation Society because they saw it as too political.[97] 'The labourers in this vineyard', Thomas Wyse observed in 1829 of the reformation movement, 'began valiantly, but threw aside their spades before noon.... The bubble burst; the joint-stock company dispersed; the defaulters escaped: saintship fell to a grievous discount: a few sufferers railed and wept ... and the rest of the nation ... shook their heads and laughed openly at the imposture'.[98]

The passing of the Catholic Emancipation Act in April 1829 brought an end to serious hopes of securing the conformity of the large majority of the Irish people to the United Church of England and Ireland. Irish Catholics were now eligible for most public offices, and the established church no longer held the same position in the constitution of the United Kingdom. Many in the established church in Ireland felt they had been betrayed by the parliamentary state – that the state had deserted the church just as it was beginning to fulfil its role as a national establishment.[99] Archbishop Magee's health failed shortly after the passing of emancipation and rumours spread that he had lost his sanity.[100] Emancipation ended the hopes of uniting the peoples of England and Ireland in a common faith, disseminated through the parish structures of a single established church and through a Bible-based popular education. Parliament had recognised that the large majority of the Irish people would remain outside the established church and, with this decision, the established church in Ireland became an anomaly. Shortly after the passing of Catholic emancipation, parliament moved to create a national system of education in Ireland, withdrawing state support from the scripture education societies and accepting the principle of non-denominational education, with scripture education removed to the end of the day and attendance made voluntary. In early 1832, under the pressure of renewed unrest over tithe, the Whig government began plans for the radical reduction of the established church in Ireland, plans which originally involved the appropriation of some revenues of the Irish church for the use of non-denominational education and poor relief. While the Irish Church Temporalities Act, passed in 1833, did not include appropriation of church revenues, it did provide for the gradual abolition of ten bishoprics and the suspension of numerous

---

97. O'Ferrall, *Catholic emancipation*, p. 207; Madden, *Memoir of Daly*, p. 111.
98. Wyse, *Historical sketch*, pp i, 230.
99. Massy, *Footprints*, pp 176–7; O'Ferrall, *Catholic emancipation*, pp 258–60.
100. A.H. Kenney, 'Memoir of William Magee' in *The works of William Magee, archbishop of Dublin* (2 vols., London, 1842), i, lxix–lxxx.

parishes, and it ensured that the established church in Ireland effectively ceased to exist as a *national* establishment. New reformation missionaries revived the proselytising campaign during the 1830s, now with different methods, including the organisation of converts into colonies under the protection of sympathetic landlords.[101] Reformation missionaries remained active through the Victorian era and had some localised success, especially through the work of the evangelical Anglican, Alexander Dallas.[102] The movement of the 1820s, however, with its aim of securing the conformity of the large majority of the Irish population to the established church, could not be revived.

The reformation movement of the 1820s had failed, first, because it had not managed to inspire and unite more than a minority in the United Church. Despite the zeal of the Bible and reformation societies, the majority in the church had kept their distance from the movement, preferring peaceful coexistence with the Catholic majority. Reformation leaders such as Magee, Daly and Farnham had been unable to convince the majority in the established church that it could extend its influence and authority over the whole of the Irish population. The movement had also been hampered by continued distrust between the evangelical and high church wings of the church, with the high church group in particular suspecting that the Bible and reformation societies were less than sound on the doctrine of the visible church. The high church bishop of Limerick, for example, while giving support to the reformation campaign in 1827, was quick to turn upon the evangelicals after the failure of the movement.[103] Second, the reformation had not managed to win wide support or confidence from either British public opinion or the Irish Protestant landed classes. Despite the joining of the two established churches at the Act of Union of 1801, few in England ever regarded it as a true incorporative union, and most Anglicans were prepared to cut their ties with the Irish establishment once that church was in difficulties. Most Irish Protestant landowners, moreover, had retained a pragmatic concern for their interests, and had declined to risk their relations with their Catholic tenants by giving much support to Bible societies, to zealous Church of Ireland pastors or to Farnham's Reformation Society. But above all the reformation

---

101. J.G. MacWalter, *The Irish reformation movement in its religious, social, and political aspects* (Dublin, 1852), pp 170–82; E. Nangle, *The origins, progress, and difficulties of the Achill Mission* (Dublin, 1839).
102. Bowen, *Protestant crusade*, pp 195–256.
103. By mid April, Jebb was denouncing Richard Murray, the evangelical clergyman who had gained numerous converts in Askeaton, and proclaiming 'the moral rottenness of Evangelicalism'. See J. Jebb to R. Jebb, (Trinity College, Dublin, Jebb Papers, Ms 6396–7/339); Stunt, 'Evangelical cross-currents', p. 219.

had failed because it had confronted an Irish Catholic population that already had a strong sense of its identity and that was being instilled with a new pride by O'Connell and the Catholic Association. Before 1824, the reformation campaign had not been unrealistic in its goal of extending the influence and authority of the established church over an Ireland in which the Catholic church seemed institutionally weak and a heavy burden on the Irish peasantry. Once the movement was under way, however, it soon became clear that despite the institutional weakness of the Catholic church – the sparsity of churches, schools, priests and nuns in many districts – the large majority of the Irish population was strongly Catholic in its beliefs and devotional practices. After 1824, the Catholic Association had not only rapidly mobilised the Catholic population in defence of their identity, but also brought many Catholic priests to identify with the national movement for Catholic emancipation. By contrast, the reformation movement increasingly assumed the aspect of a religious mission supporting an alien political force in Ireland. 'An Irish peasant, at the present day', observed the liberal *Edinburgh Review* in March 1829, 'would answer the new reformation missions, as the Indian Chieftains did the Spanish priest who recruited for converts in the rear of the army of Pizarro'.[104] The reformation movement had been rooted in the perception that Irish Catholics were ignorant, priest-ridden, and underdeveloped – a people who had not yet been brought into the benefits of the Protestant, London-centred state. The impoverished condition of the Irish majority was the result of sinful neglect by the Protestant state. They needed to be educated, converted, and civilised from above by a paternalistic establishment. The fatal weakness of the 'Second Reformationists', the liberal *Dublin Evening Post* had observed in August 1827, was that 'they despised their enemies too much'.[105] Recent work by Emmet Larkin has suggested that the beginnings of the 'devotional revolution' in Irish catholicism must be traced to the eighteenth century.[106] The defeat of the reformation movement of the 1820s certainly supports this position. It also demonstrated clearly that the era of state-imposed Christianity had passed and that the failure of the sixteenth-century Reformation in Ireland could not be reversed in the nineteenth century.

---

104. 'The last of the Catholic question', *Edinburgh Review*, xlix (March 1829), p. 237.
105. *Dublin Evening Post*, 4 Aug. 1827.
106. Larkin, 'The rise and fall of stations'.

9

Social Catholicism in England in the Age of the Devotional Revolution

JOSEF L. ALTHOLZ*

IN HER STUDY OF THE SOCIAL CATHOLIC MOVEMENT IN ENGLAND,[1] Georgiana McEntee disposes of the period before the primacy of Henry Edward Manning (1865) in only five pages. This cursory dismissal of early Roman Catholic activity in the social field[2] has been common among historians.[3] It is not entirely unjustified, considering the limited extent of this activity, its relatively unsystematic character, and the much greater achievement of Manning. However, there was a certain amount of thought and action which may fairly be called 'social Catholic' in the period before 1865. A study of the

---

* A version of this article was read in 1970 in Moscow at the session of the Commission d'Histoire Ecclésiastique Comparée in which Emmet Larkin delivered his paper on the devotional revolution. In revisiting the subject, I have been able to take advantage of the considerable development in the social history of catholicism in England since 1970.
1. G.P. McEntee, *The social Catholic movement in Great Britain* (New York, 1927).
2. As late as 1964, the term 'social catholicism' was 'not at all familiar in England': A.R. Vidler, *A century of social catholicism, 1820–1920* (London, 1964), p. ix. Vidler gives the standard definition of continental social catholicism, centred upon the reaction to the consequences of the industrial revolution, especially class stratification and *laissez-faire*. This definition does not apply to the movement in England, for reasons indicated in the conclusion of this article, which argues that the English movement was nonetheless an appropriate counterpart. Specific influences from the early French movement are indicated.
3. There is a protest against this in Gerard Connolly, 'The transubstantiation of myth: towards a new popular history of nineteenth-century catholicism in England', *Journal of Ecclesiastical History*, xxxv (Jan. 1984), p. 103.

nature of this activity and the reasons for its limited character may yield some insights into the history of both English and Irish catholicism and of the social Catholic movement.

The Roman Catholics of England, emerging from persecution at the end of the eighteenth century, were a relatively small group, centred upon a number of noble and gentry families. Excluded from public life for centuries, they had cultivated unobtrusiveness; even after emancipation they took little part in the life of the nation. Largely rural, they were largely untouched by the social consequences of the Industrial Revolution. The converts from the Oxford movement after 1845 did not much alter this situation. What did make a difference was the immigration of the Irish, already substantial before 1845 and overwhelming after the Famine. The Irish immigrants were poor, they were urban, and they were numerous.[4] The Catholic poor were, in fact, the Irish poor, much more numerous than the English Catholic community which was called upon to supply them with the services of religion. Except for religion, there was no affinity between the two groups. Two things were clear: that the social concerns and energies of English Catholics would have to be devoted to ameliorating the condition of the Irish poor, and that they were unready for this work.

The first movement of social concern among English Catholics was notable for its romanticism. Its leaders were two early, pre-Tractarian converts who were influenced by a combination of French liberal catholicism and the romantic revival of medievalism. Kenelm Digby's *Broad stone of honour*[5] was an appeal for the revival of 'chivalry', the spirit which predisposed to heroic and generous actions. This aristocratic resuscitation of the ideal of medieval charity was buttressed by numerous quotations from Lamennais and Ozanam. Digby's ideas were put into practice by Ambrose Phillips de Lisle, a friend of Montalembert and translator of his life of St Elizabeth, a favourite patron saint of Victorian charitable institutions. On his Grace Dieu estate (the original of St Geneviève in *Coningsby*), Phillips de Lisle founded a monastery and several churches and schools. His concern, however, was less social than evangelistic, and his charities were part of a larger project for the conversion of England.[6] The founding of a Trappist monastery in a Leicestershire forest

---

4. Philip Hughes estimated that there were 679,067 Roman Catholics in England in 1851, of whom some 250,000 were native born, the rest being Irish. Philip Hughes, 'The English Catholics in 1850', G.A. Beck (ed.), *The English Catholics 1850–1950* (London, 1950), pp 42–85. Later estimates are slightly higher.
5. Originally published in 1822, later in four volumes in 1826–27. See W.G. Roe, *Lamennais and England* (London, 1966), p. 120.
6. See Robert Kent Donovan, 'The denominational character of English Catholic charitable effort, 1800–1865', *Catholic Historical Review*, lxii, no. 2 (Apr. 1976), pp 200–23.

(where there were hardly any Catholics) was not a solution for the needs of the Catholic poor; the almsgiving at Mt St Bernard's was intended to impress Protestants. Phillips de Lisle's friend, the sixteenth earl of Shrewsbury, was somewhat more practical in his extensive charities.[7] However, Shrewsbury, a friend of the architect Pugin, contributed more to the revival of Gothic church-building than to the needs of the poor.

In their scheme of aristocratic benevolence under the aegis of the Catholic faith, these men present a remarkable parallel to the early social catholicism of the Continent; but their practice followed the medieval pattern in which donations to churches, to schools or directly to the poor were all equally 'works of charity'. They showed no consciousness of actual social conditions, and they were easily distracted by schemes of church reunion and Gothic architecture. But the anachronistic romanticism of Digby and Phillips de Lisle nonetheless provided an ideological basis for the charitable work of the next, ultramontane generation. They revived the medieval ideal of holy poverty, of giving to the poor simply because they were poor, which allowed English Catholics to overcome the contemporary Protestant distinction between the 'deserving' and the 'undeserving' poor and ultimately to accept the Irish poor as proper objects of charity, not to be forced to mirror a middle-class respectability but to be accepted within their own context.[8]

More realism was shown by the editors of two Catholic periodicals founded in the 1840s. Frederick Lucas, editor of the London-based *Tablet*, a convert from the Quakers, recognised that the Irish were the special concern of British catholicism and took a pro-Irish stand on political as well as social issues. In his social theory Lucas was a disciple of Ozanam,[9] and he took part in the formation of the English branch of the Society of St Vincent de Paul in 1844, from which several local 'conferences' later developed. Lucas also crusaded against pew-rents, which limited the access of the poor to churches. His pro-Irish politics, however, alienated him from some English Catholic aristocrats who shared the prejudices of their class. Lucas eventually transplanted himself and the *Tablet* to Dublin, entering Irish politics but ceasing to be a factor in English catholicism. Replacing the *Tablet* was the *Rambler*,

---

7. Shrewsbury's 'hospital' at Alton included an almshouse for the aged poor, two schools and a mechanics' institute. See Denis Gwynn, *Lord Shrewsbury, Pugin and the gothic revival* (London, 1946).
8. See Sheridan Gilley, 'Heretic London, holy poverty and the Irish poor, 1830–70', *Downside Review*, lxxxix (Jan. 1971), pp 64–89.
9. Donovan, 'Denominational character', pp 206–7, cites illustrative passages from the *Tablet*, Aug. 8, 1840. Ozanam visited London in 1851. For Lucas, see Edward Lucas, *The life of Frederick Lucas, M.P.* (London, 1896). See also Josef L. Altholz, 'The *Tablet*, the *True Tablet*, and nothing but the *Tablet*', *Victorian periodicals newsletter*, ix (June 1976), pp 68–72.

founded in 1848 by the Oxford convert John Moore Capes. The events of 1848 made Capes aware of 'social decay' and the danger of revolution: 'If we will not care for the poor man from love, we must do it from dread.'[10] Anticipating the ultimate victory of democracy, he sought to prepare the lower classes for it by education and religion. He was zealous in urging schools and missions among the poor. Capes' social catholicism, not merely political in origin, had some curious manifestations: he opposed sabbatarian legislation because it interfered with the innocent amusements of the poor. The *Rambler* serialised harrowing 'tales' of 'Scenes of Life in London', notably the novel *Kate Geary*, showing much sympathy for the Irish. Strikingly, the *Rambler* opposed the Gothic church-building of Pugin because this expensive style did not meet the actual need for numerous cheap churches, built among the poor and suited to their devotions.[11] The *Rambler* later became famous as the organ of the liberal Catholics Sir John Acton and Richard Simpson, but these intellectual and political liberals did not continue Capes' social concerns.

The most authoritative statements of a Catholic social position were made by the newly-appointed Cardinal Wiseman, archbishop of Westminster, in 1850 and 1851. The most eloquent statement was, in fact, a rhetorical device. In the controversy over the new hierarchy, Wiseman sought to demonstrate that, in taking the title of Westminster, he was not encroaching upon the rights of Westminster Abbey. The Abbey was not the Westminster he claimed:

> Close under the Abbey of Westminster there lie concealed labyrinths of lanes and courts and alleys and slums – nests of ignorance, vice, depravity and crime, as well as squalor, wretchedness, and disease; whose atmosphere is typhus, whose ventilation is cholera, in which swarms a huge and almost countless population, in great measure, nominally at least Catholic ... This is the part of Westminster which alone I covet, and which I shall be glad to claim and visit, as a blessed pasture in which sheep of holy Church are to be tended.[12]

---

10. 'The fallen king', *Rambler*, 2 Mar. 1848, p. 178. In another article Capes observed: 'The great problem for the statesman of this day is the reconciliation of rich and poor, or rather of riches and poverty'. 'Rich and poor', *Rambler*, 22 Apr. 1848, p. 345. See J.L. Altholz, *The liberal Catholic movement in England* (London, 1962), pp 10–11.

11. The very passionate controversies of the 'Goths' and 'anti-Goths' suggest that this artistic question touched some sensitive religious and social chords. See Altholz, *Liberal Catholic movement*, pp 11, 14–16, and Bernard Ward, *The sequel to Catholic emancipation* (2 vols., London, 1915), ii, pp 170 ff.

12. Nicholas Wiseman, *An appeal to the reason and good feeling of the English people on the subject of the Catholic hierarchy* (London, 1850), pp 30–1. This is one of the earliest instances of the use of the word 'slum', which at that date meant a specific slum building.

This was followed by an extensive review of *Mayhew's London labour and the London poor* in June 1851, staking broad ground: 'We shall be satisfied if we shall have awakened Catholic sympathies in favour of a great work which seems committed to our Church, that of evangelising the poor in London.'[13]

Wiseman had a genuine if somewhat diffuse concern with the problems of the Catholic poor, a subject on which he spoke in several sermons. He made efforts to import religious orders to work in London, sisters to teach and operate institutions and priests primarily to conduct missions among the poor, in one of which he took a personal part. Italian Passionists and Redemptorists were effective missionisers with their new devotions, but most of the orders were limited in parish work by their rules (or, in the case of the Jesuits, by social climbing at Farm Street). To remedy this, Wiseman formed his own diocesan order, the Oblates of St Charles, placed it under Manning and directed it to the then slum district of the Potteries in Bayswater; it was thus Wiseman who turned Manning to his mission to the Irish poor, which was not his first choice. But Wiseman gave little further attention to social issues. His interest was primarily evangelistic and he could be distracted by other concerns.[14] His true contribution was to give a decisively ultramontane turn to English catholicism, bringing with it the enthusiasm and devotions which could rouse Irish immigrants whose religious practice in Ireland, in the days before the 'devotional revolution',[15] had been far from regular.

Practical charity was more extensive and of older standing than these limited theoretical expressions. The first Catholic charitable societies had begun under Bishop Challoner in penal days, as early as 1764, and an important consolidation was achieved in 1813.[16] The basic charities were chapels and schools, which were also the basic institutional needs of the church. Catholic

---

13. Wiseman, 'The industry of the poor', *Dublin Review*, xxx (June 1851), p. 532. Even here, Wiseman displayed little more than complacency at the staunch though untutored Catholicity of the London Irish. The *Dublin Review*, Wiseman's organ, devoted very few articles to social questions. Before 1850, the only notable article was by the French liberal Catholic de Coux in July 1836.
14. One of Manning's biographers accounts for Wiseman's lack of leadership by tracing it to his unwillingness to offend the Catholic aristocracy: 'Social reform would have alienated the "Old Catholics".' V.A. McClelland, *Cardinal Manning: his public life and influence, 1865–1892* (London, 1962), p. 6n. This explanation is simplistic. Wiseman was socially conservative in his own right, with no interest in democracy or social reform; and he was ready to alienate the Old Catholics in other matters. His lack of leadership was largely due to indolence, illness and various distractions. There is an uncritically favourable account of him in Edward Norman, *The English Catholic Church in the nineteenth century* (Oxford, 1984), and a judiciously favourable one in R.J. Schiefen, *Nicholas Wiseman and the transformation of English catholicism* (Shepherdstown, 1984).
15. See Emmet Larkin, 'The devotional revolution in Ireland, 1850–75' in *A.H.R.*, lxxvii (1972), pp 625–52.
16. See John Bennett, 'The care of the poor' in Beck, *English Catholics*, pp 559–84.

noblemen and squires customarily supported a chapel and occasionally a school on their estates, the domestic chaplain doubling as mission priest. Over sixty primary schools for the poor had been founded by 1829. London had imported Irish Christian Brothers as early as 1826. The number of schools increased steadily, especially after the first orders of nuns arrived in 1839; Wiseman was particularly active in recruiting nuns and brothers from France, Belgium and Ireland.

It was at the parish level that effective work with the Irish poor began. In Lancashire, two parish priests, Daniel Hearne and Henry Gillow, managed to involve the Irish themselves in the process of education and social work.[17] Their London counterpart was John Moore, a priest at Virginia Street, Wapping, who formed a guild which combined special devotions with medical and burial provision, and whose members collected the pence which built the chapel.[18] Other guilds were formed, but more characteristic of London parishes were the confraternities, which performed a variety of services to the parish such as fund-raising and teaching evening and Sunday schools while requiring their members to perform their regular mass, confession and communion obligations – not yet as part of an ultramontane devotional revolution but as the response of a post-tridentine priesthood to the observed irregularity of Irish religious practice. Parallel to the confraternities were the Catholic temperance societies encouraged by parish clergy from the late 1830s, which contributed to the immensely successful London mission of Fr Mathew in 1843. There were parochial provident societies of various kinds, culminating in the formation of Catholic Young Men's Societies in the early 1850s.[19] Many of these organisations, especially the benefit and temperance societies, were imitative of Protestant or working-class efforts of this period; the Catholic case differs in that the social effort was deliberately tied to catholicism and integrated into the life of the parish.

Both the scale and the character of Catholic work at the parish level were changed by the new ultramontanism which arrived in London along with Wiseman in the late 1840s. 'Wiseman decided early that local missions in the midst of Catholic residential areas were the only means of turning migrants into active Catholics.'[20] He encouraged efforts already underway to place

---

17. Gillow even proposed a justification for trade unionism. See Connolly, 'Transubstantiation of myth', loc. cit., p. 102.
18. Sheridan Gilley, 'Catholic faith of the Irish slums: London, 1840–70' in H.J. Dyos and Michael Wolff (ed.), *The Victorian city: images and realities* (2 vols., London, 1973), ii, p. 846.
19. Ibid., pp 847–8. Parallel stories of the case of Cardiff are told by John Hickey, *Urban Catholics* (London, 1967).
20. L.H. Lees, *Exiles of Erin: Irish migrants in Victorian London* (Ithaca, 1979), p. 175.

chapels and schools directly in the slums.[21] But the most original feature of the new approach was the preaching of open-air missions, begun in 1848 by an English priest, Joseph Hodgson, in Southwark, where he was joined by two Passionists, who introduced the Italian device of *svegliarini* – emotional street preaching. This technique of street missions was widely imitated because it was successful among the Irish, just as the more structured missions had been effective in Ireland itself. These missions (some of them conducted in the courts of the rookeries) were followed up in the parishes by characteristic ultramontane special devotions which were added to the repertoire of the confraternities and newer devotional societies.[22] There is a distinct similarity here to the 'devotional revolution' in Ireland, though the English did not consciously borrow from the Irish example[23] and the result was not quite such a total devotionalisation of the immigrant Irish.[24]

The difference that the new ultramontanisms could make was illustrated by the Brompton Oratory, led by the flamboyant F.W. Faber, who popularised all the ultramontane devotions in his Italianate church and added some of his own, including unabashedly romantic vernacular hymns, creating a 'religious culture which was heartily popular because it was so heartily vulgar'[25] – and therefore attractive to the Irish. Brompton itself was an upper-class district, and Faber was backed by a circle of wealthy laity led by the earl of Arundel and Surrey, later (1856) the fourteenth duke of Norfolk, described by Montalembert as the most pious layman of the century. In a somewhat self-conscious attempt at class unity, the oratory's original chapel in the Strand was opened indifferently to all classes. The Irish who flocked to the chapel brought with them odours and fleas intolerable to their social betters, and the experiment had to be abandoned.[26] It was replaced by the

---

21. Gilley, 'Catholic Faith', p. 845, cites the work of John Kyne of the Lincoln's Inn Fields parish, whose schools and chapels in the slums were supported by Wiseman.
22. Ibid., p. 838.
23. Wiseman and his predecessor in the London district did not bring in Irish priests. The Lancashire bishops sought them out from All Hallows College, Drumcondra. The parallel function of the parish church as a social focus in Lancashire and Ireland is noted by W.L. Lowe, 'The Lancashire Irish and the Catholic Church, 1846–71', *I.H.S.*, xx no. 78 (Sept. 1976), pp 129–55.
24. Lees concluded that the pattern of nearly total mass attendance never developed among the London Irish, speaking of 'two Catholic populations: a minority of active participants and the majority, whom the priests saw irregularly' on the major ritual occasions. *Exiles of Erin*, p. 182. The literature on Irish Catholics in England makes frequent comparative references to Larkin, 'Devotional revolution'.
25. Sheridan Gilley, 'Vulgar piety and the Brompton Oratory, 1850–1860' in Roger Swift and Sheridan Gilley (ed.), *The Irish in the Victorian city* (London, 1985), p. 263.
26. A similar problem was faced by Frederick Oakeley at Islington, where he attempted to secure equality by seating rich and poor on opposite sides of the aisle. The fleas did not respect the arrangement, and the experiment was abandoned in favour of separate workingmen's masses at an earlier hour.

initiative of an individual Oratorian, William Anthony Hutchinson. Like Faber a convert, Hutchinson organised ragged schools among the central London rookeries. To gather the children, eventually almost one thousand in number, he formed a St Patrick's Society of Irish workers; to employ them, he set up child street-sellers in business and trained them for adult jobs. His empire of charity, backed by Lord and Lady Arundel, expanded to include an orphanage, a reformatory, a refuge for ex-prostitutes and an industrial school for cripples. But a scheme of model lodging-houses failed, his patron the duke of Norfolk died in 1860, and Hutchinson himself died in 1863, leaving his schools and enterprises to the archdiocese. His relative success was due to his willingness to deal with the Irish poor on their own terms, combining 'sophisticated understanding of Irish social conditions and ultramontane devotions and theology'.[27]

At the national level, however, the real impetus for Catholic charitable activity came from the policies of the state and the competition of Protestants. From 1833 the government had granted funds for school building to the National Society (Anglican) and British and Foreign Society (Non-conformist) schools, and in 1846 the grants were expanded to cover the training and support of teachers. This stimulated Catholics, unhappy at being excluded and fearful that the Catholic poor might be drawn into Protestant schools, to demand similar assistance for their own schools. Under episcopal sponsorship the Catholic Poor School committee was organised in 1847, chaired by an eminent squire, Charles Langdale. In December 1847, the government was persuaded to authorise grants to be made to inspected Catholic schools through the Committee. The bishops were jealous of government influence, and it was stipulated that Catholic schools would be inspected only by a Catholic inspector and that religious education *per se* would be excluded from inspection.[28] The grants, though small in comparison to those received by other bodies, were an effective stimulus to the growth of Catholic education for the poor.[29] Similarly, Catholics later took advantage of the

---

27. Sheridan Gilley, 'The Roman Catholic mission to the Irish in London, 1840–1860', *Recusant History*, x, no. 3 (Oct. 1969), p. 138.
28. The first inspector was T.W. Marshall. As a result of the increase of schools, a second inspector, S.N. Stokes, was appointed in 1853. Stokes had previously been secretary of the Poor School Committee, in which post he was succeeded by T.W. Allies. All these men were converts. The committee was mixed clerical and lay, appointed by the bishops. Some bishops still refused government inspection and support. Even Wiseman sought to limit the inspectors: see Wiseman to Langdale, 4 Feb. 1854 (Archives of the Archdiocese of Westminster). In 1858, the bishops refused to co-operate with the Royal Commission on Education on the grounds that there was no Catholic commissioner or assistant commissioner.
29. In 1855, the Catholic share of the grant was £13,272 out of £369,602. By 1867 there were 507 day schools with 67,143 children, 138 evening schools with 9686 pupils, 618 teachers, 631 pupil teachers, and a total income of £55,842, of which £21,591 came from government grants. Beck, *English Catholics*, pp 51–2.

availability of government funds for teacher training colleges to build one for men in 1850 and two for women by 1856.

The second stimulus for Catholic social concern came from the fear of 'leakage' and the real danger that poor Catholic children would be protestantised in public institutions. In workhouses, where many poor children were brought up, only Anglican chaplains and teaching were provided. This led to the growth of Catholic orphanages and 'refuges' starting in 1847, as well as constant pressure by Catholic politicians to force the admission of priests into the workhouses.[30] When laws authorising reformatories and industrial schools were passed in 1854, Catholics were unusually prompt in setting up such institutions, in order to rescue their children from Protestant influences.[31] There followed a struggle with Protestant-dominated boards of guardians to ensure that Catholic children would be sent to Catholic institutions when these were available.[32] Similar struggles led to the appointment of Catholic chaplains in the army in 1858 and in prisons in 1862.[33] By Wiseman's death, a substantial fabric of Catholic charitable activities had been built up.[34]

None of these institutions was original with Catholics; they followed governmental or Protestant models. The most striking thing about Catholic philanthropy is its imitative and defensive character. Catholic schools and orphanages were built because, if they were not, Catholic children would be educated in Protestant schools and workhouses and thus lost to the faith. Like other religious minorities (notably the Jews), English Catholics were prone to see motives of proselytism in the benevolent efforts of the Protestant majority.[35] In fact, there was relatively little proselytism of the Irish in

---

30. Lucas had been among the first, in 1853, to raise in Parliament the question of the denial of religious services to Catholics in workhouses and prisons. An act of 1859 authorised priests to instruct Catholic children in workhouses, but boards of guardians had to be prodded repeatedly into complying with this law. The need for government support in such matters affected Catholic politics: see J.L. Altholz, 'The Political Behavior of the English Catholics, 1850–1867', *Jn. Brit. Stud.*, iv (Nov. 1964), pp 89–103.
31. A reformatory and an industrial school for boys were set up in 1855; by 1865 there was another reformatory and two more industrial schools. One of the reformatories, praised by Dickens, was at Phillips de Lisle's Abbey of Mt St Bernard.
32. The government was more sympathetic than local bodies. The Reformatory and Industrial Schools Act of 1866 required that Catholic children be sent to Catholic schools, which would receive aid from the rates.
33. £500 was allotted to pay the salaries of Catholic prison chaplains, the first of whom was Fr. Nugent, the 'apostle of Liverpool', later to be active in a number of social causes.
34. The extensive work of dioceses other than Westminster is only beginning to be studied. One of the principal difficulties of Catholic charity was the uncertain legal status of bequests involving priests, under the law against 'superstitious uses.' This was partially cleared up in 1866 by an act allowing the registration of Catholic charitable trusts.
35. As early as 1816 the *Orthodox Journal* warned its readers against 'public charities.' The fear of 'compulsory apostasy' was pervasive: see J.L. Altholz, 'A Note on the English Catholic Reaction to the Mortara Case', *Jewish Social Studies*, xxiii (Apr. 1961), pp 111–18.

England; but public institutions were Anglican as a matter of course, and minorities had to take care of themselves. Without the stimulus of public and Protestant competition, the Catholics would have done much less, notwithstanding the ultramontane revival.

The other characteristic of Catholic philanthropy is its narrowly denominational emphasis, greater than any other Christian denomination. It is impossible to separate Catholic charity from other aspects of the growth of the church in England. The building of schools was inseparable from the building of churches (often, in fact, it was the same building). Both were responses to the explosion of the Catholic population, primarily Irish, and nobody distinguished between the spiritual and the social purpose. English Catholic philanthropy was pre-eminently religious, concerned primarily with the spiritual and only incidentally with the physical needs of the poor.[36] The rapidly growing Catholic minority had to concentrate all its resources on its own denominational needs. National social reform was a luxury it could not afford. The impulse which elsewhere produced what was known as 'social catholicism' was represented in England by the upbuilding of the institutional church. The unimaginative habitual loyalty of the 'Old Catholic' aristocracy and gentry, so maligned by Manning, could claim an institutional achievement matching any social Catholic movement on the Continent, though lacking their larger implications.

These activities were inadequate and unsystematic, and they seem insignificant before the work of Manning. The great merit of Manning was his recognition that the Catholic poor were Irish and urban. With this central vision undistracted by romantic or political considerations, he could attack social problems with vigour and effect. Yet even Manning, until near the end of his life, shared the limitation inherent in all English Catholic social efforts, a concern with the special needs of the Catholic poor rather than with the general problem of poverty.[37] The English Catholics made no contribution to the needs of the nation as a whole and rarely expressed any concept of social concern or Christian benevolence applicable outside their own body.

How, then, may these thoughts and works be described as 'social catholicism'? In the usual sense in which social catholicism is defined as a

---

36. 'Give them schools, and give them priests.' [W.G. Todd], 'The Irish in England', *Dublin Review*, xli (Dec. 1856), p. 518. Even Lucas regarded the physical needs of the Catholic poor as secondary; 'We want Priests and Churches, Schoolmasters and Schoolhouses; and then a long train of benevolent institutions for supplying the needs of their bodily and human existence.' Cited in *Catholic emancipation 1829 to 1929: essays by various writers* (London, 1929), p. 167.

37. Manning remarked that, when he became a Catholic, he 'ceased to work for the people of England, and had henceforth to work for the Irish occupation in England.' Cited in J.J. O'Connor, *The Catholic revival in England* (New York, 1942), p. 46.

conscious programme for ameliorating the social problems arising from industrialisation, there was almost nothing of the sort among the English Catholics. Yet it may be argued that the charitable activity of this minority denomination represented an appropriate counterpart to continental social catholicism. In Catholic countries, the institutional church – priests, churches, schools and other elements – was already in place. Catholic leaders could thus afford to turn their attention to larger national issues. The English Catholics, however, were a minority, powerless to influence national policy on the 'condition-of-England question', but with a specific and growing poor population for whom they had a direct responsibility. To the extent that they addressed themselves to that responsibility, theirs was a work of social catholicism. Its result was not the amelioration of social conditions but the building of the institutional church in the atmosphere of the devotional revolution.

10

The Genealogy of Irish Modernism:
The Case of W.B. Yeats

THOMAS WILLIAM HEYCK

THE PURPOSE OF THIS PAPER IS TO ILLUMINATE one of the two main paths in the intellectual origins of Irish modernism – the case of William Butler Yeats. The number of Irish writers who can with any assurance be regarded as participants in the modernist movement in the arts of the late nineteenth and early twentieth centuries is not large; but among those of the early generation, by general consensus, stands Yeats, who is considered with Joyce, Pound, Eliot, and Woolf to be in the pantheon of English-speaking modernists, and who was a crucial influence on later Irish modernists like Joyce himself, Sean O'Casey, Denis Johnston, and Samuel Beckett. Any account of the genealogy of modernism in Ireland must, therefore, explain the intellectual influences shaping Yeats's thought; and that is my main object in this essay. Of course, the influences on Joyce's thought constitute the second main path to modernism in Ireland; but Joyce's intellectual development was so different from Yeats's that it should be the subject of a different study. Here, Yeats is the focus; and in particular I hope to shed light on the relationship between Yeats, the Irish literary revival, and the development of a modernist outlook.

That there was any significant relationship between the Irish literary revival and modernism seems paradoxical, for the literary revival was a late flowering of romanticism, while modernism was, at least according to its most famous manifestos, classicist and anti-romantic. This is only one of the paradoxes that seem to populate the relationship. Modernism was cosmopolitan (or internationalist), while the literary revival was intensely Irish and therefore in a sense parochial. Modernism was aggressively anti-historical and synchronic in its approach to understanding modernity, while the Irish revivalists sought inspiration from the historical roots of Irish nationality. Modernism was explicitly apolitical, while the Irish literary revival was profoundly political, engaged as it was in the establishment of cultural autonomy for Ireland.

The complexity of such issues is shown by the twists and turns of writings on the topics of Yeats and the Irish literary revival as well as on modernism itself. The subject of modernism was initially defined and its history written by the modernists themselves and by critics reared on modernist principles.[1] Modernist scholars incorporated Yeats as well as Joyce into the history of international modernism and largely set their Irishness aside. In the leading text on the modernist movement, *Modernism, 1890–1930*, edited by Malcolm Bradbury and James McFarlane, Yeats is discussed as a British, or even English, modernist; London receives a chapter in the section on 'A geography of modernism', but Dublin does not.[2] In Ireland, meanwhile, there has been ambivalence about the relations among Yeats, Irish nationality, and modernism. Yeats himself, as we shall see, expressed reservations about modernist literature, and some of his admirers even at the time of his death denied that he was a modernist and insisted that he was above all a nationalist poet.[3] However, critical debate in the newly founded Irish Free State, dominated as it was by the Irish-Ireland philosophy, tended to reject Yeats as a national poet and to insist that he had been merely the voice of the alien minority – the Anglo-Irish ascendancy – not the 'real' Ireland. Such critics, looking for a voice of authentic (that is, Catholic, middle class, urban) Ireland, often posed Joyce as a kind of adversary to Yeats.[4] Ironically, however, Joyce was

---

1. See Astradur Eysteinsson, *The concept of modernism* (Ithaca, 1990), chs. 1 and 2.
2. Malcolm Bradbury and James McFarlane (ed.), *Modernism: a guide to European literature, 1890–1930* (London, 1976). For other examples of criticism that emphasises Yeats's modernism, as opposed to his Irish nationalism, see: Harold Bloom, *Yeats* (New York, 1970), which treats Yeats as a romantic visionary poet; and Hugh Kenner, *A colder eye: the modern Irish writers* (New York, 1983), which firmly and wittily sets Yeats in Irish context, but says little about nationalism and emphasises instead Yeats's linguistic contributions to 'International Modernism'.
3. See, for example, the commemoration issue of the Abbey Theatre's journal, *The Arrow* (Summer 1939), especially articles by F.R. Higgins, 'As Irish poet', pp 6–8; Austin Clarke, 'Poet and artist', pp 8–9; and Richard Hayes, 'His nationalism', pp 10–11.
4. See Terence Brown, 'Yeats, Joyce, and the Irish critical debate' in *Ireland's literature: selected essays* (Totowa, NJ, 1988), pp 77–90.

from the time of T.S. Eliot's review of *Ulysses* accepted in western literary circles as a leader of international modernism.[5]

Meanwhile, another scholarly tradition grew up that places Yeats firmly within the Irish historical context and thus usually plays down both the modernist dimensions of his work and non-Irish (including English) influences on his thought. These works see Yeats mainly in terms of Irish nationalism. Malcolm Brown, for example, declares that 'Modern Ireland provides us with the classic case of an impressive literature brought to birth by politics'; and as for Yeats, if he had not become a nationalist, most of the best of his poetry would never have appeared.[6] Other scholars have placed Yeats within the Anglo-Irish literary tradition, focusing on the contributions of the Protestant minority to Irish culture.[7] Most of the scholars who 'historicise' Yeats in these ways assume that the Irish literary revival, the Irish national consciousness that arose from it and Yeats's contributions to them were good things – most, but not all. Seamus Deane, a left-wing critic who is acutely conscious of the Troubles in Northern Ireland, has raised serious questions about Yeats's creation of certain destructive myths. In *Celtic twilights*, Deane argues that Yeats created glamorous fictions about both the Protestant ascendancy and the Irish peasantry and enlisted them in a conservative vision of an Irishness, 'which expresses itself in hostility towards the modern world'. Similarly, Deane argues, Yeats not only defended the Irish aristocracy but also created 'an image of the hero as artist surrounded by the philistine or clerically-dominated mob'. Deane suggests that it is time for the Irish to abandon this powerful but unhealthy intellectual heritage.[8]

The most recent work on Yeats continues the process of emphasising the Irish historical context but does so by interpreting him in terms of the global decolonising process. In a very influential publication of the Irish Field Day enterprise, Terry Eagleton, Frederic Jameson and Edward Said treat Yeats as a poet of decolonisation. For example, in his widely-read chapter on 'Yeats and decolonization', Said does not deny that Yeats was a modernist as well as an Irishman immersed in the politics of his day, but he insists that Yeats was

---

5. Eliot, '*Ulysses*, order and myth' in Robert H. Deming (ed.), *James Joyce: the critical heritage* (2 vols., New York, 1970), i, 268–71; first published in *Dial* (1923), pp 480–3.
6. Malcolm Brown, *The politics of Irish literature: from Thomas Davis to W.B. Yeats* (London, 1972), pp vii and 14. See also: Richard J. Loftus, *Nationalism in modern Anglo-Irish poetry* (Madison, 1964); and Richard Fallis, *The Irish renaissance* (Syracuse, 1977).
7. See, for example, A. Norman Jeffares, *Anglo-Irish Literature* (New York, 1982); and Julian Moynahan, *Anglo-Irish: the literary imagination in a hyphenated culture* (Princeton, 1995).
8. Seamus Deane, *Celtic twilights: essays in modern Irish literature* (London, 1985), chs. 2 and 3, especially pp 30–1.

also an 'indisputably great *national* poet who articulates the experiences, the aspirations, and the vision of a people suffering under the domination of an offshore power'. Of course to state that Yeats was a nationalist poet says nothing new, but by 'national' Said means anti-colonial; thus he prefers to set Yeats alongside anti-colonial writers like Tagore, Neruda, and Vallejo rather than Anglo-Irish writers like J.M. Synge and Lady Gregory or modernists like Pound and Eliot.[9] David Cairns and Shaun Richards have offered a similar but more subtle reading of Yeats that moves entirely within the cultural politics of Irish nationalism.[10] On the other hand, the critic John Wilson Foster has attempted to 'claim the Irish Revival itself as more generously Modernist than previously thought', at the same time as he seeks to broaden and perhaps soften the definition of modernism.[11] A new volume on *Irishness and (post)modernism*, edited by John Rickard, complexifies the issues even more. The essays in this volume examine the intersection of Irish national identity and culture on the one hand, with 'the development of a transnational, global avant-garde culture' of modernism and even post-modernism on the other.[12] The results are surprising. Margaret Mills Harper, for instance, finds both the nationalism and the modernism of Yeats to be ambiguous, and concludes that *A vision*, where Yeats held in a single system both national and modernist impulses, was in fact not his own work but a collaboration between Yeats and his wife Georgie.[13]

Two new works offer interpretations of Yeats as anti-colonial poet without engaging in the reductionism that seems to characterise much post-colonial criticism. In *Inventing Ireland*, Declan Kiberd brilliantly treats Yeats's lifelong search for a *style*, a unique and authentic 'mode of expression', as a central aspect of cultural anti-colonialism. Yeats sought to break with traditional literary forms precisely because literature was such a powerful instrument in anglicising the Irish. Yet in his mature work, *A vision*, Yeats provided a cultural vision for the new Irish Free State that included, as his own life did,

---

9. Said, 'Yeats and decolonization' in Terry Eagleton, Frederic Jameson, and Edward Said, *Nationalism, colonialism, and literature* (introduction by Seamus Deane, Minneapolis, 1990), pp 69–95. For Deane's view, see his 'Introduction', p. 5, which appears to endorse Said's interpretation. Said's essay was first published in his *Culture and imperialism* (New York, 1993). Despite the attention it has received, Said's essay is marred by insufficient knowledge of Irish history and the attempt to understand modern Irish history in terms of Franz Fanon's anti-imperialist ideology. See the criticisms by Julian Moynahan in his *Anglo-Irish*, pp x–xiii.
10. David Cairns and Shaun Richards, *Writing Ireland: colonialism, nationalism and culture* (Manchester, 1988).
11. John Wilson Foster, 'Irish modernism' in *Colonial consequences: essays in Irish literature and culture* (Dublin, 1991), pp 44–59.
12. John S. Rickard, 'Introduction', in *Irishness and (post) modernism* (Lewisberg, 1994), p. 13.
13. M.M. Harper, 'Twilight to vision: Yeats's collaborative modernity', ibid., pp 61–83.

a fusion of both 'Anglo' and 'Celtic' qualities.[14] Finally, Terry Eagleton in his book, *Heathcliff and the great hunger*, argues that while Irish nationalism and European modernism appear to be contradictory, in fact their sources had much in common – ultimately, a relationship with the cultural politics of capitalist society.[15]

The general thrust of the recent works relating Yeats, Ireland, and modernism is to emphasise the colonial context and thus the Irishness of Irish modernism. This is a healthy development, in my judgement, insofar as it recognises that national cultural contexts shaped all the varieties of modernism. As Bradbury and McFarlane admit, even while insisting on the international quality of modernism, '… many of the multiform movements of which it was made did have national dimensions and origins in specific regions of European culture'.[16] However, in the case of late-Victorian and Edwardian Ireland, the notions of colonialism and decolonisation do not fit perfectly as explanations of either the literary renaissance or modernism, partly because Ireland was not exactly an overseas colony, and partly because, grouping all the writers in the Irish literary renaissance as simply anti-colonial ignores the complexity of Irish society, partly because anti-colonialism does not give sufficient attention to English intellectual influences, and partly because it tends to ignore the central issue of religion. The context of decolonisation has, therefore, difficulty in explaining how Yeats took the intellectual turns that resulted in what critics regard as the specifically modernist aspects of his work, and it pays insufficient attention both to key English sources of his thought and to his religious concerns. What I will do in this paper is offer a more balanced account, and show how Yeats's intense involvement with issues concerning aestheticism, nationalism, and religion combined in very different and often strange ways to produce his peculiarly Irish modernism.

Before turning to the intellectual influences on Yeats, it is necessary to get a clear notion of modernism itself, and then for comparative purposes sketch out the genealogy of modernism in Britain. Modernism was an extremely complex cultural movement, and its definition remains controversial. Until recently, scholars have not even been able to agree on what *kind* of phenomenon it was – an alteration of artistic fashion, or a sweeping transformation

---

14. Declan Kiberd, *Inventing Ireland: the literature of the modern nation* (Cambridge, MA, 1995), pp 115–29, 290–3, 306–15, and 317–18.
15. Terry Eagleton, *Heathcliff and the great hunger: studies in Irish culture* (London, 1995), chs. 6 and 7.
16. Bradbury and McFarlane, *Modernism*, p. 13.

of thought in general; one of the 'extended periods of style and sensibility which are usefully measured in centuries', or one of those 'over-whelming dislocations, those fundamental convulsions of the human spirit that seem to topple even the most solid and substantial of our beliefs and assumptions ....'.[17] A volume edited by Dorothy Ross attempts (not entirely successfully, in my judgement) to extend the boundaries of modernism to include the social sciences.[18] However, a sensible definition between these extremes seems to be gaining ground. As one recent theorist observes, there is now general agreement among scholars that modernism is 'a legitimate concept broadly signifying a paradigmatic shift, a major revolt, beginning in the mid and late nineteenth century, against the prevalent literary and aesthetic traditions of the Western world'.[19]

Modernism, then, means something more concrete than 'contemporary'. It refers to a phase in the history of European and American high culture that lasted from about 1890 to about 1930. But it was not all-encompassing: not all writers and artists of the time shared in the revolt. Virginia Woolf was certain that *she* did, and that Arnold Bennett did not; and in general the modernists had a keen sense that they faced a persistent old guard.[20] If it has been difficult to say just what ideas and attitudes modernism denoted, both the modernists themselves and subsequent critics and scholars have felt fairly sure about recognising who was a modernist and who was not: Pound, Eliot, Woolf, Gide, Mann, Lawrence, Yeats, and Joyce were perhaps the key literary modernists, and Cézanne, Matisse, Picasso, Kandinsky, Braque, Boccioni, and Delaunay the crucial modernist painters.[21] Scholarly analyses of their work have revealed, not a set of qualities that applies to every modernist, but a set of what might be called – to use Wittgenstein's language – family resemblances, some of which characterised each modernist and made them all recognisable as participants in a revolt against the prevailing sensibility of the nineteenth century.

These qualities can be broken into four broad categories. First, there were critical attitudes towards the culture and values of nineteenth-century society. The modernists were hostile to the bourgeoisie, to its values of getting and spending, its conventional piety, its narrow morality, and its facile optimism.

---

17. Ibid., p. 19.
18. Dorothy Ross (ed.), *Modernist impulses in the human sciences, 1870–1930* (Baltimore, 1994).
19. Eysteinsson, *Concept of modernism*, p. 2.
20. Virginia Woolf, 'Modern novels'; 'Mr Bennett and Mrs Brown'; and 'Character in fiction', all in *The essays of Virginia Woolf, Volume III: 1919–1924*, ed. Andrew McNeillie (London, 1988), pp 30–7, 384–9, and 420–8 respectively.
21. See, for example, Bradbury and McFarlane, *Modernism*, and Christopher Butler, *Early modernism: literature, music, and painting in Europe, 1900–1916* (Oxford, 1994).

The modernists inherited from the romantics a sense of art and the life of the mind as activities superior to those of ordinary life; and they felt bitter and disillusioned at the inability of intellectuals over the course of the nineteenth century to stem the advance of industrial capitalism. The modernists, therefore, were alienated from middle-class society and its values, but they were also alienated from what they identified as mass society – the growing numbers of half-educated and semi-literate members of the working class, whom they did not know or understand and with whom they had no sympathy.[22] For these reasons, the modernists believed in the necessity of an avant-garde to provide cultural leadership, or at least a defence of the realm of the imagination and spirit. They liked to shock the bourgeoisie with 'outrageous' art, behaviour, or display of unconventional values.[23] At the same time, they explicitly broke with the established culture and prevailing artistic standards, moralistic and utilitarian as they tended to be; and they rejected the increasingly powerful scientific ideology and positivism, by which they as artists felt marginalised. Thus the modernists characteristically were torn by a contradiction between the passion of their rejection of bourgeois life and mass society on the one hand, and their pose of aloofness and detachment on the other.[24]

The second category of modernist attributes had to do with their sense of their own times as unique. Modernists believed that they lived in a period of profound transition, and that this period amounted to a radical break from the past. This notion became especially acute during and after the Great War, but it existed even before the turn of the century.[25] The modernists for this reason tended to turn their backs on history, to reject as irrelevant the characteristic historical orientation of the nineteenth century, and to adopt a synchronic, as opposed to diachronic, approach to understanding.[26] They explicitly claimed modernity for themselves, even if there was much about their times that caused them severe anxiety. They felt that their own world had lost all secure grounds for values and beliefs, and especially the religious bases for thought and action, and that science had failed to provide an

---

22. See John Carey, *The intellectuals and the masses: pride and prejudice among the literary intelligentsia, 1880–1939* (London, 1992).
23. See Irving Howe, *The idea of the modern in literature* (New York, 1967), p. 13; Daniel Fuchs, 'Saul Bellow and the modern tradition', *Contemporary literature* (Winter 1974), p. 75.
24. James McFarlane, 'Berlin and the rise of modernism, 1886–1896' in Bradbury and McFarlane, *Modernism*, p. 113.
25. Richard Ellmann and Charles Feidelson, *The modern tradition* (Oxford, 1965), p. vi; Howe, *Idea of the modern*, p. 15; M.H. Abrams, 'Modernism and postmodernism', *A glossary of literary terms*, (6th ed., New York, Harcourt Brace, 1993), p. 119.
26. Bradbury and McFarlane, 'The name and nature of modernism' in *Modernism*, p. 50.

adequate substitute. They saw their own times as profoundly problematic and sought to devote their art to the problematic and even to cause turmoil itself. They saw their world as harsh, dissonant, and chaotic, and believed that their art should not only picture life explicitly as fragmented but also should implicitly reflect the fragmentation in its underlying structures.[27]

A third set of modernist characteristics had to do with modes of understanding and consciousness. Modernists felt that reason, in the sense of a calculating faculty that simply manipulates sense data, was inadequate and misleading as a means of understanding the world or reality. Like the romantics, the modernists believed that reason, so valued in the nineteenth century, undervalued the imagination, and indeed all intuitive modes of understanding. They emphasised unconscious feeling over self-conscious perception, passion and will over intellection.[28] They tended towards irrationalism and trusted the 'irrational association of ideas'.[29] In keeping with their rejection of natural science, they rejected the empiricist assumption that all knowledge is based in sense perception, and they tended to magnify subjectivity in perception and art alike. They were, therefore, idealists, though rarely systematic philosophers. They believed, as one scholar says, that all artistic creativity is 'subjective, intuitive, and expressionist in character'.[30] The modernists tended to magnify the 'self', and to adopt a Nietzschean idea of the artist as genius or superman, but they also thought that the self was divided. Whereas conventional Christian thought in the nineteenth century imagined the self as the site of a struggle between reason and the passions, the modernists replaced that dualism with another – the notion that reason is the 'inherently unreliable arbiter of a "system of relations between various passions and desires", some of which may even be unconscious or repressed'.[31] Suppression of certain emotions (such as the sex drive), they believed, leads to self-deception and the advocacy of conventional moral inhibitions for the purposes of self-interest. The artist has the task not only of exposing these deceptions but also liberating the artist's self by artistic innovations such as free verse or the abandonment of visual perspective.[32]

---

27. Jacques Berthoud, 'Literature and drama' in Boris Ford (ed.), *The Cambridge guide to the arts in Britain*, vol. 8; *The Edwardian and the inter-war years* (Cambridge, 1989), p. 85; Abrams, 'Modernism and postmodernism', p. 119.
28. Ellmann and Feidelson, *Modern tradition*, p. vi, citing an essay by Lionel Trilling.
29. David Lodge, 'Historicism and literary theory', *Working with structuralism* (London, 1981), p. 71; Butler, *Early modernism*, p. 4.
30. Butler, *Early modernism*, p. 3.
31. Ibid., p. 90, quoting Nietzsche's *The will to power*. For the influence of Nietzsche in general, see James McFarlane, 'The mind of modernism' in Bradbury and McFarlane, *Modernism*, pp 77–9.
32. Butler, *Early modernism*, pp 15–16, 90–1; Howe, *Idea of the modern*, p. 14.

The fourth category of modernist attributes is the one by which they are best known – technical innovation in artistic production. This follows logically from their perception of their world at that particular moment of history. They gave up on representational discourse and rejected the idea that art should be a mirror of nature or society. They adopted instead highly self-conscious, non-representational styles and techniques. Moreover, in literature, the modernists engaged in fracturing conventional syntax and 'radical breaches of decorum, [and] disturbance of chronology'.[33] The modernists not only undertook formal experiment in literature and the other arts, but also they tended to judge the sincerity of an artist or authenticity of a work of art according to its technical novelty.[34] In the drive for innovation, modernists produced a wealth of artistic movements, some of them mutually contradictory, and most of them highly abstract and obscure to a reader or viewer not among the artistic elite; Bradbury and McFarlane name the main ones: 'Impressionism, Post-Impressionism, Expressionism, Cubism, Futurism, Symbolism, Imagism, Vorticism, Dadaism, Surrealism'.[35] Perhaps the broadest and most important of these was symbolism, for modernists generally not only structured their work by symbolism rather than narrative or logical argument, but also adopted a symbolist aesthetic. Modernists expressed more than one notion of a symbolist aesthetic: some thought there is a realm of reality beyond the ordinary material world, to which symbols alone can give access; others held that the human imagination constitutes the world we perceive, and this world is evoked by symbols; most felt simply that symbolism was the true language of art, and that all artists ought to resort to this language and exclude from art 'impurities' derived from other modes of discourse.[36]

The modernists felt that symbols not only invoked the supernatural world, but also came supercharged with associations from all earlier literature. If the interpretation of symbols in this regard required immense erudition of the reader, they thought, then all the better, for this fact accorded with their rejection of the ordinary reading public and popular culture, and their commitment to the ideas of esotericism and the avant-garde. By the same token, they embraced primitivism, both because it was shocking and because

---

33. Lodge, *Working with structuralism*, p. 71. See also Abrams, *Glossary*, p. 119; Bradbury and McFarlane, *Modernism*, pp 23–5.
34. Abrams, *Glossary*, p. 119; Howe, *Idea of the modern*, p. 19.
35. Bradbury and McFarlane, *Modernism*, p. 23.
36. See Ellmann and Feidelson, *Modern tradition*, p. 7; David Perkins, *A History of modern poetry: from the 1890s to the high modernist mode* (Cambridge, MA, 1976), pp 48–52.

it seemed to give access to a collective unconscious that the positivist mind of the nineteenth-century bourgeoisie had neglected. The symbolist aesthetic and the inclination towards primitivism led many modernists to mythopoeic allusions or to use the myth as their structuring device. The classic example, of course, was Joyce's *Ulysses*, and Eliot saw Joyce's use of myth as 'a way of controlling, of ordering, of giving shape and significance to the immense paradox of futility and anarchy which is contemporary history'.[37] But the modernists transformed the myths they used: they adopted a tone of irony, which, especially after the Great War, seemed the only appropriate posture for such fragmented times as modernity, and they changed the nature of their heroes from the person of great action to one whose mind is a 'psychic battlefield'.[38]

Finally, the modernists in their technical innovations sought to make art reflect the real setting of modern life – the modern city. They abandoned Nature as either the subject or locale of their art and looked to urban life instead, in all its squalor and impersonality. They thought of the cities of which they wrote as modernity in all its corruption and incoherence manifested in bricks and concrete – full of restless movement and change, the source of vulgarity and anomie, and the nemesis of heroism. In such settings the stream-of-consciousness style adopted by many modernists seemed the only appropriate one. Moreover, the modern cities to them were all alike; hence their art was cosmopolitan, not provincial. The modernist artist typically perceived himself or herself as an outsider in the modern city, an exile real or imagined. This too, contributed to the lack of roots and the internationalism of modernist ideology.[39]

The roots of the *British* form of modernism lay in the aesthetic revolt of the late nineteenth century. The targets of this revolt were numerous, and all of them had to do with the intellectuals' perception of the marginalisation of art and the imagination. The rise of natural science and its claims to cultural leadership; the decline of orthodox Christianity and the consequent loss of both a common cultural context and an authoritative source of inspiration; the failure of serious writers to effect dramatic changes in industrial society; the fracturing of the reading public as a result of the rapid expansion of

---

37. T.S. Eliot, '*Ulysses*, order and myth' in Deming, *James Joyce*, pp i, 271.
38. Howe, *Idea of the modern*, p. 34; for the significance of irony as the modern mode of speech, see Paul Fussell, *The great war and modern memory* (New York, 1975).
39. On modernism and the city, see Bradbury and McFarlane, *Modernism*, ch. 3; and Butler, *Early modernism*, ch. 4.

literacy; and a perceived debasement of public taste – together these cultural trends combined to produce a disaffection between artists and society.[40] This disaffection generated not only the bitter, naturalistic novels of George Gissing, but also the withdrawal of the pre-Raphaelites into archaic romance and the escapist poetry of Algernon Swinburne and William Morris. By the 1870s, various writers and artists had produced an ideology of aestheticism – a tendency to make art the substitute for Christianity, the sense that one should make one's life a work of art, and the claim that art should never be judged by standards external to itself. Art is for art's sake only.[41]

Aestheticism in Britain found home-grown inspiration but also drew on French theory as well. Walter Pater, an agnostic and believer in a religion of beauty, urged his readers to live for moments of intense aesthetic experience: 'To burn always with this hard, gemlike flame, to maintain this ecstasy, is success in life.'[42] James McNeill Whistler (an American expatriate in London) insisted that art should be free from all social and moral claims: 'Art should be independent of all clap-trap, should stand alone, and appeal to the artistic sense of eye or ear, without confounding this with emotions entirely foreign to it, as devotion, pity, love, patriotism, and the like.'[43] As Oscar Wilde put it in his Preface to *The picture of Dorian Gray*, 'There is no such thing as a moral or an immoral book. Books are well written, or badly written, that is all ... All art is quite useless'. Accordingly, a group of young poets in London, meeting as the Rhymers' Club and looking to Rossetti and Pater for inspiration, sought to expel all 'rhetoric' or 'generalisation' from their poetry, in order to focus on the pure discipline of poetry.[44]

One line of descent from the British aesthetes of the 1880s to the mature modernism of the 1920s went through the Bloomsbury Group, who – save for Virginia Woolf – do not usually receive enough credit as theorists and practitioners of modernism. This close-knit circle of fashionable, elitist, writers and artists formed a self-conscious avant-garde who felt that their mission was to preserve civilisation (that is, the fine arts), and to spread it outwards into a barbaric culture.[45] Strangely enough, the strongest theoretical influence on them

---

40. See; T.W. Heyck, *The transformation of intellectual life in Victorian England* (London, 1982); Graham Hough, *The last romantics* (London, 1947); John Lester, *Journey through despair, 1880–1914* (Princeton, 1988); Frank Miller Turner, *Between science and religion* (New Haven, 1974); Stefan Collini, *Public moralists: political thought and public life in Britain, 1850–1930* (Oxford, 1991).
41. Hough, *Last romantics*, chs. iv and v.
42. Walter Pater, *The renaissance: studies in art and poetry* (New York, n.d.), p. 197.
43. J.M. Whistler, *The gentle art of making enemies* (New York,1890).
44. Hough, *Last romantics*, pp 204–6; Perkins, *History of modern poetry*, pp 37, 40–1.
45. For a favourable account of Bloomsbury that takes them at their own words, see: J.K. Johnstone, *The Bloomsbury group* (New York, 1963).

was the Cambridge philosopher G.E. Moore, who was the farthest thing from a poet. Moore and his friend Bertrand Russell led the British 'realist' revolt at the turn of the century against philosophical idealism, and by his rigorous analytical procedures Moore led British philosophy into its 'linguistic turn'. But he also exerted a powerful influence on the men (at least) of the Bloomsbury Group, many of whom had been his friends and students at Cambridge – and his companions in the university's secret elite intellectual society, the Apostles. In his *Principia Ethica* (1902), which became the bible of Bloomsbury, Moore swept away all past systems of ethical philosophy (including both the Christian and utilitarian ethics cherished by the Victorians) by means of severe analysis of ethical reasoning. The 'Bloomsberries' regarded this demolition as a liberation, a new renaissance. Moreover, in his final chapter Moore announced what he regarded as the things above all others good in themselves: 'By far the most valuable things, which we can know or can imagine, are certain states of consciousness, which may be roughly described as the pleasures of human intercourse and the enjoyment of beautiful objects.'[46]

Whether Moore recognised it or not, this statement of values, which he imbibed from the Apostles, was the pure milk of aestheticism; and it was enormously inspirational for all the members of Bloomsbury.[47] Since Moore argued that the two states of mind above all others good in themselves were immeasurably increased by scholarly learning and cultivated good taste, his teaching inclined the Bloomsbury Group towards the notion that they constituted a cultured elite; and his method of reasoning inculcated in them a precise, severe, analytical style of thought. In addition, the Bloomsbury Group learned a formalist aesthetic from Roger Fry, another Cambridge graduate but one who had pre-dated Moore. Fry, who along with Clive Bell introduced post-impressionist painting into Britain, became the mentor of Virginia Woolf, who in turn became perhaps the leading writer of modernist novels among the British. Fry believed that painting operates solely because of the relations among its forms and colours, regardless of any story or thing represented in the painting. The emotion aroused from contemplation of this formal relationship can (and should) be isolated from all other emotions that the painting evokes; this 'aesthetic emotion' stimulated by the 'significant form' is more important than any emotions associated with ordinary life.[48]

---

46. G.E. Moore, *Principia ethica* (Cambridge, 1902), p. 188.
47. For a statement of Moore's influence, see J.M. Keynes, 'My early beliefs', in his *Two memoirs, Dr. Melchior: a defeated enemy and My early beliefs*, ed. David Garnett (London, 1949), p. 83; Johnstone, *Bloomsbury group*, ch. ii; and Paul Levy, *Moore: G.E. Moore and the Cambridge apostles* (London, 1979).
48. Kenneth Clark (ed.), *Last lectures by Roger Fry*, (New York, 1939), p. xiv; and Quentin Bell, *Roger Fry* (Leeds, 1964), pp 8–11.

Virginia Woolf adapted this aesthetic philosophy to fiction: a novel, she believed, should not be a naturalistic description of the surface facts of social life, nor a story in logical, linear form, but an attempt to catch the significant form, the permanent 'reality', that lies behind the transitory sense impressions yielded by the material world.[49]

Formalism, then, was one key element in the modernist aesthetic of the Bloomsbury Group. It allowed them to re-arrange the formal ingredients of a story, biography, or picture in order to stimulate the aesthetic emotion – witness both Lytton Strachey's *Eminent Victorians* and Virginia Woolf's *To the lighthouse*. But there was a second route in England towards this formalist aesthetic that characterised modernism. This route lay through the ideas of certain early twentieth-century theorists, most notably T.E. Hulme, Ford Madox Hueffer, and Ezra Pound, who were the central figures in intense discussions in London about art and poetry in the six or seven years before the First World War.[50] Hulme shared with the aesthetes a rejection of science and materialism and consequently for a time became a Bergsonian in philosophy and a radical expressionist in aesthetics. He also advocated for poetry exactitude in presentation and exclusion of ornamentation – a hard, spare diction focusing on the image, which he saw as the 'very essence of intuitive language'.[51] Eventually, however, a need for order and discipline turned Hulme away from Bergson and towards classicism, so that he came to advocate not only precision in the image but also the discipline of 'dry, hard, classical verse'.[52] Hueffer, who was England's strongest proponent of impressionist poetry, likewise considered that poetry should be perfectly clear, precise, unsentimental, and objective – poetry that scrupulously avoided the Victorian sin of moralising and that reflected the changefulness and fragmentation of modern life.[53]

Pound came to England from America in 1908 seeking a poetic community and much impressed by Swinburne, English aestheticism, and symbolism; but he evolved into a poet, critic, and propagandiser of very different ideas. In conversation with Hulme, Hueffer, and others, Pound came to think that poetry should be shorn of all imprecision and abstraction, and that its diction

---

49. See, for example, her depiction of the task of the writer in *A room of one's own* (New York, 1957), pp 113–14.
50. For a discussion of London as the setting for intellectual debates on art and modernity, see Malcolm Bradbury, 'London, 1890–1920' in Bradbury and McFarlane, *Modernism*, pp 172–90.
51. Quoted in M.H. Levenson, *A genealogy of modernism: a study of English literary doctrine, 1908–1922* (Cambridge, 1984), p. 46; see also Perkins, *History of modern poetry*, p. 459.
52. Quoted in Levenson, *Genealogy of modernism*, p. 86.
53. Ibid., ch. 4.

and syntax should be much more natural.⁵⁴ By 1912–13, Pound was aggressively promoting his 'Imagist' doctrine – the self-consciously 'modern' idea that poetry should be objective, impersonal and centring on the image, which he saw as the essential constituent of poetry; thus to him poetry should be non-representational but rather a series of exact images which are neither mimetic nor morally or socially engaged. An image, he wrote, is 'that which presents an intellectual and emotional complex in an instant of time'.⁵⁵ This was a formalist doctrine that preserved a sense of the constitutive role of the poet's mind or emotion.⁵⁶

In 1914, Pound met his fellow American expatriate, T.S. Eliot, and discovered that Eliot, who became the most influential of all English modernist poets and critics, had 'actually trained himself *and* modernised himself *on his own*'.⁵⁷ Eliot had learned from Irving Babbitt, one of his teachers at Harvard, and no doubt from his own background in the New England aristocracy, to despise middle-class culture and to accept the need for order and discipline as checks on unrestrained individualism.⁵⁸ In addition, before settling in England in 1914, Eliot had come under the influence of symbolism, and, through Arthur Symons' *The symbolist movement in literature*, the modern French symbolist ideas and poetry of Rimbaud, Verlaine, and above all Laforgue. From the latter, Eliot said, he learned 'the poetic possibilities of my own idiom of speech', as well as ironic self-deprecation and the means of distancing himself from experiences too painful or embarrassing to reveal directly.⁵⁹ An almost pathologically shy and repressed person, Eliot in his most famous critical essay, 'Tradition and the individual talent' stressed the 'impersonality' of poetry and denied that poetry is a 'turning loose of emotion, but an escape from emotion; it is not the expression of personality, but an escape from personality'. By the same token, Eliot argued that a poet should write with the 'Tradition', the whole corpus of European literature seen as a 'simultaneous order' in his mind; indeed, a poet's best work is often where the poet's ancestors in the Tradition assert themselves.⁶⁰ His own poetry from 'Prufrock' through *The waste land* not only resorted to allusions

54. Perkins, *History of modern poetry*, p. 461.
55. Quoted in ibid., p. 333.
56. Levenson, *Genealogy of modernism*, p. 133.
57. Quoted in Perkins, *History of modern poetry*, p. 466.
58. For Eliot's intellectual development, see: John Margolis, *T.S. Eliot's intellectual development, 1922–1939* (Chicago, 1972); Lyndall Gordon, *Eliot's early years* (Oxford, 1977), chs. 1–4; and Bernard Bergonzi, *T.S. Eliot* (New York, 1972), chs. i–iii.
59. Bergonzi, *T.S. Eliot*, pp 7–8.
60. T.S. Eliot, 'Tradition and the individual talent' in *The sacred wood* (first published in 1920, 7th ed., London, 1950;), pp 47–59, especially pp 48–9.

to a vast range of works in the tradition, but also adopted the device of fragmented or shifting voices, so that the poems are often so obscure as to be accessible only to a learned few. As is well known, Pound assisted Eliot in editing *The waste land* (1922), the most famous of all modernist poems, and removed almost completely any connective tissue such as narrative or logical argument. With Eliot's poetry and critical theory, then, British modernism found its mature expression: art that was analytical, anti-historicist, severe, disillusioned, ironic, learned, fragmented, formally innovative, obscure, impersonal, and anonymous in its urban settings – and derived, it should be noted, without reference to struggles over national identity, political controversy, or rival religious allegiances.

Yeats agreed with some aspects of British modernism, but not others. As he wrote in 1923, he condemned 'though not without sympathy, those who would escape from banal mechanism through technical investigation and experiment'.[61] Yeats always hoped for an Irish literature that had strong connections with the people, and he felt that this desire, common among Irish poets, separated modern Irish poetry from modern English poetry:

> The English movement, checked by the realism of Eliot, the social passion of the War poets, gave way to an impersonal philosophical poetry. Because Ireland has still a living folk tradition, her poets cannot get it out of their heads that they themselves, good-tempered or bad-tempered, tall or short, will be remembered by the common people.[62]

This assessment by Yeats of the differences between English and Irish literary modernism points tantalisingly to the intellectual influences that shaped his own work, some of which also shaped modernism elsewhere, but some of which were uniquely Irish.

The first, and perhaps most important, of all these influences, came from Yeats's family and its position within Irish society – that is, as a part of the Anglo-Irish Protestant minority. It is not enough to say that Yeats was an anti-colonial writer: he was an anti-colonial from a particular social group – the descendants of the Protestant colonists in southern Ireland. Conor Cruise O'Brien identifies six groups in late nineteenth-century Irish society: 1) *the pre-colonials* – the 'unspoiled' peasants of the west, largely unaffected by anglicisation; 2) *the colonised* – the country people of the rest of Ireland, 'profoundly affected by

---

61. From a leading article in the new Irish literary review, *To-Morrow*, quoted in Richard Ellmann, *Yeats: the man and the masks* (New York, 1948), p. 246.
62. W.B. Yeats, 'Modern poetry: a broadcast' in *Essays and introductions* (New York, 1961), p. 506.

modernisation and Anglicisation'; 3) *the urban lower- and middle-class colonised* – Catholics of Celtic descent who were conscious of their own anglicisation as something that should be shed; 4) *the colonists* – descendants, mostly Ulsterite, of the original Protestant settlers who held fervently to their Unionism; 5) *the English* – more recent immigrants who showed little interest in things Irish; and 6) *the alienated colonists* – descendants, mostly in the southern provinces, of the original Protestant settlers, who identified with the native Irish and condemned other Irish men and women to the degree that they were anglicised, and yet who tended to disagree with the lower- and middle-class colonised about the new Ireland that should be created.[63]

Yeats, who was born in 1865, came from the sixth group, and thus grew up among the Anglo-Irish Protestants who were accustomed to ruling Ireland, and who thought of themselves as the source of all order, decency, progress, and culture in Ireland.[64] Unlike the Ulster Protestants, many of these people by mid century felt that their time as a landed ruling class was coming to an end. Most Anglo-Irish Protestants were proud that their ancestors had led Irish patriotism in the eighteenth century, but now, as the days of the southern Protestant landlords seemed numbered, many of them sought to identify, not with the Catholic nationalists, but with the 'pre-Catholic' elements surviving in Irish society.[65] Yeats himself for a time was to throw his lot in with the peasantry; nevertheless, although his mother's family were merchants and his father's family retained little connection with the landed aristocracy, Yeats imagined himself part of the Protestant nobility, and he took pleasure in family tales of heroic ancestors who fought against James II and the United Irishmen.[66] He ignored completely (or was unaware of) the lowly social origins and acquisitiveness of most of the Protestant settlers of the seventeenth century. 'I am delighted', he wrote, 'with all that joins my life to those who had power in Ireland or with those anywhere that were good servants and poor bargainers ...'.[67] In the 1920s, disillusioned with the culture of the Irish Free State, Yeats strongly reasserted his pride in his Anglo-Protestant ancestry. In 1928, arguing against the Free State's ban on divorce, which he regarded as offensive to the Protestant minority, he declared:

---

63. Conor Cruise O'Brien, *States of Ireland* (London, 1972), pp 73–4.
64. These views Yeats stated explicitly in his famous speech to the Irish Senate in 1925 against the bill banning divorce, quoted in part in Joseph Hone, *W.B. Yeats: 1865–1939* (London, 1967), pp 369–71. See also Donald Torchiana, *W.B. Yeats and Georgian Ireland* (Evanston, 1966).
65. O'Brien, *States of Ireland*, p. 71; F.S.L. Lyons, *Culture and anarchy in Ireland, 1890–1939* (Oxford, 1979), pp 28–30.
66. For a strongly critical view of Yeats's aristocratic fantasies, see Deane, *Celtic twilights*, ch. 2.
67. W.B. Yeats, *The autobiography of William Butler Yeats* (New York, 1953), pp 12–13.

We against whom you have done this thing, are no petty people. We are one of the great stocks in Europe. We are the people of Burke; we are the people of Grattan; we are the people of Swift, the people of Emmet, the people of Parnell. We have created the most of the modern literature of this country. We have created the best of its political intelligence.[68]

Yet Yeats's family provided another, complicating, source of intellectual influence: his father, John Butler Yeats.[69] Yeats was later to write to his father, admitting 'with some surprise how fully my philosophy of life has been inherited from you in all but its details and applications'.[70] That influence on Yeats's philosophy came in several different areas. First, John Butler Yeats (a not-very-passionate home ruler) taught his son to dislike England because of its domination by commerce and industry. 'With us [the Irish]', he wrote, 'intellect takes the place which in the English home is occupied by the business faculty'.[71] Second, contradictorily, he passed on to his son a substantial package of romantic attitudes and philosophy drawn from the English romantic poets and the pre-Raphaelites. John Butler Yeats 'disliked the Victorian poetry of ideas ...', especially that of Tennyson, and he admired poetry that was 'an idealisation of speech, and at some moment of passionate action or somnambulistic reverie.'[72] Third, he taught William to reject Christianity. Although both John Butler Yeats's father and grandfather were Church of Ireland clergymen, he had become a freethinker while at Trinity College, Dublin. As a follower of J.S. Mill, he set his young son to doubting conventional Christianity, arguing that 'religion is the denial of liberty ... and all the ethical systems yet invented are a similar denial of liberty, that is why the true poet is neither moral nor religious'.[73] In the long run, Yeats's religious instincts and temperament were far too strong to be suppressed, but when he turned again towards religion, it could not be either protestantism or catholicism, which his father's positivistic logic had destroyed for him.

Meanwhile, a third powerful intellectual influence on the young Yeats was English culture itself. This had negative as well as positive dimensions. The

---

68. This speech is frequently quoted; see, for example Ellmann, *Yeats: the man and the masks*, pp 248–9. See also the discussion in Torchiana, *Yeats and Georgian Ireland*, pp 147–50. Conor Cruise O'Brien has argued that Burke actually descended from Catholic stock: *The great melody: a thematic biography and commented anthology of Edmund Burke* (Chicago, 1992).
69. On John Butler Yeats, see: W.M. Murphy, *Family secrets: William Butler Yeats and his relatives* (Syracuse, 1995); and *Prodigal father: the life of John Butler Yeats, 1839–1922* (Ithaca, 1978).
70. Quoted in Ellmann, *Yeats: the man and the masks*, p. 13.
71. Quoted from a letter to William Butler Yeats, in Hone, *Yeats*, p. 66.
72. Yeats, *Autobiography*, pp 40, 95.
73. Quoted in Ellmann, *Yeats: the man and the masks*, p. 19.

negative dimension was simply that England, and especially London, where the Yeats family lived when Yeats was still a boy and then again in the later 1880s, made Yeats feel uncomfortable and alienated. He compared it unfavourably with the rural charm of County Sligo, where he often vacationed with his mother's family. Even when he was in his twenties, Yeats felt lonely and out of place in London. He wrote his friend Katherine Tynan that London was hateful and 'always horrible to me'.[74] His experiences in London confirmed the anti-English attitudes bequeathed to him by his father. The positive effects of England on Yeats's intellect stemmed not only from the general fact that English culture was dominant in Ireland and therefore shaped the education and outlook of the Irish middle and upper classes, but also from the Yeats family's immersion in English literature. As Yeats recalled late in his life:

> ... I remind myself that though mine is the first English marriage I know of in the direct line, all my family names are English, and that I owe my soul to Shakespeare, to Spenser and to Blake, perhaps to William Morris, and to the English language in which I think, speak, and write, that everything I love has come to me through English ... [75]

His earliest models of poetry were Spenser and Shelley. In Spenser he found the entrancing image of medieval English culture, before its beauty, haughty imagination, and noble bearing were overthrown by the 'timidity and reserve of a counting house'.[76] From Shelley he took his idea of both poetry and the poet. He was inspired by Shelley's concept of intellectual beauty, finding his ideal notion of the poet in Shelley's *Alastor*, which he interpreted as the poet's solitary search for a vision of ideal beauty.[77] Moreover, Yeats saw in Shelley the image of the rebel who would stamp his will on the world and the philosopher of the imagination over reason. In Shelley and then in Blake, Yeats discovered the idea that there is a supernatural world beyond ordinary reality, to which only imaginative symbols give access.[78]

Such views put Yeats in line with another English influence – the late-romanticism of the aesthetic movement in London. In the latter 1880s and early 1890s Yeats, already a published poet, met Oscar Wilde and William

---

74. John Kelly and Eric Domville (ed.), *The collected letters of W.B. Yeats* (Oxford, 1986), p. 231; see also: Ellmann, *Yeats: the man and the masks*, p. 76.
75. Yeats, 'A general introduction for my work' in *Essays and introductions*, p. 519.
76. Yeats, 'Edmund Spenser' in *Essays and introductions*, p. 365.
77. See: George Bornstein, *Yeats and Shelley* (Chicago, 1970); and A.M. Dalsimer, 'My chief of men: Yeats's juvenilia and Shelley's Alastor', *Éire-Ireland* viii, no. 2 (Summer 1973), pp 71–90.
78. Yeats, 'The philosophy of Shelley's poetry' in *Essays and introductions*, pp 78–95.

Morris and became familiar with the writings of Ruskin, Pater, and Swinburne. Their criticism of Victorian society, and of Victorian ideas of literature and art, grew out of Ruskinian principles and the pre-Raphaelite sensibility, and therefore resonated with Yeats's own ideas. In 1891, Yeats and the Welsh writer, Ernest Rhys, founded the Rhymers' Club, the gathering of young poets much under the influence of aestheticism, including Ernest Dowson, Richard Le Gallienne, Lionel Johnson, and Arthur Symons. Although Yeats did not agree entirely with them, the Rhymers had a major and lasting influence on him. They made him aware of his ignorance (he never attended a university and always reflected the eccentric learning of the autodidact) and thus stimulated him to undertake a serious study of literature and philosophy. They taught him to think that, as Johnson put it, 'Life is a ritual'; and Yeats's manner of aloof formality owed something to that lesson. They argued against a poetry that conveyed general ideas, abstractions, or philosophies: as Symons told him, 'We are concerned with nothing but impressions'. When Yeats, who was full of philosophies of poetry, spoke of general issues, they warned him against 'rhetoric' and said that he talked like a man of letters and not a poet. They insisted that poetry should be rid of all '"impurities", curiosities about politics, about science, about history, about religion'.[79] The Rhymers were devotees of the doctrine of art-for-art's-sake, and although Yeats did not accept the doctrine completely, he was profoundly influenced by aestheticism in two general senses: he would always insist that literature meet the highest aesthetic and intellectual standards, and that literature should never preach any moral doctrine. He said in 1908 that even in writing the supremely patriotic play *Kathleen ni Houlihan* he had not tried to preach or to moralise to anyone: 'All artists were precisely the same. "Art-for-art's-sake" meant art for the sake of sincerity, for the sake simply of natural speech coming from some simple, natural child-like soul.'[80] Aestheticism, then, had a powerful influence on Yeats in convincing him that in art, purely aesthetic judgements must take priority over public issues and commitments.

Aestheticism influenced Yeats in several other crucial directions. One was to confirm him as a symbolist poet. By the mid 1880s, Yeats, like many young British intellectuals who hankered for a philosophy that would both show the connectedness of all things and provide a rationale for spiritual reality, was experiencing a fierce reaction against positivism and scientism, the whole style of thought that limited knowledge to verifiable observations. He was strongly

---

79. Yeats, *Autobiography*, pp 101–2. See also Graham Hough, *Last romantics*, ch. v and vi; and Ellmann, *Yeats: the man and the masks*, pp 140–4.
80. Reported by the *Irish Times*, 11 Feb. 1908; quoted in Ellmann, *Yeats: the man and the masks*, p. 255.

attracted to the notions of Shelley and Coleridge, who held that symbols offer insight into the unseen realm. His early poem, *The wanderings of Oisin* (begun in 1886, published in 1889) was a symbolist work; and his three-volume edition of Blake's poetry (done with Edwin Ellis between 1889 and 1893) was most notable for its analysis of Blake's symbolism. Yeats learned much about current symbolist theory from one of the members of the Rhymers' Club, Arthur Symons, who was in close touch with the Parisian symbolist poets. Symons's book, *The symbolist movement in literature*, which was dedicated to Yeats, taught Yeats and his colleagues about the poetic doctrines of Mallarmé and Verlaine, and thereby validated their antagonism to bourgeois society, their rejection of positivism, and their belief in poetry without the 'impurities' of rhetoric or abstractions. Symbolism to Yeats meant, among other things, the power to evoke emotions and ideas, and therefore stood in opposition to literature that tends 'to lose itself in externalities of all kinds'.[81] Perhaps even more important to Yeats, symbolism gave access to the spiritual realm, the reality of which he was certain. He believed primitive peoples had been in contact with this spiritual realm, but that modern people denied its existence. Hence symbolism, a cosmopolitan doctrine, to Yeats was a means of connecting with the wisdom and experience of a mysterious but real folk memory, the 'Great Memory', which has magical curative powers.[82]

Yeats's symbolism seems to rest on an idealist metaphysics – the belief that there is a real spiritual realm and, further, that reality is in some sense mental – but in fact the metaphysics provided a rationale for what he already believed. Late in life (1931), he wrote approvingly of the Irish idealist philosopher, Bishop Berkeley; indeed, he almost seems to have identified idealism as Irish metaphysics.[83] Likewise, in the 1920s, through the poet Thomas Sturge Moore, Yeats carried out a long and fascinating debate with the ideas of G.E. Moore and Bertrand Russell (who were regarded in Britain as the destroyers of idealism) about the reality of mental phenomena, in which he argued a Berkeleian position.[84] The obvious question for the historian, then, is: when and where did Yeats learn idealist metaphysics? He does not appear to have studied idealist philosophers systematically until the 1920s, when he read McTaggart, Kant, Whitehead, Hegel, Croce, and Berkeley, among others. The best answer is probably that he discovered it in

---

81. Yeats, 'The symbolism of poetry' in *Essays and introductions*, pp 155 and 160.
82. Yeats, 'Magic' in *Essays and introductions*, especially p. 50. See also, Hough, *Last romantics*, p. 229.
83. Yeats, 'Bishop Berkeley' in *Essays and introductions*, pp 396–411.
84. See Ursula Bridge (ed.), *W.B. Yeats and T. Sturge Moore: their correspondence, 1901–1937* (New York, 1953), especially pp 59–86.

his twenties, when he studied Blake. He wrote to Sturge Moore that when he was still in his teens, an Indian thinker had persuaded him that everything we perceive, including both material objects and illusions, exist in an external world; however, he wrote, 'Blake drove it out of my head', and he became convinced that everything that exists is in the mind – *esse is percipi*.[85] To Yeats, this confirmed his sense that mental images, visions, and spirits are as real as any material objects, and not distinguishable from them.

Aestheticism also helped Yeats conclude that, given the prevalence of materialism, artists must form a new priesthood in the new religion of art. Because of their sense of estrangement from bourgeois society and their opposition to utilitarian poetics, the aesthetes of the late nineteenth century rejected the 'prophetic' and 'preacherly' roles that had been assumed by the Victorian men of letters. But Yeats felt that the role of priest, one who mediates by means of esoteric knowledge between the supernatural and the people, was still available – indeed, he thought a priestly role was essential for artists to combat the dominant scientific cast of mind. Writers all over Europe, he felt, were struggling 'against that picturesque and declamatory way of writing, against that "externality" which a time of scientific and political thought has brought into literature'.[86] Only artists are capable of shouldering the burdens once carried by priests and leading culture back to ancient wisdom, 'by filling our thoughts with the essences of things, and not with things'.[87] What this left unsaid was the assumption that Christianity could not serve the function, because Christianity itself had shared in the unhealthy overemphasis on reason; indeed, Yeats thought, Christianity several hundred years before had deliberately overthrown the enchanters and magicians of primitive civilisations.[88] Moreover, to Yeats the idea of poets as a new priesthood was bound up with a desire to establish (re-establish, in his view) an organic connection between artists and society. This amounted to an outright rejection of decadence. The proper function of the poet, he came to think, was like that of the priest: to inculcate in 'the people ... an ideal of life upheld by authority'.[89]

Finally, aestheticism led Yeats to enlarge his dislike of England. The aesthetes despised everything about the Victorians, including their materialism (in the

---

85. Bridge, *Yeats and Sturge Moore*, pp 67–8.
86. Yeats, 'The autumn of the body' in *Essays and introductions*, p. 189.
87. Ibid., p. 193. See also Yeats, 'Ireland and the arts' in *Essays and introductions*, p. 203.
88. Yeats, 'The happiest of the poets', *Essays and introductions*, p. 64. See also S.F. Miller, 'Hopes and fears for the tower: William Morris' spirit at Yeats' Ballylee', *Éire-Ireland*, xxi, no. 2 (Summer 1986), pp 43–56.
89. Yeats, *Autobiography*, p. 298.

ordinary sense), their commerce, and their industry. Impressed by two of the aesthetes' favourite books, Ruskin's *Unto this last* and Morris's *News from nowhere*, as well as by Fabian socialist criticisms of capitalist society, Yeats elevated the dislike of English values he had learned from his father and from English romantic poets into a profound hatred not just for the Victorians but for conventional English culture and ideals generally. In a speech in 1898, he declared: 'We hate them [English ambitions, ideals, and materialism] now because they are evil. We have suffered too long from them, not to understand, that hurry to become rich, that delight in mere bigness, that insolence to the weak are evil and vulgar things.'[90] To his own resentment of being marginalised as an Irishman in England, Yeats was adding the aesthete's revulsion towards capitalist industrialism; and the result was a characterisation of English culture as shallow, uninterested in ideas or beauty, mechanistic, unspiritual, power hungry, and limited by the values of the counting-house.[91]

Curiously enough, Yeats's vision of Englishness strongly resembled that of Matthew Arnold, and yet it stood in direct opposition to the sense of English national character as late-Victorian and Edwardian English intellectuals were themselves coming to define it – Englishness as rooted in England's green rolling hills and therefore as rural, reverential, and traditionalist.[92] Like the other aesthetes, all of them latter-day Arnoldians, Yeats attributed the opposite of all the supposedly materialistic English qualities to the Irish; to him the unspoiled native Irish had retained their spirituality. Paradoxically, then, Yeats was to use the English aesthetes' late-romantic critique of Victorian culture as the intellectual basis of Irish nationalism and so link up with the stereotypes of Anglo-Saxon and Celtic racial qualities adopted by nineteenth-century Irish nationalists, who were themselves in a sense participating in English cultural hegemony over Ireland by accepting the English definition of Irishness as 'feminine' and Englishness as 'masculine'.[93]

---

90. Quoted in Ellmann, *Yeats: the man and the masks*, p. 112.
91. See, for example, Yeats's remarks in 'At Stratford-on Avon', p. 98; 'The symbolism of poetry', p. 154; 'The theatre', p. 171; 'The Galway plains', p. 213; and 'Edmund Spenser', p. 365; all in *Essays and introductions*.
92. For Matthew Arnold's view of Englishness and Irishness, see his 'On the study of Celtic literature' in R.H. Super (ed.), *The complete prose works of Matthew Arnold* (Ann Arbor, 1962), iii, esp. 235, 241, 243–5, and 257; and *Culture and anarchy* (Cambridge, 1960), ch. iii. For the emerging sense of Englishness as rural and traditionalist, see: Robert Colls and Philip Dodd, *Englishness: politics and culture, 1880–1920* (London, 1986); and contemporary statements such as E.M. Forster's *Howard's end* (1910) and Ernest Barker (ed.), *The character of England* (Oxford, 1947).
93. L.P. Curtis, Jr., *Anglo-Saxons and Celts: a study of race prejudice in Victorian England* (Bridgeport, CT, 1968). There is no direct evidence that Yeats read the relevant essays by Matthew Arnold, but it is almost inconceivable that he was not at least aware of them, given the strong influence of Arnold on the aesthetes. For the contrasting masculine/feminine qualities of Englishness and Irishness, see Cairns and Richards, *Writing Ireland*, ch. 3: 'An essentially feminine race'; and Kiberd, *Inventing Ireland*, pp 317–8.

At the same time as he was soaking up aestheticism, Yeats was delving into another cosmopolitan influence – the occult. In part, Yeats's devotion to the occult was a means of rebelling against his rationalist father, and in part it was an expression of Yeats's religious temperament, which, because of his father's critique of Christianity and the family's Anglo-Irish heritage, could not find an outlet in either protestantism or catholicism. Thus his interest in the mystical, like his symbolism, expressed a reaction against the scientific thinking he had learned from his father and an expression of the search for the supernatural that was one of the central concerns of his life.[94] Its importance to Yeats is clear; he wrote to a friend in July 1892 with only slight exaggeration: 'The mystical life is the centre of all that I do & all that I think & all that I write. It holds to my work the same relation that the philosophy of Godwin held to the work of Shelley & I have all-ways considered my self a voice of what I believe to be a greater renaissance – the revolt of the soul against the intellect – now beginning in the world'.[95]

Thus Yeats studied theosophy in Dublin in the mid 1880s, helped found the Dublin Hermetic Society in 1886, joined the Esoteric Section of Madame Blavatsky's Theosophy lodge in 1887, conducted magical experiments that led Madame Blavatsky to ask him to resign in 1890, and joined MacGregor Mathers' Order of the Golden Dawn soon afterwards. He retained his interests in magic and the occult for the rest of his life, and shortly after his marriage to Georgie Hyde-Lees in 1917 he engaged with his new wife in experiments in 'automatic writing', whereby she took dictation from various spirits in answer to questions that Yeats put to her/them. The result was the book of revelations called *The vision*, which was not only a vision for the new Irish state that fused the Celtic and the Anglo-Irish, but also elaborate analyses of human personalities, their relation to the phases of the moon, and a prophecy of the end of the Christian cycle of history.[96]

Scholars who have studied Yeats's career have often asked whether he really believed in the occult; but there now seems to be no doubt that he did. He had visions and supernatural experiences throughout his life, beginning in youth, including a seance in which a spirit working in him caused him to shake and threw him against a wall.[97] His belief in the occult was like other

---

94. Yeats, *Autobiography*, p. 54. See also, Hone, *Yeats*, pp 69–72; Ellmann, *Yeats: the man and the masks*, p. 41; and Virginia Moore, *The unicorn: William Butler Yeats' search for reality* (New York, 1973).
95. Yeats to John O'Leary, week ending 23 July 1892, in Kelly and Domville, *Collected letters*, pp i, 303.
96. For discussions of Yeats's occultism, see: Ellmann, *Yeats: the man and the masks*, ch. xv, 'Esoteric Yeatsism'; Graham Hough, *The mystery religion of W.B. Yeats* (Brighton, 1984), especially chs. i and ii; Murphy, *Family secrets*, 'Appendix: The Yeatses and the Occult'. For a discussion of *A vision*, see Kiberd, ch. 18.
97. Yeats, *Autobiography*, p. 64.

people's belief in science: Yeats would refuse to reject propositions about the supernatural until he had good reason to abandon them. He wrote in 1902: 'I believe in the practice and philosophy of what we have agreed to call magic, in what I must call the evocation of spirits, though I do not know what they are, in the power of creating magical illusions, in the visions of truth in the depths of the mind when the eyes are closed …'.[98]

The occult served Yeats in ways other than offering a religion that explicitly rejected natural science. For one thing, it gave him a means by which to study symbols and symbolic systems. He felt that with enough intense study, he would be able to open doors to systems of symbols such as those set out by Blake, Swedenborg, and Böhme.[99] For another, Yeats felt that symbols could evoke visions and dreams, and the occult offered him the means of controlling and utilising that process.[100] Likewise, Yeats had long been attracted to the fairy stories he had heard from his mother and the peasantry in and around his mother's family home in County Sligo; and the occult suggested ways of incorporating fairies into a belief system, for the occult helped him understand fairies as 'the lesser spiritual moods of that universal mind, wherein every mood is a soul and every thought a body'.[101] Next, as Yeats's reference to the 'universal mind' indicates, the occult helped him see that the images that come before the mind well up 'from a deeper source than conscious or subconscious memory'.[102] Yeats thus came by a second route to believe in the Great Memory, an 'Anima Mundi described by Platonic philosophers … which has a memory independent of embodied original memories, though they constantly enrich it with their images and their thoughts'. The anima mundi (literally, soul of the world) to him was an aggregation of 'ideas and memories' of a kind that leads birds to build nests; it had been accepted by primitive people but rejected by the narrower modern mentality; and it was the source of images of great emotional power.[103] Finally, study of the occult helped Yeats give further definition to his concept of the poet as a kind of religious practitioner. If aestheticism led him to think of poets as a new priesthood, the occult revealed the poet, like the musician and the artist, as the modern successor to the ancient magician; indeed, Yeats contended that poetry and music arose 'out of the sounds the

---

98. Yeats, 'Magic', *Essays and introductions*, p. 28.
99. Yeats, *Autobiography*, p. 153.
100. Ibid., pp 156 and 161.
101. Quoted in Ellmann, *Yeats: the man and the masks*, p. 67. See also Gale C. Schricker, 'Old nurse; W.B. Yeats and the modern fairy tale', *Éire-Ireland* xix, no. 2 (Summer 1984), pp 38–54.
102. Yeats, *Autobiography*, p. 112.
103. Ibid., pp 158–61; 164.

enchanters made to help their imagination to enchant, to charm, to bind with a spell themselves and the passers-by'.[104]

Yeats's rejection of England and materialism, his commitment to symbolism and the occult, and his desire as a member of the Anglo-Protestant ascendancy to identify with the native Irish all converged with his long-standing delight in Irish fairy and folk tales to turn his attention towards Ireland's ancient literature. The same romantic impulses against industrial society that led William Morris to Norse sagas and would later lead C.S. Lewis and J.R.R. Tolkien to create new English 'legends', led Yeats back to Irish folk and legendary literature. An earlier generation of Anglo-Irish was already involved in the study of ancient Irish literature – most notably Sir Samuel Ferguson, who published translations of the famous Ulster Cycle; James Clarence Mangan, who versified translations of bardic poetry done by others; and Standish James O'Grady, whose *History of Ireland: heroic period* (1878) was a landmark retelling of the Ulster Cycle as history. Yeats thus joined a Celtic revival that was already flourishing among the Anglo-Irish Protestants – a revival that in the hands of writers like O'Grady made a place for the Anglo-Irish in Irish life by offering them as aristocratic-warrior ('masculine') leaders for the ('feminine') Celtic people.[105] In the late 1880s, Yeats published several volumes of Irish fairy and folk tales, and in the 1890s he joined Lady Gregory in gathering folklore among the peasantry of Galway. From this interest in peasant folktales, he moved to admiration of the heroic traditions of ancient Celtic Ireland.[106] Yeats's interest in ancient Celtic literature not only enabled him to feel at one with the as yet 'unspoiled' segment of the Irish people, but it also gave him a means of persuading modern readers to suspend their rational scepticism and thereby heal the wound between the reason and the spirit.[107] It helped him write of simple, powerful emotions. Moreover, Celtic literature put him in touch with what he regarded as 'the ancient religion of the world', that 'Great Memory' or 'Anima Mundi' which was the source of wisdom and imagination.[108]

Finally, and not least important, the study of ancient Celtic literature inspired Yeats with a vision of a poetry that had roots among the common people, as Irish bardic poetry once had. He wrote in 1916: 'I love all the arts that can still remind me of their origin among the common people, and my

---

104. Yeats, 'Magic' in *Essays and introductions*, p. 43.
105. Cairns and Richards, *Writing Ireland*, pp 51–7.
106. Mary Helen Thuente, 'Yeats and Celtic Ireland, 1885–1900', *Anglo-Irish studies*, iv, (1979), pp 91–104.
107. Schricker, 'Old nurse', pp 40–2. See also; Hough, *Last romantics*, pp 230–3.
108. Yeats, 'The Celtic element in literature', *Essays and introductions*, p. 176.

ears are only comfortable when the singer sings as if mere speech had taken fire ...'.[109] Yeats, consciously an heir to the Anglo-Protestant ruling class, responded sympathetically to the tradition of the Celtic bards, themselves a hereditary aristocratic class of intellectuals who had preserved the legends and celebrated the triumphs of their clans. Given his views of the artist or poet as a modern magician, a new kind of priest, Yeats naturally merged the idea of the bard with another element in the ancient Celtic hereditary intellectual aristocracy – the Druids – which would be crucial to his self-assigned role in Irish nationalism.[110]

Given Yeats's dislike of England and English values, it seems inevitable that he would become an Irish nationalist, even though most of the earlier generation of Celtic revival scholars had been unionists. As it happened, his nationalism was awakened by John O'Leary, a handsome, dignified old Fenian of great integrity whom Yeats met in Dublin in 1885. O'Leary, who carried great authority among other nationalists because of his earlier imprisonment and exile, took an interest in Yeats and lent him books by Thomas Davis and the other Young Irelanders.[111] Davis's writings had transformed O'Leary's life in the 1840s. Yeats was strongly moved by Davis's poetry, though he like O'Leary did not feel that it was good poetry. For Yeats, Davis's poems reflected the dry rhetoric of the eighteenth century; however, Yeats admired the fact that 'they spoke or tried to speak out of a people to a people; behind them stretched the generations'.[112] In conversations with O'Leary, Yeats learned to maintain high standards in personal and poetic integrity, for O'Leary told Yeats one of the crucial lessons of his life: 'There are things a man must not do to save a nation.'[113] O'Leary meant that a person was not to lie, or surrender dignity, or neglect justice on behalf of the nation; but Yeats interpreted him also to mean that one must not produce or support bad literature in the national cause. He would stick to this view even after he fell in love with Maud Gonne in 1889 and was moved by her to a more extreme nationalist sentiment. Yeats, therefore, set out in the later 1880s and 1890s to produce a new nationalist literature, but one that had more imagination and musicality than that of Young Ireland. This new literature would both inspire and unite Irish patriots by providing a vision of

109. Yeats, 'Certain noble plays of Japan', *Essays and introductions*, p. 223.
110. On Yeats and Druidism, see: Moore, *Unicorn*, ch. iii. For Yeats and the idea of bards and brehons, see Kiberd, *Inventing Ireland*, p. 318.
111. On O'Leary and his influence on Yeats, see Marcus Burke, *John O'Leary: a study in Irish separatism* (Athens, 1967), especially pp 182–8.
112. Yeats, 'A general introduction to my work', *Essays and introductions*, p. 510.
113. Yeats, 'Poetry and tradition', *Essays and introductions*, p. 247.

an ideal Ireland and models of noble thoughts and behaviour for the people to admire.[114] The Irish literary movement that he sought to lead would, like the ancient bardic literature, speak to the whole people, it would be rooted in the old Celtic legends and stories, it would depict the aristocracy as the appropriate leaders for the nation, and it would unify the society by means of intense images and symbols familiar to all. From such considerations, Yeats wrote in 1914, 'from O'Leary's conversation, and from the books he leant or gave me has come all I have set to since'.[115]

Driven by the two Irish traditions to which he felt heir – that of the Celtic bards and druids, and that of Anglo-Irish Protestant leadership – Yeats set out in about 1890–91 to organise a new Irish culture: 'I began to plot and scheme how one might seal with the right image the soft wax before it began to harden.'[116] The moment was appropriate, he felt, because the division of the home rulers between Parnellites and anti-Parnellites offered an opportunity for a different kind of nationalist movement.[117] He believed that the literary movement would unite the native Catholics with the Anglo-Protestants; and he assumed that the new national literature would be in English, partly because he knew no Gaelic but mainly because the new Irish literature must partake of the cosmopolitan standards taught to him by aestheticism:

> I had noticed that Irish Catholics among whom had been born so many political martyrs had not the good taste, the household courtesy and decency of the Protestant Ireland I had known, yet Protestant Ireland seemed to think of nothing but getting on in the world. I thought we might bring the halves together if we had a national literature that made Ireland beautiful in the memory, and yet had been freed from provincialism by an exacting criticism, an European pose.[118]

From this desire came Yeats's famous activities in founding various literary societies, reading rooms and lending libraries for a new Young Ireland, a new series of nationalist books, and – above all in importance – a national literary theatre. The story of his work in the national literary revival has been told many times and does not need re-telling here. With regard to the development of his ideas, two points only need attention. The first is that he learned much about Gaelic rhythms and ways of speaking from Douglas Hyde, Lady

---

114. Ibid., pp 256–7; *Autobiography*, pp 240, 300.
115. Yeats, *Autobiography*, p. 62.
116. Ibid., p. 62.
117. John S. Kelly, 'The fall of Parnell and the rise of Irish literature: an investigation', *Anglo-Irish studies*, ii (1976), pp 1–24.
118. Ibid., p. 62.

Gregory, and J.M. Synge, all of whom wrote English prose and verse reflecting the Gaelic language. And the second is that in working with Lady Gregory, George Moore, and Edward Martyn in establishing the Irish Literary Theatre, which evolved into the Abbey Theatre, Yeats was continuing his efforts, deeply influenced by his studies of the occult and ancient Celtic culture, to form a new artistic priesthood, but one now for national purposes. In the latter 1890s, Yeats sought to establish what can be regarded as a new class of druids, an Irish 'Mystical Order', who would study a philosophy, ritual, manuals of devotion, sacred texts of imaginative literature, and 'holy symbols' (all created by Yeats), and who would then provide the authoritative leadership for a cohesive Irish culture by mediating between the supernatural and the material worlds. He even found a castle on Lough Key that he thought suitable for the Mystic Order's place of retreat, study, and contemplation.[119]

The plan for an Irish Mystical Order came to nothing, but it seems clear that Yeats believed the Irish national theatre could be a secular and practical form of the same enterprise. He wrote in a theatre magazine in 1899: 'In the first day, it is the Art of the people; and in the second day, like the drama acted of old times in the hidden places of temples, it is the preparation of a Priesthood. It may be, though the world is not old enough to show us any example, that this Priesthood will spread their religion everywhere, and make their Art the art of the People'.[120]

Yet if Irish nationalism was one of the central branches in the genealogy of Yeats's modernism, so also was Yeats's clash with conventional Irish nationalism. When Yeats sought to create a new Irish literature and culture, he came into conflict with conventional forms of Irish nationalism, and especially the Irish-Ireland variety, which held that nothing critical should be uttered about the Irish people or their virtues.[121] More generally, it can be said that while Yeats was trying to establish a new priesthood for a new Ireland, mainstream Irish nationalism already had a religion – the church of Rome. Moreover, Irish catholicism in the early twentieth century was the product of what Emmet Larkin has called 'the devotional revolution' – reinvigorated, respectable, ultramontane, and identifying 'Irish' with 'Catholic'.[122] The peasantry that Yeats imagined still retained their natural spirituality; the

---

119. Yeats, *Autobiography*, p. 153. See also Ellmann, *Yeats: the man and the masks*, pp 119–26.
120. Quoted in Ellmann, *Yeats: the man and the masks*, p. 130.
121. The best account of this conflict is F.S.L. Lyons, *Culture and anarchy*, chs. 2 and 3.
122. Emmet Larkin, 'The devotional revolution in Ireland, 1850–1875' in *The historical dimensions of Irish catholicism* (Washington, DC, 1984).

peasantry imagined by the political nationalists were virtuous because they obeyed the Catholic priests. Thus the religion Yeats sought to establish foundered on the religion to which Irish nationalism was already attached. In terms of his thought, this clash for Yeats opened a gap between his own ardent but lofty nationalism and his cosmopolitan aestheticism. The result was a bitter disappointment that he expressed in a hard, disillusioned, ironic poetry – still symbolist but now more concrete in topics and imagery – that was more like modernist verse than was his earlier dreamy romantic writing.

There were three stages in the clash between Yeats and mainstream Catholic Irish nationalism. The first arose in 1892 over the issue of what books were to be provided for the lending libraries set up by the National Literary Society. Yeats hoped for a series of books that would be, as he wrote to *United Ireland*, 'no mere echo of the literature of '48, but radiant from the living heart of the day'.[123] But the former Young Irelander, Charles Gavan Duffy, wanted the series to include simply the writings of the Young Irelanders themselves. Yeats, feeling that even Thomas Davis's poetry was second rate, thought that the time had come for the 'de-Davisisation' of Irish nationalist literature. Duffy and his friends won the consequent squabble; and worse, some young nationalist intellectuals came to think that Yeats was acting on behalf of unionism, while he expressed weariness with 'this endless war with Irish stupidity'.[124] Moreover, this early quarrel raised the question whether there could be, as Yeats devoutly hoped, a genuinely Irish literature in English. In his famous address to the National Literary Society entitled 'The necessity for de-anglicising Ireland', the eminent Gaelic scholar Douglas Hyde argued that any valid Irish literature must be in Gaelic. Yeats admired much in Hyde's speech as well as his poetry translating Gaelic literature into English; but he felt that any focus on Gaelicisation would insure that Ireland's literature would be provincial.[125] And at stake was an even bigger issue: whether Irish national literature should be, as Hyde and the Gaelic Leaguers tended to think, mainly propaganda for the nationalist cause, or whether it should be, as Yeats desired, literature that met the standards of the European aesthetic movement.[126]

The second and most famous clash with conventional Irish nationalists had to do with plays produced by the National Theatre. As early as 1899, a

---

123. Yeats to the editor of *United Ireland*, 14 May 1892, in *Collected letters of W.B. Yeats*, i, 297–8.
124. Yeats to Katharine Tynan Hinkson, 7 Apr. 1895, in *Collected letters of W.B. Yeats*, pp i, 458. See also Yeats, *Autobiography*, pp 137–42.
125 See Yeats to *United Ireland*, 17 Dec. 1892, in *Collected letters of W.B. Yeats*, pp i, 338–40.
126. See Lyons, *Culture and anarchy*, pp 42–7.

Catholic priest who had heard that Yeats's *The Countess Cathleen* was heretical in proposing that Cathleen, a symbol of Ireland, would sell her soul to keep her people from starving, disrupted rehearsals until Yeats could gather other priests' opinion to the contrary.[127] But the more famous battles occurred in connection with the performances of J.M. Synge's plays, *In the shadow of the glen* (1903) and *Playboy of the western world* (1907). The nationalist journalist Arthur Griffith wrote that *In the shadow of the glen* slandered Irish women, because 'all of us know that Irish women are the most virtuous in the world'. Further, Griffith argued, 'Cosmopolitanism never produced a great artist nor a good man yet and never will'.[128] As for *Playboy of the western world*, the unruly audience at the first performance almost shouted down the third act, and the *Freeman's Journal* declared that it was 'an unmitigated, protracted libel upon Irish peasant men, and worse still, upon Irish peasant girlhood'.[129] Deeply hurt when Maud Gonne married John MacBride in 1903, Yeats now became fiercely angry with Irish nationalism and, inevitably, with the middle-class, Catholic Irishmen who made up the rank and file of both the home rule party and the cultural nationalist movement in the early twentieth century. One result was that Yeats turned more strongly towards aristocratic views, supported by the counsel of Lady Gregory and his own reading of Nietzsche in 1902–3.[130]

The last straw was the Hugh Lane controversy in 1913. Sir Hugh Lane, nephew of Lady Gregory, offered to give his splendid collection of modern French paintings to the city of Dublin, on condition that Dublin provide suitable housing for them. But many middle-class Dubliners opposed the project, and Lane withdrew his offer. Yeats was furious with Dublin's rejection of this impressive expression of high culture, and especially with William Martin Murphy, who owned the *Independent* newspaper and who had been critical of Yeats and the National Theatre as well as a leading opponent of accepting Lane's gift. Murphy struck Yeats as the very embodiment of philistine Catholic nationalism.[131] By then, though Yeats remained an Irish nationalist at heart, he was clearly alienated from the nationalist political movement, and the poetry of his two pre-war volumes, *The Green helm and other poems* (1910) and *Responsibilities* (1914) expressed many of the attitudes that scholars later associated with modernism – disillusionment,

---

127. Yeats, *Autobiography*, pp 250–1.
128. Quoted in Lyons, *Culture and anarchy*, p. 67.
129. Quoted in ibid., p. 69.
130. Ellmann, *Yeats: the man and the masks*, pp 176–8; O'Brien, *States of Ireland*, p. 71.
131. Lyons, *Culture and Anarchy*, pp 75–6.

harshness, and alienation from mass culture. What he wrote of Ireland was also true of himself: 'Romantic Ireland's dead and gone / It's with O'Leary in the grave.'[132]

It has been argued that Yeats achieved the modern bleakness of the poems in *Responsibilities* only with the help of the young American poet, theorist, and artistic promoter, Ezra Pound.[133] Yeats and Pound spent three successive winters together in Stone Cottage (Sussex) from 1913–14 through 1915–16. In fact, as James Longenbach has contended, Yeats probably had as much influence on Pound as Pound on him.[134] Pound came to Europe in 1908 thinking that Yeats was the greatest living poet and hoping to establish a poetic community like the Rhymers of the 1890s. When he and Yeats worked together between 1913 and 1916 – discussing poetry and philosophy, reading each other's works – the two articulated many of the most influential principles of modernism and canonised the great modern writers (Pound, Yeats, Eliot, and Joyce). Disillusioned by his experiences with popular Irish nationalism, Yeats taught Pound about the occult as well about the necessity of not compromising with the general public. Pound in turn helped eliminate any vestiges of abstraction and dreaminess from Yeats's poetry in favour of exact and concrete images, or as Yeats put it, 'to get back to the definite and the concrete away from modern abstractions'.[135] Pound also introduced Yeats to the highly stylised, symbolic, and non-naturalistic Noh plays of Japan, in which both men saw similarities to the occult and Irish folklore. By 1912, Yeats had already committed himself to a poetry of 'simple rhythmical language' and 'swift natural words' expressing the emotions of a passionate life. Pound accentuated this development, and the Noh drama confirmed Yeats's aristocratic, exclusivist tendencies. When T.S. Eliot saw Yeats's new play, *At the hawk's well*, which reflected the Noh style, he accepted Yeats as a modernist – as an 'eminent contemporary'.[136]

This was an appropriate observation. Yeats wrote in 1922: '... the dream of my early manhood, that a modern nation can return to Unity of Culture, is false; though it may be we can achieve it for some small circle of men and

---

132. Yeats, 'September 1913', from *Responsibilities*, in Richard J. Finnerman (ed.) *The collected poems of William Butler Yeats* (new ed., New York, 1989), pp 108–9.
133. For example, this is generally the interpretation in Ellmann, *Yeats: the man and the masks*, pp 210–15. See also Perkins, *A history of modern poetry*, p. 584.
134. James Longenbach, *Stone cottage: Pound, Yeats, and modernism* (Oxford, 1988).
135. Longenbach, *Stone cottage*, p. 19; and ch. 2, 'The bourgeois state of mind'.
136. Ibid., p. 215.

women, and there leave it till the moon bring round its century'.[137] Though Yeats had never pursued self-conscious 'modernity' in his work and never adopted or even agreed with every aspect of modernist art – the free verse, the technical experimentation for its own sake, the discarding of traditional metres, the determination 'to express the factory, the metropolis' – he had arrived at what was later identified as modernist poetry and drama by his experiences with English culture, with late romanticism and its critique of industrial society, with symbolist theory and technique, with Irish nationalism, and with the occult. By the time he wrote *A vision*, he explicitly compared his ideas to 'the cubes in the drawing of Wyndham Lewis and to the ovoids in the sculpture of Brancusi'.[138] He had taken a very different route from the one followed by the Bloomsbury Group, for he rejected the analytical philosophy of G.E. Moore and never adopted a formalist aesthetic. He did come to advocate a kind of 'impersonal' poetry, but his impersonalism took the masks of traditional poetic forms and voices.[139] And his modernism differed from the English in that it developed in large part because of his profound concern with religion: he had moved from the idea of a new priesthood of art to the notion of a mystical order of druid/poets that would fuse the cultures of Ireland into one; and Ireland would be elevated by a literature providing models of noble sentiments and behaviour. But his ambition withered in the barren soil of Irish nationalist pieties, and Yeats turned to bitter denunciation of Irish culture, to aloof and aristocratic attitudes, and to identifiably modernist writing. Thus the genealogy of Yeats's modernism included a strange crossing of cosmopolitan aesthetic attitudes, provincial Irish public commitments and disputes, and a profound, if bizarrely non-modern, religion.

---

137. Quoted in ibid., p. ix.
138. W.B. Yeats, *A vision* (New York, 1966), pp 20–1, quoted in Kiberd, *Inventing Ireland*, pp 316–17.
139. Yeats, 'A general introduction for my work' in *Essays and introductions*, p. 522.

11

The Peak of Marianism in Ireland, 1930–60

JAMES S. DONNELLY, JR

ALTHOUGH THE CULT OF MARY was already well established in Ireland before independence was achieved in 1921–22, this devotional orientation reached its apogee roughly in the three decades between 1930 and 1960. The neglected history of this major religious and cultural development can be charted by focusing the spotlight on the important signposts. These include the appearance of new Marian shrines and grottoes or enlarged pilgrimages to old ones; fascination with Lourdes and (from the 1940s) with Fatima; the impressive religious mobilisation achieved by sodalities, confraternities, and other bodies with a distinct Marian focus; and the proliferation of books, pamphlets, periodicals, films, and even plays tied to the cult of Mary.

In this essay I have three objectives. First, I will examine the cults of both Lourdes and Fatima within Ireland during this period, for their very scale allows us to distil the characteristic features and to gauge the depth of the Irish Marian passion. Second, I propose to scrutinise the techniques used to promote the overall cult of Mary in Ireland. (Here I give some attention – admittedly, all too brief – to the work and influence of the Children of Mary and the Legion of Mary, each of which had a very different social profile.) And third, I intend to explore the reasons for the tremendous upsurge in

Marian devotion. In so doing, I will concentrate on the three factors which appear to have been of the greatest importance: the ideological impact of the Spanish civil war, the perceived threats from socialism and communism, and the quest for 'moral purity' in the face of radically shifting social and sexual mores. Traditional Irish Catholics (the great majority) and their spiritual leaders thus saw international events and forces as threatening to destroy their religious and cultural values. What is particularly striking is the breadth and intensity of the Irish Catholic responses to these challenges and threats. My general argument in all this will be that in its Marian aspect the Irish 'devotional revolution', which firmly established itself, according to Emmet Larkin at least, in the period 1850–75, reached its fullest flowering in the years 1930–60, and that in this later period the Marian cult provided its central symbols, values, and devotional practices.

The Irish fascination with Lourdes after 1930 was hardly a new phenomenon. It had already struck deep roots in the late nineteenth century and seems to have been growing lustily under strong institutional patronage in the two decades immediately before independence. The first official Irish National Pilgrimage to Lourdes, organised by the hierarchy in 1913, attracted the support of 'not less than three-quarters of a million' adults and children who were formally enrolled in the nationwide Irish Association of Our Lady of Lourdes. Through their prayers, reception of the eucharist, and small financial contributions, these 750,000 associate members became entitled to share in the spiritual and temporal benefits of the pilgrimage as well as in certain additional papal privileges, including fifteen plenary indulgences.[1] Given such enthusiasm, it is scarcely surprising that in 1918, when helping to mobilise nationalist resistance to the British threat of military con-scription, the Irish bishops declared a special national novena in honour of Our Lady of Lourdes.[2]

But it was in the 1930s that Lourdes became almost a national obsession among Irish Catholics. At the very beginning of the decade, at Inchicore in Dublin, the Oblates of Mary Immaculate opened within the grounds of their church a massive replica of the famous grotto of Massabielle at Lourdes, adding a 'Rosary Square' (capable of accommodating 100,000 people) to

---

1. Notices about the Association of Our Lady of Lourdes were sent to every parish in Ireland 'to be hung at the doors of churches, convents, schools, halls, etc.' Associates received a leaflet and a membership card, and the clerical organisers sought to bring membership of the association 'within reach of every school-going child in Ireland'. See *First Irish National Pilgrimage to Lourdes, September 1913: official record* (Dublin, 1914), pp 37–42.
2. Michael MacDonagh, *The life of William O'Brien, the Irish nationalist: a biographical study of Irish nationalism, constitutional and revolutionary* (London, 1928), p. 235.

complete the imitation of the French original. Though the Oblate Fathers had long been associated with devotion to Our Lady of Lourdes, the enormous popular response to this new 'Irish Lourdes', as the shrine quickly became known, must have far surpassed even their expectations. In just two years after its formal opening in May 1930, 'it was estimated that a million people had visited the shrine, which was the inspiration of many similar shrines at churches all over the country'.[3] Throughout the 1930s and beyond, the Inchicore grotto was a Mecca for Lourdes enthusiasts, especially on the Lourdes feastday (11 February), which was associated with an annual novena at Inchicore in honour of the Lourdes Virgin, and during the month of May, when the Oblate Fathers orchestrated an impressive Sunday series of Marian processions.[4] The May processions at Inchicore regularly drew thousands of girls and boys from all over Dublin, many of them wearing their Children of Mary costumes in 'Our Lady's colours' of white and blue, along with other thousands of adults, usually belonging to one or another of the numerous city confraternities and sodalities in attendance.[5] Special May processions, often with a Lourdes emphasis, occurred at innumerable other sites throughout the country.

The Oblate Fathers were adept at developing the Lourdes consciousness in a variety of ways as well. Like others, they organised large pilgrimages to the French Lourdes. The opening ceremonies of one such pilgrimage in 1935, sponsored jointly with three Franciscan orders and involving just over a thousand pilgrims, were held at Inchicore with considerable fanfare and publicity. An especially noteworthy feature of this enterprise was the filming of the entire pilgrimage by the Very Rev. Daniel Collier, the Oblate superior of the Retreat House at Inchicore, who obviously intended to broadcast the Lourdes message and the work of his own order in this way as soon as the big event was over.[6] Lastly, the Oblate Fathers took a leading part in spreading devotion to the family rosary after the outbreak of war in 1939. They organised what was called an 'uninterrupted' rosary novena for peace and the protection of neutral Ireland. By February 1941 it was claimed that 'over 100,000 families from all parts of Ireland' had notified the Inchicore Oblates of their commitment to pursuing this devotion in their own homes.[7]

---

3. Peter Costello, *Dublin churches* (Dublin, 1989), p. 156.
4. *I.C.*, 16 Feb. 1935. See the centenary history of the *Irish Catholic* by John J. Dunne, *Headlines and haloes* (Dublin, 1988), pp 31–40, 107–8. See also Stephen J. Brown, S.J., *The press in Ireland: a survey and a guide* (reprinted, New York, 1971, originally published 1937), pp 169–71, 242–59, 263–8.
5. *I.C.*, 2, 9, 16 May 1936, 27 May 1937.
6. *I.C.*, 3, 17 Aug. 1935.
7. *I.C.*, 6 Feb. 1941.

What was happening at Lourdes itself in the 1930s helped greatly to seize the attention and stimulate the interest of Catholics in Ireland and elsewhere. The year 1933 saw the seventy-fifth anniversary of the famous 1858 apparitions, and the anniversary celebrations at the shrine, duly reported by the Catholic press throughout the world, were said to have been conducted 'with a magnificence and fervour which had not hitherto been equalled'.[8] These anniversary celebrations were capped at the end of the year, when Pope Pius XI canonised Bernadette Soubirous in Rome on 8 December, the feast of the Immaculate Conception. This was followed in 1934 by a heavily publicised solemn triduum of masses at Lourdes to celebrate Bernadette's elevation to sainthood. Concurrently, Pius XI had declared 1933 to be a holy year in honour of the nineteenth centenary of Christ's crucifixion and redemption of the human race. The privileges of the holy year promulgated in Rome in 1933 were then, as usual, extended in 1934 to the whole world (pilgrims no longer needed to visit Rome to obtain them), and finally, the Vatican decreed that the holy year should officially be brought to a close at Lourdes on 25–28 April 1935 with another and even more impressive solemn triduum of masses and other religious events.[9] Thus, as one commentator declared, Lourdes itself would see 'the final achievement of the solemn commemoration of the nineteenth centenary of the death of Christ on Calvary', and the forthcoming triduum there would 'group the prayer of the entire world, under the aegis of the Immaculate Virgin, for international peace and all the great intentions of the holy year'.[10] There could have been no disappointment with the turnout or the impact. Huge throngs journeyed to Lourdes for the triduum in April 1935. Estimates of the number of pilgrims differed, ranging from a low of 200,000 to a high of 400,000 or even 500,000.[11] The crowning ceremonies were a pontifical high mass, a special sermon by the papal legate Cardinal Pacelli, and a radio address by Pius XI broadcast from Rome. Almost a half-dozen years after this event, a deeply impressed observer would claim that Cardinal Pacelli, now Pius XII, had 'electrified the three hundred thousand pilgrims assembled in Lourdes ... by the incomparable eloquence of his language and even his gesticulations'.[12] What a fitting encomium: no pope ever did more than Pius XII was soon to do to propagate the cult of Mary. All of this activity, of course, helped to boost the pilgrimage traffic to Lourdes. By 1935 it had reached 1.1 million,

---

8. *I.C.*, 9 May 1936.
9. *I.C.*, 2 Feb., 2, 9 Mar. 1935, 9 May 1936.
10. These were the words of the bishop of Tarbes and Lourdes, Monsignor Gerlier (*I.C.*, 2 Feb. 1935).
11. *I.C.*, 4 May, 22 June 1935.
12. *I.C.*, 27 Feb. 1941.

including as many as 20,000 invalids, who were the object of special attention both at the shrine and in their home countries.[13]

These events at Lourdes struck a responsive chord in Ireland. They formed the essential background to the revival of the long-neglected Marian shrine of Knock beginning in the mid 1930s. After visiting the French shrine, Liam Coyne and his wife Judith, to whom most of the credit for Knock's revival is due, openly wondered if Knock could ever be 'like Lourdes'.[14] The enthusiasm for Lourdes in Ireland was especially manifested in connection with a whole series of great annual pilgrimages organised by a variety of Catholic bodies. One of these pilgrimages – the Ozanam, named after the Ozanam committee of the Society of St Vincent de Paul in Dublin – had started going to Lourdes in 1926,[15] but numerous others began their annual journeys in the 1930s: the Maria Assumpta in 1931, the Children of Mary in 1934, the Franciscans in the same year, and the Catholic Young Men's Society in 1936.[16] By the mid 1930s there were at least half a dozen big pilgrimages, each having from 400 to 1200 pilgrims and thousands of associate members furnishing support at home.[17] One of the biggest of the entire decade was the Franciscan pilgrimage of 1935, which used a transatlantic liner to take 2600 pilgrims (including 150 priests, over 130 invalids, and 50 medical doctors) to Lourdes in two batches in September of that year.[18] Not far behind was the Fifth Irish National Pilgrimage to Lourdes in 1937. Led by Cardinal-Primate Joseph MacRory and four bishops, and accompanied by as many as 180 priests, it was described, perhaps not quite accurately, as 'the greatest pilgrimage ever to leave this country for Lourdes'.[19] Enhancing the attractions of these large pilgrimages to Lourdes was the inclusion of visits to other famous French shrines, several of them with a Marian focus.[20]

---

13. In 1935 about 750,000 pilgrims came to Lourdes by train, and 350,000 more arrived by other means (*I.C.*, 9 May 1936). This was apparently the first year that the total topped the million-mark.
14. Interview with Mrs Judith Coyne at Knock Shrine, 15 Aug. 1993. For a brief account of Liam Coyne, see the obituary notice by the noted Irish Mariologist Father Michael O'Carroll, CSSp, in *Knock Shrine Annual, 1954*, pp 63–6. See also Liam Ua Cadhain, *Cnoc Mhuire in picture and story* (rev. ed., Dublin, 1957). This was the sixth impression of an expanded work first published in 1945; it was based on the original work of 1935.
15. *I.C.*, 21 July 1938.
16. *I.C.*, 1, 29 June, 17 Aug. 1935, 4 May 1939.
17. *I.C.*, 21 Mar. 1936. This issue listed five large Irish pilgrimages to Lourdes scheduled for the summer of 1936: Catholic Truth Society of Ireland; Irish Association of Mary Immaculate; Legion of Mary; Maria Immaculata (Holy Ghost Fathers and parish clergy of Rathmines, Dublin); and Ozanam (Society of St Vincent de Paul). To these should be added the large pilgrimages sponsored and organised by the Catholic Young Men's Society and the Children of Mary. See also *I.C.*, 15 Aug. 1936.
18. *I.C.*, 27 Apr., 3, 31 Aug., 14, 21 Sept. 1935.
19. *I.C.*, 16 Sept. 1937. See also *I.C.*, 23 Sept. 1937.
20. *I.C.*, 23 Mar., 29 June 1935, 25 Apr., 17 Sept. 1936, 21 July 1938.

Stimulating the growth of popular enthusiasm for Lourdes was vigorous promotion through the media and by other methods. For a long time in the mid 1930s every weekly issue of the *Irish Catholic* contained a substantial article on the shrine under the title 'Notes from Lourdes', in which recent pilgrimages were discussed.[21] Besides enlisting the help of newspapers and periodicals, pilgrimage promoters and organisers also resorted to the use of lectures, slides, photography, and film in their efforts to attract recruits and spread devotion. The well-known Jesuit priest Fr Timothy Halpin employed lantern slides of Lourdes to illustrate his popular lectures to Children of Mary sodalities in Dublin; later, he was one of the clerical leaders of the all-Ireland Children of Mary pilgrimage to the shrine in 1936.[22] Even more effective were films of actual pilgrimages, such as that taken by Fr Michael G. Murphy, CC, Rathmines, of the 1936 Immaculata and Legion of Mary pilgrimages. Using a new colour process and showing all the ceremonies at the shrine, the film attracted large audiences when screened at the Mansion House in Dublin as part of promotional efforts for the 1937 Irish National Pilgrimage to Lourdes. On one of these occasions in September 1936, the lord mayor, Alderman Alfie Byrne, TD, joined a large number of priests and laity in viewing the innovative film.[23]

Pilgrimage organisers also made use of unusual photography, as when the managers of the Immaculata pilgrimage of 1935 arranged for the famous photographer Captain John Noel to show at the Olympia Theatre in Dublin what was advertised as 'the most complete set of pictures ever made' at Lourdes.[24] Noel's photographs, synchronised with sacred music, told the story of both Lourdes and the life of St Bernadette, including striking scenes of her canonisation at St Peter's Basilica in Rome. All the pictures were produced by a novel technique called 'the colour dissolvograph' and supposedly re-presented 'the highest development yet attained of artistic photography'.[25] Besides his Olympia Theatre engagements, Noel was also scheduled to display his Lourdes photographs 'throughout the Irish provinces'.[26]

Those wishing to publicise Lourdes in Ireland in the 1930s were not slow to appreciate the potential of the new media of mass communication and entertainment. The film entitled 'Lourdes and St Bernadette', praised for its fine camera work, good acting, and effective musical accompaniment, and

---

21. See, e.g., *I.C.*, 15 Oct. 1936.
22. *I.C.*, 22 Oct. 1936.
23. *I.C.*, 1 Oct. 1936.
24. *I.C.*, 30 Mar. 1935.
25. *I.C.*, 23 Mar. 1935.
26. *I.C.*, 23, 30 Mar. 1935.

featuring dramatic recreations of the 1858 apparitions, was sponsored by Irish missionaries. The Holy Ghost Fathers, whose main work lay in Africa, arranged for its screening in Cork and other southern counties during the summer of 1935.[27] Radio too was harnessed to the task. Lourdes figured prominently in the Radio Éireann programme 'Famous shrines of Our Lady' by Maura Laverty, broadcast in May 1937 and accompanied by the Irish Radio Orchestra.[28] And the Coynes were quick to tap the resources of radio to promote the revival of their 'Mayo Lourdes' at Knock.[29]

But probably nothing else made a greater impact than Franz Werfel's famous novel *The song of Bernadette* and especially the subsequent film based on it. This reverential novel seems to have been the number one bestseller in Ireland from 1942 to 1946.[30] What prompted special remark in Ireland as elsewhere was that a non-Catholic, indeed a Jew, 'should show such comprehensive and sympathetic knowledge of Catholic devotion and practice'.[31] The film version of Werfel's book of course reached an even wider audience, especially in the 16 mm format which, beginning in 1948, made it accessible in many schools, parish halls, convents, and male religious houses.[32] One expert witness insisted in March 1950 that 'The song of Bernadette' in 16 mm was still 'doing very well on private exhibition runs' in Ireland,[33] and its success continued into the following decade. In this way films about Lourdes, and now about Fatima too, were reaching a mass Irish audience.

While Lourdes was the object of intense religious enthusiasm in Ireland during the 1930s, Fatima was generally overlooked. Admittedly, the Dominican Bishop Finbar Ryan had already begun to propagate this devotion and evidently enjoyed some success. His illustrated lecture on the Fatima apparitions of 1917, given at the Gaiety Theatre in Dublin in October 1937, 'was packed to capacity',[34] and the first of numerous editions of his popular book *Our Lady of Fatima* appeared in October 1939.[35] But as Ryan himself conceded in his Gaiety lecture, the Portuguese bishop who presided over the Fatima shrine had pleaded with him on a recent visit: 'I would like you to tell

---

27. *I.C.*, 13 July 1935.
28. *I.C.*, 29 Apr. 1937.
29. *I.C.*, 2 May, 8 Aug. 1936.
30. *I.C.*, 21 Oct. 1943, 2 May 1946.
31. *I.C.*, 17 Oct. 1946.
32. *I.C.*, 4 Nov. 1948.
33. *I.C.*, 9 Mar. 1950.
34. *I.C.*, 14 Oct. 1937.
35. By 1951 there had been five editions of this highly popular book. See Archbishop Finbar Ryan, *Our Lady of Fatima* (5th ed., Dublin, 1951).

the people of Ireland about Fatima …; the only country that does not seem to have any devotion to Our Lady of Fatima is Catholic Ireland'.[36] This situation was soon to change dramatically: in the 1940s and 1950s Fatima came to rival and even to surpass Lourdes as an Irish Catholic obsession.

The turning point came in October 1942, when in a radio broadcast at the close of the silver jubilee of the Fatima apparitions, Pope Pius XII consecrated the church and indeed the entire world to the Immaculate Heart of Mary.[37] Although the pope did not say so explicitly in this address, one of the messages or prophecies associated with the Fatima Virgin was that world peace would come when 'my Immaculate Heart will triumph'.[38] According to another well-known message, devotion to Our Lady of Fatima, and especially recitation of the rosary, was said to be the key to the conversion of Russia. Like several of his recent predecessors in the papal chair, Pius XII was a rosary enthusiast, and in a second broadcast on 1 January 1943, he urged Catholics everywhere to join in the devotion known as 'the Five First Saturdays', as supposedly requested by the Blessed Virgin at Fatima.[39] Mary was alleged to have promised there 'to assist at the hour of death with the graces necessary for salvation all those who …, on the first Saturday of five successive months, go to confession, receive holy communion, say five decades of the rosary, and keep me company for a quarter of an hour, meditating on the fifteen mysteries of the rosary'.[40] These emphatic papal boosts to the cult of Fatima were to be followed by numerous others, and they yielded striking results in Catholic devotional life around the world, not least in Ireland.

Consecrations to the Immaculate Heart of Mary, with special ceremonies and prayers, now became the order of the day. Archbishop Joseph Walsh of Tuam opened the 1943 pilgrimage season at Knock shrine in May by dedicating his archdiocese, and the ceremony was broadcast on Radio Éireann.[41] Cardinal MacRory announced his decision to follow suit in the archdiocese of Armagh early in July.[42] Then, acting collectively, the entire hierarchy decided to consecrate all the dioceses and parishes of Ireland to Mary's Immaculate Heart on 15 August, the feast of the Assumption.[43] On that day there were 'nationwide ceremonies of consecration'; in Dublin

---

36. *I.C.*, 21 Oct. 1937.
37. For the text of this radio address, see Ryan, *Fatima*, pp 237–47.
38. *I.C.*, 25 Feb. 1943.
39. *I.C.*, 1 Apr. 1943.
40. Ryan, *Fatima*, p. 179.
41. *I.C.*, 29 Apr., 13 May 1943.
42. *I.C.*, 17 June 1943.
43. *I.C.*, 1 July 1943.

Archbishop McQuaid presided at a solemn high mass in the Pro-Cathedral, with government ministers and members of Dublin Corporation conspicuously in attendance.[44] Parents were urged to renew their dedication frequently within the family circle after recitation of the rosary, and the practice was also taken up by sodalities and confraternities, whose members often said the prayer of consecration on Marian feasts.[45] The pope later repeated his initiative of 1942 during the holy year of 1950.[46]

But the most remarkable ceremonies of this type were the great public invocations of the Blessed Virgin as patroness of the Irish Defence Forces (army, naval services, and air corps) and as Queen of the Most Holy Rosary on 7 October 1951, the feast of the Most Holy Rosary. This too was a product of the Fatima cult. The events of 7 October reportedly originated with a group of about thirty army chaplains who had first proposed the public invocations in May 1945 at army headquarters. After a long and unexplained delay the proposal was sent in March 1951 to the Irish hierarchy with the approval of the army authorities and the minister for defence, and the bishops quickly ratified it. Supporters of the proposal, invoking historical tradition, recalled the long legacy of dedication to Our Lady and the rosary among Irish Catholic troops, allegedly extending all the way back to the late sixteenth century and continuing up to the Easter Rising of 1916.[47] They might also have recalled that much more recently, in 1949, the bishop of Meath had blessed and helped to place large miraculous-medal plaques on the exterior bodies of the Spitfire aeroplanes belonging to the Irish First Fighter Squadron based at the Gormanstown aerodrome.[48] On the appointed day in 1951, at military centres all around the country, the great occasion was marked by solemn high masses, special sermons, benediction of the blessed sacrament, the invocation itself, military parades, and the rendering of full military honours.[49]

Dublin was the scene of an especially elaborate invocation ceremony in the Military Church of Arbour Hill Barracks, with the president, the taoiseach, the lord mayor, the minister for defence, and other dignitaries in attendance. Archbishop McQuaid presided over the solemn high mass and read the special prayer of invocation which he himself had written, and which began, 'O Immaculate Virgin Mary, Mother of God, Queen of the Most Holy Rosary, humbly kneeling at thy feet today, we choose thee as Our Heavenly Patroness'.

---

44. *I.C.*, 19 Aug. 1943.
45. *I.C.*, 15 Sept. 1949.
46. *I.C.*, 3 Nov. 1949.
47. *I.C.*, 4 Oct. 1951.
48. *I.C.*, 21 July 1949.
49. *I.C.*, 11 Oct. 1951.

The families of Dublin soldiers had previously erected a handsome altar, which the troops then decorated, and local families had embellished their homes with religious emblems. As Monsignor Patrick Boylan observed of this event, surely one of the high-water marks of Marianism in Ireland, the invocation was 'surrounded by all the ceremonial dignity that church and state can give it'. And this was being done in a land where, he claimed, the Blessed Virgin was 'veritably more dear and more real than even the dearest in their own homes and households'.[50] This celebration of the feast of the Most Holy Rosary was repeated in future years, and the invocation of Mary as patroness of the Irish Defence Forces was made a formal part of the army's annual 'mission week', with all the troops reciting McQuaid's prayer.[51]

Just as Irish Catholics responded enthusiastically to Pius XII's call for acts of consecration to Mary's Immaculate Heart, they also took up with great avidity his plea for the practice of 'the Five First Saturdays' supposedly requested by Our Lady at Fatima. This devotion penetrated deeply into the Catholic community at large but was probably at its strongest in the convent schools of the country. There it was one of the standard activities of Children of Mary sodalities.[52] And usually the young sodalists felt compelled to evangelise their peers. Thus in 1946, for example, at St Mary's Boarding School attached to the Mercy convent at Moate, County Westmeath, the sodalists posted notices about each 'First Saturday' to 'remind the school of devotion to Our Lady of Fatima'. In addition, they 'had the whole school enrolled in the Holy Rosary Confraternity and sent all rosary beads to be blessed with the Dominican indulgences'.[53]

None of the devotional practices linked to the Fatima cult enjoyed a greater vogue than the rosary, both in Ireland and in the Catholic world as a whole. As rosary enthusiasts were quick to point out, this ancient devotion had been urged not only by the Virgin at Fatima but also by Our Lady of Lourdes, not to mention every pope since the Lourdes apparitions. The extraordinary vogue of the rosary in the 1940s and 1950s can be attributed above all to two factors: first, its presentation and acceptance as almost a talisman for the restoration of peace, the conversion of Russia, and the world-wide defeat of communism; and second, the use of both new and old techniques of publicity and propaganda, eventually in a concerted campaign, to promote this devotion. There was nothing complicated about how the rosary was supposed to work.

50. Ibid.
51. *I.C.*, 24 Feb. 1955.
52. *I.C.*, 27 Feb., 12 June 1947.
53. *I.C.*, 10 Oct. 1946.

Preaching at Knock shrine in October 1951, Fr J.G. Deehan, OMI, told the pilgrims that the message of Knock was 'the same message as that of Fatima', to which he gave a distinctly anti-communist interpretation. The formula for peace, he declared in this time of the Cold War, was 'a pair of rosary beads' lying ready for use 'on the table of every home in Ireland'.[54]

This was also the doctrine preached literally all over the world by the Mayo-born priest who unabashedly called himself 'Our Lady's Salesman', Fr Patrick C. Peyton, CSC. Fr Peyton regularly connected his great and long-continued family rosary crusade with the 'promises' made at Fatima in 1917 – world peace and Russia's conversion in return for daily recitation of the rosary.[55] It was Fr Peyton who, with the help of Cardinal Spellman of New York, pioneered the use of the radio in promoting his family rosary crusade in the United States. Simultaneously with Billy Graham, he developed the device of the mass religious rally, and he used it to promote the rosary on all five continents. In 1955 he reportedly addressed crowds totalling over a million at sixty-six rallies in southern and south-east Asia as well as conducting seventy rallies in South Africa.

Long before Fr Peyton stumped Ireland with his rallies in 1954, all of the important aspects of his life story and his rosary crusade commanded headlines and lengthy coverage in the Irish press. When he appeared in August 1946 at Knock shrine, not far from his native parish of Attymass, he recounted for a 'huge crowd' of pilgrims his American experiences and his work to 'bring the daily family rosary to ten million homes' there. This mission he traced back to the practice of his 'little home in Mayo where eleven men and women never missed a night without kneeling together to say the rosary'.[56] In the many pleas made in the mid and late 1940s for a 'radio rosary' in Ireland, proponents often cited Fr Peyton's American example and his reported appeal for Radio Éireann to broadcast it.[57] Peyton himself had discussions in Dublin with the minister for posts and telegraphs about the possible rebroadcast by Radio Éireann of the 'Family theatre' and 'Family rosary' programmes that had proved so popular in the United States and elsewhere.[58] Some of them eventually were, and phonographic recordings of the famous Hollywood dramatisations of the mysteries of the rosary also circulated in Ireland.[59]

---

54. *I.C.*, 18 Oct. 1951.
55. *I.C.*, 29 Oct. 1948.
56. *Knock Shrine Annual, 1947*, pp 31–9. See also *I.C.*, 5 Sept. 1946.
57. *I.C.*, 24 Oct. 1946.
58. *I.C.*, 7 July 1949.
59. *I.C.*, 9 Mar. 1950.

In addition, Fr Peyton furnished the immediate inspiration for the rosary crusade which was launched from Knock shrine soon after his well-publicised appearance there in August 1946. The main ingredient in this highly successful annual enterprise was a promise by the household head to recite five mysteries of the rosary every day for a year together with all of the other available members of the household. Everyone who enrolled in the campaign received a certificate which could be hung up in their homes; their names were entered in a special register placed in Our Lady's Oratory at Knock, and their intentions were remembered in a special novena of masses at the shrine ending on Rosary Sunday (the first Sunday in October).[60] By Rosary Sunday in 1947 as many as 135,000 individuals were said to have enrolled in the Knock-shrine rosary crusade,[61] and by the same date in 1948 the number of enrolees had almost doubled to 262,000.[62]

Besides this vigorous campaign mounted by the promoters of Knock shrine, there was also an official National Rosary Crusade conducted under the auspices of the Irish Dominicans. Their efforts were concentrated on expanding the membership of existing Confraternities of the Family Rosary, which reportedly numbered over 150 early in 1952, and on establishing new branches. In this work where there were rivals, the Dominicans did not scruple to advertise publicly that it was 'only through membership in this confraternity that all the many indulgences attached to the rosary may be gained'.[63]

What especially invigorated the Dominican campaign in the early 1950s was the appointment of Fr Gabriel M. Harty, OP, as national director. A zealous young priest attached to St Mary's Priory, the Dominican House of Studies in Tallaght, Harty was a keen student of the history of the rosary and much in demand as a lecturer.[64] His message was regularly an anti-communist one: he would ask his audience to imagine what would happen in the morning if they woke up to find Ireland under a communist regime.[65] He was also notable for illustrating his lectures with films on Lourdes and Fatima and and for using mime to bring the mysteries of the rosary to life, as when 600 Guinness employees packed the Rupert Guinness Memorial Hall in Dublin in September 1954 to see a rosary mime pageant which he had inspired.[66]

---

60. *Knock Shrine Annual, 1947*, pp 49–53; *I.C.*, 5 June 1947. For the elaborate registers, see *I.C.*, 25 Sept. 1947.
61. *I.C.*, 2, 9 Oct. 1947.
62. *Knock Shrine Annual, 1949*, p. 5.
63. *I.C.*, 24 Jan. 1952.
64. *I.C.*, 16 Sept. 1954. Fr Harty's long career as a promoter of the rosary devotion in Ireland is surveyed in his recent book, *Make the wild rose bloom: an Irish rosary* (Tallaght, County Dublin, 1992).
65. *I.C.*, 25 Feb. 1954.
66. *I.C.*, 9, 16 Sept. 1954.

Concentrating his formidable energies on Dublin, Harty took his campaign into the factories, shops, and offices of the capital and its environs. We find him lecturing to electricity workers at the Pigeon House Generating Station,[67] to Guinness employees from the St James's Gate Brewery,[68] to government workers at Dublin Castle (under the headline 'Dublin Castle again honours the rosary'),[69] and to the staffs of two leading insurance companies.[70] While representing the Irish Dominicans at the International Rosary Congress organised by his order at Fatima in May 1954,[71] Harty told the delegates, to their astonishment, that 'the rosary was being said in the offices and factories of Ireland every evening'.[72] Although his assertion prompted disbelief, Harty assured the delegates that his account was correct, and there was substantial evidence to support him. At the Pigeon House Generating Station 200 electricity workers were said to gather at 1.20 p.m. every day to recite the rosary.[73] The Guinness Employees' Rosary Group, with about 200 members drawn from the St James's Gate Brewery, used their lunch break to say the rosary together at the nearby church of St James.[74] It was also highly significant that CIE workers erected an illuminated statue of the Blessed Virgin at Transport House on Bachelors Walk.[75] Indeed, the CIE workers of the Dublin area had flocked to join a new branch of Our Lady's Sodality and had driven up its membership to over 1200 within a short time in the early 1950s.[76] And during the Marian Year of 1954 a special fund entitled the 'Workers' Gift to Mary' reportedly attracted contributions (an hour's pay was the recommended donation) from 'over 10,000 workers'.[77]

But there was apparently a widespread belief among members of the Irish hierarchy that much of the country was being left untouched by the Dominican-led National Rosary Crusade, and that further efforts were necessary to rally the Catholics of Ireland to the rosary. Archbishop Walsh of Tuam and Cardinal D'Alton of Armagh were especially eager to link 'Our Lady's Salesman' Fr Peyton to Family Rosary Crusades in their archdioceses. Once they had extended invitations, other prelates quickly followed suit.[78] In

---

67. *I.C.*, 25 Feb. 1954.
68. *I.C.*, 9, 16 Sept. 1954.
69. *I.C.*, 24 Feb. 1955.
70. *I.C.*, 25 Nov. 1954.
71. *I.C.*, 18 Mar., 20 May 1954.
72. *I.C.*, 25 Nov. 1954.
73. *I.C.*, 25 Feb. 1954.
74. *I.C.*, 9 Sept. 1954.
75. *I.C.*, 29 July 1954.
76. *I.C.*, 23 Dec. 1954.
77. *I.C.*, 19 Aug. 1954.
78. Ibid.

the end Peyton presided over and addressed a total of more than twenty rallies extending over almost four months, beginning at Tuam on 25 April and ending on 15 August at the richly symbolic shrine of Our Lady's Island in County Wexford. The largest turnout occurred, somewhat ironically, at the rally in Belfast, where as many as 100,000 people attended, including (so it was claimed) many non-Catholics 'sharing a common love for Our Lady' and an appreciation of 'the unique value of the rosary'.[79] The closing rally at Lady's Island reportedly drew 'Lourdes-like crowds' of some 40,000 people,[80] and many of the other meetings attracted from 20,000 to 30,000 persons.[81] Altogether, the total attendance at the twenty-odd rallies approached or perhaps even slightly exceeded half a million.

Once again, the familiar verbal cadences of the Cold War entered freely into the sermons and speeches. Speaking at Loughrea, where a crowd of 30,000 ('unknown since the days of Daniel O'Connell') turned out, Bishop William Philbin of Clonfert declared that 'the church of God was being persecuted today as it never has been persecuted before in all of the 1900 years of its history'.[82] In a similar vein Bishop Daniel Mageean of Down and Connor asserted at Belfast: 'Rarely if ever before was mankind in such immediate danger. Our civilisation, our Christian heritage, is facing a crisis unknown in its long history'.[83]

The exuberant rallies embraced a wide array of religious displays and symbols, usually with a Marian focus. At Tuam, where nuns, other religious, and the Children of Mary were strongly represented, 'a beautiful tableau of the rosary' was formed 'by white-dressed children'.[84] At Ennistimon, County Clare, one of the smallest rallies (6000 people), 'nearly every house ... had been turned into a shrine, with religious pictures, crucifixes, lights, and flowers'.[85] The Galway rally boasted what were called 'spectacular features' – 'a rosary pageant and a tableau of the Hail Mary'.[86] A famous local relic provided the central focus at Loughrea; the main ceremony there was a procession in which the ancient wooden statue of Our Lady of Clonfert was carried from the cathedral to the town green and back.[87] And at Lady's Island

---

79. *I.C.*, 17 June 1954.
80. *I.C.*, 19 Aug. 1954.
81. *I.C.*, 29 Apr., 13, 20 May, 3, 24 June, 15, 22 July 1954.
82. *I.C.*, 20 May 1954.
83. *I.C.*, 29 Apr. 1954.
84. Ibid.
85. *I.C.*, 13 May 1954.
86. Ibid.
87. *I.C.*, 20 May 1954.

on the feast of the Assumption, 40,000 people joined in 'the three-miles-long ancient processional circuit of the island'.[88]

Before the rallies began, it was claimed that Fr Peyton's strategy would differ from his usual custom of promoting family prayer in each area 'with the precision of a military campaign or a super-sales drive'.[89] But whether the intense organisational effort occurred before, during, or after the rallies, it was much in evidence. Following the inaugural meeting at Tuam in April 1954, it was said that over 30,000 family-rosary pledges were 'now framed, signed, and hanging up in western homes'.[90] During the rally at Ballaghaderreen, County Mayo, Bishop James Fergus of Achonry went so far as to declare that 'all' the families of his diocese had signed the pledge.[91] Bishop Mageean of Down and Connor was slightly more reserved. He claimed at the Belfast rally that 162,544 Catholics in his diocese had signed the pledge cards to say the rosary every day, or a total of 98.5 percent of all Catholics in the diocese over seven years old.[92] If Fr Peyton was largely preaching to the converted, he was also boosting adherence to unprecedented levels. The rosary devotion was now at its peak in Ireland. Nearing the end of the campaign at Clonmel in late July, Fr Peyton flourished the not at all incredible claim that with the help of God (and his Irish rallies) he had 'already reached his target of ten million families pledged to say the rosary daily together'.[93] Irish Catholics could thus think themselves part of a great world-wide religious tide that would soon sweep away its enemies.

Throughout the years 1930–60 Catholics in Ireland and elsewhere in the world saw themselves as gravely menaced above all by communism and by moral pollution, particularly in the form of the new modern sexuality. In the way that Irish Catholics perceived their world, there was a widespread and persistent tendency to fuse or elide these two great threats. The enormous upsurge in Marian devotion and in Marian organisational activity in these same years was essentially a defensive strategy to combat and ultimately to defeat these anti-Christian forces, which seemed to aim at turning the world into a vast cesspool of paganism, materialism, naturalism, and hedonism.

Of course, Irish Catholic perceptions of the communist threat underwent various shifts in focus during this period under the impact of European and

---

88. *I.C.*, 19 Aug. 1954.
89. *I.C.*, 8 Apr. 1954.
90. *I.C.*, 29 Apr. 1954.
91. *I.C.*, 27 May 1954.
92. *I.C.*, 17 June 1954.
93. *I.C.*, 22 July 1954.

world events. But events in Ireland itself, or at least perceptions of reality there, also helped to shape ideological outlooks. Although in retrospect the Irish domestic threat from communism – or what was almost as bad, socialism – can only be described as ridiculously feeble, the work of detecting, exposing, and combating it absorbed an extraordinary amount of energy. Feeding the widespread paranoia was the conviction that Ireland's native communists worked secretly, surreptitiously, and under false pretences. Among the alarmists were members of the hierarchy, such as Bishop Michael Fogarty of Killaloe. At one confirmation ceremony in County Clare in May 1935, Fogarty declared, 'There is Russian money working in the country – working very cleverly – and it behooves everyone to be on his guard against communism'.[94] Other alarmed observers spoke loosely of 'the musk rats of Russia' who were said to be 'burrowing in Ireland',[95] or grandly claimed that 'in every town in Catholic Ireland [there] are the subterranean chambers and galleries of the crimson mole'.[96]

In the search for domestic communists much suspicion attached itself to the trade-union movement, particularly in Dublin, where the small Irish Communist Party was headquartered, but also in other towns where serious unemployment made workers discontented.[97] What caused even more concern in the early and mid 1930s was firm belief that the leaders of the IRA had been captured by a radical socialist philosophy. Socialist republicanism took organised form with the establishment first of Saor Eire and then of the Republican Congress.[98] In a joint pastoral letter read in every church throughout the land in October 1931, the bishops condemned Saor Eire as 'frankly communistic' and identified it with the overthrow of 'Christian civilisation …, class warfare, the abolition of private property, and the destruction of family life'.[99] A few years later, the Republican Congress came under similar ecclesiastical censure.[100] Although socialist republicans were

---

94. *I.C.*, 18 May 1935.
95. *I.C.*, 18 Apr. 1936.
96. *I.C.*, 10 June 1937.
97. *I.C.*, 23 May, 22 Aug. 1936.
98. Richard English, 'Socialism and republican schism in Ireland: the emergence of the Republican Congress in 1934' in *I.H.S*, xxvii, no. 105 (May 1990), pp 48–65.
99. Quoted in Keogh, *Vatican, bishops, Irish politics*, pp 180–1.
100. The Republican Congress, which represented a socialist minority of perhaps 6000 to 8000 persons within the anti-Free State republican movement, was itself split in September 1934 'on the issue of whether to concentrate on the fight against imperialism or on the narrower goal of establishing a workers' republic'. This split almost killed the Congress, but it was 'temporarily resuscitated by the Spanish civil war, energetic opposition to Franco being generated by the Congress in Ireland and in Spain'. See F.S.L. Lyons, *Ireland since the Famine* (New York, 1971), pp 527–8; English, 'Socialism and republican schism', pp 58, 63.

bitterly opposed, and sometimes physically assaulted, by the orthodox IRA, leading Catholic churchmen in certain parts of the country denounced IRA policy as communistic or warned the laity of their duty to combat 'communism and the slanderous attacks made on the church under the guise of nationalism'.[101]

The burden of opposition was not left to the official church alone. Among the lay Catholic bodies working to expose and thwart domestic communism in the 1930s were the Ancient Order of Hibernians, which published a pamphlet entitled *The red danger* in 1936 to heighten public awareness,[102] and the Irish Christian Front, which sought to mobilise behind its own anti-communist banner those who already belonged to sodalities, confraternities, and CYMS study circles.[103] The Front was a decidedly alarmist organisation given to making wild charges. A member of its executive insisted in May 1937 that communist cells 'were working in every walk of life in Dublin', and also declared, almost in the same breath, that nudist clubs 'were thriving there'.[104]

But far more important in rousing Irish Catholics and their leaders to the dangers of communism in the late 1930s was the Spanish civil war, a bloody conflict whose ideological divisiveness throughout the western world is legendary. In every country with a vigorous Catholic press, including Ireland, the news, photos, feature stories, and editorials concerned with the war were deeply biased, with the emphasis in Catholic newspapers falling overwhelmingly and unremittingly on the atrocities committed against the Catholic church and its personnel by the 'Red' republican forces.[105] Typical of the Irish situation was the treatment of the war in the regular weekly column of the *Irish Catholic* given over to Our Lady's Sodality, by far Ireland's largest Marian organisation. There readers were told in November 1938 that according to Cardinal Goma, the Spanish primate, the war had resulted in 'the murder of over 6000 priests, ... the destruction of almost 20,000 churches, and ... the universal desecration of everything that pertained to the worship of God'.[106] Addressing sodalists in a later issue, the writer of the same column began: 'You are to imagine that a fanatical Spanish communist comes face to face with one of Murillo's Madonnas; he punctures it with bullets and throws it into the flames'.[107] In their sermons, speeches, and

---

101. *I.C.*, 6 Apr. 1935. See also *I.C.*, 30 Mar. 1935.
102. *I.C.*, 23 May 1936.
103. *I.C.*, 22 Oct. 1936.
104. *I.C.*, 13 May 1937.
105. Phillip Knightley, *The first casualty: from the Crimea to Vietnam: the war correspondent as hero, propagandist, and myth maker* (New York and London, 1975), pp 198–9.
106. *I.C.*, 17 Nov. 1938.
107. *I.C.*, 13 July 1939.

school lessons all around the country, bishops, priests, brothers, and nuns re-echoed such atrocity stories and drew stark conclusions from them.[108] In an illustrated lecture to 400 people under CYMS auspices at Newmarket, County Cork, in December 1938, a visiting priest showed pictures of 'horrible acts of sacrilege and desecration' systematically carried out by 'the Reds' in Spain, and he spoke of how the 'bodies of nuns were taken from [the burial] vaults of convents and torn asunder to show hatred of religion'. He ended by declaring, 'We may thank God for Franco', to which his audience responded with 'prolonged cheers'.[109] Again and again in the late 1930s, Irish Catholics were asked to join in special religious ceremonies 'in reparation for the sacrileges and murders committed in Spain'.[110]

Although the Russian and Mexican revolutions also played some part, it was above all the Spanish civil war which elicited a distinctly apocalyptic note in the pronouncements of Catholic bishops and priests. In a pastoral letter of September 1936, Bishop Edward Mulhern of Dromore declared, 'The campaign of outrages at present carried on in Spain is but a part of a well-organised movement for the destruction of the church and religion and civilisation throughout the world'.[111] The war in Spain, insisted a Newry priest to the local Holy Family Confraternity, 'was one for the preservation or the total destruction of Christianity. The pope and Cardinal MacRory had said so, and all Catholics would accept their statements'.[112] Leading the diocesan Legion of Mary pilgrimage to Knock shrine in May 1938, Bishop Patrick Morrisroe of Achonry underlined its significance: 'In these days when rulers of the world are seeking to end the reign of Christ, to hamper his church, and kill Christianity itself ..., we are assembled here to pay honour to Our Lady of Knock'. Mary, he prayed, must again crush the head of the serpent – the serpent of paganism.[113] Later, as the Second World War began, a Dominican priest gloomily told a congress of Dominican Tertiaries in Galway that it was 'satan's hour'. Was it any wonder, he asked, that 'the Almighty has apparently doomed a wicked and unbelieving world to the fate it has richly deserved'.[114]

This apocalyptic note continued to be struck during wartime, but it was after 1945, with the commencement of the Cold War, that anti-communism really flourished in Ireland, along with an intensified Marianism that took Our Lady

---

108. See, e.g., Patrick Galvin, *Song for a poor boy: a Cork childhood* (Dublin, 1990), pp 25–6.
109. *I.C.*, 22 Dec. 1938.
110. *I.C.*, 8 Oct. 1936. See also *I.C.*, 24 Sept. 1936.
111. *I.C.*, 24 Sept. 1936.
112. *I.C.*, 1 Oct. 1936.
113. *I.C.*, 19 May 1938.
114. *I.C.*, 7 Sept. 1939.

of Fatima as its central icon. Once again, the orthodox pointed the accusing finger at the Dublin trade-union movement, which was said to have its share of leaders 'associated with Marxist activities'.[115] There was also a new concern about agricultural labourers, and in the eyes of some pious observers, domestic communists had allegedly made their 'greatest advance' among farm workers in certain rural areas.[116] But as before the war, what was called communism in Ireland was more likely to be some form of socialism, as when in March 1947 Bishop Daniel Cohalan denounced a local branch of the Socialist (i.e., Labour) party as 'a live communist cell in Cork [city] exercising its activities under the cloak of socialism'.[117] Other overheated commentators also complained about 'camouflaged communism' masquerading as socialism and working 'through bicycle clubs, hiking clubs, youth movements, and debating societies'.[118] But even such a militantly anti-communist organisation as the CYMS had to admit in 1948 that 'communism in Ireland is practically negligible'.[119] And when Sean P. MacEoin claimed in his 1948 book *Communism and Ireland* that the country was 'flooded' with communist propaganda, the book reviewer for the *Irish Catholic* bemoaned this and other similar exaggerations.[120] Still, even those prepared to discount the existence of any serious domestic threat sometimes thought that the greatest danger lay in complacency.[121]

Few Irish Catholics, however, were in any doubt about the menace of communism abroad. A whole series of religious activities in the late 1940s and 1950s had as their objective the conversion of Russia – the Pax Christi Crusade of Prayer, special devotions to the Immaculate Heart of Mary and Our Lady of Fatima, the various rosary crusades, and others as well.[122] The Catholic press of the time was full of such articles as Aodh de Blacam's 'The world in transition: re-conversion or ruin', which took aim in 1947 at both 'the atheists of Russia and the atom-bombing agnostics of America and England',[123] or 'Fatima and communism', the writer of which saw devotion to Mary's Immaculate Heart as 'the decisive weapon against the communist peril'.[124]

The fate of Hungary and Poland aroused great interest and concern among Irish Catholics in the post-war years. Accounts of the persecution of the

---

115. *I.C.*, 27 May 1948.
116. *I.C.*, 30 Sept. 1948.
117. *I.C.*, 20 Mar. 1947.
118. *I.C.*, 30 Sept. 1948.
119. *I.C.*, 20 May 1948.
120. *I.C.*, 30 Dec. 1948.
121. *I.C.*, 20 May 1948.
122. *I.C.*, 8 May, 18 Sept. 1947, 27 May 1948.
123. *I.C.*, 17 Apr. 1947.
124. *I.C.*, 18 Sept. 1947.

church there and elsewhere in eastern Europe became standard features of the press. For example, the *Irish Catholic* of 19 June 1947 carried the article 'A lesson for Ireland: how the Reds did it in Hungary' – one drop in a great ocean of such journalistic pieces.[125] As elsewhere, so too in Ireland the treatment of Cardinal Mindszenty and Archbishop Stepinac became the chief focus of this Catholic concern. In an impressive mobilisation on May Day – Our Lady's Day in Ireland – in 1949, some 150,000 Catholics gathered in Dublin to protest against the imprisonment of the two prelates and the general persecution of the church in eastern Europe. The throng reportedly included the members of over 200 confraternities and 42 sodalities; thousands knelt in the street or on sidewalks for the recitation of the rosary in one of the dramatic closing events of this great demonstration.[126]

Intensifying this concern with Catholics suffering behind the Iron Curtain or in what was also called 'the church of silence' was the communist victory in China in 1949 and the outbreak of the Korean war two years later. The communist assault on the Catholic church in China deeply resonated in Ireland, partly because China had been the focus of considerable Irish missionary enterprise and partly because the Irish-born Legion of Mary had grown lustily there.[127] Reports that the Chinese communists had not only banned the Legion but also engaged in atrocities, martyring 10,000 Legionaries and imprisoning 100,000 of them,[128] had political and religious effects similar to the republican atrocities of the Spanish civil war. Irish missionaries expelled from China became vocal witnesses to the sufferings of Catholics there upon their return to Ireland, and some missionaries were treated to a hero's welcome when arriving home.[129] For the great majority of Irish Catholics, strong anti-communism must have become almost second nature by the 1950s. Leaving aside the other media, the barrage of stories in the press, religious and secular, was relentless. In the *Irish Catholic* for the month of October 1955 alone, the headlines blared:

'Persecution in China is thorough – not even Carmelite nuns escape'[130]
'How Yugoslavia is warring on the church'[131]

---

125. *I.C.*, 19 June 1947.
126. *I.C.*, 5 May 1949.
127. See *The Irish Jesuit directory and year book, 1935* (Dublin, 1935), pp 178–89. See also *I.C.*, 13 Sept. 1951, and Edmund M. Hogan, *The Irish missionary movement: a historical survey, 1830–1980* (Dublin and Washington, DC, 1990), pp 46–7, 91–7.
128. *I.C.*, 7 June 1951, 10 June 1954.
129. See *Maria Legionis* (Sept. 1954), pp 1–9.
130. *I.C.*, 13 Oct. 1955.
131. *I.C.*, 20 Oct. 1955.

'Schools in East Germany go red'[132]
'Atheistic literature in Poland'[133]
'17 Catholic laymen killed in Shanghai' [and] 'Mao Tse-Tung over high altar'[134]
'Religion is never respected by Reds'[135]

In this fertile soil did Marianism in all its rich colours and varieties flourish in Ireland.

If communism constituted a grave danger to Christian civilisation and the integrity of family life, so too did numerous other kinds of moral pollution. An exaggerated concern with moral purity was not a new feature of Irish culture in the middle decades of the twentieth century. It was already conspicuous in the 1920s when the newly independent state began to censor films (1923) and publications (1929), and this characteristic was in fact older still. But the Irish Catholic quest for moral purity seems to have intensified considerably in the years 1930–60, when it was intimately connected with the contemporaneous upsurge in Marian enthusiasm.

What is especially striking about the moral-purity concerns of the time, apart from their frequent shrillness, was the broad range of dire threats seen to be confronting the moral order of Catholic Ireland. A host of evils – unregulated dance halls, seductive dances, indecent Hollywood movies, trashy novels, sensationalist newspapers, other 'evil literature', courting in public, dressing and undressing at the beach, excessive drinking (especially by women in mixed company), and physically revealing female dress – all were the subject of a great deal of complaint, discussion, and counteractive enterprise. Church officials waged a ceaseless campaign against 'the craze for pleasure' and 'the passion for amusement', especially among the young, a social category which was especially broad in these years because of delayed marriage. By some these distressing social and cultural trends were seen as more menacing than communism and by others as emanations or kindred spirits of communism. Whatever the precise nature of the threat, the Catholic church in Ireland mobilised its own personnel and much of the laity as well to combat vigorously the moral pollution by which it felt itself to be surrounded.

Among the moral evils allegedly corrupting Irish youth, perhaps none aroused more concern or elicited more criticism (at least before 1945) than the 'commercialised' dance hall and the 'dance madness' associated with it. Critics identified the commercial dance hall with an absence of supervision

---

132. Ibid.
133. Ibid.
134. *I.C.*, 27 Oct. 1955.
135. *I.C.*, 3 Nov. 1955.

which encouraged sinful conduct. Overcrowding, the lack of proper ventilation, and the use of dim coloured lights were all notorious for playing 'strange tricks with the dancers', as one critic delicately put it in 1940, 'especially when liquor was indulged in'.[136] In the age-old way drinking and dancing frequently went together, and this linkage was the subject of constant censure. The Public Dance Halls Act of 1935 outlawed both the provision of intoxicants in dance halls and the admission of inebriated patrons, but critics persistently complained that these clauses of the law were rarely enforced. Dancers would trot off to local pubs or hotels to drink, or would draw heavily on their own supply outside, and then they would return intoxicated to the dance hall.[137] What was especially alarming to many people about the drinking problem was the allegedly large increase in public consumption by young women. Condemning this new habit among females, the Jesuit Fr Joseph Flinn, president of the Pioneers in Ireland, observed in 1937, 'It has become the vulgar fashion of a decadent age to set up as a criterion of smartness the imbibing of fiery cocktails at social gatherings'.[138] 'Degenerate' males plied girls and young women at dances with port or 'gin-and-it' in the expectation of sex in return.[139]

The dances themselves were widely condemned as suggestive or obscene and likely to lead to sexual immorality. Jazz dancing and jazz music, popularised by the now almost ubiquitous radio, became the particular target of attack, with prelates and priests using pastoral letters and sermons to inveigh against them. Continuing its battle against contamination by British civilisation, the Gaelic League waged an 'anti-jazz campaign' in the 1930s in an unsuccessful effort to eradicate this 'denationalising' influence and 'present-day instrument of social degradation'.[140] Other traditionalists developed or repeated this theme of native corruption from foreign sources by deploring 'the frequently immoral wrigglings imported from Africa and nearer home' and sometimes called 'jazz'. Still other critics bluntly decried 'nigger music'.[141] Normally intelligent people, obsessed by the moral depravity of jazz, could become almost irrational about its supposed effects. Thus in a diatribe against jazz dancing in the *Irish Catholic* in 1940, Marie McGrath, the holder of a Ph.D. degree, gave full vent to an overheated

---

136. *I.C.*, 7 Nov. 1940.
137. *I.C.*, 5 Nov. 1942.
138. *I.C.*, 2 Dec. 1937.
139. *I.C.*, 25 Nov. 1937.
140. Jim Smyth, 'Dancing, depravity, and all that jazz: the public dance halls act of 1935' in *History Ireland*, i, no. 2 (Summer 1993), p. 54.
141. *I.C.*, 7 Nov. 1940; Smyth, 'Dancing', p. 54.

imagination: 'Caught in the vibration, everything worthwhile – duty, love, honour, purity, religion – is shaken from him [the youthful dancer]. His physical health is undermined, if not ruined; his mental outlook is distorted; his spiritual life is reduced to very nothingness. He himself becomes an object of despair.'[142]

Like the Gaelic League, many other critics of 'the current craze for jazz' called for a return to native dances, described as 'clean and sprightly' in contrast to the 'inherently suggestive and seductive' foreign product.[143]

Strongly contributing to the perceived moral dangers of commercial dance halls were their late hours (until 2 or 3 a.m.), which gave rise to the phrase 'all-night dances'. This evil was compounded by the spreading use of motor vehicles, which allowed some young people to attend dance halls located miles away from home. The presence of such strangers, insisted the critics, only exacerbated the already difficult problems of monitoring social and moral behaviour.[144] And, of course, in country places those without cars might need an hour or two to walk or cycle home. Many priests, nuns, and members of the laity became obsessed with the opportunities for sexual misconduct on the road home after dances.[145] As one commentator put it, 'The later the hour at which dancing ceases, the longer and darker the roads leading from the hall, [and] the more tumultuous the moral risks involved in attending dances in Ireland, be they of home or foreign origin'.[146] With such troubling thoughts in mind, the Irish bishops collectively urged in 1935 that all public dance halls close as early as 11 p.m.[147] Others recommended the revival of the decayed custom of cross-roads dancing, with the dances scheduled for the afternoons of Saturdays, Sundays, and holidays, so as 'to rid us of the twin menace of the commercialised dance hall and the all-night dance'.[148]

From an early stage, however, clerical and lay leaders realised that what were needed were parish halls where a range of social activities, including dances, could be closely supervised. The essence of the traditionalist agenda was well enunciated by Archbishop Thomas Gilmartin of Tuam in May 1938: 'We want local halls under proper supervision, limited in number to the needs of the locality and exorcised from the commercial spirit, where our youth can meet for good reading and games and our own virile dances, under

---

142. *I.C.*, 7 Nov. 1940.
143. Ibid.
144. *I.C.*, 7 Sept. 1935.
145. *I.C.*, 16 Sept. 1937.
146. *I.C.*, 7 Nov. 1940.
147. *I.C.*, 7 Sept. 1935.
148. *I.C.*, 7 Nov. 1940.

rules which represent the Catholic culture of our native land'.[149] Intensifying such attitudes was the failure of the Public Dance Halls Act of 1935 to realise the hopes of its proponents and supporters. Many district justices ignored the pleas of local priests for drastic reductions in the number of licensed dance halls or in the lateness of their time of closing.[150] A sympathetic district justice in County Donegal said disgustedly of the law early in 1938, 'It has added enormously to the amount of dancing, and I think the whole act has proved a failure'.[151] In particular, besides the deficiencies of its liquor clauses, there was also a chorus of complaint that the provision prohibiting the admission of children under eighteen years of age was 'more honoured in the breach than in the observance'.[152] As a measure of control, declared another critic in November 1942, the 1935 act was a 'farcical tragedy'.[153]

Parochial halls of the kind described by Archbishop Gilmartin in 1938 could counteract both the abuses of the commercial dance halls and the defects of the 1935 law. As early as 1938 the CYMS, an organisation which placed the cult of Mary at the centre of its devotional life, proclaimed as one of its goals the building of a hall in every 'church area' in the country, where boys and girls could engage in 'lawful' recreations of all kinds under the watchful eyes of the local clergy.[154] Later, other leading Catholic bodies committed themselves to this objective, including Muintir na Tire and the Legion of Mary. The first Muintir parish hall opened in mid 1941 at Murroe, County Limerick, the native parish of the organisation's founder, Fr John Hayes. It cost £1400, furniture included.[155] The hope expressed by the editor of the *Irish Catholic* that the Murroe hall would be only the first of 'a long chain of similar institutions in rural Ireland' proved well-founded.[156] 'It became the ambition of every [Muintir] guild to have a hall, an ambition since fulfilled by great numbers of them', observed Stephen Rynne in 1960. In fact, as Rynne pointed out, 'in the muddled public mind Muintir na Tire is often mistaken for a hall-building association'.[157]

What Muintir na Tire did in country parishes the Legion of Mary often did in cities and towns, which constituted its principal social base. In its early

149. *I.C.*, 19 May 1938.
150. *I.C.*, 9 Sept. 1937.
151. *I.C.*, 6 Jan. 1938.
152. *I.C.*, 8 Sept. 1941.
153. *I.C.*, 5 Nov. 1942.
154. *I.C.*, 21 Apr. 1938.
155. *I.C.*, 17 July 1941.
156. *I.C.*, 24 July 1941.
157. Stephen Rynne, *Father John Hayes, founder of Muintir na Tire, People of the Land* (Dublin, 1960), pp 168–9.

years the Legion had shown little interest in recreational centres for youth, but this became one of its main activities beginning in the late 1940s. Archbishop John D'Alton himself presided when the Legion opened its youth centre in Dundalk in late 1949. In his address D'Alton put this Legion enterprise in the context of 'one of the fiercest struggles that had ever taken place between the forces of Christ and anti-Christ'.[158] Strong Marian influences were often evident in similar undertakings elsewhere. When the new St Finbarr's Boys' Club was opened under Legion auspices in the West Cabra district of Dublin early in 1950, the parish priest consecrated the club and its eighty-odd initial members to the Immaculate Heart of Mary. And the Legionaries directing the club were said to believe that its atmosphere 'should be dominated by the ideal of the purity of Our Lady', as represented by the 'boy *beatus*' Dominic Savio.[159] A drama group called 'The Marian Players' helped to raise money for a new boys' club in Bantry.[160] Kanturk owed not only its boys' club to the Legion but also its Edel Quinn Memorial Hall (named after the famous Legion missionary to Africa, a Kanturk native), which had as its inaugural social event a well-attended 'rosary dance' early in 1955.[161] And the Legion's De Montfort Men's Club at Teach Mhuire in Dublin had the rosary as 'the central act of the nightly club programmes'.[162]

If the commercial dance hall was at the top of the list of perceived moral dangers, the cinema and, to a lesser extent, the stage were not far behind. As Terence Brown has aptly remarked, 'in village hall and city cinema in Ireland the 1930s was the decade of an enthusiastic discovery of celluloid dreams from California'.[163] And the fascination with Hollywood films showed no signs of abatement in succeeding decades. Already in 1943 Ireland had 260 cinemas licensed to show motion pictures and paying about £300,000 a year in entertainment taxes.[164] By the end of World War Two the Sunday-night cinema show was nearly universal, being 'well known in provincial trade circles as a "packed out" night almost irrespective of programme content'.[165]

Guardians of traditional morality could take some comfort from the fact that state-imposed censorship of films had begun as early as 1923. The film

---

158. *I.C.*, 8 Dec. 1949.
159. *I.C.*, 26 Jan. 1950.
160. *I.C.*, 19 Oct. 1950.
161. *I.C.*, 27 Jan. 1955. See also *I.C.*, 15 Feb. 1951; Leon-Joseph Suenens, *A heroine of the apostolate (1907–1944): Edel Quinn: envoy of the Legion of Mary to Africa* (Dublin, 1954).
162. *I.C.*, 24 May 1951.
163. *Ireland: a social and cultural history, 1922 to the present* (Ithaca, NY, and London, 1985), p. 118.
164. *I.C.*, 4 Mar. 1943.
165. *I.C.*, 18 July 1946.

censors were busy, viewing a total of nearly 1600 films in 1935 and rejecting eighty-eight. Even traditionalists conceded that the Irish film-censorship regime was quite strict, but for many it was not tough enough to combat the 'soul poison of screen shows'.[166] An extreme view was that of the journalist Aodh de Blacam, a fierce critic of Hollywood films for sentimentalising lust; in 1938 he urged 'a Father Mathew total-abstinence pledge against the cinema until it is brought under Christian control by any means that can be devised'.[167] But it was generally conceded that some Hollywood films, above all 'Snow White and the seven dwarfs', satisfied 'the sternest critical standards',[168] although it was smugly pointed out that Walt Disney had made this film with a big loan from a Catholic and Jesuit-trained Los Angeles banker.[169] This prompted the *Irish Catholic*'s film critic to remark about 'Snow White' in 1938 that 'it is no coincidence that it is a Catholic who revives our flagging hopes for films as an art'.[170] Even with strict censorship some felt that the country needed an 'Irish Purity League' modelled on the famous Legion of Decency in the United States, one of whose founders was Archbishop John McNicholas of Cincinnati, a native of Kiltimagh, County Mayo.[171] Though lacking such an organisation, priests, nuns, and parents who wanted to exercise moral supervision in this critical area were not without weapons. From late 1938 they could refer to the *Catholic Film News* of London, a twopenny monthly film guide approved by both Cardinals Hinsley and MacRory, the English and Irish primates respectively, and distributed in Ireland by Eason's of Dublin. Touting it as 'by far the best publication concerning the cinema in these islands', the *Irish Catholic* assured priests that they would find it 'particularly valuable'.[172]

But from an early stage what Irish Catholic leaders, clerical and lay, really wanted was to be able to challenge the secular cinema on its own ground by controlling the distribution and screening of films and even, to some degree, their production as well. In 1937 there was public discussion of the possible establishment of an Irish film industry that would 'operate in accordance with the wishes of the Holy Father', as expressed in his encyclical *Vigilanti Curia*.[173] Towards the end of 1938 the Catholic Film Society of Ireland came

---

166. *I.C.*, 29 Oct. 1936.
167. *I.C.*, 14 July 1938.
168. *I.C.*, 21 July 1938.
169. *I.C.*, 8 June 1939.
170. *I.C.*, 21 July 1938.
171. *I.C.*, 29 Oct. 1936, 18 May 1950.
172. *I.C.*, 22 Dec. 1938.
173. *I.C.*, 1 Apr. 1937.

into existence. It sought to 'propagate the truths of religion through films' and to create a 'public demand for a higher moral and cultural standard in entertainment films'.[174] In practice it encouraged the formation of local branches, where members could be trained in production, distribution, and projection.[175] But by its own admission the Catholic Film Society was dogged by difficulties and could not have been helped by the fact that it was based in Youghal, County Cork.[176]

Much more successful was the National Film Institute, established in Dublin in 1943, with Archbishop John Charles McQuaid's backing and headed by an energetic priest, Fr John Redmond. Although it especially concerned itself with what schoolchildren saw, it also aimed to be a central clearinghouse for all matters relating to films and motion pictures in Ireland.[177] At the beginning of 1948 the National Film Institute had a library of 480 films, a series of courses for teachers, and a mobile unit which had given almost 700 presentations in the previous year.[178] Although this was an impressive record, it was greatly exceeded in significance by the development and diffusion of portable 16 mm sound projectors during the late 1940s. This equipment could be rented or purchased at affordable prices; one Dublin company was selling RCA 16 mm sound projectors, with perfect 'cinema quality', for £210 in 1947, and these eventually came with portable generators which both ran the equipment and lighted the auditorium. Suitable films could usually be obtained from the same companies that sold or rented the equipment. One large Dublin firm – the Atlas Cine Supply Co. – had a library of 500 films in 1947, and its stock was liberally sprinkled with films on religious subjects.[179] As such firms avidly pointed out, the parish hall could now easily become the parish cinema, and priests were told how they could pack the parish hall, not once but three times a week, with such 'wonderful' films as 'The song of Bernadette', 'How green was my valley', 'The keys of the kingdom', and 'A bell for Adano', not to mention comedies, musicals, and westerns.[180] 'Hopalong Cassidy is coming to your parish hall', promised one advertisement making a presumably irresistible pitch.[181]

---

174. *I.C.*, 15 July 1943.
175. *I.C.*, 5 Jan. 1939.
176. *I.C.*, 15 July 1943.
177. *I.C.*, 29 July, 5 Aug. 1943.
178. *I.C.*, 19 Feb. 1948.
179. *I.C.*, 6 Nov. 1947, 23 Dec. 1948.
180. *I.C.*, 23 Dec. 1948, 17 Feb. 1949.
181. This was one of the more inspired advertising slogans of the Atlas Cine Supply Co. of Dublin.

We have already seen how the widespread desire to supplant the commercial dance hall had led to the erection of new parish halls throughout the country, and here in the case of the cinema was another stimulus from the side of moral purity. At the local level priests were apparently seizing the opportunity which the cheap new technology presented. Although the claim was no doubt self-serving, one equipment vendor declared in late 1948 that 'all over the country the parish halls are installing 16 mm sound projectors'.[182] Encouraging this trend was a change in the law in 1949 which freed halls located at least three miles from any settlement of 500 or more people from the liability to pay entertainment tax. It was said that once this legal change took effect on 1 June of that year, the 16 mm film and equipment business 'was never so busy'.[183] These innovations obviously strengthened clerical supervision of many forms of entertainment in rural areas. They also broadened the uses that were made of the cult of Mary, widened its diffusion, and intensified its impact.

Among the greatest dangers which the cinema and the commercial dance hall presented was their perceived threat to female purity. This preoccupation with female chastity was in fact much wider and expressed itself in numerous other ways as well. In no small degree the obsession with sexual purity was rooted in the acute awareness of the repressed and unsatisfied sexual longings created or sharpened by the extraordinary delay of marriage. It was of course in the late 1930s that the average ages of spouses at the time of marriage reached their peaks in Ireland, and many people were never marrying at all.[184] This widely deplored social trend, along with other factors, was held to encourage immodesty in dress. As usual, women were generally seen as more guilty because their immodest dress dragged men, incapable of resisting, into serious sin.[185] The devil was certainly blackening souls at the beach, as indicated by headlines in 1935 calling attention to 'The campaign of immodesty at the seaside' and 'Seaside scandals that must be stopped'.[186] One shocked moralist condemned what he described as 'nudism' on the beach at Youghal, with men naked to the waist and women 'in the most scanty underwear or in tight-fitting, abbreviated bathing costumes …, sprawling on the beach …'.[187] Another alarmed critic denounced the sun-bathing or air-bathing

---

182. *I.C.*, 23 Dec. 1948.
183. *I.C.*, 30 June 1949.
184. B.M. Walsh, 'Marriage in Ireland in the twentieth century' in Art Cosgrove (ed.), *Marriage in Ireland* (Dublin, 1985), pp 133–6.
185. *I.C.*, 27 Aug. 1942.
186. *I.C.*, 24 Aug. 1935.
187. *I.C.*, 17 Aug. 1935.

clubs being established by 'those who are keen on introducing a particularly disgusting pagan cult – the cult of the body, the cult of nakedness – into our midst'.[188] There were numerous demands for an end to mixed bathing; many traditionalists called for the establishment of separate bathing places for the two sexes.[189] Even louder and more insistent were demands to prohibit the long-standing practice of undressing and dressing more or less in public view at the beach. Catholic Action groups were urged to tackle this pressing problem,[190] and so too were public bodies. In Kerry the county council reportedly adopted a by-law in the summer of 1937 which not only prohibited dressing and undressing outside sexually distinct shelters but even banned 'mixed bathing and mixed sun-bathing in public bathing places'.[191]

Exhortations about immodest dress and the need for purity became a stock item in clerical sermons in the 1930s. Speaking at a confirmation ceremony in his diocese in May 1936, Bishop John O'Kane of Derry declared that he 'knew of no abuse so widespread today as that of immodesty in dress ... If it ever happened that the Irish church became wrecked, he did not believe it would be as a result of communism or rebels against the church, but would come through failure of the observance of purity.'[192] Putting the same point more positively but no less insistently, the main preacher at Knock shrine on the feast of the Assumption in 1937 told the thousands of listening pilgrims, 'If the young women of Ireland were pure and modest, there need never be any fear for the faith in Ireland'.[193]

If sermons are any guide, sexual purity became in this period, even more than in the past, one of the major preoccupations of the two great Irish Marian organisations, the Children of Mary and the Legion of Mary. In a Lenten lecture at Limerick in 1935 the Jesuit priest Fr H.V. Gill extolled the virtues of purity and chastity – this time in both sexes – and at once added emphatically, 'it is here that the Sodality of Our Lady has its great part to play'.[194] And in his allocution to an Acies of the Legion of Mary at Castlebar in the same year, Fr Michael Carney declared that he 'looked to the Legionaries everywhere to have as one of their great aims the creation of a high Catholic standard of social decency – particularly in matters of dress and dances, and other public recreations and amusements'. Carney especially

---

188. *I.C.*, 3 June 1937.
189. *I.C.*, 8 July 1937.
190. Ibid.
191. *I.C.*, 2 Sept. 1937.
192. *I.C.*, 23 May 1936.
193. *I.C.*, 19 Aug. 1937.
194. *I.C.*, 13 Apr. 1935.

urged 'every Catholic girl' to read the recently published little book *O women, what you could be!*[195]

But the most insistent calls for 'dress reform' or 'the apostolate of dress' came from the self-styled Modest Dress and Deportment Crusade. This was organised in 1942 by the Sisters of Mercy based at the Mary Immaculate Training College in Limerick city.[196] It could fairly be said that the MDDC had rather extreme views about proper female attire; these views were propagated in its two pamphlets, *The vice of to-day* and *Short skirts or slacks*.[197] The MDDC insisted that it was immodest for women to show their knees, which must be covered when sitting. Skirts should therefore be at least four inches below the knee (this standard would also guard against rheumatism), and slacks must not be worn at all because they threw the female figure 'into undue prominence'.[198] These specific injunctions were supported by rather crude appeals to nationalism. Irish women were invited to 'show their power in the state at large' by withdrawing Irish society 'from the anglicising influences which are ... degrading it and divesting it of every trace of national characteristic'.[199] The MDDC also called on the women of Ireland 'to establish an "Irish fashion" which will reflect glory on our race and defeat the projects of the anti-God campaigners'.[200]

Although it sought to reach out to all Irish women, the MDDC directed its appeal especially to Children of Mary sodalities, branches of the Legion of Mary, and all other associations consecrated to Our Lady.[201] Apparently, then, even many of these Marian devotees had succumbed to 'indecent fashions'. Despite its rather extreme views, the MDDC boasted in the summer of 1942 of having received the formal approval of the Irish Catholic hierarchy.[202] The organisation was more important for what it represented than for what it accomplished. It was a short-lived enterprise and probably did not exercise any substantial influence over female dress. But it is nevertheless significant as an illustration of both the intensity of the wider concern for sexual purity and of the close linkage between that concern and Marian devotion. In the 'new Christian order' advocated by the MDDC, 'Mary must take her old place as model for maid and wife and mother, and this is what the MDDC aims at'.[203]

195. *I.C.*, 15 June 1935.
196. *I.C.*, 10 Sept. 1942.
197. *I.C.*, 31 Dec. 1942.
198. *I.C.*, 29 Oct. 1942.
199. *I.C.*, 6 Aug. 1942. See also *I.C.*, 5 Feb. 1942.
200. *I.C.*, 26 Nov. 1942.
201. *I.C.*, 5 Feb., 23 Apr. 1942.
202. *I.C.*, 6 Aug. 1942.
203. *I.C.*, 1 Apr. 1943.

The Marian cult had first become a highly prominent feature of popular Irish catholicism in the second half of the nineteenth century. Its diffusion in Ireland during these decades, orchestrated by priests and nuns, was part of the general and enthusiastic propagation of the cult in the Catholic areas of western Europe as a whole, as David Blackbourn has demonstrated so effectively in the opening chapter of his impressive book *Marpingen*.[204] In Ireland the spread of the cult was undoubtedly tied closely to the 'devotional revolution'. As I have argued elsewhere, the Marian current was transmitted in the post-Famine decades 'largely through such quintessential aspects of the "devotional revolution" as the parish-mission movement, the dramatic expansion of female religious orders, their monopoly over girls' secondary education, and the associated growth of sodalities and confraternities, many of them with an explicitly Marian focus'.[205]

These institutional props remained important to the vitality of the cult in the years 1930–60, when, as I have tried to show in this essay, Marianism reached its apogee in Ireland. What propelled this extraordinary surge in Irish popular devotion to Mary was the deep ideological impact of the Spanish civil war, the perceived dangers of international communism and socialism, and the battle to preserve 'moral purity' amidst the corrupting influences of changing social and sexual mores. So exuberant and pervasive did the Marian cult become between 1930 and 1960 that it now furnished the central symbols, values, and rituals of Irish catholicism in this period. Although in some ways this peaking of Marianism in Ireland represented a further elaboration of the original 'devotional revolution', it should also be viewed as a development which disclosed certain shortcomings or failures of that religious regime. Insofar as the 'devotional revolution' put the parish unit, the priest as pastor, and the sacraments at the centre of religious life, this major nineteenth-century restructuring of what popular religion was supposed to be about was apparently insufficient, or had become insufficient, to satisfy the religious needs and longings of many Irish Catholics in the mid twentieth century. To a considerable degree the flowering of Marian devotion in Ireland in these years was extra-parochial and extra-sacramental, as demonstrated by the enthusiasm for pilgrimages to faraway and even foreign shrines or by the extremely widespread participation in national and international rosary campaigns. Thus the peaking of Marianism indicated that the tridentine

---

204. David Blackbourn, *Marpingen: apparitions of the Virgin Mary in nineteenth-century Germany* (New York, 1994), pp 3–41.
205. J.S. Donnelly, Jr., 'The Marian shrine of Knock: the first decade' in *Éire-Ireland*, xxviii, no. 2 (Summer 1993), p. 96.

system of what has been called 'parochial conformity' – a system bound up with the 'devotional revolution' – was not answering (at least not fully) the spiritual needs of large numbers of Irish Catholics. In this sense the intense Marianism of the years 1930–60 constituted in part a search for means of religious expression which the parochial structure and the sacramental system were incapable of supplying.[206]

The religious style and the cultural and political attitudes discussed in this essay were by no means unique to Ireland in this period. Other countries on both sides of the Atlantic had large numbers of traditional Catholics who shared similar views and whose religious responses had a great deal in common with those of Irish Catholics. Thus in these respects it is quite misleading to speak of Ireland in this period as having trod an isolated and provincial road, as many historians are inclined to do. What may look provincial when viewed from the perspective of the late 1960s and later, or from the standpoint of secular liberalism before that, was in fact closely connected to the dominant currents in western catholicism from the 1930s through the 1950s.[207]

---

206. I owe the thrust of the argument in this paragraph to my good friend Fr Joseph McLaughlin, CSSR, of St Michael's College in Colchester, Vermont, who in his extremely helpful comments on this essay brought to bear his deep knowledge of the work of early modern historians who have been re-examining the impact of the Reformation and Counter-reformation on European religiosity.
207. Terence Brown perhaps exaggerates Irish cultural provincialism and resistance to outside influences during the 1930s, 1940s, and 1950s in his generally excellent survey, *Ireland: a social and cultural history, 1922 to the present*. The outside influences ought to be taken to include not only the liberal and secular ideas which met such stiff resistance in Ireland but also the conservative political and religious ideas which found an enthusiastic welcome. In narrowing the international perspective in this fashion, Brown is hardly alone.

Emmet Larkin: A Memoir

LAWRENCE J. MCCAFFREY

EMMET LARKIN AND I HAVE BEEN FRIENDS for over forty-five years. We met at the National Library of Ireland in July 1953 while researching our Ph.D. dissertations, he for Columbia, I for the University of Iowa. His topic was James Larkin (no relation), the Irish labour leader; mine was Isaac Butt and the beginning of the home rule movement. In addition to an interest in Irish history, we had much in common: parents who came from Ireland, urban backgrounds, service in the Second World War, and educational opportunities provided by the GI Bill of Rights.

After Emmet and I returned to the United States we frequently corresponded, and we would meet for a drink and perhaps lunch or dinner at American Historical Association (AHA) meetings. Increasingly the contents of our letters and conversations dealt with the American Committee for Irish Studies (now the American Conference for Irish Studies – ACIS).

ACIS origins go back to the summer of 1957 when I was working at the National Library. In early September, a few days before I returned to St Paul, Minnesota, where I was teaching at the College of St Catherine, I had dinner at the home of R. Dudley Edwards, professor of Irish history at University College, Dublin. He had shown a keen interest in the work and careers of Emmet and me, and had been most hospitable to us when we were in

Dublin. During after-dinner drinks, Dudley suggested that Americans and Canadians in Irish history should establish a North American branch of the Irish Historical Society, and urged me to initiate the process. I promised to discuss his idea with Emmet and Gilbert Cahill, a friend of mine from graduate school days at Iowa, teaching at the State University of New York-Cortland.

In a three-way correspondence, Emmet, Gil, and I decided to present Dudley's suggestion to others working in Irish history at the December 1958 AHA meeting in Washington, DC. Thomas N. Brown, from the British-Irish desk at the State Department and later the University of Massachusetts at Boston history department, Helen Mulvey, Connecticut College, and Arnold Schrier, University of Cincinnati, joined us in my tiny room at the Mayflower Hotel. We agreed to start a North American Irish Historical Society. But in letters between Brooklyn College, where Emmet was an instructor in history, and Iowa City where I was a visiting lecturer in history at the University of Iowa (1958–59), and then Urbana-Champaign where in September 1959 I became an assistant professor of history in the Division of General Studies at the University of Illinois, Emmet and I expressed second thoughts about the feasibility of such an enterprise. On this side of the Atlantic few people were researching and writing Irish history, and an even smaller number were actually teaching it. During the Chicago meeting of the AHA in 1959, Emmet, Gil, and I decided on an interdisciplinary Irish studies rather than an Irish history organisation. We had been teaching humanities and western civilisation courses. These experiences frustrated ambitions to teach our specialised fields, but they did expand our intellectual horizons, and encouraged an appreciation and enthusiasm for interdisciplinary instruction and learning. In addition, we were widely read in Irish literature, and appreciated the insights that it brought to our interpretations of Irish history. We endorsed George Dangerfield's observation in *The strange death of liberal England* that 'Ireland is one of the few countries – perhaps the last – where the boundaries between art and politics have never been fixed'.

Moving from the idealistic and theoretical to the practical and realisable, Emmet and I were aware that due to the genius and significance of writers such as William Butler Yeats, James Joyce, John Millington Synge, and Sean O'Casey, Anglo-Irish literature had attracted the talents of a large number of research scholars. We knew that if an Irish studies organisation could enlist most or all of them, it would profit in prestige as well as numbers.

Following the Chicago meeting, Emmet recruited two Anglo-Irish literature friends, John Kelleher of Harvard and David Greene of New York

University, for ACIS. Meanwhile, I sent ACIS announcements to the leading journals of history and literature, emphasising its interdisciplinary purpose and inviting all readers interested in Irish studies to join.

ACIS's official existence began in the spring of 1960 with Gil as president, John and David as vice-presidents, Emmet as treasurer, and me as secretary. James McCrimmon, head of the Division of General Studies at the University of Illinois, a charming and generous Scotsman with an empathy for fellow Gaels, provided me with a modest budget and a part-time student secretary, Danute Gudaitis, so that I could send out a quarterly mimeographed *Newsletter*.

Shortly after ACIS began to function we were joined by Hal Orel, a student of Yeats and Thomas Hardy at the University of Kansas, and Emmet and I added him to the list of vice-presidents. Then we were fortunate to attract such important social scientists as the anthropologist John Messenger (Indiana University and later Ohio State), and his wife Betty, a folklorist, as well as political scientist Alan Ward (University of Connecticut and later the College of William and Mary). They added to ACIS's interdisciplinary profile and played important leadership roles in its growth and development.

ACIS became visible in joint sessions with the Modern Language Association (MLA) and the American Historical Association at December 1961 meetings in Chicago and Washington. Emmet, who had moved in September 1960 from Brooklyn College to Massachusetts Institute of Technology (MIT) as an assistant professor of humanities, Gil, and I attended both meetings, as did R. Dudley Edwards and our close friend, Alf Mac Lochlainn, keeper of manuscripts and later director of the National Library of Ireland. Ambassador Thomas Kiernan gave an Irish government nod of recognition to ACIS by inviting Emmet, Gil, and me to the embassy for a conversation about the organisation followed by lunch at the Cosmos Club. The ambassador also was kind enough to attend a reception we hosted at the AHA meeting, following our session in which Emmet had read a paper on 'Church and state in nineteenth century Ireland'.[1] With AHA and MLA session successes and a steadily increasing membership, Emmet and I decided that the time had come for ACIS to hold yearly national conferences. Purdue University hosted the first in 1962, and subsequently published some of the papers, including one by Emmet, 'The quarrel among the Roman Catholic bishops over the national system of education, 1838–41'.[2]

---

1. Subsequently published in *Church History*, xxxi, no. 3 (Sept. 1962), 294–306.
2. In Browne, Roscelli and Loftus, *Celtic cross*, pp 121–46.

Since then ACIS has met on a number of American college and university campuses and at University College, Dublin, University College, Galway, and the Queen's University of Belfast. On two of these occasions Emmet and I had the privilege of being honoured by the Irish themselves. At the Dublin meeting of June 1987, the National University of Ireland conferred honorary Doctor of Literature degrees on Emmet and me for our historical scholarship and for establishing the American Conference for Irish Studies. Six years earlier, at the ACIS national conference hosted by the University of Pittsburgh and Carnegie Mellon University, Sean Donlon, Irish ambassador to the United States, on behalf of his government, had awarded Emmet and me attractive and valuable facsimiles of the Book of Durrow in recognition of our 'outstanding work over the years to promote Irish Studies in the United States', especially our 'energetic participation from the beginning in the American Committee for Irish Studies'.

Although we turned the secretary and treasurer offices over to other people in 1966, for a number of years Emmet and I continued to serve on the ACIS executive committee. I was president from 1976 to 1979, and Emmet from 1979 to 1982.

Because of ACIS's expansion, and the considerable expense involved in attending national conferences, with Emmet's support I proposed the establishment of regional branches and meetings. In 1976 the midwest became the first regional branch and held a successful meeting at Loyola University of Chicago. Previously there had been an independent New England Irish studies group. Largely through Emmet's diplomacy, in 1978 it decided to officially affiliate with ACIS. In addition to the midwest and New England, regional organisations now exist in the mid Atlantic states, the south, and the west. Since national conferences have become so large, and their sessions so specialised in terms of topics, regional meetings have retained the intimacy, social camaraderie, and some of the interdisciplinary associations and communications that were such a prominent feature of national meetings in the early stages of ACIS.

Emmet, Gil, and I designed ACIS as a North American organisation. It functioned that way until 1967 when for a number of good reasons Canadians broke away and established their own Association for Irish Studies. The separation has been friendly with the two organisations sharing some members, and, on occasion, holding joint conferences.

On Emmet's initiative, in the 1960s ACIS launched two major projects. He obtained financial support from the American Council of Learned Societies,

Chicago's Newberry Library, the British Museum, and the National Library of Ireland to microfilm Irish and British materials in the Vatican archives. Each institution involved has copies, giving scholars in Britain, Ireland, and the United States access to important sources without long, expensive journeys to Rome. In 1966 an anonymous donor in Ireland, who wanted to contribute to the development and promotion of Irish studies, contacted Professor Roger McHugh of the English Department of University College, Dublin. Roger then got in touch with Emmet, and together they designed an interdisciplinary Irish studies reprint series. Under Emmet's direction and editorship, the MIT and University of Chicago presses reprinted eleven significant essays in Anglo-Irish literature, Celtic studies, and Irish history.

When Emmet and I review the history of ACIS and ponder its present and future, we share a pride of accomplishment mixed with apprehensions and disappointments. We regret that ACIS's interdisciplinary flavour has diminished as evidenced by the multi-layered, specialised topic sessions at national and some regional meetings. In many areas of the humanities and social sciences an emphasis on theory, accompanied by vocabularies and rhetoric incomprehensible to non-specialists, have obstructed interdisciplinary communication. And, unfortunately, political agendas and ambitions that have been such a disruptive force in college and university faculties and academic organisations have infected and factionalised ACIS.

Although it has failed to satisfy all of our original expectations, ACIS deserves credit for advancing Irish studies in the United States, Canada, Britain, and Ireland itself. Irish subjects certainly have a stronger standing in American colleges and universities than they did forty years ago. Graduate and undergraduate Anglo-Irish literature courses are more popular than ever. Irish history is flourishing as a research area, and as an attractive offering for students. Ireland has inspired more historical research and publication from American scholars than other European countries apart from Britain, France, Germany, and Russia. Since Emmet and I entered the Irish history field, it has established an identity related to but independent of British history. Irish-American history and literature are progressing well on their own and as aspects of American ethnic studies programmes. While history and literature scholars produce most Irish studies publications, those in the social sciences and Celtic studies also make significant contributions.

Of course ACIS cannot claim full credit for current Irish interests. They also reflect continued excellence in Irish literature, the appeal of Irish traditional music, Ireland's relevance as a case study in the interactions between political and cultural nationalisms and religion and nationality, efforts to comprehend the reasons for agitation and violence in Northern Ireland, and the emphasis on ethnicity and cultural pluralism in the United States. But without ACIS scholars would not have been in a strong position to take advantage of a friendly climate. It has provided a focus and a forum for those in Irish and Irish-American studies. ACIS has captured the attention of university administrators, grant agencies, and publishers. The energy and enthusiasm that it generates and the respectability that it confers on its subject inspires and encourages many young people to pursue graduate studies in Irish and Irish-American topics. ACIS achievements in the United States have inspired the establishment of interdisciplinary Irish studies organisations and curricula in Britain and Ireland as well as Canada.

In 1966, when Emmet moved from MIT to the University of Chicago as associate professor of history and bought a home in Woodlawn, I was teaching at Marquette University in Milwaukee. Separated by such a short distance, we had numerous opportunities to visit. In 1970, after a year of teaching at the University of Maine, Orono, I accepted a position at Loyola University of Chicago and moved to Evanston. Over the past twenty-eight years the Larkins and McCaffreys have shared many social occasions, and Emmet and I frequently talk on the telephone. These circumstances gave me a unique opportunity to observe Emmet's intellectual development over the years since the publication in 1965 of his highly acclaimed first book, *James Larkin, Irish labour leader, 1876–1947*.[3]

Before his Larkin study was in print, Emmet had started to research and publish material on the Catholic church in nineteenth-century Ireland. Since his first article on the subject, 'The Roman Catholic hierarchy and the fall of Parnell',[4] twelve others have appeared in various journals and books of essays. In 1975 the American Philosophical Society issued *The Roman Catholic church and the creation of the modern Irish state, 1878–1886*, the first of his projected twelve-volume 'A history of the Roman Catholic church in Ireland in the nineteenth century, 1780–1918'. It won the American Catholic Historical Association's John Gilmary Shea Prize for the best book of the year in Catholic history. Emmet has published seven of the intended twelve volumes, and at present he is diligently constructing the eighth.

Emmet's most widely read, and perhaps most influential book, *The historical dimensions of Irish catholicism*,[5] is not part of his twelve-volume

---

3. (London and Cambridge, MA, 1965), reprinted (London, 1989) with new foreword by the author.
4. *Victorian Studies*, iv, no. 4 (June 1961), 315–36.
5. (New York, 1976), reprinted with revised foreword by the author (Washington, 1984, 1997).

289

series. It brings together three essays that Emmet previously published in *The American Historical Review*. The importance of two of these articles, 'The devotional revolution in Ireland, 1850–1875' and 'Church, state, and nation in modern Ireland'[6], can be gauged in part by the number of contributors to the present volume who address the issues which they raise.[7] The other article – the first to be written – 'Economic growth, capital investment, and the Roman Catholic church in nineteenth century Ireland',[8] has been more porblematic. In it Emmet attempted to measure the impact which an increasingly powerful post-Famine catholicism had through its extensive investment in buildings – churches, rectories, convents, and schools. He argued that this vast capital investment in religion retarded the growth of the general Irish economy. This argument was greeted with considerable scepticism by economic historians and others, and in his 'Introduction' to *The historical dimensions* he changes his mind, deciding that the church supplied desired and needed religious and educational services, and by erecting buildings actually stimulated a stagnant agrarian economy by providing alternative employment opportunities and by distributing consumer purchasing power in the form of salaries.

The seven published volumes of Emmet's study of nineteenth-century Irish catholicism are based upon extensive research in Ireland, Britain, and Rome. Because of the available archive sources, he has devoted most of his attention to the hierarchy and clergy. His books feature lengthy quotations from the correspondence of church leaders. Emmet describes his extensive use of quotes as a 'mosaic' technique in which prominent churchmen discuss events and motives in their own words while he integrates their perspectives and his own analyses into a coherent whole.

Emmet's style of presentation, the emphases he places on certain subjects, his concentration on the hierarchy, and some of his principal theses have not escaped criticism, even from those who admire the ambition of his project and the significance of its impact. Commentators have complained that although the mosaic approach adds authenticity, it gives a source book tone to his work and deadens the pace of the narrative. One critic has complained that Emmet's style, affected by his source material, has become increasingly 'high ecclesiastical'. Other complaints include charges that Emmet has been so focused on original sources that he has ignored some important secondary

---

6. *A.H.R.*, lxxvii, no. 3 (June 1972), 625–52 and lxxx, no. 5 (Dec. 1975), 1244–76.
7. For assessment of the significance and impact of the two Larkin theses, see the 'Introduction' to this volume.
8. *A.H.R.*, lxxii, no. lxxii, no. 3 (Apr. 1967), 852–84.

works that would broaden the social and economic context of his effort, and that he has paid too much attention to ecclesiastical politics and not enough to other facets of Irish catholicism. Some critics are not persuaded that Emmet has proved his contentions that the alliance between catholicism and nationalism created a de facto Irish state or that it fostered liberal democracy.

Despite objections to his mosaic style, his concentration on the hierarchy, and his theses that changes in post-Famine catholicism amounted to a devotional revolution and that catholicism reinforced liberal democratic elements in Irish nationalism, almost all of Emmet's critics, those not jealous of the significance of his endeavours, concede that his work on nineteenth-century Irish catholicism is of major importance, has stimulated historical and social science research on Ireland's most important institution and cultural force, and has offered information and insights into many other aspects of Irish history. They praise 'the meaty content' of Emmet's books and articles; their brilliant, thought-provoking analyses; and their challenge to other researchers in Irish history. Josef Altholz described *The Roman Catholic church and the creation of the modern Irish state* 'as a landmark in the historiography of modern Ireland. In the sweep of its vision, the rich detail of its counter-point, and the warmth of its human sympathies, it is a treat for the student of modern history'.[9]

For personal and intellectual reasons, Emmet began his research on Irish catholicism with an adversarial attitude toward his subject. His father, Emmet Senior, a Chicago native raised in east Galway, was an IRA guerrilla in the Anglo-Irish and civil wars. Both the British and Irish governments imprisoned and the church excommunicated him as she did all rebels against the Free State. Sharing his father's grievances, Emmet, in his post-childhood years, ceased to believe in or practice the catholicism of his mother and sister. His research on and writing of the Larkin biography intensified his distrust of the Catholic influence in Irish life. The indifference of Irish bishops and priests to the plight of the urban poor, and their antagonism to the Irish labour movement, particularly during the 1913 general strike and employers' lockout, offended Emmet's admiration for James Larkin and his own passion for social justice.

Once into his subject, the objectivity of Emmet's research and analyses overcame the subjectivity of his emotions. He has never shied away from exposing the frailties of many bishops and priests, and their frequent displays of authoritarianism, bigotry, narrow vision, and puritanism, but he has

---

9. Review in *Journal of Modern History*, xlviii, no. 3 (Sept. 1976), 544–5.

concluded that the general effect of Irish catholicism has been more positive than negative. It has provided an impoverished and oppressed people with consolation, hope, discipline, and cultural and national identity. It also has offered them social, medical, and educational services when the state was indifferent to their poverty and ignorance. And although the Catholic church on most of the Continent was allied to aristocratic privilege and property, Emmet has argued persuasively and strongly that in Ireland she accepted the liberal democratic tenets of Irish nationalism and functioned as a stable force in pre- and post-Treaty times. He is certainly aware that Catholic influences have been pervasive in the Free State and Republic, but he insists that the confessional state represents majority opinion as much as it does clericalism.

Emmet's view of the past, like that of all creative historians, has been affected by personal experience as well as research. Emmet's association with the University of Chicago, one of the most prestigious universities in the United States, has encouraged respect for traditional institutions, especially the Catholic church, the oldest in the western world. His coming to Chicago coincided with the beginnings of unrest on campuses throughout the country. It troubled him that students displayed so little respect for a vocation and a way of life that he valued so much.

At the same time that students were defying university authorities and contemptuously dismissing the humanities as no longer germane to their interests and needs, and some faculty members, unaware of the long-term consequences, joined the crusade for academic relevance, many Catholics, reacting to Paul VI's *Humanae Vitae* rejection of contraception, were denouncing Rome. To Emmet, the Catholic church, for all of the sins of her past and present and the stubborn inflexibility of the Vatican, like the university, has been a source of continuity and stability in an increasingly chaotic, fragmented world. He has continued to fret about the clerical scandals that further weaken the church's hold on the laity as he does about deconstructionists and other academic theorists who increasingly separate the university from the world of reality, and about weak-spined American politicians who respond to public opinion polls rather than consciences or the priorities of the common good. These concerns do not indicate that Emmet has shifted his allegiance from liberalism to conservatism, they do mean that his liberalism remains communal rather than individualistic with a healthy regard for the links between past, present, and future.

Over the past twenty-five years it has been fun to watch agnostic Emmet muster an exaggerated chagrin when his Catholic friends, with whom he once debated religion, vigorously denounce Rome and various Irish and American prelates. I often tease Emmet that at heart he is a papist who has rejected Catholic doctrine but believes in the pope.

Many of our conversations about religion, politics, and academic life take place at dinner parties, usually at his Woodlawn home. Emmet and his wife, Dianne, offer guests lavish hospitality, featuring generous and delicious portions of food and drink. At the head of the table, Emmet presides like a bishop at a diocesan consistory. In the midst of heated discussions he displays a wonderful sense of humour, enjoying teasing others and being teased himself. Because he is so involved in and enthusiastic about his research, and identifies so closely with some of the clerical personalities he writes about, that in affectionate jest some of his friends refer to and address him as Reverend Doctor Larkin or his eminence, Emmet Cardinal Larkin.

Emmet's career is an effective rebuke to those who insist on a dichotomy between a distinguished publishing record and effective teaching. He has demonstrated that the former enhances rather than detracts from the latter. Emmet delights in both undergraduate and graduate teaching. He diligently prepares his courses in British and Irish history, shifting emphases from year to year, offering new and original interpretations, constantly adding to his reading lists. People who have been there have told me that Emmet's classroom is an exciting place to be. He captures their attention with energetic lectures that contain the same inventive insights that he brings to his research and writing.

This festschrift includes contributions from some scholars who have completed their dissertations under Emmet's guidance. Their quality indicates that he has attracted talented people to the University of Chicago, and that he has done much to help them develop their potential. When I read articles, books, and dissertations produced by Emmet's students, I am impressed by the quality of the research, the intelligence of the presentation, and the clarity and grace of the writing.

While he demands a great deal from the people he teaches and directs, Emmet is deeply concerned about their total welfare. He and Dianne graciously entertain graduate students in their home. Young people who come to the University of Chicago to work with Emmet find a caring friend as well as a mentor. He does not impose his enthusiasm for nineteenth century Irish religious history on his students. Realising that the Ph.D. is a long, arduous, and sometimes frustrating process, and that students must be personally interested and devoted to their dissertations to complete them in a satisfactory manner, Emmet encourages advisees to select subjects that will engage their intellectual curiosity. As a result of his flexibility, he has directed research that ranges over a wide spectrum of British and Irish history.

Although he is now over seventy, Emmet's intellectual energy and curiosity have not been diminished by minor physical disabilities. Every autumn he enthusiastically responds to the beginning of the academic year. He continues to add new material and interpretations to his lectures, counsels undergraduate and graduate students, supervises seminar papers and dissertations, prepares papers and lectures for academic conferences and public forums, when called on to do so offers advice to the ACIS executive committee, and researches and writes his multi-volume history of Irish catholicism in the nineteenth century.

Emmet still spends part of each summer in diocesan and religious order archives in Britain and Ireland and is planning another journey to Rome. Every research excursion results in further discoveries, new ideas, and increased enthusiasm for his subject. In his written work and in his classroom and public lectures, Emmet continues to offer fresh insights into Irish catholicism. Lately he has shifted his focus from the hierarchy to the clergy working in parishes as pastors, curates, and missionaries; to nursing and teaching nuns and brothers; and to the devotional world of the laity.

I consider Emmet to be the leading historian of Ireland working in the United States, and no one on either side of the Atlantic has contributed more to the advance of Irish historiography. Although he has excelled as a publishing scholar and teacher, and has played a major role in the development of Irish studies in this country, these academic interests and achievements rank far below his family on Emmet's priority list. Not only has he proven that research and writing are compatible with teaching excellence, he has demonstrated that it is possible to achieve professional distinction and still be an attentive and loving husband and father. His greatest pleasures are the time he spends with Dianne and his daughters, Heather and Siobhan. I am sure that their love and respect is more important to him than all the praise and awards that he has earned and received for his research, writing, and teaching.

Principal Works of Emmet Larkin
(to 1998)

HELEN MULVEY

'The Roman Catholic hierarchy and the fall of Parnell' in *Victorian Studies*, no. 4 (June 1961), pp 315–36.

'Church and state in Ireland in the nineteenth century' in *Church History*, xxxi, no. 3 (Sept. 1962), pp 294–306.

'Mounting the counter-attack: the Roman Catholic hierarchy and the destruction of Parnellism' in *Review of Politics*, xxv, no. 2 (Apr. 1963), pp 157–82.

'The quarrel among the Roman Catholic hierarchy over the national system of education in Ireland, 1838–41' in R.B. Browne, W.J. Roscelli, and Richard Loftus (ed.), *The Celtic cross: studies in Irish culture and literature* (West Lafayette, IN, 1964), pp 121–46.

'Socialism and catholicism in Ireland' in *Church History*, xxxiii, no. 4 (Dec. 1964), pp 462–83. Repr. in *Studies*, lxxiv, no. 293 (Spring 1985), pp 66–92.

James Larkin: Irish labour leader, 1876–1947. Cambridge, MA, and London, 1965. Paperback, London, 1968. Repr., London, 1977, 1989.

'Launching the counterattack: part II of the Roman Catholic hierarchy and the destruction of Parnellism' in *Review of Politics*, xxviii, no. 3 (July 1966), pp 359–83.

'Economic growth, capital investment, and the Roman Catholic church in nineteenth-century Ireland' in *A.H.R.*, lxxii, no. 3 (Apr. 1967), pp 852–84. Repr. in *The historical dimensions of Irish catholicism* (see below).

'A reconsideration: Daniel Corkery and his ideas on Irish cultural nationalism' in *Éire-Ireland*, viii, no. 1 (Spring 1973), pp. 42–51.

'The devotional revolution in Ireland, 1850–75' in *A.H.R.*, lxxvii, no. 3 (June 1972), pp 625–52. Repr. in *The historical dimensions of Irish catholicism* (see below).

The Roman Catholic church and the creation of the modern Irish state, 1878–1886. Philadelphia and Dublin, 1975.

'Church, state, and nation in modern Ireland' in *A.H.R.*, lxxx, no. 5 (Dec. 1975), pp 1244–76. Repr. in *The historical dimensions of Irish catholicism* (see below).

The historical dimensions of Irish catholicism. New York, 1976. Repr. with new introduction, Washington, 1984. Repr. Washington and Dublin, 1997.

The Roman Catholic church and the Plan of Campaign in Ireland, 1886–1888. Cork, 1978.

The Roman Catholic church and the fall of Parnell, 1888–1891. Chapel Hill, NC, and Liverpool, 1979.

The making of the Roman Catholic church in Ireland, 1850–1860. Chapel Hill, 1980.

(Ed.) William L. Feingold, *The revolt of the tenantry: the transformation of local government in Ireland, 1875–1895.* Boston, 1984.

The consolidation of the Roman Catholic church in Ireland, 1860–1870. Chapel Hill and Dublin, 1987.

'The problem of Irish clerical avarice in the nineteenth century' in *Éire-Ireland*, xxiv, no. 3 (1989), pp 33–41.

'The Irish political tradition' in T.E. Hachey and L.J. McCaffrey (ed.) *Perspectives on Irish nationalism.* Lexington, KY, 1989.

The Roman Catholic church and the home rule movement in Ireland, 1870–1874. Chapel Hill and Dublin, 1990.

(Trans. and ed.) *Alexis de Tocqueville's journey in Ireland, July-August, 1835.* Washington and Dublin, 1990.

The Roman Catholic church and the emergence of the modern Irish political system, 1874–1878. Washington and Dublin, 1996.

(Ed., with Herman Freudenberger) *A Redemptorist missionary in Ireland, 1851–1854: memoirs by Joseph Prost.* Cork, 1997.

'Cardinal Paul Cullen' in Jeffrey Paul von Arx (ed.), *Varieties of ultramontanism.* Washington, 1998.

Index

Aberdeen, G.H. Gordon, 4th earl of 53, 55, 57
Acton, John E.E.D., 1st baron 212
Affre, Denis Auguste, archbishop of Paris 32
Alexander II 40
Altholz, Josef 13, 291
American Conference for Irish Studies 15, 284–9, 294
American Council of Learned Societies 287
American Historical Association 284, 285, 286
Amnesty Association 75, 76
Ancient Order of Hibernians 268
Anglade, Professor François 25
anglicanism 2, 7, 12, 68, 123, 159–61, 180–208, 236
Antonelli, Cardinal Giacomo 35
Arnold, Matthew 241
Arnold, Thomas 202
Arran, Arthur Saunders, 2nd earl of 19
Association for Discountenancing Vice and Promoting the Practice of the Christian Religion 187

Babbitt, Irving 233
Barnabò, Cardinal Allessandro 34
Beckett, Samuel 220
Bective, Thomas Taylour, 1st earl of 19
Bedford, Francis Russell, 7th duke of 48
Behan, Brendan 16, 33, 41

Bell, Clive 231
Belvedere, Lord 19
Benedict XIV 18
Bennett, Arnold 225
Beresford, George, 2nd earl of Tyrone 19
Beresford, Henry de la Poer, styled Lord Tyrone 19
Beresford, J.G., Church of Ireland archbishop of Armagh 187
Bergson, Henri-Louis 232
Berkeley, George, Church of Ireland bishop of Cloyne 239
Bernstein, George L. 9
Bessborough, J.W. Ponsonby, 4th earl of 48
Bessborough, John George Brabazon, 5th earl of 59, 62
Biletz, Frank 11
Birmingham, George A. 90, 91, 98, 104, 117
Birmingham, Fr James 27, 31
Blackbourn, David 282
Blake, William 237, 239, 240, 243
Blavatsky, Helena Petrovna 242
Blomfield, C.J., bishop of Chester 202
Boccioni, Umberto 225
Böhme, Jakob 243
Bonar Law, Andrew 137
Bourke, Thomas P. 37
Bowen, Desmond 183
Boyce, D. George 136
Boyd, Elizabeth 120

Boylan, Patrick, Monsignor 261
Brabazon, John George, 5th earl of Bessborough 59, 62
Bradbury, Malcolm 221, 224, 228
Brancusi, Constantin 251
Brand, Henry 58, 59, 60, 61, 63
Braque, Georges 225
Brian Boru 74
Bright, John 54, 63
British and Foreign Bible Society 189
Brompton Oratory 215
Brown, Malcolm 222
Brown, Rev. Stephen J. 83
Brown, Stewart J. 12
Brown, Terence 276
Brown, Thomas N. 285
Browne, Michael, bishop of Galway 145
Browne, Noel 145, 146
Bulfin, William 119, 120
Bullock, Shan 91, 104
Burke, Edmund 236
Burke, Rev. Thomas N. 68
Butenev, Count 40
Butler, Mary 122
Butt, Isaac 10, 68, 69, 75, 76, 77, 78, 79, 284
Byrne, Alfie 257
Byrne, Edward, archbishop of Dublin 141

Cahill, Gilbert 284–7
Cairns, David 223
Canning, George 203
Cantwell, John, bishop of Meath 26
Capes, John Moore 212
Cardwell, Edward 55, 57, 58
Carew, Lord 45, 50
Carhampton, Henry Lawes Luttrell, 2nd earl of 19
Carlisle, G.W.F. Howard, 7th earl of 55, 56, 58, 59, 60, 61, 62
Carney, Rev. Michael 280
Carson, Sir Edward 137
Cassidy, Hopalong 278
Castlereagh, Robert Stewart, Viscount 20, 96
Catholic Association 183, 193, 194, 195, 197–8, 203, 204, 208
Catholic Film Society 277–8
Catholic Young Men's Society 256, 268, 269, 270, 275

catholicism
    and Anglican conversion initiatives 180–208
    and Irish national identity 65–80, 91–4, 103–4, 108–29, 234–6, 246–9
    and Irish political system 43–64, 130–57
    and political violence 16–42
    practice of 5–8, 158–79, 217–19, 252–83
    social 209–19
    the honouree of this book and 291–3
Caulfield, James, bishop of Ferns 23
Causeway, County Kerry 27
Cézanne, Paul 225
Challoner, Richard, vicar apostolic of London district 213
Chalmers, Rev. Thomas 191
Children of Mary 252, 254, 256, 257, 261, 265, 280, 281
Church Missionary Society 194
Church of Ireland. *See* anglicanism
Clanricarde, Lord 48
Clapham Sect 188
Clarendon, G.W.F., 4th earl of 32, 48–53, 56, 60, 61, 63
Clark, Jonathan 182
Clement XII 18
Clifden, Henry Agar, 2nd viscount 19
Cobden, Richard 63
Cohalan, Daniel, bishop of Cork 270
Coleridge, Samuel Taylor 239
Colley, Linda 182
Collier, Rev. Daniel 254
Collins, Michael 136, 139, 140, 147–9, 150
Connolly, Thomas 19
Corish, Professor Patrick 5, 171, 178
Corkery, Daniel 87
Cosgrave, W.T. 147, 148
Costello, John A. 146
Coughlan, Fr 28
Coyne, Liam 256, 258
Croce, Benedetto 239
Croke, Thomas William, archbishop of Cashel 39, 65, 69–72, 76, 79, 141
Crolly, Professor George 41
Crolly, William, archbishop of Armagh 175
Crommelin, May de la Cherois 104
Cullen, Paul Cardinal 3, 4, 5, 6, 10, 17, 29, 30, 33–42, 51, 58, 60, 61, 64, 65, 68, 69, 72–3, 76, 141, 158, 174, 178

Cumann na nGael 154
Curtis, Patrick, archbishop of Armagh 181, 200, 204

D'Alton, John Cardinal 264, 276
Dallas, Rev. Alexander 207
Daly, Rev. Robert 195, 206, 207
Dangerfield, George 285
Daunt, O'Neill 79
Davis, Thomas 245, 248
Davitt, Michael 125
Dawson, Charles 78
de Blacam, Aodh 270, 277
de Lisle, Ambrose Phillips 13, 210, 211
de Valera, Eamon 139, 140, 143–5
Deane, Seamus 222
Deehan, Rev. J.G. 262
Defenders 21
Delahogue, Professor Louis 25
Delaunay, Robert 225
Devonshire, Duke of 61
devotional revolution 12–15, 74, 158, 174–9, 208, 213, 247, 253, 283
Digby, Kenelm 210, 211
Dignan, John, bishop of Clonfert 145
Dillon, John 65, 150
Doheny, Michael 32
Donlon, Sean 287
Donnelly, James S., Jr 14
Dowson, Ernest 238
Doyle, James Warren, bishop of Kildare and Leighlin 24–6, 28, 35, 41, 181, 193, 195, 198
Drummond, Thomas 46
Dudley, Lord 19
Duffy, Sir Charles Gavan 33, 77, 248
Duggan, James, bishop of Chicago 36
Duigenan, Patrick 16, 41
Duncannon, Lord 46
Dupanloup, Felix, bishop of Orleans 70, 77
Dysert, Lord 19

Eagleton, Terry 222, 224
Edgeworth, Maria 94
Edwards, R. Dudley 284, 286
Eliot, T.S. 220, 222, 223, 225, 229, 233–4, 250
Ellis, Edwin 239
Elrington, Charles 188

Elrington, Thomas 188
Emmet, Robert 66, 74, 78, 236
Enniskillen, Lord 19

Faber, Rev. F.W. 215
Fairbairn, Sir William 74
Farnham, John Maxwell, 5th baron, 190, 199–201, 202, 205, 207
Farrell, Brian 140
Fatima 252, 258–62, 264, 270
fenianism 3, 4, 9, 16, 17, 33–9, 41, 67, 68, 72, 74, 75, 76, 78, 86, 90, 99, 129, 245
Fergus, James, bishop of Achonry 266
Ferguson, Sir Samuel 244
Fianna Fáil 140, 144, 154, 156
Fine Gael 144
Fitzgerald, J.D. 56
Fitzgerald, Lord Edward 74
Fitzgerald, Rev. Philip 32
Flinn, Rev. Joseph 273
Fogarty, Michael, bishop of Killaloe 267
Ford, Ford Madox. *See* Heuffer
Fortescue, Chichester 56, 59
Foster, John Wilson 223
Francis, M.E. 86, 101
Franco, Francisco 269
freemasonry 18, 39
French, Edmund 29
Fry, Roger 231

Gaelic League 108, 116, 119, 121, 122, 125, 273, 274
Gandhi, Mohandas K. 66
Gardiner, Luke 19
Garibaldi, Giuseppe 57
Gellner, Ernest 66
Gibson, Thomas Milner 58
Gide, André-Paul-Guillaume 225
Gill, Rev. H.V. 280
Gillespie, Raymond 7
Gillow, Rev. Henry 214
Gilmartin, Thomas, archbishop of Tuam 274, 275
Gissing, George 230
Gladstone, W.E. 38, 57, 60, 65, 69, 75, 130, 131, 142
Gonne, Maud 245, 249
Gordon, G.H., 4th earl of Aberdeen 53, 55, 57

Index

Gordon, James E. 194, 200
Graham, Rev. Billy 262
Grattan, Henry 19, 74, 236
Greene, David 285
Gregory XVI 39, 41
Gregory, Augusta, Lady 223, 244, 247, 249
Greville, Charles 46
Grey, Sir George 52
Grey, Henry, 3rd earl 45, 63
Griffith, Arthur 109, 115, 117, 136, 139, 140, 249
Gudaitis, Danute 286
Guinan, Rev. Joseph 89

Haas, Lord 52
Hagan, John, rector of Irish College, Rome 143
Hales, Seán 149
Halpin, Rev. Timothy 257
Hancock, W.K. 147
Hardy, Thomas 286
Harper, Margaret Mills 223
Harty, Rev. Gabriel M. 263, 264
Hatchell, John 58, 59, 62
Hatherton. *See* Littleton
Hayes, Rev. John 275
Headford. *See* Headfort
Headfort, Thomas Taylour, 1st marquess of 19
Healy, T.M. 155
Hearn, Francis 22
Hearne, Rev. Daniel 214
Hegel, G.W.F. 239
Hempton, David 183
Heyck, T.W. 14
Heywood, Samuel 20
Hibernian Bible Society 189, 191, 194–5
Hill, Myrtle 183
Hinkson, Katherine Tynan 85, 105
Hinsley, Cardinal 277
Hobsbawm, Eric 66
Hodgson, Rev. Joseph 215
Home Government Association 76
Home Rule league 74
Horsman, Edward 55, 56, 59
Howard, G.W.F., 7th earl of Carlisle 55, 56, 58, 59, 60, 61, 62
Hueffer, Ford Madox 232
Hughes, Fr 28
Hulme, T.E. 232
Humbert, General Jean 23
Hutchinson, William Anthony 216
Hyde, Douglas 122, 246, 248
Hynes, Eugene 6, 175

Irish Christian Brothers 193, 214
Irish College, Rome 29, 34, 36
Irish Historical Society 285
Irish Republican Army 38, 135, 146, 147, 149, 150
Irish Society for Promoting the Education of the Native Irish through the Medium of their own Language 189, 190

James II 235
Jameson, Frederic 222
Jebb, John, Church of Ireland bishop of Limerick 187, 188, 197, 201, 207
Johnson, Lionel 238
Johnston, Denis 220
Joyce, James 220–2, 225, 229, 250, 285

Kandinsky Wassily 225
Kant, Immanuel 239
Keane, William, bishop of Cloyne 37
Kearney, Hugh F. 10
Keenan, Desmond 5
Kelleher, John 285
Kennedy, bishop of Killaloe 31
Kenny, Patrick D. 11, 109, 110–20
Kenyon, Rev. John 28, 31
Keogh, William 53
Kerr, Donal 9
Kiberd, Declan 223
Kickham, Charles 84, 106
Kildare Place Society 189
Killen, W.D. 160, 161, 171
King, Locke 52
Kirby, Tobias, rector of Irish College, Rome 36, 37
Knock 256, 262
Krause, William, 199
Kyne, John, bishop of Meath 260

La Touche, David 19
Labour Party 155
Lacordaire, 30
Laffan, Rev. Patrick 32

Index

Lamennais, Félicité de 210
Land League 39, 72, 98, 107, 120, 130, 131
Lane, Hugh 249
Langdale, Charles 216
Lansdowne, Lord 45, 55
Larkin, Dianne 293, 294
Larkin, Emmet 1–15, 17, 65, 103, 108, 110, 130–57, 158, 178, 182, 192, 208, 247, 253, 284–96
Larkin, Emmet, Sen. 291
Larkin, Heather 294
Larkin, James 284, 291
Larkin, Siobhan 294
Laurence, Richard, Church of Ireland archbishop of Cashel 187
Lavelle, Rev. Patrick 34–9, 42
Laverty, Maura 258
Lawrence, D.H. 225
Lawson, J.A. 61
Le Gallienne, Richard 238
Ledóchiwski, Cardinal Miescyslaw Halka 77
Ledru Rollin, Alexandre 30
Lee, J.J. 11
Legion of Mary 15, 252, 257, 269, 271, 275–6, 277, 280, 281
Leinster, William Robert Fitzgerald, 2nd duke of 19
Lemass, Seán 145
Leo XIII 41
Lewis, C.S.,244
Lewis, George Cornewall 30, 49, 159
Lewis, Wyndham 251
Littleton, E.J. 159
Liverpool, Lord 203
Lloyd George, David 134, 136
Logue, Cardinal Michael 125–6, 141
Longenbach, James 250
Louis Philippe 27, 29
Lourdes 252–8, 261, 263, 265
Lucas, Frederick 54, 211
Luttrell, Henry Lawes, 2nd earl of Carhampton 19
Lynch, Liam 140, 147
Lysaght, Sidney Royce 90, 92, 93, 94, 99
Lyttle, W.G. 104

MacBride, John 249
MacBride, Seán 145

MacCann, James 112, 113, 121, 123, 125, 126
MacDermott, Rev. Michael 28
MacDonagh, Oliver 39, 42
Macdonnell, Alexander 62
MacEntee, Seán 145
MacEoin, Sean P. 270
MacEvilly, John, archbishop of Tuam 141
MacHale, Rev. James 203
MacHale, John, archbishop of Tuam 4, 26, 27, 35, 65, 72, 73, 77, 78, 80, 181, 200
MacNeill, Eoin 122
MacNeill, Máire 177
MacRory, Cardinal Joseph 256, 259, 269, 277
Magee, William, Church of Ireland archbishop of Dublin 180–2, 187, 188, 191, 196, 197, 206, 207
Mageean, Daniel, bishop of Down and Connor 265, 266
Maginn, Edward, coadjutor bishop of Derry 27, 38
Maguire, Rev. Thomas 195, 202
Mahon, Major Denis 28
Mallarmé, Stéphane 239
Malta, University of 30
Maltby, Edward, Church of England bishop of Durham 51
Mangan, James Clarence 244
Mann, Thomas 225
Manning, Cardinal Henry Edward 209, 213, 218
Mansergh, Nicholas 132
Martin, Rev. John 24
Martyn, Edward 247
Mathers, MacGregor,242
Mathew, Rev. Theobald 214
Matisse, Henri-Émile-Benoit 225
Maynooth, St Patrick's College 22, 25, 31, 33, 35, 41, 97, 115, 181
McBride, Lawrence 10
McCabe, Edward, archbishop of Dublin 141
McCaffrey, Lawrence J. 15, 284–96
McCormack, Widow 32
McCrimmon, James 286
McDonnell, Rev. Eneas 195
McEntee, Georgiana 209
McFarlane, James 221, 224, 228

301

INDEX

McGettigan, Daniel, archbishop of Armagh 76
McGrath, Marie 273
McGrath, Thomas 6, 7, 8
McHugh, Roger 288
McMahon, Marie Edmé de 77
McMahon, Rev. Mathias 27
McManus, L. 90
McNicholas, John, archbishop of Cincinnati 277
McNulty, Edward 97
McQuaid, John Charles, archbishop of Dublin 141, 146, 259, 260, 278
McSwiney, Peter Paul 69, 71, 72, 73, 76, 77, 79
McTaggart, John McT.E. 239
Meagher, Thomas Francis 28
Melbourne, William Lamb, 2nd viscount 45–7, 52
Mellowes, Liam 140
Messenger, Betty 286
Messenger, John 286
methodism 7
Metternich, Prince Klemens 29, 39, 40
Mill, John Stuart 236
Miller, David W. 5, 125
Mindszenty, Cardinal József 271
Minto, Lord 28
Mitchel, John 28
Modern Language Association 286
Monsell, William 38, 50, 58, 60
Montalembert, Charles de, Count 210, 215
Mooney, Thomas 78
Moore, G.E. 231, 239, 251
Moore, George 247
Moore, Rev. John 214
Moore, Thomas Sturge 239, 240
Moran, D.P. 96, 104, 109–10, 112, 117, 122, 128
Moriarty, David, bishop of Ardfert 37, 38
Moriarty, Rev. Philip 35
Morpeth. *See* Carlisle
Morris, William 230, 237–8, 241, 244
Morrisroe, Patrick, bishop of Achonry 269
Muintir na Tire 275
Mulcahy, Richard 148
Mulgrave, C.H. Phipps, 6th earl of 47
Mulhern, Edward, bishop of Dromore 269
Mulvey, Helen 15, 285

Murphy, James 83
Murphy, Rev. John 17, 42, 97
Murphy, Rev. Michael G. 257
Murphy, William Martin 249
Murray, Daniel, archbishop of Dublin 4, 30, 31, 32, 34, 41, 42
Murray, Professor Patrick 33, 35, 41
Murray, Rev. Richard 197

National Association 72, 76
National Literary Society 248
Nehru, Pandit Jawaharlal 66
Neruda, Pablo 223
Newman, Cardinal John Henry 42
Nicholas I 39, 40
Nietzsche, Friedrich 227, 249
Noel, Baptist 194
Noel, John 257
Norfolk, Henry Fitzalan-Howard, 15th duke of 123
Norfolk, Henry Granville, 14th duke of 215
Normanby. *See* Mulgrave

O'Brien, Conor Cruise 132, 234
O'Brien, James 38
O'Brien, Rev. Dr 27
O'Brien, William, 150 155
O'Brien, William Smith 17, 28, 30, 32
O'Byrne, M.L. 83, 92, 96, 97
O'Casey, Sean 220, 285
O'Clery, Michael 88
O'Coigley, Rev. James 23
O'Connell, Daniel 9, 26, 28, 29, 30, 40, 43–50, 55, 56, 57, 61, 62–4, 65, 67–80, 97, 109, 111, 131, 183, 193, 194, 197, 198, 203, 208
O'Connell, Daniel, jun. 50
O'Connell, John 56
O'Connor, Rev. John 38
O'Connor, Rory 140
O'Connor, T.P. 120
O'Donovan, Gerald 97
O'Ferrall, Richard More 47, 52, 58
O'Grady, Standish James 88, 91, 94, 100, 102, 244
O'Hagan, Thomas, 1st baron 61, 62, 69, 75, 76
O'Higgins, Kevin 147, 148

Index

O'Higgins, William, bishop of Ardagh and Clonmacnois 26
O'Kane, John, bishop of Derry 280
O'Leary, John 75, 78, 79, 245, 246, 250
O'Leary, Canon Peter 39
O'Loghlen, Sir Colman 76
O'Malley, Rev. Thaddeus 30
O'Neill De Tyrone, Viscount 77
O'Neill, Hugh 74
O'Sullivan, Rev. Owen 27
O'Sullivan, Philip 88
orangeism 181
Orel, Harold 286
Our Lady's Sodality 264, 268, 280
Ozanam, Antoine Frédéric 210, 211

Palmerston, H.J. Temple, 3rd viscount 28, 44, 50, 54, 55, 57–63
Parnell, Charles Stewart 11, 65, 79, 80, 94, 109–11, 120, 130–57, 236
Pater, Walter 230, 238
Paul VI 292
Pearse, Padraic 121
Peel, Sir Robert 47, 59–62, 65, 199
Pender, Margaret 93, 101
Peyton, Rev. Patrick C. 262, 263, 264–6
Phelan, William 191
Philbin, William, bishop of Clonfert 265
Picasso, Pablo 225
Pioneers 273
Pius IX 28, 29, 35, 40, 41
Pius VI 21, 41
Pius VII 41
Pius XI 144, 255
Pius XII 255, 259
Ponsonby, J.W., 4th earl of Bessborough 48
Pope, Rev. Richard 195, 200, 202
Portarlington, John Dawson, 1st earl of 19
Pound, Ezra 220, 223, 225, 232–4, 250
Power, Rev. William 22
presbyterianism 2, 7, 110, 159, 160, 181, 184
Pugin, A.W. 211

Radetzky, Josef 29
Radziwill, Prince 77
Ranger, Terence 66
Redington, Thomas 48, 49, 52, 53
Redmond, John 65, 137, 139
Redmond, Rev. John 278
Reformation Society 201, 202, 205, 207
Renehan, Laurence, president of Maynooth 31, 35
Rhys, Ernest 238
Richards, Shaun 223
Rickard, John 223
Roebuck, J.A. 49, 63
Roman Catholic Church. *See* catholicism
Ross, Dorothy 225
Rossetti, Dante Gabriel 230
Rousseau, Jean-Jacque 20
Ruskin, John 238, 241
Russell, Bertrand 231, 239
Russell, Francis, 7th duke of Bedford 48
Russell, John, Lord 32, 35, 45, 47–50, 51–3, 57, 59, 60, 117, 159
Russell, Odo 36
Ryan, Archbishop Finbar 258
Ryan, W.P. 11, 109, 110, 112, 119, 120–8
Rynne, Stephen 275

Sadleir, John 50, 54, 56
Said, Edward 222
Saint-Aulaire, Louis, Count de 39
Saor Eire 267
Saunders, Arthur, 2nd earl of Arran 19
Savio, Dominic 276
Schmidt, Leigh Eric, 7
Schrier, Arnold, 285
Scrope, George Poulet 27
Shakespeare, William 237
Sheehan, John 26
Sheehan, Canon Patrick A. 84, 86, 93–9, 102, 104
Sheehy, Rev. Nicholas 18, 42
Sheil, Richard 194
Shelley, Percy Bysshe 237, 239
Shrewsbury, John Talbot, 16th earl of 13, 211
Simeon, Charles 191
Simpson, Richard 212
Sinn Féin 115, 138–40, 143, 146, 148, 150, 151, 154, 155, 156
Smith, Sydney 203
Smithson, Annie MP 92
Smyth, Patrick 88
Society of St Vincent de Paul 211, 256
Somerville, Sir William 50, 52

INDEX

Soubirous, Bernadette 255
Spalding, Martin, archbishop of Baltimore 34, 38
Special Constabulary 135
Spellman, Cardinal Francis 262
Spenser, Edmund 237
St Germans, C.G. Eliot, 3rd earl of 53, 56
St Patrick's Society of Irish workers 216
Stanley, Rev. Arthur 62
Stepinac, Archbishop Alojzije 271
Stewart, Robert, Viscount Castlereagh, 20, 96
Strachey, Lytton 232
Struwe, Count 40
Sullivan, A.M. 78
Sullivan, T.D. 78, 79
Sunday School Society for Ireland 189
Swan, Anne S. 98, 101
Swedenborg, Emanuel 243
Swift, Jonathan 236
Swinburne, Algernon 230, 232, 238
Symons, Arthur 233, 238, 239
Synge, J.M. 223, 247, 249, 285

Tagore, Rabindranath 223
Taylor, Cooke 32
Taylour, Thomas, 1st earl of Bective 19; 1st marquess of Headfort 19
Thurles, Synod of, 1850 33
Thurston, Ernest Temple 97
Tolkien, J.R.R. 244
Tone, Theobald Wolfe 21, 23, 66
tractarianism 51, 210
Trelawny, Sir John 62
Trench, Power le Poer, Church of Ireland archbishop of Tuam 188, 195
Troy, John Thomas, archbishop of Dublin 18–23, 34, 41, 42
Tufnell, Henry 49–51
Tynan, Katherine 237
Tyrone. *See* Beresford

Ulster Volunteer Force 135
ultramontanism 10, 14, 34, 51, 60, 63, 69, 79, 214–16, 247
United Irishmen 21, 24, 235

Vallejo, César 223
Varshney, Ashutosh 66
Vatican Council, 1869 40
Verlaine, Paul 233, 239
Villiers, Charles 58

Walsh, Joseph, archbishop of Tuam 259, 264
Walsh, William J., archbishop of Dublin 65, 125, 141
Ward, Alan 286
Waters, Martin 120
Werfel, Franz 258
Whately, Richard, Church of Ireland archbishop of Dublin 159
Whelan, Irene 183
Whelan, Kevin 174
Whistler, James McNeill 230
White, Luke 61
Whiteboys 18, 19
Whitehead, Alfred North 239
Whitworth, Sir Joseph 74
Wilde, Oscar 230, 237
Wiseman, Cardinal Nicholas 14, 57, 212–14, 217
Wittgenstein, Ludwig 225
Wood, Sir Charles 49
Wood, James, bishop of Philadelphia 36
Woolf, Virginia 220, 225, 230–2
Wyse, Thomas 198

Yeats, Georgie Hyde-Lees 223, 242
Yeats, John Butler 236
Yeats, William Butler 14, 220–51, 285
Young Ireland 17, 26, 28, 31, 32, 48, 248